It's Good
to Be the
King...
SOMETIMES

W World Wrestling Entertainment™

It's Good to Be the King...

SOMETIMES

Jerry "The King" Lawler

with Doug Asheville

POCKET BOOKS

New York   London   Toronto   Sydney   Singapore

This book is a publication of Pocket Books, a division of
Simon & Schuster, Inc., under exclusive license from
World Wrestling Entertainment, Inc.

ISBN: 0-7434-5768-4

First Pocket Books paperback printing October 2003

10 9 8 7 6 5 4 3 2 1

POCKET and colophon are registered trademarks of
Simon & Schuster, Inc.

Cover photo by Rich Freeda, 2003 World Wrestling Entertainment

Visit us on the World Wide Web
http://simonsays.com
http://www.wwe.com

Printed in the U.S.A.

For information regarding special discounts for bulk purchases,
please contact Simon & Schuster Special Sales at 1-800-456-6798
or business@simonandschuster.com

To my Dad,
who was a wrestling fan,
but died without ever seeing me wrestle.
I hope he would have been proud.

To my family, who I love.
And to all the boys in the business
who make wrestling so enjoyable!

It's Good
to Be the
King...
SOMETIMES

Good Ole J.R. looks right at home in his trademark black Stetson cowboy hat as he makes his way to the announce position at ringside. Many of the wrestling fans in the crowd on this night are wearing cowboy hats as well. And they are drinking beer. And they are chewing tobacco. And they are spitting on the floor. And they are cussing up a storm . . . and those are the women!

For this is West Memphis, Arkansas, considered by many to be the redneck capital of the world, or at least the Mid-South. Where livestock is still thought to be an appropriate wedding gift. West Memphis, Arkansas, the little backwoods burg that sullies the good name of the civilized city of Memphis, Tennessee, which lies just a stone's throw away. Provided you can throw a stone across the Mississippi River. Memphians have long looked down on West Memphians as trailer park-dwelling hangers-on, who, whenever they wanted to do anything of value or substance, had to cross the state line and come into Tennessee.

The University of Oklahoma fight song, which is J.R.'s entrance music, fades down as he settles into his seat and adjusts his headset. "Gimme a little more Me!" J.R. barks into his microphone as the soundman turns up the volume on J.R.'s voice. It's got to be loud to hear yourself over a wrestling crowd that is screaming at the top of its lungs. And scream they do as the royal music that signifies the coming of "the King" fills the arena. Ah, "the King," complete with crown, in all his glory, giving a royal wave to the locals as he sits down next to J.R. and prepares to broadcast yet another historic match.

"What about this arena we're in tonight, J.R.? Have you ever seen one any smaller? I dropped a washcloth on the floor of my dressing room and had wall-to-wall carpeting! And what about this crowd, J.R.? I've had more people come to see me wash my car than are here tonight. What gives? Who's wrestling tonight anyway?"

"Well, King," J.R. replies, "what gives, is that this arena, as rundown and dilapidated as it is, was once a movie theater called the Avon. And most of the seats down in front of the screen have been taken out to make room for the wrestling ring. And the reason the crowd is so small is because these wrestlers tonight are just a bunch of young unknowns trying to get started in the business."

"So then why are you and I here, J.R.? We're WWE Superstars. We don't belong in the same arena with a bunch of nobodies! And hey! Look at what's hanging over the ring! Is that a washtub?"

"Sure is, King. That's what they use for a ring light. A galvanized metal washtub with three light bulbs in it."

"And look at the way these fans are dressed, J.R. Don't they know these styles went out in the seventies?"

"King, we're IN the seventies! You and I have traveled back in time to call the first-ever professional wrestling match of a young kid named Jerry Lawler. Tonight he will step into a wrestling ring for the first time in his life. He'll have a partner named Jerry Vickers, and they'll be taking on a masked tag team known as the Executioners. This is a historic match we're about to broadcast, King!"

"First of all, J.R., I've never heard of Jerry Lawler, and second, how could any match held in the podunk town of West Memphis, Arkansas, be historic? Did you hear the mayor's mansion burned down here last week? Yep, perty near took out the whole trailer park! Ha, Ha, Ha!"

"Very funny, King. Now be quiet, here comes Lawler and his partner out to the ring now."

"What do you mean, here comes Lawler? Where is his entrance music? Where is his pyro?"

"King, I told you, this is 1970. No one has entrance music. Or pyro. It just isn't done yet."

"You mean this isn't 'sports entertainment.' It's still just 'wrestling'?"

"Now you're catching on, Einstein! Uh-oh. Here come Lawler's opponents, the dreaded masked Executioners!"

"Wow, J.R. Those masked men look huge compared to Jerry Lawler. What do you think Jerry weighs?"

"I know what he weighs, King, a hundred and eighty-five pounds."

"A hundred and eighty-five pounds! J.R., you eat more than that for breakfast! These Executioners scrape runts like Lawler off the bottoms of their shoes! I mean, look at his chest, J.R. He's so skinny, his nipples touch. And who's that guy with Lawler? He's not much bigger himself."

"Well, King, that's Jerry Lawler's partner, Jerry Vickers. He's a young man from Kansas City who's come down here to try to get noticed by the big organization. But right now he's taking any bookings he can."

"Yeah, and he's obviously taking any partners he can, too! I can't get over how small this Lawler kid is. I'll bet he uses Chap Stick for roll-on deodorant! Hey, I think the match is about to start, was that the bell?"

"Do I have to keep reminding you, King? This is not the WWE. This is a low-budget, no-frills, wrestling show. The promoter, Aubrey Griffith, has to run these matches on a shoestring. Instead of a bell, they just clang a hammer against the metal ring post. Anyway, it kinda sounded like a bell."

"Yeah, J.R., and these guys 'kinda' look like wrestlers! Well, here they go. Vickers and Executioner number one locking up. Somehow I have a feeling this isn't going to last long."

J.R. begins the commentary as the match gets underway. "Standing side headlock by Vickers on the Executioner to start the match . . . Executioner fires Vickers into the ropes . . . Vickers comes off and hits the Executioner with a nice shoulder tackle. Vickers back into the ropes, the Executioner drops down, and catches Vickers coming off with a big hip toss, and now the Executioner grabs a headlock of his own on Vickers. Now Vickers shoots the masked man into the ropes, big shoulder tackle . . . here comes the Executioner again off the ropes . . . this time Vickers drops down, then catches the Executioner with a hip toss, and he follows that up with a body slam on his opponent and the Executioner retreats to his corner, like a scalded dog, and gets a sympathy hug from his partner, Executioner number two! The Executioner tags in his partner . . . Executioner and Vickers lock up . . . Vickers snatches a headlock and pulls the big masked man toward his corner. And there's a tag on Lawler! Well, here we go, King, business is about to pick up . . . this is what we're here for . . . Jerry Lawler's first time in a wrestling ring. Now let's see what kind of wrestler he is."

"I can tell you what kind of wrestler Lawler is, J.R. He's a 'crossword' wrestler. He came into the ring vertically, but he'll leave horizontally! I predict this match will either be stopped by the ref, or the Red Cross!"

"Oh, you 'predict' do you, King? Who do you think you are, Nostradufas? Be that as it may, Lawler has the advantage right now. He's got a headlock of his own on Executioner number two. Look out, the Executioner has backed Lawler into the ropes . . . Wow! What a big forearm smash by the Executioner to Lawler's chest. That looked like it may have knocked the breath out of Jerry . . . and now, another big smash to Lawler's chest . . . Jerry is slumping back against the ropes. Now the Executioner with a big boot to Lawler's midsection . . . Lawler's down . . . more hard kicks from the masked man. King, the Executioner is stomping a mud hole in Lawler, and he's about to walk it dry!

"Now what's the Executioner doing? He's grabbed Lawler by the hair and by the back of his tights . . . Hey, wait a minute! The Executioner is running across the ring with Lawler in tow, and now he's throwing Jerry . . . OH MY GOD!! . . . Did you see that, King? The Executioner just threw Lawler between the middle and top rope, right out onto the concrete floor, and the poor kid landed right on his head!"

"I saw it, J.R. . . . It looked like Lawler didn't even try to grab the ropes or break his fall in any way! Did you hear that sickening thud when his head hit the floor? That was great! That may have been the funniest thing I've ever seen! And look, J.R., Lawler's not moving! He may be dead, J.R, I think he is! I think this kid has just kicked the oxygen habit . . . He'll be checking into the 'Wooden Waldorf' . . . He'll be playing harp duets with Hoffa . . . He's no longer eligible for the census . . . He's . . ."

"Would you shut up, King! This is not funny. Jerry Lawler is hurt!"

"Oh, excuse me, J.R. I forgot, it's only funny until someone gets hurt. . . . Then it's hilarious! Ah ha ha ha!"

"Well, you can laugh all you want to, King, but Lawler is still lying on the floor, unconscious. The other wrestlers have come out and the promoter is out here trying to revive Jerry . . . they are picking him up and carrying him back to the dressing room, and it looks like this match is officially over!

"In just over six minutes, your winners, by a count out, the Executioners!"

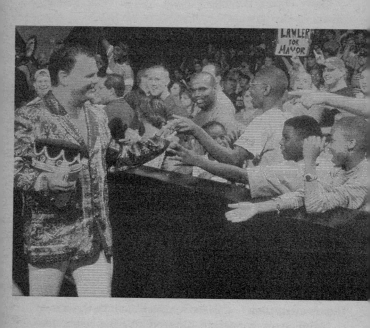

1

Sunday, May 19, 2002. It's *Judgment Day* at the Gaylord Entertainment Center, Nashville, Tennessee. *Judgment Day* is a big-time WWE Pay-Per-View, broadcast all over the world, so all the *Raw* and *SmackDown!* stars are here. We've spent the last three weeks of television building up these matches. One of the featured bouts is Kurt Angle and Edge in a hair-versus-hair match. Meanwhile, suspended dramatically above the ring is the steel cage that Triple H and Chris Jericho will use for their hell-in-the-cell battle. But the big showpiece is Undertaker and the Hulk, who'll climax weeks of feuding in a match for the Undisputed WWE Championship.

The place is packed—bulging with 18,000 fans—and the King rejoices in the rousing welcome he gets from his loyal home-state subjects. Nashville was always my "home away from home," so to speak. Among the crowd is a bunch of Tennessee Titans football players like Kevin Dyson, Randall Godfrey, and the tackles Joe Salave'a and Adam Haayer. Haayer went to college in Minnesota with the latest and greatest beast in sports-entertainment, Brock Lesnar. WWE wrestling has always been popular among athletes. Whatever city we're in, if it has a professional sports team, there are usually some players at the show. Same goes for entertainers; I think they can all appreciate what we do. Wrestlers have to have what it takes to succeed in both those worlds.

This Sunday was the start of a big few days for me. I was doing the commentary on the PPV with my trusty compadre J.R. The next night, *Raw* was coming live from the Pyramid in the King's hometown of Memphis.

This was the deal. Pay-Per-View events from state-of-the-art facilities in front of 18,000 adoring fans. Live shows on national TV out of the biggest arena this side of the Superdome in New Orleans. The King has come a mighty long way in the thirty years since the greenhorn almost got himself killed in front of twenty-eight people in a busted-down movie theater in West Memphis, Arkansas. Of course, the kid who got thrown out of the ring wasn't the King yet, but Jerry Lawler certainly felt that bump well enough. Once he'd regained consciousness.

It was natural for me to be thinking about my dim and distant wrestling past that particular weekend. For one thing, Vince and J.R. were busting my balls about remembering stories for my book. Look, I should say up front that I have not been blessed with a great memory. I barely remember what I had for breakfast, much less everything that's happened in my entire life. I think I need one of those jobs the Arnold Schwarzenegger character in *Total Recall* got. "Tell me what I remember again . . ." Like I could swear I never wrestled Mick Foley. I've seen him wrestle a million times and commentated on hundreds of his matches, but I don't remember ever actually wrestling him myself, but I'm told I had a match with Mankind at *King of the Ring* in 1997. I'm shown evidence of it, so I guess "It's true, it's true," as Kurt Angle might say.

But it's driving around this part of the Mid-South, routes like Memphis-to-Nashville and Memphis-to-Tupelo, that brings back a pile of memories for me. I've spent a big part of my adult life in cars, driving to and from shows in one place or another. When I first started in the business, I'd think nothing of driving five, six hundred miles to a match, often at insane speeds, and just as often up to no good along the way. I pass the spot on the road to Nashville where my great friend and manager Sam Bass was killed in 1976 and that whole crazy period is immediately right back with me.

In 1976, I'd only been in wrestling a few years but Jerry Lawler was already the King. A monarch has no need for modesty, so I'll say it: At that time, I was the biggest deal in the most important wrestling territory in the whole country. In a year, my partner and I would split from the established local promoter and I would get an ownership stake in the business in the Mid-South. I had the solid platform for a great career that's still going as strong as ever, both locally and nationally, following a short hiatus.

It's a real high-pressure job. For an event like *Judgment Day*, most of the wrestlers have a ten- or fifteen-minute match and they're done. Twenty minutes tops. J.R. and I have to go out and be up and try to be entertaining for the entire show. Our job is to keep everybody excited, every minute, for three straight hours. You have to further the story lines, keep the people informed, and get the matches and the individual wrestlers over. (In wrestling, putting someone "over" means to make them look good.) J.R. and I have a lot of responsibility. Punch the mute button one time and try to watch the show that way. I defy you to make it through one match.

On Pay-Per-View days, there's a production meeting where writers, agents, and the TV crew go over what will happen that particular night. It's all timed out to the second. The referees have earpieces so they can tell the guys, "You'll go home [finish the match] in the next minute." Vince McMahon personally oversees these production meetings. But I don't go to them.

That's always been a pet peeve of mine: I hate to

rehearse. If anyone makes me do it, I'll never say the same thing live I did in rehearsal. I like to be spontaneous and say the first thing that pops into my mind, which isn't always a good idea. I don't even like to know what's planned for the show, much less rehearse what I'm going to say. I find it's more sincere if I am reacting honestly to what I see. That way, I'm experiencing the matches the same way the fans and people at home are. I've always thought that part of my success comes from the fact that I seem to say exactly what a lot of the fans are thinking, and that has to be spontaneous. J.R. certainly goes to the meetings. Everybody goes but me.

These production meetings are at eleven o'clock in the morning. They write the shows during the week, or sometimes as late as the night before, and change them two or three times before the meeting. And they also change the show two or three times after the meeting. One of the reasons I give for not going is that they rewrite the show so many times.

Truth of the matter is, I used to have to go to the production meetings. There was one meeting I was at where they were talking about an angle—plot twist—with Undertaker back when he was this evil entity. (I miss that Undertaker, he was my favorite.) He had recently abducted Stephanie McMahon and he had several subjects that were creatures of the night around him. They'd gone to the ring and grabbed another wrestler, Midian, and they were going to induct him into Undertaker's circle and bring him over to the dark side.

In the production meeting, I was sitting beside Michael Cole, who was taking notes on everything. Vince was saying they were going to lay Midian out on a table and Undertaker was going to stand over him wearing his black hood chanting some evil spell. Undertaker and his acolytes were then going to levitate Midian, make him float in the air. A magician had shown them how to do that with a big metal arm you couldn't see lifting up Midian. Michael Cole and I looked at each other and said this was going to be neat.

Comes time to do the show and someone grabs Midian to prepare for the initiation and Michael and I are ready. But at some point in the day, the technical people found out that the levitation thing wasn't working properly for some reason, so it was decided not to even try it. Michael and I are at the ring and the dark ceremonial stuff is going on up on a stage some way away. Midian is on a table as we anticipated and Undertaker waves his arms over him, also as planned. Michael and I are calling the action, and Michael says, "Oh my gosh, King, look, he's levitating! He's floating in air!" I could see well enough to see that he wasn't moving at all. I looked at Michael and said, "What?" He said, "He's floating. Isn't he?" I said, "I don't think so."

Fortunately, that was *SmackDown!*, and it was being taped, which meant we could go back and add voiceovers, and do what we call a "fix." But had that been *Raw*, where the show is totally live, everybody would have looked like complete idiots. Well, at least Michael would have looked like a complete idiot. After the show, we went back and someone said, "Oh! We forgot to tell you guys. We threw out the levitation deal." That story has remained something I use in my argument against rehearsing. Too many things can go wrong if you're not doing it off the cuff.

At *Judgment Day 2002*, Edge won the hair match. He literally had more to lose and Kurt actually looked pretty good bald. This match allowed me to use some good hair jokes on Edge. "My cat's coughed up better-looking hair than Edge has. I've seen better-looking hair in my shower drain than Edge has." And, "What kind of shampoo do you think Edge uses? Pennzoil or Quaker State?" I said Kurt would actually be doing Edge a favor by shaving off that straggly hair and letting Edge start over from scratch. To be honest with you, all the while J.R. and I were calling this match, I actually thought Kurt was going over and they really were going to shave Edge's head. I hadn't gone to the meeting, and I just thought that cutting Edge's hair would have been the cooler thing to do.

The hell-in-the-cell was very good, but nothing near the legendary match between Mick Foley and Undertaker in 1998, which was just unbelievable. It would be next to impossible to replicate the kind of bumps Foley took that day. Triple H and Jericho sacrificed their bodies in the match, and fortunately, neither one of them was injured. In fact, the worst casualty at *Judgment Day* was the referee Tim White. Triple H was running at Chris Jericho, and Jericho moved out of the way and the ref got nailed into the cage. It looked good, a big bump, and it seemed like he was really hurt. After the match we found out he *was* hurt. He had to be taken to the hospital with a dislocated shoulder that required surgery.

In the main event of *Judgment Day 2002*, Undertaker beat Hogan to become Undisputed Champion and Hogan made a long, emotional goodbye speech to the crowd. It left the fans wondering if this was the last time they'd see the immortal Hulk Hogan, but it promised good things for the next night, because at a *Raw* after a Pay-Per-View all sorts of new angles are usually set up leading to the next big showdown.

Because *Raw* was coming from Memphis, I became an unofficial branch of Ticketmaster for a couple of days. It always happens, people you haven't heard from in years call the day of the event expecting me to get them great seats . . . and for free! This is another one of my pet peeves. When I'm out shopping or eating somewhere, I'm standing there to pay for something, and as I give the cashier my money, that same person will inevitably ask me, "Hey, King, you got any free wrestling tickets?" I usually say, "I didn't just get this burger for free, did I?"

It was a relief to get to the Pyramid to escape the phone calls from people wanting tickets. The Pyramid is a strange building. Acres and acres of stainless steel built Egyptian-style, right on the banks of the Mississippi. At one point, the city of Memphis thought it was going to get the Rock and Roll Hall of Fame and they were going to put it in the little pointy end of the Pyramid on top of the arena. But the Hall went to the King's second-favorite city, Cleveland, so the top of the Pyramid is hollow.

There were far fewer people in the backstage area, both crew and wrestlers, than there had been in Nashville the night before because all the wrestlers who normally appear on *SmackDown!* had gone to Birmingham for a show, leaving just the *Raw* teams for Memphis. Before the fans were let in, I was in the empty arena as some of the guys warmed up. WWE security walks around the arena both ringside and backstage before the doors are open to head off overeager fans. There's always a few individuals who think they can get to a restricted area just by walking quickly and looking official. I saw a couple of guys in yellow T-shirts like the Pyramid staff wears walk in at the top of the stands. One of the WWE security guys shouted up, "Who are you with, concessions?"

"We don't do concessions," the guy shouted back. "We serve beer." Okay, this is Memphis.

It was a special thrill for the King to take his seat beside J.R. at the announcer's table that night. The fans chanted "Jer-ry, Jer-ry," and there were a bunch of signs: "Raw Is War but Lawler Is King, Welcome Home King of Memphis," and "Lawler Will You Marry Me?" (I didn't get a chance to check out who was holding that one. I hope it wasn't a guy.) There was also a sign that read, "Vince Sux Cock." How disgusting. I was embarrassed that a sign like this would appear in my hometown. I was about to go over there and talk to the person. "S-U-C-K-S, you half-wit, not S-U-X!" Don't people know how to spell these days? Anyway, before I could move, the sign was gone.

It turned out that Vince had a surprise for me—Raven, who used to do the commentary for *Sunday Night Heat*, and is really a strange-looking freak with his dreadlocks, or whatever they are, sticking out all over his head—joined J.R. and me to do a bit of color commentating of his own. The idea was that Raven would help out but he would be showing up the King, telling him how the TV should be done. He would piss me off to the extent that we'd have to settle it in the ring.

The viewers on TV just saw Raven show up and sit down next to me at the table, but we did a more elaborate setup from the ring for the live fans because they didn't get to hear any of what Raven was saying. It was stuff about me and Stacy and about my ability as a commentator. He actually seemed to object to the King's interest in puppies. I got to have my say and I was happy to conclude of Raven that "the last time I saw something like you, I flushed it."

Raven actually annoyed a lot of people that night, and they weren't all wrestling fans. Jerry Brisco, who's been in the business for years and who now works for Vince as an agent, told me that when Raven heard about the match, he went to Vince and said he didn't think he should get beat because he wanted to get back into wrestling full-time. Vince changed the finish to allow Raven to get counted out instead of getting pinned. This made a lot of people pretty hot. There's a hierarchy and a code. Someone tells you to do something, you go do it. The word spread quickly 'round the dressing room that Raven didn't want to do a job (get beat) for the King in the King's hometown. I know wrestlers who got hot too.

X-Pac, for one, came to me and said it would be an honor for him to put me over in my hometown. I appreciated that, but it didn't surprise me that Raven didn't want to get beat. A lot of guys think that it damages their character's reputation. It is no big deal to me because my character is now more a commentator than a wrestler.

We had the match. I took some bumps from Raven until I dropped my strap, which is the sign that the King has taken enough and means business. I slapped him 'round the ring and set up the original finish where I was going to do a fist-drop from the second rope, and then cover him for the one-two-three. But instead of waiting to get nailed and counted out, Raven jumped out of the ring as I was standing on the rope with my fist cocked, ready for the dive. It looked kinda goofy and was really anticlimactic, but, whatever, I've had matches finish in much stranger ways in Memphis. Plus I got the win anyway. Getting your hand raised after a match is all that matters, it don't matter how you did it.

SmackDown! tapes on Tuesdays and goes out on Thursday. For fans who haven't been to a live show, there are matches that go on before the TV cameras are running that are just for the benefit of the fans in the house. So they're called house matches or dark matches. I was booked to do a house match at the *SmackDown!* taping in Tupelo, Mississippi, the night after *Raw* in Memphis.

I drove down with my mom and my then girlfriend, Joni. I've wrestled in Tupelo many, many times, though never at the 10,000-seat arena they have now, the BankcorpSouth Center. I hadn't known who I was wrestling until I got to the arena. I learned that my opponent was Prince Albert, who I knew from his days wrestling in Memphis where he got started in the business. He was called Baldo then. He began getting all pierced and tattooed and he had this Prince Albert gimmick going. (Anyone who doesn't know should go ask someone what a Prince Albert is. It's quite an eye-opener. And also the word "gimmick" needs explaining. It can mean a wrestler's shtick. My "gimmick" is being the King. Or, it can be substituted for a body part. As in she kissed my gimmick and I kissed hers.) I like Albert a lot and we had a very good match. Albert had no problem putting me over, and I appreciated it. The fans in Tupelo gave me a rousing welcome like I hadn't heard in years.

My mom and Joni had been watching from the Pre-Tape Room, which is where they put together some of the vignettes and posed shots of the wrestlers used in the graphics before the matches. When I got back there, Hulk Hogan was in the room fixing himself a cup of coffee. Now Hulk and I go way, way back and I know him as Terry. I wanted to introduce Terry to my mom. Terry was great—really gracious and friendly. He told my mom that her son had given him his first real break in the business. He recalled the time he had worked in the

Between innings relaxing with my mother.

Mid-South Coliseum in Memphis almost thirty years before. At the time, he was an inexperienced, young wrestler and I had, in his words, "thrown him to the lions." It was very cool of Hulk to say those nice things about me to my mom.

My wrestling journey that began that day in West Memphis goes on. I want to share the stories of the King, and Jerry, if I can remember a few of them. They go right across the country and to many parts of the world. There are as many peaks and valleys as there are in the Dow Jones average. Success, fame, money, girls, car wrecks, lawsuits, divorce. It's good to be the King alright, but it's not *always* good to be the King.

There's only one place where my story of the journey can begin . . .

Me, Mom and Larry

Memphis, Tennessee. The Bluff City on the mighty Mississippi. The HQ of Federal Express. Site of the first Holiday Inn, and are you ready for this? The home of the first-ever Piggly Wiggly supermarket. Just off I-55 on the way out of the city is Graceland, where the King of rock 'n' roll, Elvis Aaron Presley, lived and where he died in 1977.

Every place you look in my hometown, the King of wrestling has lent his royal presence at some point in time. I made records at Sun Studio like Elvis. I broke Elvis Presley's consecutive sell-out record at the 11,500-seat Mid-South Coliseum—for my wrestling, not for my singing. Right when Elvis died, we were fixing to set up something that would bring the two Kings together for a showdown to decide the "Real" King of Memphis, and it's one of my great regrets that that never came to pass.

I've lived in Memphis all my life apart from a few years my family spent near Cleveland, Ohio, when I was a kid and some time in Nashville. When the family came back, I finished high school and almost immediately started wrestling. It's taken up the biggest part of my life since I was about nineteen. You can make the case for Memphis being the wrestling capital of America. Memphis wrestling is a tradition that goes back way before World War II and the Memphis region was the last major independent that hung on when Vince McMahon and the WWE were rolling over all the local territories in the 1980s. While it might not be as strong as it was in its heyday, Memphis wrestling is still going. And the King has been the man since the early seventies.

Before we get to how that came to be, I want to take you 'round some of the King's Memphis. To me, it's sorta' like introducing a lifelong friend. Just beyond Beale Street, which is the home of the Blues, is the old Lorraine Motel where Dr. Martin Luther King was assassinated in 1968 and which is now the National Civil Rights Museum. I was just a kid working as a shoe salesman at Kinney shoe store that day when someone came in and yelled, "Close the store and go home . . . someone just shot Martin Luther King!"

It would probably sound cool to say I was from a "tough" neighborhood. You know, the kind where a cat with a tail was a tourist. But that wasn't the case. In reality, mine was more like the *Leave It to Beaver* kind of neighborhood. Before we moved to Ohio, our family lived in a house on Vernon Avenue. And when we

came back, minus my brother, Larry, who stayed up there, we went back to the same house. My mother lived in that house a total of forty-seven years.

I went back to Vernon Avenue recently. I guess I remember it like it was when I was a kid. Seeing the sights on my old street brought back a lot of memories. Ours was a little white wooden house. I can remember my dad, in the middle of summer, up on a ladder, no shirt on, sweatin' like crazy, scraping the old paint off the side of the house and spreading on the new paint. It seemed like that house always needed painting. Now it's kind of a yellowish color. Vinyl siding courtesy of Jerry Lawler's Siding Company back in 1989. (That's right, at one time, I lent my name to a local siding company.)

I'm sitting in my car looking over at the Paynes's house. The Paynes always kept the nicest, most well-manicured lawn in the neighborhood. Suddenly a woman stuck her head in through the open car window. She was holding a lit cigarette right in the car and I hate smoke. "Last time I saw you 'round here," she said, "it was snowing. It was the eighties." Good grief, it was Judy Killebrew. She was born and raised in the house next door to Mr. Payne's and she still lives in that same house. Judy's little brother Chris used to be one of the kids I terrorized when I got old enough to be the King of my street.

I got out of the car and walked around. Here's the famous drainage ditch three houses down from mine. It tunneled under the street, made a sharp turn, and came out behind a house on the other side of the street. That ditch is probably less than four feet in diameter, but as kids, we used to have a club in there. We used trees to try to "dam up" the tunnel and make the water back up in the ditch when it rained. We had a meeting place down there and it was really cool if we had a candle or a flashlight to goof around with. As we got a little older, we finally allowed a girl to join our club, and then, if I remember right, it became the "pull down your pants club"!

There's the bit of ground behind the church, that me and the guys played football on every Sunday. That's where my friend Jerry Bryant was running a hundred miles an hour trying to catch one of my passes and went straight into a tree. We all laughed and laughed and old Jerry was lying there in critical condition. I swear I can pick out the tree Jerry collided with. That tree is still there, but Jerry Bryant isn't. He was a great athlete and I later trained him and got him into wrestling. Jerry Bryant loved wrestling, and was pretty darned good at it, but not long after he'd gotten into it, he was told he had Lou Gehrig's disease. There was nothing anyone could do. We just had to sit by and watch as a talented young man, in the prime of his life, wasted away and died. I still think of Jerry every time I go out to play touch football.

My family went to a Methodist Church just a few blocks from our house. Just past it was a little strip shopping center on Macon Road that had the best bakery. Weekday mornings my dad would have to get up real early to go to his job at the Ford plant and sometimes he'd wake me up at 4 A.M. We'd come down here and they'd be making hot doughnuts right there in front of you . . . you know, like they do now at Krispy Kreme. We'd buy some and eat them right there in the bakery, before they had a chance to cool off. Man, were they ever good. Then dad would take me back home. He'd go to work, and I'd go back to bed.

From the time I was eight years old, until I was fourteen, my family lived in Ohio. When we got back from Ohio, I went to Treadwell High School, which was the biggest city school in Memphis. I graduated from Treadwell in

1967, but my picture's still hanging up in one of the hallways. Pro basketball player Penny Hardaway also graduated from Treadwell. He told me he used to look up at my picture and think, "If the King came from this high school, I can make it big too." One thing about my school was that while I was going there, I never got into a fight. Not one. But since I made it big in wrestling, I wish I had a buck for every time I heard about how someone beat me up when they were in high school with me.

I doubled back past Vernon Avenue and drove a few blocks to the house on Wrenwood where my first wife, Kay, the mother of my sons Brian and Kevin, lived when she was in high school. I used to sneak up to her window late at night to talk to her. I wasn't supposed to be going to see her. She had a curfew because she had school the next day, while I could stay up late then because I was a big man at Memphis State on my commercial art scholarship. If you'd have asked that eighteen-year-old young man who was standing outside his girlfriend's window, when he should have been doing schoolwork, what he thought he'd end up doing, I imagine he'd say something to do with his art—a job at Hallmark or American Greetings. Maybe drawing comics for DC or Marvel. Not even close.

I stopped for lunch at one of my favorite Memphis eating spots, Cozy Corner Barbecue. I really like several barbecue places in Memphis. There's Gridley's—at one time they were my favorite. There's also Corky's. They're very good and have locations in cities outside Memphis. Believe it or not, my favorite dish at Corky's is their hot tamales covered with chili. As Jackie Fargo used to say, "It'll make your tongue slap your brains out!" Then there's the "world famous" Rendezvous. But my personal favorite is Cozy Corner. They barbecue chicken, baloney, and Cornish hens. There's even barbecued spaghetti. But I love the ribs. Half a slab of pork ribs with slaw and beans is $8.95. You can't pick at a rib. You got to eat it and worry about being messy later. Once I start in on a slab of those ribs I don't stop for anything. Then I get a toothpick and I've got a whole other meal. I became good friends with the guy who owned Cozy Corner, Mr. Robinson, and he just died a few months ago. His family is still running the restaurant, and he would be proud to know the food is as good as ever.

There are a few people who aren't wrestling fans and who don't know about the King's exploits, but even they know about the matches I had with Andy Kaufman in the early 1980s, especially the first one we had at the Mid-South Coliseum in April 1982. That match got worldwide, mainstream publicity. Up to then Andy had just wrestled women—he was the "self-proclaimed" Intergender Wrestling Champion—but he got more than he bargained for with the King. I put him in the hospital. We later had an even more famous encounter on the Letterman show. I'll be laying down that whole story later in the book and it's the first time it's all been told.

I was still pulling pieces of pork from out my teeth when I drove 'round the old fairgrounds past the big concrete hulk of Liberty Bowl Stadium where they hold important college football games. The Memphis Chicks used to play AA ball in Tim McCarver Stadium, which is back there, too. Tim McCarver's from Memphis, thus the honor of naming the stadium after him . . . I'm still waiting for something to be named after me.

The off-white saucer of the Mid-South Coliseum that's also on the Fairgrounds lot looks kind of sad these days. We had live wrestling shows there every week, from June 19, 1971 to June 17, 1996. I feel like I spent half my life in the place, watching matches, assessing talent, wrestling, doing TV, and so on. We were the last regular tenants they really had in the place, but someone got it registered as a historic building so they can't tear it down.

It's not far from there to the Quonset hut on South Flicker Street where I used to do a radio show on old KWAM Radio, while I was still in college. That was where I first saw wrestlers up close and decided that was something I might be interested in doing. At the same time, I was hanging out at the Southern Frontier Lounge and Restaurant where you could get a twenty-ounce T-bone steak for $2.95. That's right, I said, TWO dollars and ninety-five cents for a T-bone steak! Of course, the steak still had the marks on it from where the jockey was hitting it, but for $2.95, how could you complain? That was Memphis wrestling legend Jackie Fargo's place. But I'm getting way ahead of myself. It's only a couple of miles from KWAM back to the East Memphis street I live on now and I took myself on home.

I have strong feelings for Memphis and the city has returned the affection I have for it. Except for those few citizens who've had the audacity to sue me. The city and Shelby County that surround it each proclaimed May 9, 1988 as "Jerry Lawler Day." That was the day I finally won a World Championship for myself and the city. I talked myself into actually running for mayor of the place in 1999. Out of a field of more than twenty, I came in third.

I've always been proud to be from the bluff city. I've wrestled in front of thousands of fans, in all corners of the world from Japan to Australia, and of course, every state in the Union, and it has always been a special feeling to hear the ring announcer say, "Weighing in at 234 pounds, from MEMPHIS, TENNESSEE, Jerry 'the King' Lawler!" I love Memphis, and I plan on stayin' as long as they'll have me. Plus, the King's name has always carried weight here. Everything from hot dogs, to automobiles, to fireworks has been sold using it. I think the city

is ready for another King venture. I'm thinking of a restaurant somewhat like Hooters only much hotter. I want to find someone to run it who's in the business and knows it well. We'd use my name and call the place . . . "PUPPIES," featuring, of course, good-looking girls with big breasts.

I remember reading a newspaper story in 1993. The reporter wrote about how the King was everywhere. He was watching TV one day and the ads came on. There were three, one after another: The King's Gwatney Chevrolet/Geo ad, followed by his Term-City Furniture ad, followed by his Fireworks City commercial.

Sure enough, in Memphis, there's no escaping the King.

March '63 in Ohio

My father and my mother both came from poor families. So poor, in fact, that all they exchanged at Christmas were glances. To relate it to today, if you were that poor, you'd go to Kentucky Fried Chicken to lick other people's fingers. They grew up in little towns to the east of Memphis, my mom in Whiteville, Tennessee, and my dad in Brownsville, Tennessee. My mother's family was from Germany way back. I don't know anything much about my father's family other than the fact that they came originally from Ireland, hence my middle name, O'Neil.

When I was born, of my grandparents only my mother's mother was still alive. My sons, Brian and Kevin, called my mother Grandma Lawler, while they called their other grandmother E-maw. My grandmother was always "Granny" to my brother and me.

Before we moved to Ohio, and also when we came back, we went every week to see her in Somerville, which was thirty-five miles away. Somerville was a neat place, a very "country" little town, the kind of place where every week someone would have to haul a can of paint to the top of the water tower to cover up what someone wrote about their sister. Besides the water tower, there was a little old movie theater that I think cost

"Granny"

a kid something like fifty cents to go to. I'd always be given a quarter to spend at the five-and-dime, a short walk from my grandmother's house. Almost every time, I'd buy a little metal slingshot and terrorize the neighborhood. I got a major whippin' from my mom one time when I broke out a couple of windows in the old cotton gin.

We'd sometimes spend the night. The first time we were up there, I remember telling my brother I had to go to the bathroom. He said, "Pick a corner!" She didn't have a bathroom in her house, but an honest-to-goodness outhouse. I hated that because in the summer, it would be 150 degrees in there. You'd go in and sit down and look up and without fail, there'd be the world's biggest wasp's nest. You couldn't get up and leave but you couldn't move either. You'd sit there and stare at those big ol' wasps while they sat there and stared back at you.

My father was raised by his aunt and uncle on a farm far from the town. He never really got to go to school, so he never learned to read or write. He could write his name, barely, but as far as write anything else, he wasn't able to. And he couldn't even read the word "the." That obviously limited his opportunities in terms of the jobs. Before my brother or I were born, he worked at the Memphis Zoo. He fed the animals and cleaned out cages and did just about anything else that had to be done there. Six days a week and he made a whopping seventy-five dollars a month. He later took a job on the assembly line at the big Ford Motor Company plant in Memphis. Dad was also hard of hearing—he had a broken eardrum from childhood that meant he was never in the service. He did remarkably well for someone who had a lot of drawbacks. When I was growing up, I don't ever remember it being that big a deal that he couldn't read or write.

The first memories I have are of the little house on Vernon Avenue. The family went north when I was seven years old. There was a dispute between the city of Memphis and Ford. The company wanted to expand and make the assembly plant larger. Apparently all the land around the factory was owned by the city of Memphis and I guess they felt they could just name their price. Ford just shut the place down.

Ford built another assembly plant in a little city called Vermilion, Ohio. They gave some of the workers in Memphis the opportunity to transfer to Ohio, and my dad decided to go for it. First he went up by himself. He found us somewhere to rent, and then we all moved to Ohio. The first place we lived in was in Vermilion itself. With the influx of families moving for the jobs at the plant, there was a housing shortage, so we had to set up house in a little lakefront cottage right on Lake Erie. This was the middle of February and on the day we moved in it was 5 degrees below zero. I'm not sure if the cottage even had permanent heat because it was usually only

My brother Larry and me in Ohio

rented out for the summer season. It was so cold we had
to open the refrigerator to keep warm. That winter the
lake froze over and people could drive their cars onto it.
I don't know why you'd want to do that, but people did.

Coming from Memphis with its mild winters and
year-round warm weather, the climate was a tremendous
shock. We thought we'd moved to the moon or something, it was just so different from the South. My parents
hated the weather, but my brother and I loved the snow.
My parents preferred rain because it was self-shoveling.
I would stay out in the snow so long my mother said she
had to use an ice pick to take off my clothes!

Then we moved to a little town about eight miles
away called Amherst, where we stayed for the rest of the
time we were in Ohio. We lived in two different houses

in Amherst. One was a guest house, actually, that was behind our landlord's house. They lived at 840 Main Street and our address was 840½ Main Street. We had a furnace right in the middle of the basement. I remember one year at Christmas, I got this set of fire trucks I saw in the grocery store we shopped in. I hooked this string on the front of the fire truck and for hours I ran around in circles in the basement, pulling the trucks around that furnace. I also had a great robot that walked on battery-powered legs.

From there we moved across town to the coolest house we ever lived in, 149 Axtel Street. A two-story mansion in my young eyes! Not only did it have an upstairs with three bedrooms, it had a really neat basement, which brother and I got to pretty much use as a playroom. My brother actually saved up his money and bought a pool table to put down there. In what I think was one of the worst days of his life, when they delivered it, the door to the basement was too small to get the pool table through so they had to take it back.

A lot of things happened in the world while we lived in that house. I remember the "British Invasion," as the Beatles became the biggest thing going. The man who lived across the street from us managed a variety store in a shopping center. I worked in his store drawing pictures of the Beatles on T-shirts and pillowcases and the like. Whoever I drew the pictures for had to buy the shirt or pillowcases from the store, and I'd use Magic Markers so the drawings wouldn't wash out. I'd charge a dollar per drawing and then turn right around and spend every penny I made on Beatles records.

Coming from Memphis, I'd not been around any major professional sports teams. That was one of the reasons why wrestling was always so big here—for a long time there were really no pro sports teams at all. People in

Memphis have traditionally been fans of either the St. Louis Cardinals, because they're not that far up the road, or the Atlanta teams, because they are also close, or the Dallas Cowboys, because, for some reason, they are "America's team."

But all of a sudden, as a young boy, I was living near a city that had these big teams. Amherst is only about thirty miles west of Cleveland. In the late fifties, both the Browns and the Indians were actually good. The Browns had an excellent team. They won three NFL Championships in the fifties and again in 1964. Jim Brown played for the team from 1957 to 1965, so I was around when the greatest running back of all time was in his prime.

If the Browns star was Jim Brown, the Indians had Rocky Colavito, who was most famous for hitting four home runs in one game in 1959. He had two great years in 1958 and 1959: 41 homers and 113 RBIs one year, and 42 and 111 the next. So what did Cleveland do? They traded him to Detroit for Harvey Kuenn. What were they thinking? In 1961, Colavito just blew up: 45 homers and 140 RBIs, and Kuenn wasn't even with the Indians by then.

As a kid, I only got to go one time in person, to an Indians game. For us to go into Cleveland was a major deal. It was the big city and it seemed so much larger than Memphis although it was probably only about the same size. I don't know who the Indians played the day I went or if they won or lost, but I still have the souvenir we bought, a little plastic bat with a pennant on it sporting a picture of old Chief Wahoo. That was a real exciting day for me and when we came back to Memphis, I remained a die-hard Indians and Browns fan.

Now I try to catch an Indians and Browns game in person if I can get the chance. If I'm up anywhere near Cleveland, I'll check and see if there's a game on and I'll do my darnedest to go. When the new Browns were

As the King I get to meet many of the Browns players, like quarterback Tim Couch.

started up, they were in the same division as the Tennessee Titans. It can be tricky for the King to go to a game at the Adelphia Coliseum, where the Titans play, and root for the team that isn't from Tennessee. But I was a heel long enough not to care whether people are happy with me or not.

One of the extremely cool things about being the King is that I got to meet a lot of Browns and Indians players over the years. One day, I was looking in the newspaper and it said Sam Rutigliano, Head Coach of the Cleveland Browns, was going to be speaking to the Fellowship of Christian Athletes here in Memphis. I said to myself, oh my gosh, I'd give anything to go and meet him. This must have been sometime between 1978 and 1984, because that's when Sam Rutigliano was the coach.

He was coming on a Friday, and at the time I was wrestling Friday nights in Atlanta. I'd leave early in the day and fly down. They had a late flight back I could catch after I was done wrestling and because of the time difference it got back to Memphis right at midnight. But I thought that was too late and there was no way I could meet the coach. I even asked if I could get off that Friday night but they wouldn't let me.

It had said in the paper that Coach Rutigliano was going to be staying with a guy named John Bramlett, who was an Evangelist, in Memphis. He used to play football for the Denver Broncos. I looked in the phone book and, sure enough, John Bramlett's number was there. I dialed the number, he answered the phone, and I said, "John, this is Jerry Lawler." He said, "Yeah, Jerry, how're you doing?" Another good thing about being the King, you don't have to waste too much time explaining to folks who you are. I told John I'd seen that Sam Rutigliano was going to be staying at his house after the banquet. I said I'd been a die-hard Browns fan since I was a kid and I'd love to get to meet him but I was going to be in Atlanta that evening.

Bramlett said the Coach had a real early flight out the next morning—six-thirty or something like that. But he said his kids would love to meet me. They were huge wrestling fans. He said if I got in at midnight, I should just come over straight from the airport.

I wrestled my match and was praying for the plane not to be late. Sure enough, everything was cool and on time. I landed a little before midnight, and drove straight to the Bramletts' house, arriving right after twelve. That night made such an impression on me. The house had a glass-fronted porch and the inside door was open. As I was walking up the front steps, I could see all the way back to the den. There, sitting in a chair, was Sam Rutigliano. It went through my head, "This guy is the coach of the Cleveland Browns and he's waiting up to meet *me*. How cool is that?"

It was amazing. I was the big mark—fan—for football, so to speak, and all I wanted to do was talk about the Browns and the NFL. John Bramlett's kids had stayed up and all they wanted to talk about was wrestling. All their lives they'd been around football and football players and it was no big deal to them.

Sam Rutigliano was the nicest guy you'd ever want to meet. Amazingly, his college roommate was the guy who went on to become Captain Lou Albano, who, of course, was a big-time wrestling manager. Sam had followed Lou's career and knew about wrestling. We talked and he gave me his business card, with the orange Browns helmet on it, "Head Coach, Sam Rutigliano." He said next time I was in Cleveland, I should call him and I could come out to the training ground and have a meal with the team. He said they were all wrestling fans and would love to meet me. I still have that business card Sam gave me. It's one of my prized possessions.

A few months later, once the preseason started, I called him and he treated me as if we were long-lost buddies: "Hi, Jerry, how're you doing? I told the guys about meeting you down in Memphis. Sure, come out tomorrow." I was in heaven! The Browns had their training camp at Baldwin-Wallace College at Berea, Ohio. It was the neatest thing to walk into that locker room and actually meet the guys who were my heroes. There were a lot of Browns who were wrestling fans, players like Eddie Johnson, Frank Minnifield, Hanford Dixon, Felix Wright, Bob Golic, Dave Puzzuoli, Ozzie Newsome, and Gerald McNeil. The late Eddie Johnson, especially, wanted to talk about wrestling. "Do you know this guy? Have you ever wrestled this guy?" and I'd say, "Yeah, but let's talk about football." He'd say that was just his job. And I'd say, well wrestling's my job.

Eddie Johnson's nickname was the "Assassin" and everyone knows that's a wrestling moniker. Eddie once asked me if I could get him a wrestling mask to go along with his nickname. On one of my trips to Cleveland I took him this really cool black mask and he was so proud of it he actually wore it under his helmet during an NFL game in Denver. There were pictures in the local newspaper of him with the mask on and apparently it didn't set well with head coach Marty Schottenheimer.

I had my own weekly TV talk show, the *Jerry Lawler Show*, that I would do a couple of times a year from Cleveland. I got to meet and interview a lot of guys like Brian Sipe, Clay Matthews, and my all-time favorite Brown, Bernie Kosar. I got to meet the owner, Art Modell, and his son David. Art Modell is a genuinely nice guy who still to this day loves Cleveland. Because Art moved the Browns to Baltimore, where they became the Ravens, not many people in Cleveland love him back. They'd like to see Art go down to Lake Erie and pull a wave over his head. But he was backed into a corner.

The situation was that the stadium was antiquated and he couldn't build the skyboxes modern stadiums

On the field with former Browns quarterback Bernie Kosar.

Frank Derry

have to have. He had to do one of two things: leave the city or sell the team.

I've hung out with the Indians a bunch of times too. My buddy, Frank Derry, who owns the Indians' official news publication, *Indians Ink*, gets me the red-carpet treatment in the press box at Indians games. I've sat next to Indian legend and Hall of Famer, Bob Feller. I've thrown out the first pitch at a game at Jacobs Field and that was a tremendous thrill. Got the ball over the plate too. I've been to Winterhaven—the Indians' spring training camp—and gone out on the field when the games ended and hung out. I've gone into the clubhouse before a game and Ellis Burks is there eating sushi with Matt Lawton, and Ellis looks up and gives me a big, "King!" I get the same feeling I had when I saw Sam Rutigliano waiting up for me, which is like the feeling I got as a kid watching the Tribe play. It's a schoolkid's dreams coming true. And thanks to the celebrity I enjoy from being a wrestler, I get to live out my dreams pretty often.

Dad and me

Once I returned to Memphis, I had to follow my beloved teams from afar. I quickly became more and more interested in the biggest spectator sports deal in town, and that was professional wrestling. At that time, wrestling in North America was divided into a dozen or more territories, most of which supported their live events with local television shows. The first wrestlers I remember seeing were the guys who did the Cleveland television. In the late fifties that meant wrestlers like the Tolos Brothers (John and Chris), Bobo Brazil, and the Sheik. The Sheik was by far the biggest star and the biggest villain; he headlined all the cards I saw on Cleveland television. His real name was Eddie Farhat; in 1964, he began running the territory out of Detroit. Imagine the owner of the territory being the biggest star. . . .

When I was a kid living in Memphis in the early fifties, the city was a hotbed of wrestling. They would have matches in a baseball stadium called Russwood Park, but I don't remember any of them myself. One of the top guys around the time we came back was Sputnik Monroe. He had some classic battles with a wrestler named Billy Wicks. They had a match at Russwood Park for a Cadillac one time and another refereed by former

Heavyweight Boxing Champion Rocky Marciano that attracted more than 15,000 fans.

Sputnik was a colorful character, not all that tall, not all that muscular, but he had a great look and a lot of charisma. He had thick eyebrows and wore a constant scowl on his face as if he were always smelling something rotten. But the most unusual thing about Sputnik, other than his name, was his hair. He had jet-black hair, and then right in the middle of the front of it, he had bleached a big streak of it white. He sort of looked like a skunk, but that hair was Sputnik's gimmick. He wasn't all that great a wrestler, mostly a brawler, but he did really good interviews. He called himself the Diamond Ring and the Cadillac Man.

Sputnik would hang out in the black neighborhoods of Memphis and was probably the first white wrestler to be a huge fan favorite in the black community. He once had a big bout coming up in town, so to promote the event, he bought a big goose and dyed all its feathers pink. He put a rhinestone collar 'round the goose's neck and got himself dressed up in a nice suit with a big hat. He put the goose on a leash and the pair of them walked up and down Beale Street, causing such a commotion the chief of police personally came out and asked Sputnik to stop.

When we came back, I realized that not only did Memphis have its own wrestling show on TV every week, but there were also live events every Monday night at the Ellis Auditorium downtown. My father was already a big wrestling fan and he and I went to the matches down there together once we moved back. That was almost the biggest thing he looked forward to every week. My father had a real bad heart condition—he had seven heart attacks in his life and he couldn't do much physical activity. He was put on disability at the Ford plant in Ohio, which was why we moved back to Tennessee. The biggest weekly check my dad ever got in his life, including overtime, for ten or twelve hours a day in a hot factory, was $99. I used to get fifty cents a week allowance, and thought that was a big deal. When we moved back to Memphis, we had no income other than his disability. My mother had to go to work on the assembly line at the Kimberly-Clark factory.

My dad got a job as an usher for the wrestling events at the Auditorium. His "pay" was two box seat tickets, so we got in free to the matches. We basically *had* to be there every week. I remember seeing so many people for whom wrestling was a major part of their lives every week, much more than just a habit or a hobby. Some of the old people that sat in the same box as my dad and me seemed to live just for the wrestling show. That's when I saw firsthand how passionate some wrestling fans could be. We saw the same fans there every week.

From the beginning, I was a fan of the heels, or the bad guys. I was always drawn to them more than to the babyfaces, as we call the good guys in wrestling. I thought they just had more about them: more style, more charisma, more attitude. They were the guys who took more risks and got more reaction out of the fans. My favorites were the Blue Infernos, who were the top heel team. They were a masked team so they were real mysterious to me. I found out later they were Frank Martinez and Gilberto "Pepe" Merendea. I don't know how many times I waited out back of the auditorium hoping I'd see the Blue Infernos without their masks. How I thought I was going to recognize them, I don't know.

My father was pretty sick, and I'd have to drive us down to the matches once I got my license. My dad passed away in 1969. He was buried on my nineteenth birthday. It was before I started wrestling, before I even had any idea about doing anything in wrestling. I just know that he would have been so thrilled and proud to know that I had become a wrestler and made such a success of it. That would have been great for him; he'd have loved it.

As it was, my dad and I shared years of watching wrestling together on TV and at the Auditorium. The wrestling was on Channel Thirteen in Memphis. The commentators were Lance Russell and Dave Brown, guys who'd figure prominently in my career when it got started. And so would the wrestlers who appeared on their shows and at the Ellis Auditorium, guys like the "German" tag team the Von Brauners; the evil "Japanese" wrestler, Tojo Yamamoto, and, of course, Jackie Fargo. That was the "Fabulous" Jackie Fargo, who had emerged as the top talent in the region. I loved to watch Jackie wrestle. If there was a more crazy idea you could have told the teenaged Jerry Lawler that he'd be working with Jackie Fargo and these guys one day, I don't know what it could have been.

As for that teenager, he spent a lot more time goofing off than doing schoolwork or figuring out what it might be that he wanted to do with his life. The thing about my high-school years was that they were split right down the middle. I went to ninth and tenth grade in Ohio and was just forming friendships there when we moved back to Memphis for the eleventh and twelfth grades at Treadwell High School. Having been gone for seven years, I barely knew anyone other than neighbors or people who had lived close by.

My brother Larry stayed up in Ohio. He had a job and got engaged to a girl. He got married and it was some time before they came back to Memphis. Larry was always more straitlaced and conventional than me. He was always the standard being held up for me to aspire to and I was always wanting to set a different standard. When we came back, it was just my mom, my dad, and me.

My mother remembers there were twenty-one boys living on our street, all about the same age. I guess the girls just

My brother and I had homemade costumes. I'm the pig-ghost.

ran for cover. We were all friends, but that didn't mean we didn't have fights. There were fights all the time. As a matter of fact, any guy on our street with all his teeth was considered a sissy. There were enough of us that we could have whole ball teams. We organized boxing tournaments, football games, corkball games. We all played together and that kept us out of trouble because you never had to leave the street. Actually we were all pretty good kids. Not one kid on my block went to the electric chair.

Our next-door neighbors were the Mashburns, four brothers: David, Dicky, Danny, and . . . Mike. Mike was the youngest and they must have run out of Ds. Next to the Mashburns, there was Terry and Barry Fink. Across the street from me was Cecil Speer and Bobby Brown. Next door on the other side of our house was Chucky and Jimmy Teeters. Their dad, Ted, was a tough kind of guy who used to do stuff to impress kids in the neighborhood. He'd put a firecracker in his teeth and light it. A dumb thing to do perhaps, but it made quite an impression on any kid who happened to be watching.

One of my great friends at the time was Robert Reed, and he's still a friend of mine. If you ask me, I'd say that I was a friendly, fun-loving kid who liked a good practical joke. But Reed remembers it a bit differently. He characterizes me as the "big bully" of the block. He says I terrorized the other kids, twisted their arms, and made them cry. Because I was a big kid, Reed remembers I'd say, "Let's do some boxing," and set up ropes 'round some trees just so I could whack the other guys and torture them. Reed was a pretty good boxer. He was able to take a good punch. Only problem was, he'd take it thirty or forty times a round.

One time Reed's mother called him because she wanted him to go to the store. We were playing touch football right in the middle of the street and his mother calls and our game's screwed up. Reed goes home to get his Stingray bike with its banana seat and its high handlebars. He then starts off for the corner store on Macon Road. But first, he has to cycle past his friends. Of course, he knows something's going to happen to him.

He looks along the street and doesn't see anybody so he takes off, a hundred miles an hour down the slope. I'm out of his sight, up on my porch, about twenty yards from the sidewalk. I see Reed coming, buzzing down. I was holding a football and as I see him draw even with me, I throw the football at him. I'd never have been able to do it again in a million years but the football wedged perfectly between the front wheel and the frame of the bike. Reed flips up and over the handlebars, and flies like Evel Kneivel before crashing into the street. I thought he was dead! Apparently I'd also make him and Chris Killebrew lie down in front of a jump ramp we made for our bikes. And I'd ride right over them, and skin 'em up with the back wheel. It's a miracle those guys on the street survived my reign of terror, but somehow they did.

Another thing Reed claims I did was put a fish scale

in his eye. What kind of weirdo would think of a thing like that? I told him to come over and try out this contact lens I had that would make him see better. I grabbed him in a headlock and stuck it in his eye and asked him what he could see. Not much, probably. Reed was a little younger than me, you understand, and I could get him in trouble pretty easily.

Once at school, a girl I liked named Judy Hart showed me this letter somebody put in her locker. Someone called her a "hor." I thought I had a good idea who'd done it. A couple of days later, I was talking with some friends. Reed was there and I asked him, "By the way, how do you spell 'whore'?" and he said "h-o-r." "Bam!" I dotted his eye. I thought I was being a gentleman defending Judy Hart's honor, but it turned out it wasn't even Reed who wrote the note.

I busted myself up pretty well a lot of the time. The most painful to recall was one particular time at Halloween. I think it was the people next door, the Teeters, instead of candy, gave away those peashooters that used to come with little packets of dried peas. We were going trick-or-treating and I had that peashooter in my mouth and was going to run and jump the ditch that I mentioned before. That was a big deal because it was quite a leap. I ran and jumped and somehow I missed and didn't make it across. The peashooter hit the ground first and ripped all the skin off the roof of my mouth down to my throat. I thought I was dead; it was the worst thing ever, ruined my whole Halloween. I couldn't enjoy eating any of the candy I got because I'd screwed up the inside of my mouth so bad.

When I'd get in trouble, my mom and dad weren't afraid to take it out of my hide. My parents did not spare the rod, I can attest to that. When I got out of line, my mother would haul off and hit me with the nearest thing she could get her hands on. She'd kick me and spank my bottom until it was bright red. I wouldn't be allowed food or drink for the whole day. Then at night my father would come home and really punish me! Well, that may be a little bit of an exaggeration, but that's the way it seemed to me.

My mother chased me 'round the dining-room table with a belt or switch in her hand on more than one occasion. She used to say, "This hurts me worse than it does you." I'd always come back with "Well, be sure and take it easy on yourself!" I sprayed a big hose on my brother Larry one time and knocked him clean over a fence. I think the reason he was climbing the fence in the first place was to get away from me. He sprained his arm pretty bad and had to wear a sling for weeks.

I was always doing something to drive my parents nuts. I guess that's why they tried to give me a hint by putting a sign on my bedroom door: CHECKOUT TIME IS 18.

chapter 5

Before I lost my wrestling cherry in West Memphis, Arkansas, a lot of things had to come together. Looking back, there were any number of coincidences and pieces of good fortune that took place and paved the way for me. It wasn't like Jackie Fargo walked past the house on Vernon Avenue, saw me slamming Mike Mashburn in the yard, and said, "Hey, kid! Wanna be a wrestler?" Strangely enough, what got me in close personal contact with the wrestlers for the first time was another great talent I happen to have and one that goes with wrestling like fly-fishing does with monster truck racing, and that's art.

At high school, I'll be the first to admit I wasn't a very good student. I just hated to study. I remember one of the teachers said of me to my mother one time, "Jerry does just enough to get by." I guess it was the perfect description of me and it was really the attitude I had at school: as long as I got by. School wasn't something I was enjoying so I wasn't going to go out of my way to excel at it. I don't know why I thought like that, but that was the way it was.

I did enjoy one part of school though, and that was art class. At the time, it seemed like that was a blessing and a curse all at once. The blessing was that I did great when I was drawing in art class—straight As and even-

Me and Mom

tually I won a commercial–art's scholarship. Drawing in art class is okay, but unfortunately I'd draw in other classes as well. The curse was that I was drawing most of the time I should have been studying and that would get me in trouble. Either in class or when I should have been doing homework, I'd be drawing Superheroes . . . Superman and Batman, and things like that.

When I was in the eleventh grade, I had an American history class whose teacher was also the head basketball coach. This was Coach "Bear" McLain, so named because he was a big, well, bearish individual. Nice enough guy, but pretty gruff, as most sports coaches are. Treadwell High School had a very good basketball team. They always seemed to make it to the state tournament in Nashville and in my junior year they played in the state championship game, a huge deal for a school from Memphis. For a student such as myself, Coach was a great American history teacher to have because he didn't really care about anything other than basketball. You'd go into his class and he'd say, "Okay, read pages thirty-one through sixty-one. I'm going to the teachers' lounge." And off he'd go, out the door. We'd just be there by ourselves and you might read, you might not.

One of the star basketball players sat right in front of me. His name was Curry Todd. Needless to say, Curry could get away with anything in Coach McLain's class. The Coach grew up on a farm or something and as a young kid he had been kicked in the head by a mule. At least that was the story. He did have this big scar right above his left eye. Curry loved to make fun of the coach's scar. I don't know how many times he did this, but Coach McLain would leave the room and Curry would turn to me and say, "Hey, Lawler, draw a picture of Coach getting kicked by the mule." I'd draw a cartoon picture of Coach getting kicked in the head, blood flying out and everything. Curry'd keep looking over as I was doing it and laughing.

One day, I was just finishing up the picture. It was a particularly good rendition with Coach flying through the air, his head all busted open and cut up. Then I glance up and I see this pair of pants right in front of my desk. I look up all the way and, *Oh God, there's Coach McLain standing over me looking down at my drawing!* It was the scariest thing ever. He grabbed me by the shirt and yanked me up out of the desk, ripping my shirt as he did it. I knew I was dead. He dragged me out into the hallway, pushed me up against a locker, and he said, "Boy, I'll break you down like a shotgun." I was trembling. I was scared to death that he'd paddle me, which they still did back then. Coach was the worst, he'd knock you from one end of the hall to the other.

Fortunately, Coach McLain had mercy on me and took me down to the principal's office. Mr. Maybry, our principal, was an older man, I mean like "real" old. Sometimes you'd see him walking down the hall and you'd wonder if his undertaker knew he got up! Amazingly, this was the first time I'd ever been taken to his office. He says, "Lawler. What's your telephone number?" I said, "My telephone number?" And he said, "Yeah, I need to call your mom." I thought, my God, that's the worst thing you could do! Just beat me. Paddle me. Let Coach McLain paddle me. Hang me from the goalposts by my testicles. Just don't call my mom.

No such luck. Principal Maybry called and got my mom on the phone. He said, "I've got your son Jerry here in my office. He's down here all the time. We have a lot of problems out of him, Mrs. Lawler . . ." What? No, no, no! Holy mackerel, he was setting me up, the old codger. When I got home there was this long switch lying across the table and I got the worst beating I ever did receive.

That's how my drawing would get me into trouble. But I was the King of the art class.

I got a job after school sacking groceries and drawing signs at the local Hogue and Knott grocery store. If they had a promotion, like Green Giant green beans at twenty-nine cents a can, I'd make the little sign with the price on it and draw a picture of the Green Giant. They had the best signs of any store. I'd take my time drawing the signs so I didn't have to spend much time sacking. But I eventually got sacked myself for putting aerosol cans in the incinerator. At night after the store was closed one of our duties was to burn cardboard boxes, in the incinerator. When no one was looking, I'd slip a can of hair spray or maybe a can of spray paint off the shelves, put it in the incinerator, and then run and hide or act like I was cleaning. It took a few minutes, but those cans would heat up, then they would explode with a satisfying *whump!* I'd be whistling away down one of the aisles, and all of a sudden, *Boom, boom!* Sometimes, I'd make it outside in time to watch a big fireball fly up out of the chimney. That used to be the highlight of my workday, but someone squealed on me and that was that.

The cool thing about that grocery store was that every week they'd put a poster in the window to show who was wrestling on Monday night at the Auditorium. The poster would come out on Wednesday and I'd ride my bike down there to see what the matches were going to be. One day I sat down at home and started doing some caricatures and drawings of the wrestlers I was seeing at the Ellis Auditorium. Sometimes I'd draw a storyboard of the week's top match showing the major moves and the finish.

I was happy with the results and I took the drawings to the Auditorium on Monday nights and showed them around. I think it was someone who we sat near at the

Auditorium who suggested I send a couple of them to
Lance Russell, the announcer at Channel Thirteen for
the wrestling show. Figuring I had nothing to lose, I got a
few pictures together and sent them in. I don't know
what I expected, maybe that he'd give them to the
wrestlers and they'd like them and want me to draw
more for them. I know I certainly didn't expect what
happened.

As I always did, I turned on the TV Saturday morning
for the wrestling show. Lance Russell and his colleague
Dave Brown were sitting at the desk and they started
talking about what was going to be on the show that day.
I was looking at the screen and suddenly I noticed, right
on the corner of the announcer's desk, were my drawings! Oh my gosh, what were they going to do? Were
they going to show my drawings on TV? That would be
too good to be true. Then they had the first match. Then
the second, but no mention of my artwork. The drawings
were just lying there on the corner of the desk. Then the
third match. Every show, they would always do a recap
of what had happened in the matches down at the
Auditorium the previous Monday night, then they
would announce who was wrestling who this upcoming
Monday. I was waiting, sweating like crazy, "What are
they going to do with my pictures?"

I was sure the show was going to end without a mention of my art, when, all of a sudden, Lance Russell said,
"We're going to look at the action from the Auditorium
last Monday night. And as a matter of fact we've got
some really nice cartoons done by a fan out there name
of, let me see . . . Jerry Lawler." He said the first match
was Tojo Yamamoto against Jackie Fargo and up on the
screen went my picture of Tojo chopping Jackie Fargo.
My artwork . . . full screen! I thought I'd die, it was just
great. When the program finished, I went out and told all
my neighbors about it. My drawings were on the

wrestling show, did you see? Then there was a phone call for me. As soon as I answered, the voice on the other end was unmistakable. I'd just listened to it for the past ninety minutes. It was Lance Russell! Are you kidding me?

Lance Russell asked if I'd seen the show. I said I had, yes sir. He said everyone seemed to like the drawings. Something about my capturing the essential moment really well. Then he said that, in that segment where they recapped the matches from the previous Monday, they'd show my drawings if I sent them to them every week. I almost fainted!

I did that for three or four weeks and they showed my drawings on the air. Then Lance Russell called me again and this time he asked me to come over to the studio. Lance says my dad bought me a new suit to bring me down the TV station in, but I don't remember that at all. I do know that I was an impressionable seventeen-year-old kid for whom this was far and away the biggest thing that had ever happened. Lance Russell and Dave Brown were stars in Memphis. Big stars! Their live wrestling show got huge ratings. It was the most watched show on Memphis television. They did it in front of a studio audience of only about a hundred people, but that was all the small studio would hold. You had to send away for the tickets and there was a six-month waiting list.

Lance said they wanted to acknowledge me on the air at some point as the artist whose drawings they'd been holding up these last few weeks. I thought I'd just be sitting out among the crowd they had at the broadcast and they'd stick a camera on me for a second. The prospect of that was scary enough, but during a commercial break, someone called me out of the audience and I had to go and sit right next to Lance Russell! I was about to pee my pants! They came back from the commercial and I was sitting there like a statue with my drawings in my hand. "This is Jerry Lawler. He's been doing these cartoons. Show 'em the first picture, Jerry." And my hand moved maybe an inch. I was like the deer caught in the headlights. My eyes were wide open, staring straight ahead. I couldn't blink, I couldn't breathe. It was obvious I was a TV natural.

After the show I met the "Fabulous" Jackie Fargo for the first time. As I mentioned, he was the top wrestling star in the area at the time and I was pretty much in awe of him. Jackie was born and raised in China Grove, North Carolina, and he's back living there now. Jackie puts on a real gruff air and he was not someone to back down. He lived in New York City for a few years in the fifties. First time he was there, he ordered hominy grits with his eggs for breakfast and he got his balls well busted. He said that pretty soon, he was cussing out the waiters and fighting with cabdrivers. He's always been the boss.

That day in the TV studio, he said, "Hey kid, come here." He wanted to see the picture I'd done of him. He said it was pretty good and asked if I could paint it on a wall. "On a wall? Oh, yessir, I guess." He told me that he and this guy called Eddie Bond were partners in a nightclub on Madison Avenue and I should come down there sometime. Jackie Fargo was asking me to come to his nightclub!

A few weeks later, Jackie Fargo caught me in an embarrassing moment. I'd drawn a picture of him and his brother "Roughhouse" wrestling the Blue Infernos. I'd drawn the Fargos putting the Infernos through a table with a Bubba Ray Dudley–style move. But Jackie also saw a picture I'd done for the Blue Infernos. It was just like his, only this time the Infernos were putting the Fargos through a table. He busted my chops a little about how I was going behind his back and doing artwork for his bitter enemy.

Meeting wrestlers like this was a dream come true for

The lady who saved me from the draft, my art teacher, Helen Stahl.

me. But it would take some time, and a few more twists and turns, before I got into a ring. At this point, I actually hoped that someday I'd get a career using my art. I wanted to work for Hallmark or American Greetings. When I got ready to graduate from Treadwell High School, the prospect of being drafted came around all of a sudden. I was looking at getting sent "off to Vietnam on my senior trip," as the Bellamy Brothers song goes. You could get a student deferment, but my family didn't have the money to send anybody to college at the time. My brother went to junior college and worked his way through, but I wasn't expecting to go to college at all.

Fortunately, my art teacher, Helen Stahl, one of the most wonderful women in my life, had saved a whole bunch of art that I'd done over the course of the two years that I was in her class at Treadwell. She put together a portfolio and basically submitted it for me to Memphis State University, what is now the University of Memphis. Next thing I knew, I won a full-tuition commercial-arts scholarship. I was going to get to go college for free to be an artist and not get drafted, all at the same time. I've always been grateful to Ms. Stahl for sticking her neck out for me like that. I'd never have got around to doing that for myself, and she provided another nudge for me along the road toward the Kingdom.

Just to finish that part of the story, I eventually did get drafted. A good friend of mine, Auburn Church, who was the same age as me, got drafted too and we went for our physicals on the same day. His dad worked at the Ford plant as well and moved to Ohio the same time we did so there were a lot of parallels between our families, the biggest being that my brother wound up marrying his sister. Auburn had real bad asthma his whole life. If he came to stay at my house or I stayed at his house, I couldn't sleep at night because his breathing was so loud. Before our physicals, I said to him, "Man, you're lucky, with your asthma, they'll never take you. But I'll be right over there on the front line." But I got deferred for having high blood pressure and they took Auburn right in and he went to Vietnam and wound up a career soldier. He made it through the war, then was stationed in Germany for a while, and is still in the service today. Weird how things like that happen.

I had no idea I had high blood pressure. I had to go six straight days to a doctor to have my blood pressure tested, once in the morning, once in the afternoon. Every day it was high. Not real high, but high enough to get a deferment. At the time, this was 1968, it was almost like I didn't mind being drafted. In a sense, I was looking forward to it, because it was a great adventure. Now I'm glad I didn't have to go, but it wasn't like I didn't want to. As we'll see, I wasn't exactly a hippie. I wasn't protesting the war or burning my draft card or anything. As for the blood pressure, I'd never had any trouble with high blood pressure and I never really have since. It was probably my being nervous at the prospect of going overseas and getting my butt shot off. In some states where there are athletic commissions, you still have to have a physical in order to wrestle and every now and then it will check high. It's strange now to think how a combination of high blood pressure and an art scholarship stopped me from possibly becoming a statistic in Vietnam.

JACKIE FARGO

Jackie Fargo quickly became a large part of my life. I suppose it's true to say that I idolized him. I'd seen him wrestle for years down at the Ellis Auditorium and then I got to meet him at Channel Thirteen. Jackie was an established star at this point and he was using his name to branch out in other directions. Along with the country music star Eddie Bond, Jackie was the celebrity owner of a place called the Southern Frontier Lounge and Restaurant. He was a kind of meet-and-greet guy. Jackie loved my wrestling caricatures and he must have shown them to Eddie Bond. They asked me to come down to the club and paint some right onto the walls. In all, I must have done a hundred of them. They were everywhere, all through the whole place. I did a little picture of Jackie Fargo slamming Eddie Bond, for example, and another one of him riding a bucking bronco. I worked on those for several weeks and got to hang around with Jackie.

It's pretty difficult to believe, but the young King was quite shy around Jackie. No one else, probably, just him. Jackie loved to embarrass me. One day I had actually come in through the front of the club, which was rare because I wasn't old enough to be in there. There was a very good-looking girl called Marie who worked there as

You never forget your first girl, or your first car.

a waitress. Jackie called her over. "Hey, Marie. Com'ere." Then, to me, "Kid. Can you paint her picture?"

"Sure."

"All right. I want you to paint her picture."

"Okay."

"She's gonna pose for you."

"Okay." He paused.

"In the nude."

"Oh, no, no, no. I can't do that."

"What's the matter with you, kid? You won't paint her picture nekkid?"

"Oh, no."

Sometimes Jackie would go and help out in the kitchen and flip the Fargo Burgers they served in the restaurant. I'd knock on the kitchen door. "What the hell you want, boy? I'm busy here."

"Well, if it's okay, I want to get a couple of those Fargo Burgers."

"Okay, then get the hell outta here." Here was the biggest star in Memphis cooking me a hamburger.

Soon, I was like a stooge for Jackie. I ran errands for him in my beat-up 1962 Ford Falcon that I'd wrecked the front of. The thing was forty different colors and hand-painted. One time, Jackie asked me to run him down to the grocery store to get some lettuce. Yes, sir. This was potentially very cool. I was going to drive Jackie down Union Avenue in my crappy old Ford. He got into the car and I pulled out. I glanced over at him and very carefully, he slid down in the seat as far as he could go. I looked quizzical. "You don't think I could let someone see me riding in this shitbox, do you?" he said. I was crushed.

As far as I was concerned, Jackie Fargo was the coolest guy in the world. He was not just a famous wrestler, but an all-around neat guy. It seemed to me like he had the best lifestyle. He was on live TV on Saturday mornings. He wrestled on Monday nights before a huge crowd that was fawning all over him. And there were all these fans, including a lot of pretty women following him 'round the nightclub the rest of the week.

Seeing Jackie Fargo and Eddie Bond in action probably scarred me for life. There were girls hanging 'round the Southern Frontier all the time. Jackie remembers one particular girl called "Suckin' Sue," but alas, she was before my time. I thought Jackie enjoyed what you could describe as a real wrestler's lifestyle. And it was all that. There used to be more groupies then than there are now. At this point, you have to go out and search for groupies and girls, though I'm not saying some guys today don't have a girl in every town.

The difference today is that there's no real contact with the fans at the shows. The wrestlers walk in down the runway to the ring at these arenas and they're about fifteen feet from the fans in the front row. Some fans gather at the point where the wrestlers drive into the arena but they're not even that close then. Usually half of them haven't figured out who was in the car by the time it's gone by. In the sixties and seventies, and on the local circuit, the girls were everywhere and you'd see the same ones every week. That was a big part of the business.

When I was first hanging around Jackie, I was pretty naïve. My experience with girls at high school had been what might charitably be called limited. Sex was not something we talked about 'round the dining table at home. It wasn't something we talked about anyplace. I didn't have any sisters and my brother was already married and out of the house. I didn't really know how to talk to girls or how to approach them. So I did some pretty goofy things that I thought they would find irresistibly impressive.

I wanted to show one particular girl what a tough guy I was. She was going to Treadwell High School and I had already graduated. She'd never met my friend Mike Mashburn, so we concocted what seemed to us to be a brilliant plan. Mike and I took my car and drove to the corner by the school. I got out and started walking down the street. I knew what time this particular girl got out of school and which route she went home. I saw her so I started waving to her as I crossed the street. Here comes Mike Mashburn in my car barreling down the road and I let him hit me. I went up on the hood and down onto the street. Mike stopped the car and jumped out. He picked me up, threw me into the backseat, and took off. We thought that was a great scam but I didn't get anywhere with the girl. I never learned my lesson. I pulled this same stunt for a wrestling angle twenty years later and almost got killed.

There was another girl, named Luanne Stevens, who I actually got as far as going on a date with. Mike and I scripted another scenario that I was certain would get me some action. It was what we'd call in wrestling a "work." Either Mike Mashburn or I had this small switchblade knife. Oh no, you're thinking, where the heck's he going with this?

I picked Luanne up and we drove around. It was around ten, ten-thirty at night. I knew where Mike Mashburn was going to be. I drove by and Mike flipped me off just like we'd planned. I put on the brakes and Luanne said, "Don't stop," but our fearless hero replied,

"No, that guy flipped us off, I'm not going to take that." I stopped the car and backed up. I rolled down the window and said, "You got a problem?" He said, "Yeah, I got a problem. With you." I opened the door and Luanne was saying, "No, don't get out."

I got out anyway and Mike and I started fighting. This was my first attempt to do what I figured the wrestlers did in the ring. I thought they cut themselves with razor blades. Mike had me up against the car so I took a razor blade and cut my head. Blood starts pouring down my head and Luanne hadn't seen it was self-inflicted. I slam Mike against the car and he takes off running. I stagger back around the car and get in and she says, "Oh my God, you're bleeding!" I said, "Look what he had," and I pull out the switchblade. Luanne pretty much goes into a state of shock. I said I was all right but she said, "No, he tried to kill you, he's got a knife."

We drove up to the old Southern Frontier. I figured I was going to get all these sympathy kisses and what have you but it didn't work out that way. She was too freaked out. I cleaned up my head and was ready for her, but she just wanted to go home. This wasn't exactly what I had planned. So I drive her home and she runs in and shouts, "Mom, Dad, we've got to call the police. This guy tried to stab Jerry." I was trying to say that everything was okay but her parents wanted to call the police and call my mother, which was probably worse. I finally got them calmed down and left. I saw Mike Mashburn later. When I threw him against the car he'd jammed his finger and he was going to have to go to the doctor. He was all messed up on the deal too and Luanne and I never had the night of passion I hotly anticipated.

Jackie Fargo and Eddie Bond always had some angle going on. They came up with the idea of opening a sign company, Bond-Fargo Signs, for which I'd do all the art-work and they'd do the promotion on radio shows that they both had going. I started doing the signs after school. They had a small, low building like a shed next to an alley that ran down the side of the Frontier's property and I'd paint the signs in there.

Most of the jobs involved lettering the sides of pickup trucks. But one day, the pastor from the Church of the Nazarene came in. His congregation had just bought a church and there was a big sign out front that had the name of the old church on it. The new guys bought two large pieces of Plexiglas and they wanted "The Church of the Nazarene" painted in plain blue block letters on it. It had to be done in reverse with a white coat sprayed over it so it would show up well when the Plexiglas was put in front of the neon light box.

This was a big job for the sign company: five or six hundred dollars. The Plexiglas alone cost a hundred bucks or something like that. I did the lettering and sprayed over it and was very proud of the job I'd done. The pastor comes up to take a look. I was standing there smiling away and he looks at the sign. He said, "Good work. The lettering is nice and bright." I liked being praised for my artwork. The pastor went on, "But we're the Church of the Nazarene. Not Nazirene." Rather than loyal adherents of the teachings of Jesus Christ, I'd announced his congregation as followers of Adolf Hitler. I'd ruined the whole thing. We had to pay for the Plexiglas and I think they got the sign redone somewhere else.

As I said, I thought the wrestling lifestyle that I was seeing a little of was just great. I wanted to be able to try it just once, to get into the ring one time. I'd watched wrestling closely enough to know these guys weren't really trying to kill each other. Me and my next-door neighbor Mike Mashburn had been out in the backyard body slamming each other and working on our moves for ages. We tried the stunts the wrestlers used on each other but we did it straight on the ground, which was much harder than the ring.

I was so stuck on the idea of getting into the business that I even started wrestling at Memphis State. Collegiate wrestling was not that big a deal at the school. Actually, it hardly existed at all. I think a total of five guys turned out and the baseball coach doubled up and took wrestling as well. There weren't even enough guys to make a team that could compete, but we did get a background in the sport.

My career at Memphis State did not lead to my getting a professional match. What I thought was that one day, I'd get the up nerve to tell Jackie Fargo what I was doing in terms of practicing and watching and trying out stuff. I'd ask him for a chance, or I'd ask him how I'd go about getting a chance. Jackie says now that he knew I was bursting to ask him about wrestling and he was waiting for me to make the first move. For a rib (a joke), he did once bodyslam me into a table full of diners who were friends of his, but that was about as close as I got to discussing the business with him. I never did get the nerve up to ask him about it in person.

So it happened that the first Jackie Fargo really knew about my wrestling was when he heard me discussing it on my radio show. What radio show? We have to back up here a little bit.

'm sorry to say that I hated Memphis State. Well, let me clarify that. I hated college. To me it was the biggest disappointment and waste of time. In my day, Memphis State was always referred to as "Tiger High." (The school mascot was and is a tiger.) State was more like the next year of high school than a big-time college. I quickly became very disillusioned. Art is such a gift, a God-given talent. You can either draw and paint or you can't. They can teach you techniques and certain little things to improve, but you either have that ability or you don't.

I guess I just had a different expectation of what it would be like learning art at college. I thought there would be these great artists who would be so much better than me. They would teach me new things so that I could become a more proficient artist. But when I got there, the art teachers I had couldn't even draw or paint. I didn't have one professor with real artistic ability. For the first time in my life, I failed an art class, because after a while I didn't have any interest in going to class given by someone who wasn't as good as me. I thought I could draw and paint better than any of these people, so what were they going to teach me?

So I started cutting classes, hanging out with a guy named Jim Blake I'd met at a record store he was running near the university. Jim had stores called Atlantis and Popeye's and, later, one called Yellow Submarine. Guess which band Blake really liked? Popeye's Record Shop is where I first met Blake. We were both big Beatles fans and also fans of a science fiction artist named Frank Frazetta. Another thing we had in common was that we were both fans of wrestling.

Blake's store had pinball machines in front and the record store in the back. He and I used to clear out the store after it closed, move some of the pinball machines aside, and wrestle. So, between listening to records, playing pinball machines, and wrestling, Popeye's became a pretty cool place to hang out. I wound up there when I should have been in class.

The way Blake remembers it is that I was always bragging about what a great artist I was. So he called me on it. "If you're so good," he said, "how about doing a Frank Frazetta?" I said, "I can draw as well as Frazetta," and Blake said, "Sure you can. Go home, kid." I said, "If I do one, and it's as good as a Frazetta, will you buy it?" Blake said, "If you do anything half as good as Frazetta, I'll buy it."

Now the truth is, Frank Frazetta is one of the greatest artists ever, in my opinion. I am a huge fan of his work. My all-time favorite is Norman Rockwell, but Frazetta's work is right up there with Rockwell's in my eyes. No way am I really in the same league with Frazetta, but I have done several paintings that would be fairly difficult for the average person to tell apart from his. For Blake, I set out to produce a masterpiece.

Two days later, I take the painting to the store and I show it to Blake. "What do you think of that?" He didn't say anything. He just pulled out his billfold and handed over some money. Blake was real easy but he was very happy to see that I really could paint like Frank Frazetta. From then on, whenever I needed money to go on a date or to fix whatever piece of junk I was driving, I'd draw something and he'd buy it from me. It wasn't a huge amount of money: thirty-five or forty dollars for a painting, but to me it was pretty good money. And Blake has kept every one of those pictures. He put together an art show for me in town years later and displayed all the pictures, but he put prices on them so no one would buy them: $20,000; $30,000 for an original Lawler painting. He didn't want to sell the art, he just liked to collect it.

Jim Blake also ran these underground newspapers that I did drawings for. There was *Atlantis* and *Strawberry Fields*. Another one was called *Tennessee Roc* after the legendary bird of mythology. I drew the bird for the logo and I put headphones on him like he was listening to the stereo. And there was *Nashville Skyline*. They were all newspapers about Blake's two favorite things in the world, art and music. When Blake started the Yellow Submarine, right when I was starting wrestling, I did a big eight-by-eight-foot mural of the Beatles and the Yellow Submarine. We nailed it to the wall but someone stole it from outside the store. I painted the store too with portholes and the like and made another eight-by-eight, this time a Frazetta monster painting.

To those in the know, this all sounds somewhat "countercultural," what with the underground newspapers and everything. Indeed, Blake's stores were what used to be called "head" shops. They sold pipes, papers, paraphernalia. Everything you needed to smoke dope, but not the dope itself. He even sold these light organ things that had different lights that came on depending on the volume of the music. Sometimes, I'd see other hippies come into the store, obviously spaced out, and sit and stare at those lights for hours. I got to meet some real characters around Blake's places of business. A hippie with real matted hair walked in one day wearing only one shoe. I asked, "Did you lose a shoe?" The hippie answered, "Nope, I found one!"

Jim would never smoke dope in front of me, but I suspected he did. He was a for-real, one-hundred-percent, bona fide hippie. He had the long hair like most other hippies of that time. He married a young girl named Nancy, who was sort of a hippie herself. At the wedding both the bride and the groom had really long hair. I heard that after pronouncing them man and wife, the minister said, "Will one of you please kiss the bride?" Jim and Nancy had a baby daughter who they named Mesmerry—a great hippie name.

Some years went by and Nancy grew out of the hippie thing, as did most others. But not Jim. He stayed a hippie and he's still sort of like that today, a happy-go-lucky sort of guy. Meanwhile, I was the straightest guy around Blake's places. I had short hair, except for the little "Beatle bangs" that my mom allowed me to grow over my forehead. As for the dope, I did nothing. I have never in my entire life had an alcoholic drink, smoked a cigarette, or taken a recreational drug of any kind. I never wanted to, never had the urge to. God knows, it's not from any religious conviction or moral objection. I've just never wanted to try a drink or a smoke. Someone told me that, at first, beer tastes awful, but you develop a taste for it. I just never wanted to try anything that tastes awful. Not even once, let alone enough times to develop a taste for it.

I don't think I'm better than anyone else because of this, it's just a fact about me like the color of my eyes. I can't remember my dad having a drink either. I think my mother said that when he was younger, he may have had a beer or two, but no one in my family was a drinker at all. My mother smoked when I was little and I always remember how I hated the smell. Thank goodness she stopped almost forty years ago. So I never drank, never smoked, never did any kind of drugs. Almost everyone else in the business drank some. You'd have a match and go have a beer or get a six-pack with the guys. I may have missed out on some of the camaraderie that goes along with having a beer with the boys, but I like to think of all the money I've saved over the years by never buying a beer or a pack of cigarettes.

There were things we didn't have when I was growing up that became a big deal to me later on. We didn't watch much television. Or maybe I should say, I didn't watch much television. We had one, but it was always tuned to shows my parents liked and I hated. Shows like Lawrence Welk's or Mitch Miller's stupid "sing-along" show. My dad loved *Bonanza*. I always thought it was a weird show. Three guys in high heels, living together! Anyway, my dad had to go to work so early every morning, the TV was turned off early in the evening. So I watched it a lot later on.

Another thing I saw the other kids have that we never had was soft drinks. We never had Cokes, I guess because they cost too much. We drank tea or water. I was in high school before I ever got to buy them. By that

time, everybody else wanted to drink beer but I was happy drinking Cokes. Twelve Cokes a day. Now I have a room in my house that's full of Coca-Cola memorabilia.

But it's not like I was a saint. Did I drink beer until I threw up when I was eighteen? No. Did I cut myself in the head with a razor blade and fake being stabbed to try to earn the affection of a girl? Yes. Did I smoke pot along with everybody else in the seventies? No, I did not. Did I drive through tollbooths at a hundred miles an hour in the middle of the night? You bet I did.

What with all the time I was spending away from school and my general indifference to it, next thing I knew, after my first year, I flunked out and my scholarship was taken away. My first thought was, how am I going to tell my mother? Thankfully, I was bailed out by my buddy Jim Blake, who paid for my second year so I wouldn't have to tell my mother anything. He bought enough of my paintings that I could afford college. I think tuition at the time was something like $250 a semester. That was a good amount of money but it wasn't thousands and thousands of dollars like it is today.

Jim Blake's store had record racks at the back. On Friday and Saturday nights it was a big hangout for college kids and they put a little deejay booth back there and I started doing a little DJing myself. Two of the biggest-name DJs in the country, one who ended up on the East Coast and one who ended up on the West Coast, both cut their teeth in Memphis. The first was from California and he was the hottest thing in town on the seven-to-midnight shift. He was Scott Shannon. He called himself "Super Shan," and everyone in town was listening to him. He's on in New York City right now, with his show *The Morning Zoo*. The West Coast guy, by the way, was Rick Dees.

The great thing about radio is that the listener has to use his imagination. Part of Scott's shtick on his show was the "Gazork." Shannon said at the radio station where he came from in California, he kept a monstrous creature in the basement called a "Gazork." He found that it came in very handy. If anyone ever gave him any problems, the station manager or the program director or anyone, he'd grab 'em and feed 'em to the Gazork. Shannon said he was going to bring the Gazork to Memphis. "Memphis needs a Gazork," he said. He did this week-long thing where he said it was being shipped from California and he kept track of its trip on the radio.

People would call in and tell Scott Shannon who'd pissed them off that day and he'd say, "Okay, hang on a second, I'm going to feed him to the Gazork." There'd be screaming and yelling and this big growl and chewing sounds followed by a big burp. He'd do that three or four times a night. After a couple of weeks, he ran a contest on the radio to draw a picture of the Gazork. The first prize was a color television set, which was huge.

We didn't have a color TV and here was a chance to win one just by drawing something. Second prize was a stereo and third prize was a radio or something. I thought, a color television? Fantastic. I started drawing all different kinds of stuff: great, horrible-looking monstrous things. I must have sent in thirty of them.

The first mall in Memphis had just been built, Southland Mall I believe it was. Scott Shannon announced he was going to have the judging and award the prize there. All the pictures were going to be on display. The judges were Dickie Lee, who had a number one song called "Red, Green, Yellow, and Blue," Scott Shannon, and someone else. All I could think about was that it would be great to win this color TV. The reason I wanted one so bad was because of *Batman*. It was so great, I used to pretend that I liked this girl because she was the only person I knew who had a color TV. I would go to her house and watch *Batman* as a kind of date.

The night before the contest, the telephone rang. "Is this Jerry Lawler?" It was this unmistakable voice. Scott Shannon himself. He was on the radio at the time and I'd been listening, but he called during a song.

"Jerry, this is Scott Shannon from WMPS Radio." *Oh my God!* He said, "Listen, I just wanted to call and tell you, I really feel bad about this." I said, "What do you mean?"

"Without a doubt, your drawings were the best," he said. "Head and shoulders above everything else. But you sent in so many that the other judges thought maybe this thing was rigged. There's one especially I liked and wanted to use. Anyway, I'm calling to tell you they picked a different one. You're going to win second prize. But I want to meet you and get you to do some more drawings for me. I love your artwork."

I was real disappointed I wasn't going to win the color TV, but I was going to meet Scott Shannon. The next day I went to the mall and there were hundreds of Gazork pictures, some good and some horrible, all on display. All my thirty pictures were there. There must have been a thousand people there just to see Scott Shannon because it was his first personal appearance in the city. "Ladies and gentlemen," someone says, "let me introduce, from WMPS, Scott Shannon!" Out he comes, a tall, handsome guy with long blond hair. He had on a white suit with no shirt and a white scarf around his neck.

This was another moment, after life at the Southern Frontier, that may have scarred me for life. All the girls in the place were swooning. It was like Elvis walked in, people were going crazy. And I thought, man, that is something I would love to do. Forget about art. This is what you need to be in life. You need to be a DJ.

I went up on stage and was awarded the stereo. After the appearance I got to meet Shannon and he said he'd love to have me do some artwork for him and he took my number. He was planning to do a weekly survey for the record stores that the station was going to print up. He wanted me to do a caricature of him doing something different every week on the cover of this survey. For me this was a huge honor, the greatest thing since Lance Russell gave me the break on Channel Thirteen.

I started drawing the caricatures and every week I'd take the artwork down to the radio station. The first week Scott Shannon said, "Hey thanks, see you later." Then the next week he asked if I'd like to sit and watch him do the show. After a while I'd go down there when he started the show and stay there the whole four hours watching him. Then he started letting me answer the phone and help out. Finally I got up the nerve to say this was something I'd love to do myself.

Scott said it was next to impossible to start out at a real radio station like the one he worked at without any prior on-air experience. He said I should get my foot in the door any way I could. But the tough thing was that you've got to get involved in a radio station to make a demo tape to take around to get a job. If you don't have experience you can't get a job, but you can't get experience unless you got a job. He knew I was going to Memphis State. He said they have a radio station, see if you can get an air shift. He said he'd show me enough to get an air shift. I probably knew enough already. I certainly didn't know a hundredth of what he did. I wasn't even aware Memphis State had a campus radio station.

Next day, I go out there and find WTGR, the little Tiger radio station. Oh, it was a real radio station, in the sense that there was a studio, a microphone, records to play, and even a broadcast tower. But it only had something like 2,500 watts of power, which meant you couldn't hear it if you ventured very far off campus. Every aspect of the station was run by students who were majoring in broadcasting. Even the station manager was a senior at MSU.

My major was art and I didn't know what my minor

was going to be so I started taking radio and television. I soon found out it wouldn't be as difficult to get on the air as I had thought. There were openings on Friday night and Saturday night air shifts because nobody wanted them. People wanted to be out on dates. So I took the Friday night air shift; 7 P.M. to 10 P.M. All of a sudden, I had my own radio show, but boy, did I suck.

After a few weeks, Scott Shannon asked me to do a demo tape, and let him hear it. I thought it was pretty good, but Scott said it was horrible, so I guess it *was* horrible. I was not that great at running the control board and timing out intros and stuff, when a DJ's talking when the music starts on a song, finishing right as the singer starts their vocals. I'm also sure you've heard a DJ accidentally talk a second or two too long and is still talking when the singer starts. That's called "stepping on" a song. Needless to say, on my first demo tape, I stepped on so many songs, the tape had footprints.

Scott just sat me down in front of the microphone at his station, wrote down exactly what I should say on intros, timed them out perfectly, and did all of the records and every bit of the board work. All I did was talk. He put together a demo tape that made me sound like one of the most polished DJs anywhere. When I listened to it back, I could hardly believe it was me. I thought, man, I'm good! He said I should take this tape and try all the radio stations I could find, anywhere I could get a real job. So I sent the tape out to all the radio stations in Memphis.

At that time, I hated country music. I like it now, and have actually appeared in a country music video with Clay Davidson, but then I never wanted to listen to anything other than the Beatles and the rock music Scott Shannon was playing. I got a call from Eddie Bond, who was the program director at KWAM, which was country. Yes, the same Eddie Bond who was Jackie Fargo's partner at the Southern Frontier. He said he liked my tape and they had an opening. Could I come in and talk about the job? I called Scott Shannon and said, "Oh my gosh, they called me from a country station. I don't want to do that," and he said, "Are you crazy? Take whatever job you can get. Get your foot in the door. You're not going to stay there forever." So I took the job.

That was the little nothing-happening radio station I mentioned before. It was strange how the various parts of my life were coming together. Eddie Bond, who I knew from the restaurant, gave me the job. He did the morning show and guess who was doing a two-hour show in the afternoon slot? Jackie Fargo.

The broadcast part of the station was in the Quonset hut that's still over there on South Flicker Street. The station had a "K" in the call letters because the transmitter was across the Mississippi in West Memphis, Arkansas. That was the first time I learned that all broadcast stations east of the Mississippi River begin with the letter W, and all stations west of the Mississippi begin with the letter K. Did you know that?

The transmitter was barely across the river. Sometimes, it was actually in the river when the Mississippi got close to flood stage. A couple of times, because of technical problems, we'd have to do our show from the transmitter. If the river was up, you'd have to park your car at the edge of a levee, and go in a little rowboat out to the transmitter.

One night, when I got there to do my show, I walked up to the boat and started to get in and paddle out, when I noticed at the bottom of the boat, all curled up, about a four-foot-long water moccasin! (Which is a big old poisonous snake for all you city people.) The guy that was already on the air had to pull a double shift that night, because I never made it out to the transmitter.

The embarrassing part of the deal was that I was given the seven-to-midnight shift, which meant I was on the air opposite Scott Shannon. I'm sure that during my show, I must have sounded pretty unenthusiastic. "Hey." Pause. "You're listening to K-WAM." Pause. "Nine-ninety on your dial." Pause. "Here's . . . Merle Haggard, singing his latest hit, 'Mama Tried.'" I could barely disguise the contempt in my voice. It hardly mattered. I knew there was nobody tuned in. I found out later that there was always at least one person listening.

It didn't take long for the luster of being a radio "star" to wear off, sitting in that little studio by myself, having to endure the likes of Willie Nelson and Ernest Tubb singing through their noses. Sometimes, just to avoid the boredom, I'd call up my friends and they'd come over to the station and hang out while I did the show. There was a record rack that contained all the records on the play list. After you played a song, you were supposed to put the record back in its place in the rack. I had a bad habit of waiting until my show was over to return the records to their rightful places.

I remember one night I had a stack of 45s about four feet high piled on the desk next to me. A friend from high school, Jim Barrom, was there watching me do the show and he'd brought his goofy little brother, Chris, with him. We were talking and piling the records up after I played them. I was right in the middle of doing a live commercial, reading the copy for the Western Lounge, or T. Tommy Thompson's Steakhouse, or something, and my friend's little brother stands up to go to the bathroom and knocks the entire stack of records over right on top of the microphone. Must've sounded on air like the whole radio station had caved in.

The worst part of it was, all the records got damaged or scratched up and from then on you could hear the scratches when they played on the air. It's a miracle I didn't get fired for that one. It wasn't long after that, I ran out of miracles.

I didn't really like working at the country station. I'm

thinking, nobody likes country music, so why was I playing it? One day, I got the bright idea to try and change the station's format on my own. Bob Dylan had come out with an album called *Nashville Skyline* that had a bit of country to it, including the song "Lay Lady Lay." I thought I could sneak in some good stuff every now and then. I brought the album from home, and I put on "Lay, Lady Lay" and I knew the listeners had to be loving it.

Bob Dylan was blaring out of the two big speakers in the studio there when all of a sudden Conway Twitty starts playing! What the hell, Conway Twitty? Where was that coming from? I was thinking, I had another record cued up and I'd done something, and somehow it had started playing, but no, the only record going was Bob Dylan. I was looking at the board, wondering what was going on.

All of a sudden, the hot-line phone starts ringing. I pick it up. "Hello?" It was Eddie Bond, the program director. "Jerry?"

"Yeah."

"Jerry. What is that shit you were playing?"

"Oh, er. Bob Dylan."

"Yeah? Well Bob Dylan don't get played on my radio station. I cut you off at the transmitter. You can pack your stuff up and go head on home." I got fired on the spot for playing Bob Dylan.

A week later, Eddie Bond gave me a reprieve. I got to come back, and believe me, from that point on, my show was as country as cornbread! It worked out well for me too, because I got switched to afternoon drive time. During the afternoon show the wrestling company advertised on the radio station. Not only would they run commercials about wrestling, but every Monday they had a little time slot where they would send a couple of the wrestlers by to do a live interview on the station. I was sitting in my little Quonset hut where nobody ever sees you, a faceless name on the radio. There was nothing glamorous about it, nothing like Scott Shannon walking out in front of all the girls in his white suit.

But on Mondays a big Cadillac would drive up and a couple of wrestlers would get out. They'd always have a couple of good-looking girls with them. They'd come in and do their little promo. "Tonight I'm going to kick this guy's butt." These were the guys I'd see on television every Saturday morning. These guys were big stars, and the girls would be crazy about them.

So I changed my mind again, back to where it had been before I saw Scott Shannon at the shopping mall. I got to thinking, "That's the job right there." I wanted to be a wrestler again, not stuck behind a microphone in a Quonset hut. You don't get any girls that way. I wanted to be a big star . . . on TV!

chapter 8

I nursed my dream for a long time while I worked my various jobs. It was 1970. I was still living at home and going to Memphis State where I'd fallen into the kind of just-enough-to-get-by routine I developed in high school. The sign-painting business was going and I was doing the radio show as well. In whatever spare time I had, I hung out at the Southern Frontier or at Jim Blake's record place. On weekends I'd drive around some of the local burger places like everyone else did. Looking back, it was like I was waiting for something to happen in my life.

One day, I was sitting in the shed where the sign company was situated and this guy walked in. He said his name was Jerry Vickers and he was looking for Jackie. I asked him what he needed and he said he was a wrestler who'd just got to town from Kansas City. He wanted to see how he might go about getting booked in Memphis. I told him Jackie wasn't there right now. I looked at this guy. Jerry Vickers didn't look that much bigger than me or older than me and he said he was a wrestler. He didn't want to be a wrestler, he was a wrestler. He told me he was staying with this other wrestler called Erich Von Brauner who he knew from Kansas City. I'd actually seen Von Brauner wrestle on television and at the Auditorium so I figured Jerry Vickers was legit.

I thought we could trade information. I knew about Jackie and he knew about wrestling. I said that I hung around with Jackie Fargo and wanted to try wrestling but I'd never asked Jackie about it. Jerry Vickers told me he hadn't been in the business that long, and I asked him how he got started, and if he thought it was possible for him to help me get started. I could see his wheels turning. He spotted a mark. He said that before I could get going, I needed boots and tights. "You got boots and tights?"

"Nah."

"I got some I could sell you."

"Really?"

"I've got an extra pair of boots. I'll sell them to you for fifty dollars." At that stage in my life, fifty dollars was like a thousand bucks. But as far as I was concerned, if you had real wrestling boots, that's all it took to make you a real wrestler. So I said all right. He said I should come over to his house and we could work out a little. All I needed was the basics, he said, and then I could go to Mr. Fargo and ask to get booked.

So I took my money out to Jerry Vickers's house. Fifty for the boots. They were a size too big, but I didn't care. He charged me another twenty-five for a little pair of trunks and I cared about that, but I gave him the money anyway. I was now the proud owner of real wrestling boots and tights. That probably turned out to be the best seventy-five dollars I ever spent in my life.

We went out in the backyard and Jerry showed me how to lock it up and some basic moves. I had practiced like this with Mike Mashburn for years, but it was the first time I'd tried anything with a real wrestler. Jerry Vickers told me he was wrestling that Saturday night in West Memphis, Arkansas. I said what do you mean? I'd never heard there was wrestling over the bridge in West Memphis. Apparently they had little independent shows that they had no way of advertising and were never talked about on TV. It was what was called "outlaw wrestling" set up in opposition to the main promotion in the area.

At the time the Memphis territory was controlled by two guys named Nick Gulas and Roy Welch. They promoted the shows at the Ellis Auditorium and also in the major cities in the area like Nashville; Evansville, Indiana; Huntsville, Alabama; Louisville; and so on. Jerry Vickers wanted to see if Jackie Fargo could get him an introduction to Nick Gulas or Roy Welch. But in the meantime, he was involved in this little outlaw deal across the river.

Jerry described the setup for me. He wrestled at the Avon Theater for a promoter called Aubrey Griffith. Griffith was an ex-wrestler who was still trying to make a few bucks out of the business by promoting matches. Jerry said it would be a good place for me to get some practice and he offered to drive me over and introduce me to Griffith and put in a good word for me. "But whatever you do," he said, "Don't say that you've never wrestled before. He won't book a raw rookie. If he asks you, say you've wrestled. Tell him anything. Just say you've wrestled in Florida or somewhere." He said they might use me if they thought I had some wrestling experience. It was very good of Jerry to help me out like this, and I said I'd talk to Jackie Fargo about him.

So we went to West Memphis and the Avon Theater. It turned out to be an old movie theater that had shut down. We walked in past the concession stands and opened the doors. There were seats slanted down, but in front of the screen they'd taken out fifteen or twenty rows. A dirty old ring was set up and over it was a wire with a big galvanized washtub hanging down. This was the ring light, a washtub with four three-hundred-watt light bulbs in it. But to me it looked like Madison Square Garden.

Jerry Vickers introduced me to Aubrey Griffith. He was a little stocky guy and I thought, "How could he have ever wrestled? He's not even as tall as me." Jerry Vickers told

Griffith that I wanted to wrestle. So Aubrey said, predictably enough, "Jerry, have you ever wrestled before?"

"Yeah, a bit."

He said, "Where at?"

"Florida."

He said, "Oh, really? Who'd you wrestle for down there? Who was the promoter?" I looked at Jerry Vickers. Jerry hadn't prepared me for that particular question. I felt like my face was just a neon sign saying, "He's lying, he's lying!" Jerry Vickers then jumped in and did his best to try and bail me out. Jerry said, "Didn't you wrestle for Eddie Graham down there?"

"Yeah. Eddie Graham. Eddie Graham." Like I'd heard of Eddie Graham.

I knew Aubrey Griffith could tell I was lying but he didn't embarrass me by saying so. He just thanked me for coming by and he said he had all the guys he needed right now but I should leave him my number and he'd call me if something came up. It was the classic brush-off. I thought for a second and I said, "Well, I'm on KWAM radio every Friday night. I could talk about your Saturday wrestling matches on my show." And he said, "You're on the radio?"

"Yeah."

"You could talk about our wrestling on the radio? Would I have to buy the spots?" he asked. "Oh, no. I could just say that I'm wrestling over here and talk about it, say who all's wrestling." In other words, free publicity. He paused for a second. "Okay," he said. "Tell you what. You and Jerry Vickers, main event, this Saturday night against the Executioners." Hey, I thought, all right. We're in. Jerry Vickers just looked at me like, How did he do that?

I'd talked my way right onto the card. I was very excited. I blew it out all week long on the radio, talking up the great wrestling that could be seen just over the river in West Memphis. I got the sound effects of a huge crowd from Madison Square Garden and I put together this spot with the big ring bell and the crowd from the Garden, "Saturday night! West Memphis, Arkansas! Avon Theater!" The commercial sounded like this was some huge event.

But as Saturday drew nearer, I began to realize what I'd done. I had no idea what to expect. I'd watched enough wrestling at the Ellis Auditorium and on TV, but the only guy I'd really wrestled was Mike Mashburn in our backyard. As I mentioned, I knew enough from going to the matches that there was a lot of theater involved in wrestling.

For the longest time, I'd thought it was all completely legit. Then a guy named Billy Hicks, who was one of the concessions sellers at the Auditorium, wised me up. He told me that the wrestlers actually talked about their match right before they had it. They discussed how they were going to end it and they knew who was going to win. At this point, it must have been soon after we came back from Ohio, I thought there was no way this could possibly be true. But one Monday the guy took me down into the bowels of the Auditorium and opened a door. In a room were two wrestlers who I knew had a match that night against each other BS-ing like they were old friends. Here was the proof! Now I knew for a fact that the matches weren't strictly competitive. But that's about all I knew about the business.

Come Saturday, Jerry and I drive over to the Avon Theater. The wrestlers dressed right up on the stage of the theater behind the ratty old movie screen. Movie screens are actually perforated and see-through from behind. So when you took your clothes off, you could see whatever people there were in the audience. They couldn't see you, but you'd imagine they could because you could see them plain as day.

I thought about the Executioners. The big tag-team stars in Memphis at the time were the Interns. The main two guys were Jim Starr and Tom Andrews. Before Tom Andrews, they'd started out with Billy Garrett. Their manager was Dr. Ken Ramey. They had a great gimmick; at least I thought it was great. They came out to the ring in medical scrubs, then peeled them off to reveal sterile solid-white wrestling uniforms. They wore masks so as to not be recognized when they were actually working in hospitals. Their manager, Dr. Ramey, had supposedly been a well-respected physician at one time but had lost his license for doing things like storing the patients' bedpans in the freezer. It was so camp like the kind of tongue-in-cheek humor that you'd find on *Batman* on TV. Anyway, the Interns were very well-known guys in the area.

The Executioners were a knockoff of the Interns. Their names were Charles Lipe and Joe Goforth. I looked at them as we all got dressed. Lipe and Goforth. Sounds like something Moses told people to do in the Bible. They didn't look too scary, not nearly as scary as the Interns. Aubrey Griffith came in to talk with us. He said we should go out there and have a good match and after twenty minutes or so, one of the Executioners should take the fall on Jerry Vickers. I later learned that was wrestling lingo meaning one of the Executioners would do something devastating to Jerry, and he'd be counted out. Of course, I couldn't let on that this was my first time, so I acted nonchalant. Sure thing. Sounds good. No problem.

Well, the match did not go precisely according to plan. Neither Aubrey Griffith's plan nor mine. I had come up with an idea. I'd seen the Blue Infernos do this great move in a match in Memphis. They'd got this wrestler named Young Ania and held him out straight and ran him across the ring. They threw him clean out of the ring between the top rope and the second rope. Now usually the guy being thrown would make sure he crashed into the rope or he'd grab hold of it to slow his momentum or to break his fall, so to speak. I'd seen it countless times. But Young Ania kept his arms straight by his sides and went flying out of the ring. When he landed on the floor he must have somehow broken his fall and then he tumbled forward. But it looked like it had killed him. It looked so good I thought, "I want to try that."

When the match started, Jerry Vickers was up first. After a few minutes he tagged me in. When I locked up with one of the Executioners, I asked, under my breath, if they'd be so good as to throw me out of the ring. They didn't seem to have a problem with that. I was grabbed and picked up and run toward the ropes. It brings to mind the famous last words of so many southern men, "Hey, watch this!" I kept my arms straight and waited for the impact so I could go into my tuck and roll on out.

Well, I'm still waiting. The next thing I remember, I'm lying on the ground in the dressing area behind the movie screen. I woke up a bit and looked up and there's Jerry Vickers standing over me fanning a towel in my face. I felt terrible. I told Jerry all I could remember was a loud noise. "Oh yeah," he said. "That was your head hitting the cement." I'd been knocked out cold in my very first match. But still, it was a fantastic thrill for me. Even better, I got paid for it. My first paycheck was for six dollars. It wasn't a check, but six bills in an envelope. I think they said the match lasted a total of six minutes. I reckoned that I made a dollar a minute, and that averaged out to sixty dollars an hour. Compared to the five dollars an hour I was making at the radio station, I was now in high cotton!

When I went back on the radio, I talked up the show again, just like I'd told Aubrey Griffith I would. And I went back to West Memphis to wrestle the next Saturday and the next Saturday and the next. I wouldn't shut up about the wrestling on the air and the crowds actually got a bit better. The first time I went, there may have been twenty people. By the fourth week, there were forty-five. In the end, we may have broken into three figures. Aubrey thought it was thanks to the incessant publicity on the radio. For a while, Jackie Fargo never mentioned anything. But I had a feeling he must have heard about it.

I was still painting the signs for Jackie and Eddie. My wrestling partner Jerry Vickers worked right there next to me too, but nothing to do with wrestling. He was an ambulance driver for one of the companies like Davis or Medic. These companies had one emergency phone number listed in the book, and when you called it, you'd get the dispatcher and tell him your address. The dispatcher would then call the pay phone in the area you were in that they had an ambulance parked near. I often wondered what would have happened if someone had been using the pay phone when the dispatcher was trying to reach the driver. Anyway, Jerry Vickers parked his old ambulance by a pay phone in the alley next to the shed where I painted and he waited there for the phone to ring. He sat there all day, reading, sleeping. If the phone rang, he'd have to go to the call with his ambulance. I don't think he kept that job very long. As for the main reason he'd come to Memphis, Jerry actually never wrestled for Nick Gulas or Roy Welch.

One day when I came into work at the radio station, Eddie Bond was sitting there. He was on the phone and I heard him say, "Oh, come on, Jackie. Don't do that. I'm asking you as a friend, don't do that." I go into the office and Eddie Bond gestures for me to pick up an extension. It's Jackie Fargo. "That no-good little son-of-a-bitch. He's over there putting on fake wrestling matches and talking about it on the radio. We're going to go over there this Saturday night and we're going to kick their ass. We're going to break their arms, hurt those guys." Eddie says, "Come on, Jackie. This is Jerry. He's a friend of ours, you don't want to do that." Jackie says, "Bullshit. They're hurting our business, they're gonna be sorry." They hang up and Eddie says, "Man . . . You messed up now." I felt myself breaking out in a big sweat.

When Eddie Bond left, I called Jerry Vickers. "Man, we're dead." I told him how Jackie Fargo was on the phone saying all the real wrestlers are going to come over and kill us. He says, "What are you talking about?" I said, "I just heard him on the phone telling Eddie Bond. He's hot that I'm talking about it on the radio." There was a country record out at the time by Junior Samples, who was on the TV show *Hee Haw*. It was a song about the tortoise and the hare. The tortoise said, "Your ears are mighty big," and the hare said, "That's all right. They can burn the wind." Jerry says, "I'll tell you one thing. This Saturday night, when I'm in the ring, you keep your eye on the back door. When you're in the ring, I'll keep my eye on the back door. If anyone even looks like a wrestler comes in, we'll burn the wind."

I called Aubrey Griffith and told him we'd better not run on Saturday night. "The real wrestlers are going to come over and beat us up." He just laughed. He'd worked with Fargo over the years. He said, "They're not. They're just trying to scare you. They don't want you talking about it on the radio, that's all." That Saturday, Jerry Vickers and I did the match thinking the real wrestlers were on their way at any minute, but nobody ever showed up. Aubrey Griffith said, "What did I tell you?" He said our wrestling was the same as their wrestling. They just didn't want the free publicity going out over the radio.

Next day, Jackie Fargo came into the radio station. He'd had his fun with me and now he was going to do some business. "Tell you what, kid," he said. "If I get you a match with a Memphis promoter, if I get you booked with Nick Gulas, will you quit talking about that crap on the radio?" "Oh, yes." This was what I'd been waiting for. That was the legit deal, getting a match for Nick Gulas. Jackie said, "Okay, kid. Next Saturday night, you're going to be wrestling in Jonesboro. You can ride out there with me." This was it. A real wrestling match in a real arena for a real organization. And I was going to ride to it with the "Fabulous" Jackie Fargo. I was on my way.

Terry Lawler

Tojo Yamamoto

"**K**ayfabe" is a word that's been around forever in the wrestling business. It's not a word that really exists outside wrestling at all. But once you get involved, you find out right away that if someone says "kayfabe," it means you should shut up and be quiet, or it means you shouldn't talk around a certain person. Or if you say somebody's "kayfabe," they're not part of the business; they're not inside. So you shouldn't talk around them. It's a verb, too. You can "kayfabe" the fans about a match or whatever.

These days, when the WWE crew goes into a new arena for a show, they stick up Xeroxed sheets showing everyone where the various rooms are: production, talent relations, makeup, Vince's office, and the like. There's always a sheet that shows a picture of a fat guy with a big cigar and a pair of manacles and underneath it says "K. Fabe." That's for the kayfabe room and there's one set aside at every arena. In the old days, that always signified somewhere where guys could go to talk over their finishes with their agents. Now, you'll see people doing that in the commissary, which is practically in public. But, in keeping with tradition, they still have the kayfabe room. What's it for? Well, kayfabe. I can't say.

A while back, many of the things we talk about in this book would have been kayfabe. But I think it's been a good thing for wrestling that this isn't the case anymore. I know some people disagree, but I believe it was the best thing that ever happened in the business. If wrestling people had kept trying to convince fans that everything was absolutely real, then it would have been an insult to the fans' intelligence. Television made it a lot more difficult to hoodwink anyone and the Internet now means it's tough to keep anything a secret. I don't really believe many people over the age of about twelve were being fooled, but it was only relatively recently that wrestling executives admitted it wasn't a competitive sport like, say, boxing, where I'm sure nothing's ever been fixed.

It was Vince McMahon who broke the code of silence. In 1989, there was a bill in front of the New Jersey Senate that would stop its athletic commission having anything to do with wrestling. Needless to say, it was about money. The New Jersey Athletic Commission stuck a 10 percent tax on profits from televised sports events. This amounted to a huge payout for the company for something like a Pay-Per-View and obviously Vince didn't want to pay it if he didn't have to. So he stated publicly that wrestling was not a sport, it was entertainment.

I argued the same thing before the Mississippi State Gaming Commission in 1996 when I was setting up a wrestling promotion at the Lucky Lady Casino. They wanted me to do the same background check and buy a big license that they imposed on boxing. I went before the commission and said we're not like boxing. They were concerned about the gambling aspect and I said nobody's going to be able to bet on our matches because it's a choreographed exhibition. It's not in any danger of being interfered with or compromised because it's fixed already.

For a long time, wrestling was overseen by the same athletic commissions that governed boxing. Wrestlers had to be licensed and the athletic commission would take 5 to 10 percent right off the top of every gate for doing nothing. In the old days, the independent promoters wanted the commissions to withhold licenses from their opposition. Over the years, promoters realized they could challenge the opposition in different ways, so the commissions outlived their usefulness. But they were still charging their twenty-five or fifty or a hundred dollars for a license in addition to the cut from the show.

Whatever the reason for the confession, since 1989, what everyone really knew but never admitted has been part of wrestling. The truth is out there, as Agent Mulder used to say. That doesn't mean there aren't secrets in the business. There are secrets in everything. And there's still not much that pisses off someone in the business more than an outsider saying wrestling is fake. Okay, it's choreographed or predetermined, but it's not fake. Fake is a dinosaur in a *Jurassic Park* movie. There were no dinosaurs. The guys are really doing what you see them doing. You better know what you're doing in there, or you're going to get badly hurt. And sometimes wrestlers really do get badly hurt. In 1999 one of the WWE's guys was paralyzed in a fall and some wrestlers have been killed.

Admittedly, if you punch someone in the head in the ring, you're not hitting them as hard as you would in a real fight, but most of the stuff is real. Any match you see, there are moves that require a tremendous amount of athletic skill, strength, timing, and guts, or a combination of all four. So never use the word "fake" with a wrestler. In 1985, the ABC reporter John Stossel asked "Dr. D.," David Schultz, if wrestling was fake and David slapped him and injured his eardrum. Stossel sued Dave and the company. The same year, the comedian Richard Belzer sued Hulk Hogan after he passed out from a Hogan headlock. This stuff hurts, boys and girls.

There's a practice that isn't as common as it used to be and that's "blading." This is when a wrestler hides something real sharp about his person to cut himself with during a match. The best place to cut is on the forehead because it looks really dramatic when the blood flows down and it heals up pretty quickly. You can often spot another wrestler because his forehead looks like a plowed field of scar tissue. Or a peach pit. As I said, blading has been a lot less popular at any level of the business since AIDS, but it used to be an absolutely everyday occurrence. My point is that guys who'll do this in the name of entertainment aren't faking anything. The first time I did it was that mock fight I had with Mike Mashburn in high school when I was trying to get laid. I must have done it hundreds of times since, but for slightly different reasons.

I wanted to establish these couple of things before I started writing about my thirty years in the business: some things are still kayfabe, and wrestling's not fake. Now that those are out of the way, I don't intend to write about every match I ever had. For one thing, I don't remember every match I ever had. I don't remember every match I had this year, so when it comes to writing about 1973, I have a problem. And for another thing, if I included it all, my book would be three times longer than Mick Foley's.

I have to start with my first real match, the one that Jackie Fargo promised to set up for me. He was as good as his word and Jackie drove us out to Jonesboro, Arkansas, where I was matched up against Tojo Yamamoto, who was this short, fat wrestler. He was promoted as being from Japan, but he was actually a Hawaiian guy called Harold Watanabe. Jackie says that one night Tojo and he were waiting in the snow for a cab outside a hotel in Louisville. Tojo was wearing his full sumo outfit with wooden shoes and the hairdo and everything. Someone laughed at Tojo and he said he'd break their face until Jackie reminded him what he was wearing.

Tojo was a mean guy who kept to himself. I found out

later that they would always book the young guys against him. These were guys whose potential or staying power they knew nothing about. Tojo didn't mind going out and beating someone up real bad. I think he rather liked it. If you came back after getting a licking from Tojo, they'd say you had some potential. It was like a rite of passage and many people, after wrestling Tojo, would change their occupation because wrestling wasn't quite what they thought it would be. I knew Tojo was the name guy and my job was to get mashed by him. But I had to do it convincingly—I had to "sell" his moves.

Tojo's main move was his chop. Tojo was no acrobat—this is not Rob Van Dam we're talking about—but his chop sure was effective. He chopped me on the side, then threw me on the rope and chopped me on the head coming off the rope. Chop, chop, chop. All I did was sell his chops, which was very easy to do because he hit me real hard. He didn't pull them at all. My chest was red and I had handprints all over me. He also had this move, called "The Claw," that he applied. It was horrible. For fifteen minutes, he just beat me up. Tojo and I never talked before the match. I was too intimidated and he didn't volunteer to talk to me. He didn't talk to you during the match either; you just knew instinctively when the finish was.

That's probably the biggest difference in today's wrestling. Back then, most people other than Tojo would come out and tell you what the finish was supposed to be but you'd just make up the rest of it on the fly. You'd play off the crowd and see what the crowd is responding to. Today, they lay out every single move from start to finish. Half the guys now, if they forget a move in the middle of a match, they're lost because they can't ad-lib. Now the guys will have a match and if the crowd's not responding, they'll do what they have laid out no matter what.

After my first match with Tojo, I came out of the ring and Jackie said, "Well, kid. Still wanna be a wrestler?" I told Jackie Fargo it was great. I knew that I couldn't act hurt or complain because this was my initiation. So I didn't ever moan. For my pains, they booked me Saturday nights for six straight weeks against Tojo Yamamoto. I got the same treatment every week. I'd wrestle Tojo and he'd beat me real bad. And I'd crawl out of the ring and tell Jackie Fargo how much I loved it. And the truth was, I did love it. There was something about doing the moves and stunts and bumps that was exciting, but the real rush was being out there in front of people, performing.

I was very inexperienced at this point. I think I'd shown enough to prove I wasn't about to quit if I got the wrong end of a thrashing, but that was about it. It was important to find out that I could take the bumps. People ask me about getting thrown around and hit so much. Well, all the stuff pretty much hurts. Knowing how to fall doesn't stop the hit from hurting, but it probably stops you from being injured. When you do something day in and day out, you don't think about it. If someone comes in and bodyslams me and then bodyslams someone who's never been slammed before, it's going to feel much the same to both of us. The difference is the other guy might think he's about to die because his body probably hasn't been put through that type of abuse before.

Over the years, you develop a tolerance to it. I think I have a pretty high pain threshold. You can become immune to poison if you take a little bit every day. You get to where it doesn't affect you. People say, "Don't you get sore?" You don't even think about it. Then one night you might go out bowling, and the next day you'd feel it because you're doing something different that your body's not accustomed to. But even in my first match, the first time I landed on my head, I didn't care. I guess the reason for that was that it knocked me right out. It hurt later sure enough and you come to expect it to. It's like a football player going across the middle to catch a pass. You expect to get hit and it hurts, but you get accustomed to it.

Very soon after my experience with Tojo, I had to make a decision. I couldn't wrestle and work at the sign company and do the radio and go to college. The decision wasn't really that hard for me. I quit everything I was doing and became a wrestler for Gulas/Welch Promotions. I quit college. I quit the radio. I quit the sign company. I was going to try to make it as a pro wrestler. I knew that my mom might not agree with my choice of career.

My father had already passed away by the time I started wrestling full-time. My mother was working every day at Kimberly-Clark, I think on the night shift. She never liked wrestling at all. But my decision was part of a natural progression so it can't have been a total surprise to her. She knew I was around Jackie Fargo. She liked the sign company and thought that was good for me, but I wasn't making much money doing that and I couldn't see how I could turn it into a career. When I told her I had a chance to wrestle for a big organization, I can't remember any specific conversation we had about it. She probably didn't say much. She didn't jump for joy but she didn't say I couldn't do it. I was a grown man anyway and I'd made my mind up.

To this day, she hates the fact that I'm wrestling. She calls it "that mess." Every time I see her, she says, "When are you going to stop that mess and get a real job?" She's hardly ever been able to stand watching me wrestle. The match she went to in Tupelo was probably about the tenth one she's been to in all the years I've been wrestling, and even then she watched from out back. I think she's worried about me getting hurt. She used to go with my dad to the matches at the Ellis Auditorium sometimes, but that was just because he was going. She'd just sit there and watch the other people.

When I was still living with her, there were rules. I had to be in by eleven o'clock, no matter what. One of the nights I was due to wrestle over in West Memphis, there was freezing rain in the air. In Memphis, people panic if they think the roads are going to freeze. My mother said, "You can't go." I said, "But I'm wrestling in the main event." She said the bridge would freeze over and I'd have a wreck. I had to call and say I couldn't be in main event because my mother wouldn't let me go because the roads were going to be slick.

Now I'd decided to go into wrestling full-time, there were going to have to be some changes. First off, I couldn't let my mom stop me from showing up. Second, Jackie Fargo told me my '62 Falcon wasn't going to make it in the business. I was going to have to get another car. But there was no way I could afford one. I'd paid $250 for the Falcon and I had to finance that. My car note every month was $29.00. Sometimes, I used to go to Fargo and ask for an advance on my pay because my car note was due. I'd ask for seventeen dollars, say, so I could make my car payment, and he'd say, "Seventeen dollars? You need a better car." Jackie Fargo was very proud of his cars. He says he used to wear out two new Cadillacs a year.

Jackie Fargo said I had to get a real automobile, but I said it was fine, it was a good car. He said wait 'til you go on a long trip. Sure enough, the car blew up on me pretty quickly. I called Jackie and told him he'd been right. Push rod blew right through the motor. "Uh-huh. Where were you booked?"

"It was quite a trip. Covington, Tennessee," which is like thirty miles from Memphis. But I'd never been out anywhere and it seemed like a long way to me.

Before I could start spending any money, I had to make some. I'd started wrestling, but at the beginning, I just didn't get used very often. A local promoter called Buddy Wayne would book me to referee, often down in Florence, Alabama. Buddy helped me a lot. He asked Nick Gulas if he would let me wrestle in the towns he ran and that exposure was tremendous for me. After a while, Buddy Wayne told Nick Gulas to use me more. "One day, Nick," he said, "we're going to make some money with him." He told Gulas I had some potential. Buddy kept on at Nick Gulas until he finally said, "Okay, let's put the sumbitch on then."

Someone from the Gulas/Welch office called me and said that I was booked that Saturday. Great! And it was on television! Even better. Of course I thought being on TV was the height of everything. I was sure you had to wrestle for years before you got the chance. I thought about all my friends seeing me on TV. But I soon found out that I was earmarked to be what is called the "job" guy on television. The guy who was doing the job was the one who was getting beaten. The featured wrestler would ask, "Who's doing the job?"

It's like the extra guys you've never seen before that Kirk and Spock used to take down to the planet on *Star Trek*. You knew they were in for it. I was raw meat for the local talent.

I went out that first Saturday and found that the match was against the Interns. The real Interns, not any knockoffs this time. They slaughtered me and my partner, probably in less than a minute, but, again, I loved it. I was on the lowest rung on the ladder, getting mashed every week on TV in these "squash matches." It was still a big deal around my neighborhood that I was on TV, even though I think I wrestled every Saturday for an entire year without winning a match.

In the beginning, I bluffed my way through it. I was good from the get-go. It came pretty easily to me, I have to say. Like the artwork, I had a natural talent. And when I wrestled the Interns and other local tag teams like Don and Al Greene and so on, I learned every time. No one was going out of his way to help me and I was going to sink or I was going to swim.

I was in some pretty deep water. I wasn't just wrestling once a Saturday. I wrestled on Nashville TV in the morning and then drove to Huntsville, Alabama, for the TV in the afternoon and got beat there. I'd continue on to Birmingham or Chattanooga and get beat there as well. Sometimes it was Birmingham *and* Chattanooga— four live TV shows in a day. But I'd get fifteen dollars for each one. I was going either single or tag. If they wanted someone put over, I could do it. If they needed a second guy for a tag team, they'd use me and some other jabroni (loser) like me.

After making a grand six dollars for my first match, there were some days when I might clear sixty dollars. But there were many more days when I didn't make anything. That wasn't so bad when I was living with my mom. But my need to make a more steady living got significantly more urgent in 1972 because I became a dad. Twice.

10

My girlfriend was Martha Kay Williams, who was a high school senior. She was as pretty as she could be. She was petite with long, light-brown hair. She had a great little body. We hadn't been dating for very long when she became pregnant. She called me up one day and said, "I've got some news." I was so stupid and naïve, I almost asked her if she was sure it was hers. A typical young kid, I never thought about birth control. Oh no, no need for that. As I've said, sex was never, ever talked about in my family so there'd been no little talk about the birds and the bees. Sex was never discussed. Totally taboo. But it probably had the opposite effect to what my mother intended. All of a sudden you came of age and you were able to partake of it, it was like, *Oh my God! This is great. The forbidden fruit.* I couldn't get enough of it. I guess I'd just never really thought about the consequences.

I'd still been a virgin when I started wrestling. When we moved from Ohio back to Memphis, it was right in the middle of high school. I went back to people I didn't even know. The school wasn't snobby or upper scale or anything but I didn't really go out of my way to fit in. I concentrated on my art to a great extent. The end of the sixties was a wild and crazy time and high-school kids

Kay

were experimenting with things and being rebellious but I wasn't in that mode. I didn't fit in with that kind of crowd. And I was a bit shy with girls. The King would be horrified to admit it, but it's true. Being that age should be great, but it isn't always.

I didn't have any money and girls would often go for the guys with the nice cars and the good clothes. A lot of the guys' parents would buy them a car when they were sixteen. I remember being really envious of this one guy at school named Reaume Inman. He wasn't the most handsome guy in school, but the girls flocked around him because he had the coolest car in school, a brand new Pontiac GTO. I could just picture myself behind the wheel of that GTO with a beautiful cheerleader on my arm. But unfortunately for me, I didn't get a car until after I graduated. Without a car, I didn't really have any way to date when I was in high school. My parents would say, "If you want to go somewhere, we'll take you." That's the last thing you want, your parents to drive you on a date.

When the senior prom came around, I didn't have anyone to go with. There was a girl named Hope McDaniel, who was one of the prettiest girls in senior class. She was so pretty, in fact, that most of the guys were intimidated. She was in my art class and we talked there one day. She asked who I was going to the senior prom with and I said I probably wasn't going to go because I didn't have a date. She said she probably wasn't going to go either because no one had asked her. So it was one of those mutually agreed ideas that we would go together. She was really great, but nothing came of it. I didn't dance or anything, so it was a "one-date wonder."

The first girl I was ever with came about when I was working at the radio station. Listeners would call up and request records. This woman called in and we started talking. She would call several times a night and we talked more each time she called. She wound up inviting

Hope McDaniel. I told you she was the prettiest girl in the class.

me over to her house and I went to meet her. I had no idea what she looked like. She had a nice voice, but she could have been so ugly she'd make roadkill get up and run away. When I got to her house, I was pleasantly surprised. She was older than me, in her thirties. Nice-looking. We talked awhile. She knew what she was after, otherwise she would never have asked me to come to the house. But when she found out that I was a virgin, that she'd be getting a cherry, it was like, oh boy. Her eyes lit up.

It was a memorable and pleasurable experience. In the afterglow, lying there, trying to make a little conversation, she happened to mention that her husband had just gotten out of prison the day before and he could be coming home sometime. Her HUSBAND! PRISON! I wasn't going to hang out. I set a record getting dressed and getting out. She said he wasn't getting there that minute but I said it was okay, I had to leave. She was a good teacher. I had a few more rendezvous with her when her convict husband wasn't around.

So I'd broken the ice. And the next girl was Kay. I met her at the local high school hangout. There were three drive-through places in a row. There was a Shoney's Big Boy, there was Krystal Hamburgers, and a little way down was Sandy's, another hamburger joint that actually had the best food of the three. Every Friday and Saturday night everybody who had a car would drive very slowly down Summer Avenue to Sandy's and go through Krystal and then through Shoney's. If you saw someone you knew, you'd stop, if you could find a parking space. It was a neat and safe way to hang out. The only danger came later when you hooked up with someone and went parking.

I guess Kay and I must have had most of our liaisons in the car. A couple of times we met up at my house because my mother worked nights. My mother was always lurking, trying to catch me doing something wrong. One time, we left a little spot on the couch. I know what Bill Clinton must have felt like when he realized he left a stain on Monica's dress. Next day, my mother pointed at it and said, "What's this on the couch?" My eyes bugged out like Roger Rabbit. There was nobody there but my mother and me and she knew she hadn't gotten it there. She didn't know what it was and I'm sure that what it really was never occurred to her. But if she's read this far, she knows now.

When Kay called me and said she was pregnant, I said, "You've got to be kidding me . . ." as if this were a complete impossibility. My first thought was the same as millions of young men who've been in this situation. What's my mom going to say? My mother was always extremely conscious of how things appeared to other people. She was always worrying what people would think. She drilled this into me my whole life: I just knew that the worst thing *ever* was a baby born out of wedlock. As soon as Kay was sure she was pregnant, all I could think of was getting married as quickly as possible so that when the baby was born it wouldn't raise too many eyebrows. An abortion was not even a consideration. So I said to Kay, "I think we need to get married."

We knew if we told her parents and my mom we wanted to get married they'd want to know why. It would have been pretty obvious and we didn't want to tell them what the deal was. So we eloped. I'd already refereed and wrestled a bit in Florence, Alabama. I checked, and Alabama was one of the states where you didn't need a blood test or a waiting period to get married. You could walk into the Justice of the Peace's office and get it done in about five minutes.

I picked Kay up one morning and we drove down to Florence. It was about a hundred and forty miles from Memphis. On the way there we didn't even talk about the life-altering event that was about to take place. We were in love . . . or at least, in lust. We went right to the Justice of the Peace and got married. After the little ceremony, I told Kay we couldn't afford a honeymoon at Niagara Falls, so I suggested we drive through a car wash slowly. I was trying to be funny in a pretty unfunny situation. I remember she didn't find it amusing. Instead, we checked into a motel. We knew everyone was going to be wondering where we were so we had to call our parents. They probably knew what was going on and when it came down to it, nobody raised a real stink over the fact we got married. There wasn't a great deal anyone could have done about it at that point anyway.

The way it went down pretty much guaranteed that my mother never liked Kay. Kay had taken her little boy. She tried not to show it outwardly. My mother is extremely old-fashioned. The first thing that got Kay on her bad side was the simple fact that Kay would call me on the telephone. My mother thought that was horrible. "Nuh-uh. A girl don't call a boy. That's not done." I didn't know what was wrong with it exactly, but she thought it just wasn't done. That was the beginning. From then on, she had it in for Kay. I was supposed to be home at eleven o'clock, but if I got in at eleven-fifteen, she blamed Kay. They never had a good relationship.

Kay and I got a little, and I mean little, apartment over on Jackson Avenue in Memphis. Jackson Avenue was in the kind of neighborhood where if you paid your rent on time they arrested you for robbery, but it was all we could afford. She quit high school, though she later went back and got her diploma. In January 1972, Brian was born. And, are you ready for this, ten months later, Kevin was born. It was a classic set of Irish twins. Poor Kay was pregnant again one month after having Brian. We were obviously a pretty potent combination. I used to tell Kay, "Wow, you're fertile as a turtle!" I think her father finally suggested we get a TV to watch at night. Right after Kevin was on the way, I went out and had a vasectomy. The unkind cut. From that point on, I was shooting blanks. Every time I tell someone about the operation, the first words out of their mouths are "Did it hurt?" The answer is no, not a bit. As a matter of fact, I sat there and watched it being done and it took about ten minutes. I could have jogged home after. It's a great operation until you change your mind, but now's not the time for that story.

Kay had a time being pregnant with Brian. Pregnancy is an example of a woman's ability to take physical pain. No man could go through it. No man could stand morning sickness. After the first urge to hurl, he'd say to himself, "If that woman tries to have sex with me again, I'll kill her!" Poor Kay was really sick every day. I was wrestling in these little towns and she was riding in the car on these trips, getting sick every time.

I'd just got started and I wasn't wrestling in any of the

premier venues. I didn't even get to wrestle in Memphis. There were matches Monday night in Memphis but instead of wrestling in my hometown, I was having to go on Mondays to Birmingham and then on to Johnson City, Tennessee, on Tuesday. I don't know how good your southern geography is, but these two places are pretty far apart and I had a brutal schedule.

First thing Monday morning, I'd drive over to Summer Avenue and catch a Greyhound bus to Birmingham. It left about seven in the morning, stopped in every little Podunk town in between, and crawled into Birmingham at five in the evening. The bus station was right across the street from the Boutwell Auditorium. I'd walk over there and wrestle, usually the first or second match. At that point in my career, I was known as a "curtain jerker." The show would be over at ten o'clock. I'd walk back to the bus station. At one-thirty in the morning there was a mail bus to Memphis. It was a regular Greyhound bus, but all the seats had been taken out and the entire bus was used to haul mail and cargo. There was one seat behind the driver and they'd sell me a ticket for it. There usually wasn't a line.

I'd get back from Birmingham at 6 A.M., just in time to start the drive to Johnson City, Tennessee. Johnson City is three hundred miles from Nashville, so it's five hundred miles from Memphis. If you measured a straight line from Johnson City, it was actually closer to Canada than it was to Memphis. I'd drive over, wrestle, and drive back to Nashville and stay there. I'd wrestle there Wednesday and usually go to Bowling Green, Kentucky, on Thursday before returning to Memphis. I did that for months before I told promoter Nick Gulas I couldn't do it anymore. For all that, I got twenty-five bucks out of the Johnson City run.

So, next thing we knew, Kay and I had two kids. The marriage was difficult on both of us. I was doing what I enjoyed, but I was traveling all over the place. I didn't feel good about the fact I was leaving the wife and two kids at home. Kay didn't have the kind of life she wanted either. One minute she was a high-school senior and less than a year later she was married with two babies to take care of and a husband who was gone most of the time. She did about ten years of living in twelve months. It wasn't an ideal situation by any means, but she never complained.

When I got to be more successful in Memphis, we had to move to Nashville because you couldn't live in Memphis if you wanted to wrestle full-time in the territory. Nick Gulas and Roy Welch said that if a wrestler lives in the main town, two things would eventually happen. First, the wrestler would be seen around town so often that he wouldn't seem special, or a star, and the fans wouldn't want to pay money to see him. Second, the wrestler would do something stupid or get into some kind of trouble to bring bad publicity on the business. They were trying to protect their most important assets: the wrestlers and the fans.

So Gulas and Welch made all the better Memphis wrestlers live in Nashville. Also, Nashville was a central location for the territory and it was where the office was located. Kay didn't want to move to Nashville because all her family was back in Memphis. Her mother had been great about helping with the kids, which gave Kay some semblance of a normal life. Kay didn't know a soul in Nashville—no friends, no family, and she was stuck there with the kids.

This is a very hard business to be in if you're married. I would go so far as to discourage a young guy with a family from pursuing it. He's putting a lot on the line. Look around any part of the entertainment world and it's the same: any job in showbiz is tough on a marriage. It's a very different kind of life from most any other. For one thing, you're away from home a lot and you're exposed to all sorts of easy temptations. And there are girls who'll let you know that they're yours for the asking. That's difficult enough for any guy.

I think the nature of being a star in any entertainment field adds to the problems. If someone's in the spotlight, part of your appeal, part of what you have to do to make people come and see you is to allow them to think you're available. Even if you're married, it's always been best in the business to keep it quiet. It was always drilled into me, by veterans in the business, never let anyone know you're married. It's the kiss of death as far as female fans are concerned. It's the same with boy bands or anything like that.

My longtime business partner, Jerry Jarrett, was at one time the most over babyface wrestler there'd ever been in the Memphis territory. He was the first good-looking young guy who was pushed hard and promoted and the girls went crazy over him. He was so over it was unreal. He was like a rock star. And no one knew he was married.

Jerry's mother, Christine, was helping to promote Louisville and that was the city he was probably the most popular in. One night there was a big sellout crowd and Jerry wasn't there because his wife had just given birth to a child. Christine went out and made an announcement. "Jerry can't be here tonight. His wife gave birth to a little daughter." A hush went over the place. Things went downhill from that point on. He seemed to lose his drawing power with the fans.

I think this is a combination of two things. The female fans will no longer look at the guy as being available. Even if there was zero chance of you getting it on with the guy in question, you could have that fantasy. But also, when people are paying money to come and see you, they want you to be special. They want you to be different. They don't want to think you have the same life they have. The

Second-generation rivalry: David Flair, Ric's son, and Brian Christopher, my son.

big star shouldn't be having to get up to change diapers in the middle of the night or worry about having to pay the house note. Of course they do have the same problems as other people, but most fans want to suspend disbelief and think you're larger than life. If you let them know you're married and have kids too, you're not so special.

That was another reason promoters didn't want us living in Memphis. They didn't want fans to see you trailing around town with the wife and kids. Not that I did a lot of that; I was on the road so much. I'll be the first to admit I was neither a great husband to Kay nor a great father to Brian and Kevin. Kay and I got divorced when Brian was about seven. They were both about seven. I wasn't around a tremendous amount when they were growing up. I've spent more time with Brian since he got into the business. I know him better as Brian Christopher than I did as Brian Lawler. It's more like we're a couple of the boys in the business together rather than father and son.

I can't remember Brian coming to me and saying he wanted to be in the business. I don't know if we had that conversation. I know that he started wrestling in his backyard like I did when he was in high school. He never came to me and asked for a special leg up because of my position in the business. Instead, he went to my partner Jerry Jarrett and Jerry got him started. I think it was smart of him to go that way about it and he's been successful in his career.

It's been my experience with all the other wrestling promoters' sons or wrestlers' sons that it seems like they got special treatment. About the only one I saw who didn't do that was Roy Welch. He had a son who wrestled whose name was Buddy. He changed his name to Buddy Fuller because he didn't want the stigma of being the boss' son. It's like being the football coach's son playing quarterback. Is he quarterback because he's actually good or because he's the coach's son? There have been plenty of really good second-generation wrestlers who've got ahead on their own talent from The Rock and Jeff Jarrett back through the years, but I've seen it the other way so many times.

Kevin has had a few jobs. Carpet cleaning, pizza delivering. He lives in Memphis. He was always more interested in wrestling than Brian but he was never really big enough to get as far as he would have liked. He's wrestled on occasion and refereed and run towns. He's done everything there is to do in the business but he's never been able to make much money at it mainly because of his size.

Brian was up with the WWE, of course. He was wrestling as GrandMaster Sexay and was probably best known as part of "Too Cool" with Scotty 2 Hotty. But in 2001, Brian got fired after some drugs were found in his luggage at Calgary Airport. Believe it or not, I have never really gotten the complete story of what actually happened. From what I heard, it was really nothing more than residue. If it had been any significant amount of drugs, he would have been in really bad trouble, and gone to jail.

Brian was detained for a few hours at the border and then let go. He had to pay a fine and he doesn't have a permanent record, but it was enough to cost him his job because you can't screw up the Canadian border for the WWE. They do so many shows in Canada every year, and they take so much equipment across the border for these shows. Can you imagine if the reputation got out that WWE people bring drugs across the border? They could make them stop every truck and take everything off and take it to pieces. They can't afford that, so Brian was let go. Some people think they made an example of Brian. I think they treated him just like they would anyone on the roster in the same situation. The WWE can never be accused of being indecisive when they get rid of someone. Bottom line, Brian lost a great job because he made a stupid decision and I think he knows that now. I hope he knows that.

I'm often asked why I don't acknowledge Brian as my son in the business. We've wrestled together plenty of times but never as a father-son team. Part of that's because of what I said before, that he wanted to do it on his own and I didn't want to be any kind of albatross to him. But also I wouldn't really have deserved to take the credit if he was good. In truth, I wasn't around so much when he was growing up and it wouldn't really have been right for me to say, "Look what I made." What Brian has done, and Kevin too, they've done on their own. And I'm extremely proud of both of them.

11

I met Jerry Jarrett for the first time in Huntsville, Alabama. He started wrestling a bit before me and I knew he was a young guy who was getting to wrestle in the main events. He was teamed up with Tojo Yamamoto right away while I had to start wrestling in the opening matches. What I didn't realize was that he was working in the office for Nick Gulas, doing the booking, creating story lines, and deciding who got put in the main events. And his mother, Christine, had worked for Nick for years. Because he was in the office he had some pull, so he got put in the main events (I would find out later, that's one of the advantages of being the booker), but I didn't really know who he was.

That night in Huntsville, this guy came into the dressing room and sat down beside me. I'd just finished wrestling the first match and I was taking my boots off. I knew this was Jerry Jarrett, but he didn't look anything special—about my age, a bit smaller than me. He said he'd watched my match and he started giving me some pointers about what he thought I should do. He said he thought it would be better if I did this or if I did that. I don't recall exactly what he was saying, but I do remember the reaction I had. I listened and I was thinking, "Who's this guy telling me what to do? He's not that hot himself."

So I glanced over to him and said, "Really?" He said, "Yeah." So I said, "I'll tell you what. You wrestle your way, and I'll wrestle mine. Okay?" He looked a bit shocked and he got up and left. The next week, I got sent to wrestle in Alabama again. When I got down there someone asked me if I knew Jerry Jarrett was doing the booking and the penny dropped. That's why I was out of Memphis—I'd pissed off the booker. But it was actually the best thing that ever happened to me because I got to wrestle every night, whereas before I was wrestling two or three nights a week. Had I stayed in Memphis, I probably would have kept on getting beat week in and week out.

A new territory opened in Alabama. A guy named Bill Golden called Nick Gulas, who was a friend of his, and said he wanted to run some towns in Alabama. He lived in Montgomery and he wanted to operate some venues from there. He asked if Nick had some guys he could run down there and in return he'd give Nick a percentage of his gates. Nick jumped at this opportunity because he didn't have to do any work other than receive a check each week. It was like found money. Golden ran Montgomery, Gadsden, Anniston, Tuscaloosa, Alabama, and Columbus, Mississippi.

Nick called me one day and said, "Kid, I'm going to send you down to Alabama." At that point, I wasn't doing the long run to Johnson City anymore but neither was I wrestling in the main towns like Memphis, Louisville, or Evansville. I just got squashed on TV and then squashed again in Jonesboro or Dyersburg or one of the small towns around Memphis. But even so, when I was told I was going to Alabama, I couldn't help feeling like a ballplayer being sent back to AAA.

I went down to Alabama with a bunch of guys who were about the same level as myself. I didn't feel intimidated by anybody. I knew I was as good, or as bad, as anybody down there. I began to have competitive matches rather than just being beaten. When a wrestler started out in those days, he usually began as part of a tag team. The Tennessee territory was big on tag-team matches. Tag teams were interchangeable and they mixed up the guys until they found something that worked. It was only when someone got noticed in a tag team that they were moved to being a solo wrestler and that was where people got to be stars.

The first guy I'd been teamed with on a regular basis was a wrestler named George Strickland. George had been the promoter who got Dr. Sam Sheppard into wrestling; later Sheppard married George's daughter. Sam Sheppard was the guy whose story they used for the Harrison Ford movie *The Fugitive*. It was a famous murder case up in Cleveland. His wife had been murdered in 1954 and he was convicted. He always claimed it was another guy. Unlike Harrison Ford, the real Sam Sheppard didn't escape—he was sent to prison. He spent ten years in the Ohio Penitentiary before he was released.

When Sheppard got out of prison, George actually started him wrestling. He sucked as a wrestler but people came to see him because of all his notoriety. Can you imagine what crowds O. J. Simpson would draw if he started wrestling? Strickland and Sheppard teamed together for a while and then they put me with George. He was an older guy and near the end of his career and so I think they thought putting George with a young partner would give him some new life. Plus, he was a good "ring general" for me to learn under.

When I got sent to Alabama, some other combinations opened up. Nick Gulas told Bill Golden about this guy called Steve Kyle. He'd told Steve he thought he looked just like me, so he sent him down to Alabama. Bill Golden told me Nick was sending this guy along who was the spitting image of me. He said we were like twins and we were going to wrestle as the Lawler Brothers.

So Steve Kyle arrives. Alright, there's this guy. Where's the one who looks like me? At the time I weighed about one-eighty and Steve Kyle must have weighed two-sixty. He wrestled as Steve "The Body" Lawler. How could they think we looked anything alike? I thought he was a dork. But as a team, he made the perfect straight man for me to be the crazy, flamboyant guy. He was more of a technical, on-the-ground wrestler and I would do all the flying bumps. The Lawler Brothers clicked as a team and all the towns started drawing money.

Then a guy named Sam Bass came along as a manager. He was working with a guy called Roy Bass and they were running with a cowboy gimmick as a pair of outlaws. There was another wrestler in the area, Jim White, who went as a masked wrestler called the Green Shadow. As I said, they were always mixing guys up, throwing stuff at the wall, and seeing what stuck. So they took the mask off the Green Shadow and teamed Jim White with Roy Bass and the Lawler Brothers wrestled against them.

I was especially tight with Sam Bass. We seemed to have a lot in common. We both loved to drive really fast, we both were huge fans of the band Dr. Hook, and we both loved to play ribs, or pranks, on the other wrestlers. We had a deal with a motel in Montgomery, Alabama, and we hung out a lot together and got real crazy. This was my first real time away from home and I made the most of it. One thing that was different about Sam and me, was I never drank alcohol, Sam did. It seemed Sam was often drinking. I used to say I'd never seen Sam drunk, but later I realized, I may have never seen Sam sober! Sam claimed that he hated to drink alone, so he was always trying to get us to drink with him. I was just totally against it and never succumbed, but Steve Kyle finally said he'd try some sometime.

Steve Kyle was like me; he didn't drink at all. So I got together with Sam and we planned a rib on him. Sam was drinking some strong whiskey. Sam told Steve the whiskey itself tastes horrible, but the chaser is great. You can chase it with anything. If you drink water afterward, that would taste wonderful too. I had said that I'd stand over in the bathroom with what Steve Kyle thinks is a glass of water while Sam gave Steve some of his whiskey. He'd want a drink of water after that and I was all set to offer him some. Of course, I had rubbing alcohol in the glass.

It took awhile and we slowly built up the rib. I told Steve if he had a drink, I'd have a drink. Finally, Sam pours him a shot of Jack Daniels. Steve holds his nose, and drinks it down much too fast. "Oh my God! Water, water," and he comes running across to me and I say, helpfully, "Here you are, Steve," and he gulps it down. He swallowed about three big slugs before he could spit it out. That may have been my favorite of many ribs I pulled on Steve.

We did stupid ribs like that on the road all the time. One of the first things I learned about "wrestler etiquette" was that it was considered nasty to have hair under your arms. When your opponent had you in a headlock, the last thing you wanted to have your face in was his sweaty armpit hair. Consequently, wrestlers often shave under their arms. Next time you watch a match on TV, see if you notice. I told a couple of guys I had this special stuff I used to get rid of my underarm hair painlessly. I squeezed the stuff on and told them to hold their arms down by their sides for ten minutes. It was, guess what, Superglue. It may have got the hair out, but a little less painlessly than I advertised.

While I was in Alabama, the wrestling went very well. Nick Gulas was talking to Bill Golden every day.

He was running the place like a little farm operation for Memphis. Bill told him that the Lawler Brothers were red hot. We were being featured on TV in Montgomery, and everything was going great. I'd been down there not quite a year when Nick brought me back up to Nashville. If going to Alabama was being sent to AAA, now I was being called up to the Major Leagues. I was really happy in the fact that I could move back home to Memphis and work out of there. They sent me word of what date I would be starting up in the Nashville territory, but there was one big difference. Nick Gulas teamed me with Jim White, but not Steve Kyle. We started working regularly in Memphis and all the towns put us on the schedule. Poor Steve was still stuck in the minors. I felt bad for Steve, but I had to do what the office told me to do. I think Steve secretly held that against me for a long time.

Several years later, after I had been doing very well and making good money for a long time, Steve finally got called up. The first night in the dressing room together, I tried to reminisce about the days we spent together in Alabama. Steve and I had killed a lot of time playing video games down there. One in particular was Mattel Intellivision. I remember asking Steve if he still had his Intellivision. He said, "Thanks to you, brother, I don't have *a* television." That's when I knew for sure he was a little bitter. Steve didn't last long in the Tennessee territory. He moved on, and we lost touch. I don't know where my "brother" is today.

Jim White and I seemed to click as a tag team right away. The chemistry was there from day one. Once again, he played the straight, no-nonsense kind of serious wrestler to my flamboyant, showboating type of character. Nick put a guy named Jimmy Kent with Jim White and me when I first came up from Alabama. Jim White had been managed by Sam Bass down there but Sam stayed in

Alabama and they put Jimmy Kent with us, but only for
a few months. I never disliked Jimmy Kent, but I never
liked his style of managing. He was a cheap-heat kind of
manager, and he was silly with it. "Cheap heat" is where
you find an easy way to make the fans dislike someone.
An example is German wrestlers, who are always heels
because sixty years ago, we fought them in a war. Plus,
he wanted all the attention of the team to be on him, and
I thought it should be on me. That's what had worked in
Alabama and I didn't see any reason to change it. After a
few months, Jim White and I went to Nick Gulas with
our feelings. We said that Sam Bass would be the guy for
us, so he was brought up too. Then the team really
clicked.

It was around this time that I first met Lou Thesz. For
anybody who's been associated with the business in any
way, shape, or form in the last fifty years, Lou Thesz was
synonymous with wrestling. He'd held the NWA
(National Wrestling Alliance) World Championship forever. In fact, from the late forties to the early fifties, he
won over nine hundred straight matches. He always carried himself with style, class, and dignity. He looked like
what you imagine a championship wrestler to be. He
had huge hands. He was a real grappler, but he was also
very well spoken, very well mannered. He always wore
a suit and tie and always looked the part.

Lou came into the territory toward the end of his
career, when he was in his mid-fifties, although he was
still wrestling occasionally in his seventies. He and Pat
O'Connor, another wrestler and former NWA champion,
went against Jim White and me in some tag-team
matches, so that had to be around 1973. I was in awe of
both of these guys, the biggest names ever, and we were
just getting started. I remember in one match, Lou Thesz
Jim had covered and I was supposed to go in and kick
him and make the save. After the match, Pat O'Connor

said, "You came in, it looked like you were kicking a keg of dynamite." I said, "Yes, sir, that's what it felt like." I barely touched him. Lou died in April 2002 at age eighty-six.

In the early days, the work was often unglamorous and difficult. Long trips to small towns for little money. Herb Welch was Roy Welch's brother. Since Roy owned half of the company, Herb always seemed to get booked in big matches. He was an older guy and I never liked to watch him wrestle. He didn't do a whole lot in his matches, just grab a hold and keep his opponent in it for what seemed like forever. His career was winding down as mine was getting going and we did wrestle on some of the same cards. One time we were going to be partners in a match in some town. Union City, Tennessee, perhaps. It was freezing cold and they had a little heater in the middle of the dressing room. I was still very concerned with how I was looking and I was careful to look good. I look over and Herb Welch was pulling his trunk on over a union suit. (You know, the full body, red-thermal-underwear-type thing . . . with a flap in the back!) He was going to wrestle like that and I was very embarrassed.

One other embarrassing thing Herb did that I witnessed involved a young wrestler named Jerry Barber. It was another small town, another small crowd, but the new guys—like Barber and myself—would still go out and bust our butts. On this night Jerry Barber came to wrestle even though he was sick with the flu. He had a two-out-of-three fall match that was going three falls. He made it through the first fall and he came back to the dressing room and the first thing he did was reach into his bag and grab one of those Vicks inhalers. He was so congested he could barely breathe, so he shoves that inhaler up his nose and takes about five deep breaths, then he heads back out to the ring for the second fall.

After the second fall was over, here comes Jerry again. He sticks it into his nose, breathes in as deep as he can five or six times in each nostril, and then heads back out for the third and final fall.

While Jerry was in the ring for the third fall, old Herb Welch gets up, walks across the dressing room to Jerry's bag, reaches in, and pulls out the inhaler. Then right there in front of everyone in the dressing room, he pulls his trunks down and sticks that inhaler right where the sun don't shine. (Yep, he made a rectal thermometer out of Jerry's inhaler!) Then Herb put the inhaler back into the bag, sat down, and waited for poor Barber to arrive. Sure enough, the bell rings, the third fall is over, and here comes Jerry. He staggers into the dressing room, all out of breath, goes straight to his bag, and grabs that trusty inhaler. Every one in the dressing room cringed as we looked on, but no one tipped the poor guy off. It was one of the few times I ever saw Herb Welch laugh, but when Jerry stuck that inhaler up his nose and started snorting, I thought Herb was going to bust a gut.

One of my all-time favorites was a character named "Plowboy." Once when Sam Bass and I were working together in Memphis, we went on Memphis TV with a guy we'd worked with in Alabama. The story was that Sam and I were traveling through the backwoods in Mississippi. We were driving along and we looked over and saw this guy plowing in the fields. The unusual thing was, there was no horse pulling the plow; this guy had the thing hooked up to himself and he was just walking along, making the furrows. This was Plowboy Frazier. He was huge, about six-ten and four hundred, four hundred and fifty pounds. He name was Stan Frazier and he really was from Pascagoula, Mississippi, and was as country as could be. We made up the rest of it.

Plowboy was one of the first programs we did with Jerry Jarrett. The story was that Plowboy worked for us, driving us around, carrying our bags, and pretty much being our stooge, or gofer. We didn't pay him in cash but we gave him diamond rings instead. He had these big, phony-looking rings, a new one each week, and it looked like Sam Bass and I were taking advantage of this poor dumb hillbilly. Jerry Jarrett stood up for Plowboy. He called him over during the TV show and asked about our relationship. "Jerry and Sam, they're good to me. Look at these pretty diamond rings." Jerry said, "That's nice. I'm sure those rings are worth a lot of money." Plowboy said, "Oh yeah, they tell me they're worth thousands."

So Jerry Jarrett asked Plowboy what he knew about diamonds. Did he know they were the hardest sub-

Plowboy Frazier

stance on earth? "Yeah, I heard that." Jerry asked to look at one of the rings and he pulled out a hammer. Plowboy got all perturbed, "What're ya gonna do with that?" Jerry said he wasn't going to damage the ring. He prizes a diamond out and says, "This is the hardest substance on earth, right? So hitting it with a hammer won't do anything. Okay?" "Guess." So he hits it and of course it shatters into dust and with it go Plowboy's good feelings toward

Sam and me. That started a big program with Plowboy.

We wrestled against Plowboy and Jarrett for a long time and it gave me a golden opportunity to come up with some really funny lines about hillbillies and Mississippi. (I was doing the redneck jokes about Plowboy long before Jeff Foxworthy came along.) I used to love to work with Plowboy, because I could have so much fun ribbing him. He was so big that it took a tremendous amount of effort on his part just to get up and down in a match. Whenever he would hit me, or slam me, or knock me down in any way, I would always say to him, "Cover me!" This meant he had to get down and try to pin me while I lay on the mat. The ref would count to two, and I would kick out and then Plowboy would have to try to stand back up again. Usually he would have to crawl across the ring on his knees to get to the ropes and use them to help pull himself back to his feet.

One match, after I had told him to cover me about five times already, poor Plowboy was completely blown up—exhausted. He picked me up, slammed me, and when I hit the mat and said, "Cover me," again, he just stood there, looking down at me. Suddenly, it was like a lightbulb went on right over that big head of his . . . he finally realized what I was doing. He glared down at me and then he just put his big foot on my chest. The ref jumped down and counted to two before I kicked out and for the rest of the match that's the way he would go for the cover. He was so proud of himself that he had outsmarted the King!

Eventually, we may have used more gimmicks with Plowboy than anyone. We didn't want to get rid of him by sending him to another territory, so we would just recycle him by giving him a new identity. He went on to be the Giant Rebel in a big Confederate soldier's uniform. He was also the Lone Ranger, wearing a cowboy hat and a mask, as if no one could recognize him. We put the same makeup as Kamala the Ugandan Giant (of whom more later) on him and made him Kamala II. (The best that can be said for that was at least they were both from Mississippi.) Plowboy wrestled in L.A. as the Masked Convict. He was the Giant Hillbilly for a time. And Tiny Frazier. A million things.

Ever since it got to be really powerful, the World Wrestling Federation would be able to reach out and take stuff that worked in some other part of the country. They had someone watch our TV shows every week. We did so many crazy things and they were a little more conservative. But if they saw something they thought would work, they'd try it themselves up there.

They liked the Hillbilly gimmick, so they started their own Hillbillies. They brought Plowboy up as Uncle Elmer, together with Hillbilly Jim (Jim Morris), who I started down there as Harley Davidson, and, later, Cousin Junior (Lanny Keane) and Cousin Luke (Gene Petit). This was in the mid-80s. They had a good run. Uncle Elmer Plowboy got married on national TV in a huge Hillbilly wedding, and it was for real. Plowboy married his long-time sweetheart.

Being so big, Plowboy always had circulation problems. Years later, I'd hear from him regularly, even when he wasn't wrestling much. He called me one day and said, "Well, neighbor [Plowboy called everybody, neighbor], back in the hospital." He was talking like it wasn't much of a big deal. "Ah, doing something with ma legs." We talked a couple of minutes and said we'd talk later. But he died very soon after. This was 1992 and he was only sixty-one years old. I had no idea he was in that bad shape. I made a lot of trips with him and we had a lot of fun times. I really miss the Plowboy.

When we got up to Memphis, Jim White and I were a thrown-together tag team. Tennessee had some of the best tag teams going at the time. They also had some goofy, wild ones. Quite a few of them used a country gimmick. There was a popular team called the Scufflin' Hillbillies, two guys in nothing but overalls carrying a squealing pig with them. Their finishing move was called a stump puller. The guy would put your head between his legs, sit down, and pull your legs up in the air. Another move they did was to throw you into the rope, jump down on their hands, and give you a mule kick as you came back off the rope. There have been a bunch of Scufflin' Hillbillies on the go over the years. The latest incarnation is the Godwinns.

The top tag teams were often in the featured matches. There'd be perhaps three or four matches a night, two-out-of-three falls. There seemed to be a ton of great heel teams in the Tennessee territory then. There were the Interns, managed by Dr. Ken Ramey, who we've met before. Karl and Kurt Von Brauner, two "German" heels managed by Saul Weingeroff. They had Don and Al Greene, another top team. They still had the Blue Infernos, the team that I used to watch and wrestle, but now they were unmasked and wrestling as Gypsy Joe and Frank Martinez. Lorenzo Parente and Bobby Hart, the Mighty Yankees. All of these were main-event-caliber guys who had been in the business a long time.

A lot of these heel teams were actually pretty tough guys. You didn't have to ask whether a team was heel or face, you just had to look at them. Don and Al Greene were a couple of big, mean guys. They always had a look on their faces as if they smelled something burning. When I was refereeing early on, they were always getting on me for smiling too much. I guess subconsciously I was just so happy to be doing what I was doing, I smiled. I didn't even realize I was doing it most of the time. Don Greene came to me before one match, deadly serious. He said, "You smile one time, I'm going to slap your face. You're killing our match."

"Oh, no sir." I went out and thought: don't smile, don't smile. Don Greene looked at me, his beady eyes boring into me.

Just as the match was about to start, we got to the middle of the ring and I was giving the instructions—"No hair pulling, no hitting with the fists, no eye gouging, five count for break." I checked Don Greene's equipment and he's looking right at me with a strange smirk on his face and his cheeks puffed out. Suddenly he brought his hands up to his face and with his two index fingers he pressed on both his cheeks. His mouth was full of water and he spat it right in my face. The entire crowd busted out laughing. Don busted out laughing and I did too. I didn't think it was funny, I was really laughing with relief that he hadn't killed me. They had me scared to death.

Teams like the Greenes were made up of big guys who didn't really like to take a lot of bumps. They had a slow, methodical style and way of working. They were the big, scary wrestlers who liked to dominate matches and beat people up. They wanted to smash babyfaces. That's how they got to be big.

On the other hand, there was myself and Jim White and Sam Bass. Jim White and I came along and we loved to take bumps. I was always impressed by other guys doing that. That's why I'd always liked the Blue Infernos so much; they were big bump takers. As soon as we got into the ring, I wanted someone to throw me around. The majority of our matches we would be selling our opponents to the crowd. That was our specialty. I enjoyed taking the crazy bumps and the flips out of the ring more than I did beating on the other guy. I got to be known as a big bump taker.

Pretty soon, the other teams all wanted to work with us. They'd rather have two guys take the bumps than have two other great lugs like themselves beat them up. Jerry Jarrett had teamed up with Tojo Yamamoto, who was switched to being a good guy. Tojo had been a very hot heel. They had two wrestlers beating up Jerry Jarrett on TV and Tojo came to his rescue. He told everyone that this kid was his protégé and he'd been secretly training him to wrestle. He wasn't going to let anyone beat him up. The main dynamic of the team was this bad guy everyone loved to hate suddenly became a fan favorite along with Jerry.

They became the top good-guy team. Jerry was young with long blond hair and they didn't push a lot of young guys at the time. And, as we know, he was doing the booking. He said, heck, rather than get beat up by monsters like Don and Al Greene or the Interns, I'd rather go out and work with Lawler and White and throw them around. It made him look better. When Jerry was in the ring with the big heels, because of the size difference, there wasn't a whole lot he could do other than sell— take the abuse. But Jim White and I were about the same size as Jerry, maybe just a little bit bigger. He would just barely touch us and we'd be flying all over the place and people would be screaming and going crazy.

So we started working with them. The Von Brauners and Saul went to his friend, Nick Gulas, and complained. They said we were nothing but a couple of acrobats, flipping and flying all around. But Jerry Jarrett was doing the booking and he wanted to work with us. And so did Jackie Fargo. That's how we got the top spot, by selling better than the other guys. I was never a flashy wrestler myself, but I always knew the value of selling. I've always thought that the best match you could ever have is when you get two wrestlers going against each other, and each one is trying to outsell the other.

There was one particularly memorable angle between Jarrett and Fargo and Jim White and me. That particular morning, neither Jackie Fargo nor I was in the studio. So

Jerry Jarrett and Jim White were going to have a singles match with Sam Bass in Jim's corner. I had got dressed up as a woman and I sat out in the crowd. As the match was about to start, I went up to the ring and asked Jerry Jarrett for his auto-graph. As he leaned through the ropes to sign my book, I hit him with my purse, which had a brick in it. I went into the ring, took off my dis-guise, and Jim and I proceeded to beat Jarrett up.

I remember this being Jerry's idea. I was reluctant to do it but I went through with it and I really went the whole hog. I shaved my legs, my arms, chest—every-thing. It's not easy to find a woman's shoes size twelve or thirteen. I got the whole outfit, wig and all. Sam and Jim helped me put it on in a hotel. They let me out down the street from the TV station so no one would see me dri-ving with them. I had to walk down the sidewalk and come in the front door of Channel Thirteen, as a woman! I'd looked into the mirror and thought everyone in the world would know this was some guy dressed up like a cheap transvestite. But I walked down the street and no one seemed to notice.

I went into the studio and sat down. What I remember most was trying to sit in some kind of ladylike fashion wearing a skirt and pantyhose. That meant trying to sit with my legs together. If you're a guy and you have to sit with your legs squeezed together, it's hard to do for more than about thirty seconds. I don't know how girls do it. I sat there and my legs started shaking like crazy. The first match is going on and my legs are killing me. I had to open them a touch. Across the ring, some guy was leering, trying to look up my skirt! He'd have got some kind of shock. So I had to press my legs together and basically clasp them tight. I'd never been so glad to see Jerry Jarrett come to the ring in my life. I did not make a really cute woman. I just had on some lipstick but I needed some eye makeup and stuff. Maybe a little mascara and some blush would have helped.

You get some guys you have a real chemistry with in a tag team. Jim White and I were like Abbott and Costello. Jim was the straight man and perfectly happy doing it. I was Lou. I got to do all the goofy and crazy stuff and the interviews. But Jim did all the hard work. That worked for us as a team. We won the Southern Tag Team Championship together, which I think was the first title I won. Jim and I parted company somewhere along the way. My next partner was Don Duffy, who wrestled as the Masked Scorpion. He didn't last long, just a couple of months. It just didn't work. He wanted to be the guy up front too.

After Jim White and Don Duffy, I wrestled with my old friend Don Greene just a little bit. We wrestled in Georgia as The Heavenly Bodies. In 1976, Plowboy and I beat Bill Dundee and Big Bad John to win the Southern Tag Team Championship. Again. I must have won and lost that thing thirty times. Then, later, I won the title with Dundee and I also won it with the Mongolian Stomper. Over the years, I've been in tag teams with half a phone-bookful of guys. Gorgeous George, Norvell Austin, Porkchop Cash. And on and on. But by the time Plowboy and I hooked up, I was working much more as a single wrestler. And I was the King.

chapter 12

Before the advent of WWE, or the World Wide Wrestling Federation as it was known originally, the most powerful organization in American wrestling was the National Wrestling Alliance, the NWA. The NWA was the umbrella organization over most of the local promotions, which had the country divided up into territories. Nick Gulas and Roy Welch were the promoters for Kentucky, Tennessee, Arkansas, Mississippi, and Alabama. Eddie Graham had Florida and South Georgia. There were the Crocketts, who had the Virginias and the Carolinas. Vince McMahon Sr.'s World Wide Wrestling Federation was in the Northeast and largely operated as an independent entity. In the Northwest, Don Owen was the promoter. Verne Gagne's AWA was based in Minnesota. There was a St. Louis territory, which was where the NWA headquarters was. The Sheik had a territory in Ohio, Michigan, and Illinois.

Most of the territories had regional TV shows they used to promote the live events. The owners and promoters respected the boundaries between the territories and wouldn't step on each other's toes. They also worked to keep other promoters out. Every now and then opposition promoters would spring up. The NWA promoters would rally 'round and send in more talent to beef up the card for the promoter who had the opposition. So the NWA was a real alliance. They met yearly in Las Vegas or Tahoe and talked about their issues. For a long time, the territories all made money. A promoter could make $150–200,000 a year in the mid-sixties and very small towns could draw 500 people a week.

The NWA recognized one world champion they would send around to work for all the promoters. Nick Gulas would call the NWA office and say, "When can I get a week of the World Champion?" So the NWA World Champion would fly in and Nick would have him booked Monday in Memphis, Tuesday in Louisville, and so on. Then the champion might go to the Carolinas for a week and then perhaps to the territory in Texas and Oklahoma and the part of Mississippi that Bill Watts had.

The champion's job was to make the fans think that the top wrestler could beat the World Champion. That's what the NWA looked for in their champion. Harley Race did it well. Ric Flair was great at it. He'd come into Memphis and sell the top guy in the territory until they thought Jerry Lawler could beat Ric Flair any time he wanted to. Of course, you never could beat the champion. And the more you used him, the more you'd have to come up with something special to convince people you could beat him without ever actually doing so. By hook or by crook, the champion would hold on to that belt. No matter how much the challenger had to put the champion over, the champion would have to put the local guy over even more. That's because the local guy had to keep drawing money—crowds—when the champion would be gone the next week.

It wasn't that long after I came up from Alabama before I was involved in these championship programs. About a year after Jim White left town, I began working as a single wrestler and almost right away, Jerry Jarrett came up with the notion that I should be put in title contention. Beginning in 1974, and for years thereafter, my deal would be that I would wrestle whoever the world champion was. The quest for the world title was always a big angle in the territories.

The championship changed hands pretty often. Harley Race was champion eight times and Ric Flair more than ten. Jack Brisco was the champion from July 1973 to December 1975 with a week off from losing to Giant Baba in Japan. Brisco was the first NWA champion I got to wrestle. We did a big buildup to it where I was supposed to wrestle the top ten contenders for the NWA title. Usually the Memphis promoters just used the local talent, but Jerry Jarrett convinced Nick Gulas that he should bring in top guys from around the country for ten straight weeks. Believe me, that took some doing, because Nick was as tight as the bark on a tree, and ordinarily, he wouldn't want to spend the money it would take to get these guys to Memphis. The Sheik, Bobo Brazil, Dick the Bruiser, Mr. Wrestling II, Dory Funk, Terry Funk. These were really the top names in the business at that time, but the fans in our territory only knew them from reading about them in the wrestling magazines. We billed them as the top ten contenders and I had to go through them to get a world title match.

I was so new that none of these guys had ever heard of me. That meant there wasn't a snowball's chance in hell that any of them would put me over. In other words, they wouldn't let me beat them. Most of them took one look at me and said, "No f-ing way I'm losing to him." I remember the Sheik was in and I went to the dressing room and sat down and talked to him for a couple of minutes while he was getting changed. He was a star and I'd read about him, but I'd never met him. He was nice enough. After we'd talked awhile he said, "Kid, d'you know who I'm working with tonight?"

"Er, yes. That would be me."

"You? Oh. I thought you were the ring crew or something."

If they weren't going to put me over, they'd have to get themselves eliminated from the title race. They'd have to get disqualified or timed out, or I'd get disqualified or something. They would do pretty much anything other than actually get pinned. No matter what we did in the match, I'd just go on TV the next week and make an interview where I'd claim I'd beaten the guy. We'd edit the film to where we only showed the parts of the match where I had the upper hand and it made it appear that I had dominated the match. They were good matches and it was a great program for the region. We sold out with almost all these contenders.

By the time we got Jack Brisco here in 1974, everyone in Memphis was convinced I was going to win the title. Jack Brisco was from Oklahoma, the brother of Jerry, who's a road agent now with WWE. I think the first match we had was a sixty-minute draw. Then we came back and did a match where I pulled out a chain where the referee couldn't see it for the finish. I used the chain on Jack and put it under my arm and covered Jack, one-two-three. People went crazy. I grabbed the belt and the referee came over to raise my arm as champion. He took the wrong arm and as he lifted it up, the chain fell out and he reversed the decision. So the belt went back to Jack. The fans went home thinking, "Had it not been for the ref seeing that chain, Jerry would be the world champion." That was just one of the ways we had to keep coming up with to make it appear the champion was beatable. But wrestling him for the title was huge for my credibility.

These championship matches were often real marathons. In 1976, I wrestled Terry Funk to a sixty-minute draw. In 1977, I had a sixty-minute draw with

Harley Race and another ninety-minute rematch where it appeared that I would have won but for interference by Jimmy Valiant. That's another thing that changed. You don't have ninety-minute matches anymore. I'm not saying it's a good thing or a bad thing, it's just a fact.

If you look at an old program from the Ellis Auditorium from when I used to go with my father, there'd be three matches on the card. All the matches were two out of three falls. The show would last two and a half hours, like today's shows do, but now they have eleven matches. You have a bunch of six-, seven-minute matches rather than forty-five-minute matches. Times have changed. I think people's attention spans are shorter. People want to see more action at a faster pace. They want the aerials, the high-flying stuff too. That ensures that the matches are short. There's no way you could do a match like the Hardy Boyz have for an hour. Your body just couldn't take it.

The title I was allowed to win was the NWA's Southern Heavyweight title, which I first won in 1974 against Tommy Gilbert as part of the run-up to the Brisco match. I was Southern Heavyweight Champion when the NWA World Champion came to town. I think I was Southern Heavyweight Champion thirty-three times, which sounds great, but it means I also lost the title at least thirty-two times as well. I had Southern Championship matches with everyone who was ever any good and passed through the state of Tennessee: Tommy Rich, Tommy Gilbert, Jackie Fargo, Rocky Johnson (The Rock's dad), Jimmy Valiant, Bill Dundee, Kendo Nagasaki, Jesse Ventura, Humongous, Eddie Gilbert, Randy Savage, Austin Idol, Man Mountain Link. You name him, and I probably gave him a shot at the southern title.

The World Championship was obviously the bigger deal. There was a TV show we did in Memphis with World

Champion Ric Flair around 1982 that was typical. Flair
and I were both scheduled to wrestle other guys on the
show that day, just two guys who nowadays are called
"enhancement talent." That means they were just there
to lose to us. I went out and I said I'd love to shake the
champion's hand. Flair made out like he didn't know
who I was and talked down to me and the studio audience. He said he was happy to come and show people in
Tennessee what big-time pro wrestling was like but that
he didn't feel there was any worthy competition in the
area. He claimed his match wasn't even worth breaking
a sweat over, and ordinarily he wouldn't even bother
with it, but there were women in the audience dying for
him to take off his $7,000 robe.

With my tongue planted firmly in my cheek, I started
dishing out the compliments to Flair. "You know, Ric,

you really are the best. You're so good you could beat any wrestler you wanted to, including me. You *are* the best wrestler in the world. So why not prove it? Instead of wrestling this young jabroni you're about to beat, why not wrestle me instead. The fans here in Memphis think I'm pretty good, and when you beat me, they'll know you really are great." Flair says it doesn't matter who he wrestles, he's Ric Flair the Great, Ric Flair the Legend . . . So okay, I'll give you ten minutes of my time. I then tell Ric that since it's a foregone conclusion that he is going to beat me, why not put up his title just to make the match exciting? I finally persuade Flair to put the title on the line and all of a sudden, there's a world championship match on Channel Thirteen, even though Flair said he doesn't make $500,000 a year and fly on big jets to put up his belt on local TV.

So we wrestle ten minutes and basically I put Flair over for all of it. He's killing me with slams and suplexes and he's got me in a figure-four leg lock at the bell. It's going too well for him to stop so he demands another five minutes. The referee agrees and restarts the match. He chops me a few times and I get mad. I pull down my strap and start beating on Flair. I slam him and put a huge fist-drop on him. Looked nice, I have to say. So Flair grabs his belt and runs off. He's had enough. Once again, the fans in Memphis went away from that TV show believing I should be the world champion.

The match was a classic example of two guys putting each other over by selling well—making the fans believe each hold, each move is killing you. Flair didn't actually lose and I didn't win, but I could claim I had. What really gets a guy over is selling. You don't really have to be a great worker to sell. You can let the other guy take 90 percent of the match and get beat up and just make one big comeback. I used to make sure I sold my opponent and it makes a lot of guys want to work with you.

Most wrestlers don't ever address the idea of selling. They want to be beating people up. They think they look stronger if they beat the other guy up. Well, in reality, you look stronger if you get beat up, beat up, beat up, and take everything your opponent can possibly dish out, and *still* come out on top.

Selling is almost a lost art. Hulk Hogan, when he was the champion, that was his specialty. Most of the match, he would sell for his opponent. Then right at the end, he would Hulk up, shake off his opponent's blows, do the big leg-drop, and boom, win the match. I remember a match when X-Pac sold Hulk Hogan in turn really well. Hulk Hogan just picked X-Pac up and sailed him over the top rope. It made Hulk look like Superman, but it wasn't really Hulk. X-Pac is small enough and agile enough that he just leapt and made it look like Hulk was able to toss him out of the ring with his physical strength. That's the kind of thing we would do. We would make the good guys look fantastic. This was what people wanted to see. All the towns were going crazy.

When I started wrestling as a single wrestler in Memphis, having success there was a landmark that meant a lot to me. That was the first time I wrestled Jackie Fargo in a singles match. To me, that was a big deal because of the way I'd looked up to him when I was a kid and how I'd worked for him awhile. And what made it an even bigger deal was the fact that in that match Jackie treated me as his equal. Looking back, I think he sold for me more than he did the other guys he wrestled and I think it was because he felt partly responsible for my being in the business, and he wanted me to be a success. Over the years, I loved working with Jackie. Nobody could sell like him. You'd hit him, and his head would reel back with that long blond hair of his flying. And, oh man, if he would get blood . . . his blond hair would turn completely red! I don't know how many times we wrestled each other. The last time, I think, was in Nashville in 2000.

It was when I was wrestling Jackie Fargo that I became the King. One week on Memphis TV, I was making an interview about an upcoming match with Jackie. I was just trying to come up with some colorful statements that the people could identify with. "You know, Fargo, you've been the King around Memphis for a long time," I said. "But you're looking at the kid who's going to knock you off your throne." I won that match and some kids were saying as I left the ring, "Hey, you're the King, you're the King!"

I was also wrestling in Atlanta on Fridays for the NWA. Jerry Jarrett had taken a job helping to book in Atlanta so I worked down there some. There was a guy called Bobby Shane, who was wrestling as "King" Bobby Shane. He had this real-nice big red crown and a long red robe. I got down to Atlanta the Friday after I had beaten Jackie and thought, wouldn't it be cool to walk out in TV the next week with that getup on after having the interview with Jackie and beating him?

I went over to Bobby and asked him where he had got the stuff and I told him about the interview I'd done. He said he ordered it from a place in Houston called Southern Importers. He said it took three or four weeks after he ordered them for the stuff to come in. But he said, "You know what? I'm leaving for Australia tomorrow and I'm going for two months. I'm not taking all this junk. I'm just going as Bobby Shane, I'm not doing the King gimmick. If you want, you can take it with you. It'll save me from having to pack it up. Use it while I'm gone and we'll order you some." Perfect.

So I took the stuff and wore it the next week on TV. I was the King of Memphis now, I'd dethroned Jackie Fargo. To be honest with you, most of the other wrestlers laughed at me when I put that big crown on my head . . . they all thought it was a stupid gimmick. But the fans didn't. When I walked out on TV with it on, the people went nuts! I started wearing the crown and everything every week. I figured I'd give it back to Bobby Shane when he got back. He did come back to the States but on one of his first trips back, in February of 1975, he got killed in a plane crash.

The small aircraft he was flying in crashed into Tampa Bay and Bobby got stuck inside the plane and drowned. Gary Hart, Buddy Colt, and Dennis McCord (Austin Idol) all got out. I was left with the crown and the robe. That crown got stomped in a match and my next crown wasn't lucky either.

chapter 13

Sam Bass was my best friend. Since we started working together in Alabama, we'd spent a lot of time with each other, working and hanging out, and we were a great team. He was a funny guy, a cool guy. Just a neat person all around. One of the reasons we got on so well was that he loved to drive and I hated to drive. We were a perfect match. Even if we took my car, Sam would usually drive. We would cover real long distances together, traveling from match to match.

Everyone in the business spends long hours on the road. WWE crews drive the trucks full of equipment from show to show. As soon as the lights go down, guys are scurrying around taking stuff to pieces. Three hours after the show, there'll be a WWE eighteen-wheeler pulling out on the road. The distances are huge. Just look at the *Raw* schedule—Edmonton to Dallas to Atlanta to Oakland, and so on.

In the seventies and eighties I could put 100,000 miles on a car in a year, easy. Sometimes I'd do 3,000 miles a week. Tuesdays I'd go from Memphis to Louisville and back, an 800-mile trip in one day. I did that every week for ten years, probably. Or Memphis to Johnson City and back. That's a thousand miles. When I started thinking about this book, I thought I could easily

fill two separate chapters with driving stories and a lot of them would be about me and Sam.

In the seventies, the speed limit on the Interstate was seventy-five and they wouldn't even stop you unless you were going over eighty. They'd give you eighty-five. So we'd drive a hundred miles an hour on trips. We used to say, "We don't drive a car, we *aim* it!" We said that as a joke, but it was really true. I'd be driving at a hundred miles an hour on a two-lane road and Sam would reach over and cover my eyes and say, "Beg me to let you go, beg me to let you go!" People would always say, you guys, one of these days, you're going to be in a wreck. Sam's favorite line in response was, "If I'm in a wreck, it's going to be an accident."

I said we'd do crazy things. Some of them were real crazy. Sam and I would run tollbooths at great speed, again at around a hundred miles per hour. Never touched the sides. (My brother Larry remembers me doing that once when he was in the car and the troopers came after us. But I beat them to the state line.)

Sam traded cars a lot. As soon as the "new" would wear off one, he'd trade it in for another one. He got ahold of a real lemon once. That car never ran right and he was totally sick of it. We pulled off by the side of the Interstate one night on our way back to Nashville and Sam decided to put the thing out of its misery. I can't remember if Sam drank gin or vodka. Whichever one it was, he doused it over the inside of the car, took a match, and set fire to the thing. I couldn't believe my eyes! We were standing on the side of the road watching his new car go up in flames . . . and Sam was smiling!

A truck came along, a big eighteen-wheeler. He pulled over and the driver comes running over with a fire extinguisher. Before he gets to us, Sam waves his arms and shouts, "No, no. Bring gasoline!" And without blinking, the guy just turned around. "Oh, okay."

My brother Larry swears driving with me is what made his hair gray.

He comes back with a can of gas and throws it on.

You used to see quite a few hitchhikers along the side of the road. One time, Sam and I saw one, a big old country-looking guy. I said, "Sam, watch this." I pull over and start slowing down and stop about twenty yards past him. He runs toward the car, and as he reaches it, I take off and drive a little bit, then stop again. Sam leans out and says, "Hurry up, we gotta go!" He runs up again, and I drive off again. We made him run about four times and then take off, squealing the tires and throwing gravel all over the guy. We think that's hilarious. We drive about an hour and come to a little truck stop. We're in there having something to eat. We'd forgotten about the hitchhiker, when I look up and here's the guy walking in the door. The place was pretty crowded, and luckily, he never recognized us, but he had recognized my car. When Sam and I left the truck stop and went out to my car, there was gravel all over the hood and top of it. I wouldn't pick anyone up now, which is probably best for everyone concerned.

Guys often used to drive in a convoy from town to

town. One time, Jerry Jarrett and I were driving from Memphis to Nashville after a match. Right after we got out of town, Jackie took off and drove on ahead. We didn't think anything of it. A few miles down the road, we see this figure by the side of the road. It was Jackie Fargo, buck-naked, hitching a ride. He'd squeezed his gimmick between his thighs so he looked like a real ugly, blond-headed, fat lady by the side of the road, hitchhiking! Jerry Jarrett and I laughed our heads off as we drove by.

Naturally, Jerry and I had to try and top that. I was riding with Jerry Jarrett and we knew Fargo was somewhere behind us. We pulled the car over, jumped out, took our clothes off. Jerry got up on top of the car on his hands and knees and I got up there and made like I was giving it to him doggy-style. When Fargo flew by he put his lights on bright and blew his horn. Guys just don't rib like that anymore. Could you imagine Triple H and The Rock, butt naked on the top of a car as Undertaker drove by?

I own some really cool vinyl Halloween masks that are made in Hollywood. They're really scary and realistic-looking. Sam and I once drove down the Interstate wearing Frankenstein masks. We'd drive up beside people and look into their car at them just like everything was normal. It'd scare the heck out of them. We got about ten miles before two Highway Patrol cars, one on either side of the road, pulled out and stopped us. We threw the masks down. Cops walked up to the car. "You guys wearing some kind of masks in there?" "Yeah." Apparently it's against the law to scare people on the highway, so they made us put the masks into the trunk.

We also did stuff with CB radios. We'd cuss out truck drivers and make them crazy mad. Sam and I were in my Thunderbird, which had the CB antenna built into the regular antenna so you couldn't tell I had a CB by looking at the car. Most cars had the extra antenna. We were

on the way to Louisville and we were giving this particular truck driver all kinds of grief. Stupid stuff about
what we did with his wife while he was on the road and
all. He said, "If I could ever find y'all, I'd run you in the
ditch so fast. Why don't you have the guts to tell me
where you are . . ."

We were pretty much alongside this guy when we
happened to pass Tommy Marlin, who was a referee. His
car had a special CB antenna. I said, "Sam, watch this."
"Alright you big ass, if you want some of me, I'm in this
black Ford right in front of you." Right away, there's a
truck on either side of Tommy, plus one in front, and one
behind. They pulled him over, right off the road. Poor
Tommy didn't even have his CB on, so he had no idea
what was going on. They figured out it wasn't him pretty
fast.

Fans used to like to follow the wrestlers in their cars
after the matches. I used to look forward to our weekly
trips to Jonesboro, Arkansas, because of two special sisters that liked to tag along after the matches. They were
both really cute, and very shy when you met them at the
matches, but after the show it was a different story. They
would follow along behind my car for about ten to fifteen miles, and then they would pass and get in front. As
soon as they did, I would put my lights on bright and
one of the sisters would be lying in the back window, in
full view, completely naked! She'd lie there for a few
minutes and then she would turn, like she was on a
rotisserie grill or something, and give you the complete
picture, over and over again. This would go on for about
twenty miles, and then they'd wave and pull off and
head back to Jonesboro. I guess it was their way of letting
me know they had enjoyed the show I had put on by giving me a show of their own.

I had to make a lot of trips by myself through the
years, so I was always looking for ways to pass the time

or, more importantly, keeping myself from falling asleep while driving. Of course the radio was a constant companion. I can't tell you how many hours of driving I spent listening to Indians games on the radio.

I acquired another talent while driving these trips late at night. When I got on the road I would look for a little gas station that was closed up for the night. At one time most of the soft-drink machines sold sodas in bottles. Right next to the machines would be a rack with a couple of cases of empty bottles in it. I'd pull in and take the empty bottles, load them into my front seat, and then use them for target practice going down the highway. I'd roll down the passenger side window and as I was zooming along at about eighty, I'd fire a bottle out at a roadside sign. I got so proficient, I started chunking them out the driver's window, left-handed, over the top of the car and still hitting the signs. That was a bigger challenge and required better timing. One night I pulled the bonehead move of the year by accidentally rolling down the back window instead of the passenger window. I had my bottle in hand as I approached the first sign of the night. I'm going eighty . . . the sign is in my sights. FIRE! I threw the bottle as hard as I could. Right through my passenger side window! Busted glass was everywhere, and to top it off, it was about thirty-five degrees outside so I had to drive the rest of the way home freezing my butt off. That pretty much ended my sign target practice, but to this day, I reckon I can still hit a sign with a bottle at eighty miles per hour.

I've had a few decent accidents over the years but I've been lucky. I was driving back one time from Florence, Alabama, on Highway 72. It was then, and still is, a two-lane highway. This was late at night. I was coming to the top of a hill and I could see the lights from a truck coming the other way. When we both got to the top of the hill, there was a car, even with the truck, trying to pass.

In action with Jackie Fargo

He was coming right at me. Had he swerved to miss me, it would have been a disaster. But he just kept coming in my lane. The truck driver later said he was probably drunk. I swerved right over, off the road, and swerved back across the road and back the other way. I lost control and my car turned sideways and the back hit a tree. The truck driver said the guy never slowed down.

Another time, coming from Nashville, I was riding with Jackie Fargo. Jackie had driven to the matches, from Memphis to Nashville, but on the way home he wanted to take a little nap, so he asked me to drive. I was nervous driving Jackie's car. It was a brand-new Cadillac Coupe de Ville. Jackie had fallen asleep, and I had been driving for about an hour. Then I said, "Jackie!"

"What, what?"

"Is that car on our side of the road?"

He looked up, "Get over, kid, get over." I moved over and this car zoomed right past us on the wrong side of the Interstate. Missed us by a couple of inches. That guy was probably drunk too.

The closest call was coming back from Osceola, Arkansas, one night. We had the show and were leaving on Interstate 65 coming back toward Memphis. My wife Paula was with me. (Wife? Don't worry, we'll get to that.) We'd been on the Interstate about fifteen minutes. She and I were talking and I was looking at Paula and when I glanced back at the road, I see this truck, a huge eighteen-wheeler coming across the median. The dirt and dust were flying as he regained control of his truck, but when he did he was in my lane! We were both going about seventy-five and he was in my lane coming right at me. I veered off to the right and he went by, not missing me by very much at all. I looked back and he went back across the median the way he should have been going. He must have fallen asleep. Maybe it was the guy with that CB trying to kill me.

* * *

I said I've been lucky. Sam Bass wasn't. In July 1976, I had a World Championship match against Harley Race at Mid-South Coliseum and Sam was my manager for the match. He had a brand-new Ford, whatever the biggest one was. I had a Cadillac. Although I lived in Hendersonville, which is near Nashville, most of my ties and connections and people I knew still lived in Memphis. I needed work on my car, and I had a guy I knew in Memphis I wanted to use. Sam and I went down on a Saturday to do the TV show. I left my car in the shop in Memphis and it was going to be ready on Monday. We rode back together to Nashville that Saturday night. The plan was to fly down to Memphis on Monday. They had flights for $39. We were going to pick up my car, go to matches, and come back that night in my car.

Sam calls me at nine o'clock that Monday morning. He said he thought he'd just drive his car down. The wrestlers Frank Hester and Pepe Lopez had called him and they wanted a ride. Frank and Pepe wrestled as the Dominoes (so-called because the team included one white guy and one black guy). I told Sam that we'd already made plans, why did he want to do that? I had the plane reservations and everything. The Dominoes had their own manager, J. C. Dykes, who was probably driving down. They could go with him. Sam said he'd call the Dominoes and tell them we were going to stick with our plan. But Sam was never crazy about flying. An hour later he called me back and said they really had no way of getting to Memphis. He said he was just going to go ahead and drive. Sam said he would just follow me back that night.

So I flew down and Sam drove with the guys. We got through the match and we left the Coliseum in our cars. Right before you got on the Interstate there was a place called the World's Fare. There were all kinds of places to eat in there including a hamburger place. The owner had asked me to use my name in exchange for a cut of the profits. He called the place "King Lawler's Slamburgers." Everything had some kind of wrestling name. Our announcer Lance Russell had a big nose. I called him "banana nose," so we had foot-long "banana nose hot dogs." We had big Slamburgers and then little Jabroni burgers. (By the way, I was the first person to actually use the kayfabed term "jabroni" on television back in 1974, so Rock must have smelled what the King was cooking.) The owner had asked me to drop by so I told Sam I was going in and I told him to wait; I wasn't going to be five minutes. But Sam said he'd go on ahead and drive slowly so I could catch up.

I'm in about ten minutes. I drive out onto the Interstate, pop it up to about a hundred, and start looking for Sam. I'm waiting, waiting. I get fifty miles up the road and no Sam. A hundred miles, I still hadn't caught him. By this time I know Sam's barreling along too and hadn't waited for me.

I get to the hundred-and-fifty-mile marker and I'm listening to the CB radio. We used CB radios to talk to each other and tell other drivers where the cops were waiting. Some guy comes on and says, "Look out, eastbound there's a big wreck at the 163-mile marker. Truck's on fire." You know how people say they get a feeling when something bad happens? I swear, as soon as he said there was a big wreck, I felt like a knife had been stuck into my stomach. I just knew Sam was involved.

At that point, this was about eight miles ahead of me. I was one of the first to get to the scene. It happened on a bridge. I stopped across the bridge and ran back across. The big eighteen-wheeler was on fire in the median. There was a car upside down in the middle of the Interstate. Sam's car was white and this car was green. So, I breathed a sigh of relief knowing it wasn't Sam's car. I walked 'round the car and there was a guy lying there who had been almost sliced in half. The right side of his body was separated and a big current of blood had flowed into the grass. I was just staring at this guy, lit up by the fire from the truck. It was nighttime and I couldn't see much else.

Suddenly somebody grabbed my shoulder. It was another wrestler, Cowboy Frankie Lane. He said, "Lawler! We thought you were in the car with Sam." I said, "That's not Sam's car."

"No," he said. "That's Sam's car over there." Sam's car was wedged right up underneath the truck that was burning. It was a National Cash Register truck, an eighteen-wheeler full of cash register receipt rolls. It was packed with paper. It was burning like crazy. You couldn't get anywhere near it. I looked around to see if I could see anybody. In the road, I found a pair of wrestling boots. One lying down and one sitting up. A gray boot and a black boot. I knew they belonged to the Dominoes, so I knew that was Sam's car.

Later, the truck driver reckoned Sam was doing between a hundred and fifteen and a hundred twenty miles an hour. Sam passed the eighteen-wheeler. What he didn't know, and didn't see, was that another driver had got into a wreck on the bridge ahead and was sitting sideways on it with no lights on. Sam hit him and the eighteen-wheeler hit both cars. The truck dragged Sam's car into the median and caught fire.

The truck burned for hours. They emptied a whole tanker truck of water on the truck and couldn't put it out. Someone had called ahead and said that I'd been in the car too. Jackie Fargo, Jerry Jarrett, and Tojo Yamamoto left Nashville and drove down to where the wreck was. When they saw me, I told them what had happened. We had to drive to Nashville and go to Sam's house to tell his wife, Jody. I was the one who told her.

The second hardest thing I ever did was continuing on to do that show in Kansas City after Owen Hart died. The hardest was to tell my good friend's wife that he just got killed in a car wreck.

She wanted to go back down to the wreck. We drove back down, over an hour. She was crying and so was I. All of a sudden she stopped crying. She said, "You know what, Jerry. Old Sam's pretty tricky. I'll bet you he got out. I'll bet you he's not dead." I guess she convinced herself of that to keep from accepting the truth.

I stayed until they pulled the bodies out of the car. It wasn't anything that looked like a body at all. Big charred pieces of meat. Their arms were gone, their legs were gone. Just torsos. Two of them, we figure Sam and Frank Hester were in the front seat, and they were wedged together in that section of the car. They never let Sam's wife look at him. They didn't have any kids together; they both did from previous marriages. She never remarried. Sam was only forty-one. Rubin Rodriguez, who wrestled as Pepe Lopez, was thirty-nine and Frank Hester was thirty-seven.

Sam's death was a terrible thing. He was the best friend I ever made in the business. It was Sam who gave me the new crown after the one that Bobby Shane had lent me got crushed in the ring. And it was after Sam died that some people started talking about the curse of the crown. They said, "Don't give Lawler a crown; something bad will happen to you."

14

Nineteen seventy-seven was a huge year for me, a year of major changes in my personal life and my professional life. It was my first experience at being away from home by myself. When I first started getting booked regularly to wrestle, I'd go to Nashville once a week and spend the night. I saw some sights in Nashville that were real eye-openers to me and I had a wild time. The kind of stuff I got up to wouldn't seem to suggest I was management material, but it's funny how things turn out.

The Gulas/Welch wrestling office was in the city, in the Sam Davis Hotel on Seventh Avenue. I'd stay in the hotel when I came to town. I had so much fun in that hotel doing crazy kid pranks on the other wrestlers. I looked forward so much to going every week. The place isn't there anymore, it was demolished in 1985.

When I checked into the hotel, I'd ask for a corner room in the front as high up the twelve-story building as possible. Because the office was in the hotel, almost all the wrestlers would come by the office. I'd sit up at the window in my room and throw buckets of water down on the guys as they came into the entrance. My best shot was one I landed on a lady wrestler. The Fabulous Moolah used to book girls out of North Carolina to all the different territories. On this trip there were only two of them and they'd stay just a week or two and then move on.

I saw one of these girls getting out of a taxi in front of the hotel. It was her first day in the territory, so she was coming into the office for her itinerary. She had her hair fixed in a big beehive (I mean one of those big ones a ceiling fan would love) and she was carrying a cheap piece of luggage—a cardboard suitcase with a plastic handle. She paid the driver and was walking toward the awning of the hotel entrance. I had a trash can full of water and I dumped it out the window. It was a perfect shot, right on the noggin. Her hair was plastered straight down over her shoulders and the suitcase got knocked right off the handle. She was left standing there holding a plastic handle with her hair totaled. I got into trouble for that. Nick Gulas found out that I was doing this and he called me to the office. He said Moolah was threatening to never send girl wrestlers to his territory again. I think I had to pay for a new suitcase.

Another time, I got a wrestler called Bearcat Brown. I just drowned him from my room. Another bull's-eye. He stood there shaking for a second and then he walked back to his car. I laughed as I watched ol' Bearcat. I figured he was going back home to change out of his soaked clothes. Instead, he reached in the window and took a gun out of the glove compartment! He walked back to the front of the hotel and disappeared inside. There was an old guy who worked the desk of the hotel at night. He had one tooth and I used to say they made the movie *Old Yeller* about it. Bearcat came in and said to this guy, "Give me the skeleton key." He was standing there soaking wet, shaking, because he was so mad, holding a gun, and screaming for the key. Of course, Old Yeller handed it over. He went to all the corner rooms trying to find who'd got him. Meantime, I'd gone to the back of the building, out a window, and onto the fire escape where I sat it out.

A couple of streets over from Seventh Avenue was Broadway. Up and down the street were souvenir shops for the Grand Ole Opry, which was nearby. It had music stores where you could buy guitars or banjos. There were bars and nightclubs where they played country music. It was a regular redneck paradise! And there were peep shows and adult bookstores where they showed movies. That was my first experience with this kind of stuff and it made quite an impression on me. Oh, I had hidden the occasional *Playboy* magazine under my bed like every other teenaged boy, but I'd never seen the real thing! The places had little booths laid around the wall. You could tell if one was occupied, the door was locked. You'd find an empty one and lock the door. The booth was like barely bigger than a telephone booth. On the back of the door was a little screen. You had to stand back from the door, put a quarter in, and the X-rated movie would come on. I was fascinated. I spent half my paychecks a quarter at a time on porno movies.

If you stood up against the back wall, the booths were so cheaply made, just pieces of plywood painted black, that you could see into the next booth and tell if there was somebody in there. Some of them had pretty big gaps. The movies had no sound, all you could hear was the whirr of the old 8-mm movie projector. It was great if someone had put a quarter in already and the movie was near the end. You knew you were in trouble if there were two people sitting there completely dressed. Then it would cost you seventy-five cents to get to the good part.

One night I'm watching the movie and I heard this noise. I looked over and there was this guy squeezed against the wall sliding into my booth. Suddenly he's right there with me. I said, "What are you doing?" He

said, "Do these movies get you turned on?" "No!" I
shouted. (So what was I doing there?) He reached out to
prove that I wasn't lying and I scrambled out of there. As
I ran out the front I hollered to the guy at the desk,
"There's an f-ing queer back there." The last thing I saw
as I got out the door was this guy reach down and fetch a
big old baseball bat. I was out of there. I don't think I
went back for a long time.

Downstairs at the hotel, they had a small reception area
and the wrestling office. The office had one of those
Dutch doors. The first person you asked for was named
Nina Bond. She was a big lady who lived in the hotel.
She had no life other than working for Nick Gulas. I
don't think she ever really left the place. Besides Nina,
Christine Jarrett was the main secretary. She'd worked
for Nick for thirty years or more. Nick Gulas and Roy
Welch each had an office. If I wasn't at the peep shows,
I'd hang out down at the office.

Christine's niece and nephew also worked there as
helpers. Every day they'd get lunch for everyone. They'd
eat and order stuff for the others and take it back. Sam
Bass was a terrific ribber. Sam had met some guy who
worked at the zoo in Nashville. This was how Sam's
mind worked. He asked this guy what they did if an elephant got constipated. The zoo guy said they had this
special laxative. Sam asked if he could get some of it. So
Sam had himself a vial of elephant laxative.

Now the first rib was to order the goofiest combination of food for Nina. She'd always say, "Just get me
whatever." Okay, pork chops and peach pie. Then we
put castor oil on her food. She never said anything. She
never let on that there was anything weird about her
food. She'd just eat it up. You know what's coming.
Finally, we got a plate of food and Sam takes out the laxative and puts the whole bottle on the food. She ate

everything and Sam and I waited and waited but nothing happened. We had to go and wrestle or something.

When we got back that night we heard the story and Nick Gulas was furious. When that stuff hit Nina, she jumped up from her desk and started to run and she didn't even make it to the bathroom. There was a trail all the way up to her room. Everybody was mad. The hotel people were mad. Nick Gulas was a really fastidious guy who freaked out when people were clipping their fingernails in front of him, so you can imagine how he reacted to this. We couldn't admit to that one. There were suspicions, but no one found us out.

Jackie was the master of gross ribs like this, and Tojo Yamamoto was the easiest target. Like Nick, Tojo couldn't stand a gross rib; he'd get sick to his stomach. Tojo would be in the locker room getting ready and Jackie would say, "Hey Tojo, what's goin' on?" Jackie would stand next to him and change. He'd pull his drawers down and sit there buck naked and look down. He'd say, "Hey, Tojo, want a Lifesaver?" He'd peel his foreskin back and there'd be a Lifesaver. "You're sick! You're sick!" Fargo would pop the mint into his mouth. He'd walk by with a guy's toothbrush stuck up his butt. He'd come out of the bathroom with a bit of toilet paper and flick bits of stuff at Tojo. Not what you think—he crumbled up a candy bar on the paper, but Tojo fell for it constantly.

Nick Gulas was a tough guy who took everything very seriously. But he had a good heart and he was as funny as could be despite the fact that he didn't have much of a sense of humor himself. Nick was the boss. There was no doubt about that. He ran the territory with an iron fist. He was a Greek immigrant who had come to Nashville and made good through hard work and perseverance. Nick used to walk all over Nashville putting out cardboard posters to advertise his matches. He told me he walked until there were holes in the bottom of his shoes and he'd sit down and cut a poster in the shape of his sole and put it in his shoe and keep walking. When he finally became successful, he wore expensive suits, big diamond rings, and drove the best cars. Nick had jet-black hair that he used to keep slicked back, never a strand out of place. He was real paranoid too. He had this beautiful home out in Brentwood and he had guards and guard dogs. He loved to brag, but even when he did that you couldn't help but like him. He'd say, "I got me some guard dogs out at my house. You'd better not come out to my house. I got two big dober pinchermans."

"Dober pinchermans," I'd reply, "They're nasty."

He thought guys took marijuana pills. There was this guy called Butch Boyette who wrestled as a hippie in the seventies. He really was a bit of a hippie, so that wasn't just a gimmick, and I suspected he smoked dope on special occasions. (Days that ended with the letter "y" were special occasions to Butch.) He came to the match one night and he was so messed up. His eyes were all bloodshot and he was reeking of smoke. Nick Gulas asked him what was wrong with his eyes. Butch just stared up at Nick through those bloodshot eyes and drawled, "Ah, Nick, I went swimming for about an hour. I went underwater and got all this chlorine in my eyes." A little later, Nick came in shaking his head. "That damn Boyette, I don't know if he's gonna be able to wrestle tonight or not. He took some of them marijuana pills and he stayed underwater for an hour." Nick was dead serious.

We did live interviews every week at the TV station. Nick would do the intros for the interviews and the wrestlers would come on live. If I was wrestling, he'd say something like, "Well, Nashville, this Wednesday night at the Nashville Fairgrounds, it's going to be the biggest wrestling match in the history of Nashville. Jerry 'the King' Lawler here is going to be taking on so-and-so and I know Jerry Lawler is mad as he can be because of what happened last week and I guarantee that he's chomping at the bit to get at so-and-so and he's going to rip him from one end of the ring to the other. He's going to tear his head off. Now Jerry, tell us what you're going to do to so-and-so."

One week, after Nick's lengthy lead-in, I just said, "Why should I, Nick? You just told them everything I'm going to do." He cut the interview and started screaming. "What the hell is wrong with you, boy?" Nick always referred to the "boys" as "boy."

Nick Gulas would go on some strange tirades, and could he ever cuss. He'd make a construction worker blush with his cussing! He was waiting for me to do an interview once. He asked where I was and someone said I was in the bathroom. "The bathroom?" He shouted, "You go to the goddamn bathroom on your own time. You use the fucking bathroom at fucking home, boy!" A lot of people didn't like Nick and thought he short-changed them. Nick was tight with his money. (When he pulled a dollar out of his pocket, George Washington would blink at the light.) But really his payoffs seemed bad because there was just not a lot of money in the houses. I always thought Nick paid what was there. Buddy Wayne remembers one night in Chattanooga where the take was just under $9,000. Nick Gulas said, "Hell, boy, damn good house tonight . . . right at ten grand," and that's what he told the wrestlers. He paid them what was there but he'd said it was a $10,000 house so it looked like he was shortchanging people. Most promoters would tell the wrestlers the houses were smaller than they actually were so they wouldn't have to pay out as much. Not Nick Gulas, he just liked to talk big.

Wrestling has always been a family business, something that's been handed down. Vince McMahon got into the business because his father was in it and his father before him. One of the things that happened to a lot of wrestling promoters, and which opened the door for me to become an owner of a company, was the fact that some of the families who owned these territories had sons or daughters they wanted to hand these businesses down to, and they just weren't capable.

Nick Gulas had one son, George. When George got to be about nineteen or twenty, he decided he wanted to be a wrestler. Nick himself was never a wrestler, he was a promoter and a businessman, and a shrewd one at that. He always looked at wrestlers the way Alfred Hitchcock looked at actors. With great disdain. He thought they were like cattle. He thought he made the wrestlers, by giving them the exposure and telling them what to do. To an extent that was true.

He didn't like it when his son said he wanted to be a wrestler, but George got what he wanted. Nick owned the company, he was the boss, so George wasn't going to be just any wrestler; he was going to be the star. But George wasn't a good wrestler; in fact, he was very bad. He was a tall, skinny, gangly guy about a hundred and sixty pounds. The only sport he played in school was basketball and that's what he looked like, a tall, skinny basketball player in a wrestling ring. All of a sudden George was in the main events. He didn't have to go through any period of having to lose matches. He was beating the Interns first time up. Nick Gulas booked George all around Birmingham, Johnson City, Nashville, Bowling Green, Huntsville, Chattanooga. People knew he was the promoter's son. And people resented it and it turned them off. Nick shoved his son down everybody's throat for so long that people quit coming to the matches until some towns were dead.

Jerry Jarrett had got more into the business end and he wanted to do the booking. Nick Gulas let him start booking matches and thinking up ideas for them. The territory was pretty big at that time and it was more or less divided into two ends with one crew of wrestlers working one end and another crew working the other end. Nick started letting Jerry book the other end of the territory around Memphis. Jerry was the one who started pushing me into main events. We were red-hot over in our towns: Memphis, Louisville, Evansville, Tupelo. We had the territory going gangbusters.

But it was clear that George's end was declining, while Jerry had the other end going great. Monday nights we would have the Memphis Coliseum sold out with eleven thousand five hundred people. Birmingham, in the same type of building, would draw maybe twenty-five hundred people. George heard about it and went to his dad and asked if he could wrestle in Memphis. Nick told Jerry Jarrett that he was going to

Jerry Jarrett

send George over. Jerry said, "No, Nick, I'm not going to do it." Nick said Jerry worked for him. Jerry said that George had killed Nick's end of the territory. We had things going well and Jerry wasn't going to have George kill what he'd built up.

Jerry had supposedly been buying into the company through his mother, Christine. Nick said, "I'll tell you something, boy. I still run this company and I own this company. Where George wants to work, he's going to work." Jerry said he owned part of the company too and he had some say. But Nick said Jerry didn't own anything. When Jerry checked into that he found that he really had no ownership and no say-so. So he went to Nick and said, "You know what? I quit." Nick Gulas laughed at him and said he wouldn't last a week on his own.

Jerry then came to me and told me what he was going to do. He said it was a very risky deal. I was the featured guy over here. Jerry said he was sure that Nick was going to come and offer me more money to stay with him and he wasn't in a position to match that money. But he would make me a partner. I'd not only get paid to wrestle, I'd also get a share of the profits the company made. He thought I'd make more money than if I stayed with Nick because he was fixing to bring George over here.

I thought about it, and I left Nick and went with Jerry. The chance to get an ownership stake was too good. Nick Gulas obviously wasn't going to give it to me. About a third of the wrestlers went with Jerry. Nick had been a promoter for forty years and he was tried and tested. He also had the TV contracts. Nick had been on Channel Thirteen in Memphis for years. After the split, Jackie Fargo and Tojo both went with Gulas. They were like Jerry Jarrett's closest friends and his mentors as well. They had both pushed Jerry to break away from Nick but I guess they never thought he'd actually do it.

When Jerry came to me and asked if I'd be willing to go with him and I said I would, he said he had all the top guys in the territory lined up: Jackie, Tojo, and me. Then he went to Nick and told him what he was doing and Nick hit the ceiling.

The following week we booked shows in Memphis with Jerry, Jackie, Tojo, me, and a lot of different guys. We got there that Monday night and Tojo and Jackie were no-shows. We found out they were working in Birmingham for Nick. Nick must have got to them and promised them more money and convinced them that Jerry wasn't going to make it.

After I made the decision to go with Jerry, I went to Channel Five in Memphis. I walked in off the street and I had no idea who to talk to. But I was the featured wrestler in Memphis. And the wrestling show on Channel Thirteen was doing a twenty rating. It was the highest-rated show on the station. It got higher ratings at eleven o'clock on a Saturday morning than the prime-time shows did throughout the week. It was a huge moneymaker for the station.

I asked to meet the program director. His name was Phil Slavik. I went into his office and I said, "Would you like to have a wrestling show on Saturday mornings?" He said like the show on Channel Thirteen? I said a new show. I said it would have me, and I thought we could bring the announcers and most of the talent. Suddenly he got real fidgety. He started stuttering and stammering and said he really didn't have the authority to make that kind of decision. So he went and got the general manager, Mori Griener, and I told him the same thing. The next week we had a contract to start on Channel Five, WMC-TV, Saturdays, 11 A.M. Nick Gulas stayed on Channel Thirteen but that show lasted maybe two months before everything moved over to Channel Five.

Dave Brown, the Channel Thirteen weatherman, was

the cohost of the wrestling show with Lance Russell. He was a big local personality and the popularity of his weather reports meant they had the highest-rated news at five and ten. Lance Russell was also the program director at Channel Thirteen. The two most important people at that entire television station quit and came with Jerry Jarrett and me. They both moved to Channel Five. Dave and Lance hosted the new wrestling show. And Channel Five's news, with Dave Brown doing the weather, replaced Channel Thirteen at the top of the ratings and it is still there to this day.

You'd pump up the programs on TV. Any time two wrestlers got involved in a feud or were going against each other for more than one match, it was called a "program." Today the term "program" has been replaced by "story line." Either way, the TV shows are where these program/story lines were hyped. TV always was and remains a commercial for the live shows. It was something you'd give away to get someone to buy a ticket for the live event or, now, a Pay-Per-View.

Eventually, we did a live TV show every Saturday morning in Memphis. We'd tape it and make dubs and bicycle that tape around. The following week the show we'd done live in Memphis would be seen in Louisville, Nashville, and Evansville. For a while we did a live TV in Louisville and Nashville too but it worked out better to record the show in Memphis and send the tapes around. The matches we had in Memphis we would also have the following week in all those other towns. Then we'd do something different in Memphis, and the next week that would be in all the other towns too. I always hated the fact that if you got "color," or bled in your match on Monday in Memphis, that meant you had to bleed again the following Tuesday and Wednesday, just when your cut from the previous Monday was healing up.

Lance Russell

Lance Russell was the foil for my antics for years on TV. While it might have appeared that he just stood there and held the microphone while I ranted and raved, the truth is, his priceless facial expressions and perfectly timed comments were just as important to the interviews being successful as I was. Here was the guy who once called up a high-school kid and asked him to come and show his drawings of wrestlers on TV, now interviewing that same kid. And Lance never once had a problem making it look like that kid was a big star. I made relentless fun of his somewhat prominent nose. I think as many fans referred to Lance as "Banana Nose" as they did by his real name, thanks to me. I'd say things like, "You know how we all have little noses and we have to breathe all day long . . . not Lance. His nose is so big he only has to take one breath and it keeps him going all day."

Years ago, Lance was the spokesperson on commercials for a local clothing store called Baxter's Suits.

Lance did a ton of commercials for Baxter's and all those cheapskates ever gave him was one lousy suit over a period of about ten years. One Saturday, Lance was on vacation, so Dave Brown had to interview me. I solemnly announced that Lance could not be there that day because there was a death in his family . . . his Baxter suit had died . . . It shined itself to death. I constantly ripped on his clothes and stuff. Once I actually ripped his coat, literally—I pulled it clean off his back. He got his own back once in a limited way on a Christmas special where we switched characters. Lance wore my "Lawler's Army" gear and I wore a sports coat, glasses, and a fake nose.

After Jerry Jarrett and I broke away, the territory was divided in two. We ran two cities every night. On Monday nights, we'd run Memphis, and Nick would run Birmingham, Alabama. There were two separate crews. It was almost like the WWE is doing now with *Raw* and *SmackDown!* The Birmingham crew would work Johnson City, Tennessee, on Tuesday. Wednesday they'd work Nashville; Thursday: Bowling Green, Kentucky; Friday: Huntsville, Alabama; Saturday: TV in Chattanooga, Tennessee, or in Birmingham. The other group, mine and Jerry's, would work Memphis on Monday; Tuesday: Louisville, Kentucky; Wednesday: Evansville, Indiana; Thursday would be a spot show—one that could take place anywhere; then Tupelo, Mississippi; then Jonesboro, Arkansas. They'd also do Memphis TV on Saturday. There were forty guys in each group.

The new company was called the CWA, the Continental Wrestling Association. Jerry Jarrett and I wanted to give our new company some legitimacy so we brought in Billy Graham. "Superstar" Billy Graham had a huge reputation. He had been the champion for the World Wrestling Federation, but he wasn't being used up there anymore. People knew that he'd been a credible champion, so it gave us credibility right off the bat when we made him our first champion. He lived a long way from the Mid-South, and it was really expensive to fly him in and out, so we just used him for a few shots. He was a good guy, easygoing. Great physique. Huge muscles. He was one of the first guys who had some health problems and attributed it to the steroids he said he felt he had to take to compete.

Jackie Fargo and Tojo Yamamoto stayed with Nick until he pretty much went out of business, which didn't take that long. It was sad, really. I always liked Nick. Gulas went from being one of the richest men in Nashville with a home in swanky Brentwood, and one of the top wrestling companies in the country, to dying broke in a nursing home. Jarrett's mother had to pay for the burial. George is teaching school now. I saw him at a match in Nashville recently.

I really made out from Jerry's move on Nick Gulas. I'd gone from goofing around his office in the hotel in Nashville to part owning the business in a few years. And while all this was going down, the King's private life was in turmoil. Oh, and in 1977, the other King died.

chapter 15

The Mid-South Fair was a big deal every year in Memphis with all sorts of exhibits and amusement rides. About two weeks before the Fair in 1977, this guy came to me and said he used to work for Elvis Presley. They'd bought this photo machine that would take a picture and develop a poster-sized photo in five minutes. They were going to use it with Elvis at his concerts. Well, that wasn't going to work anymore, since Elvis was no longer with us; he had died a few weeks before. He thought that he might rent a booth at the Fair and work with me. He said he'd take care of everything at the booth and all I'd have to do was show up and smile for the camera. It sounded like a pretty easy gig to me.

I get out to the Fair on the first day. There were two girls there to help with the pictures, one to take the pictures, one to take the money. The guy was doing the developing. Now these two girls were just absolute knockouts. Beautiful faces and great bodies on both of them. One was a blonde and one was a brunette. The brunette's name was Tina Diana, and the blonde was Paula Caruth. I just couldn't stop staring at these girls and I remember thinking, "Well, you wouldn't expect anything other than beautiful girls to be hanging around Elvis Presley." I quickly found out that the blonde . . .

Paula, was the girlfriend of the son of Dr. George Nichopoulos, who'd been Elvis's doctor. She'd never heard of me and she said her friend told her I was some redneck wrestler from Mississippi. I could tell she wasn't too impressed with me and for some reason that drove me nuts. I guess I figured she should be swooning over the only "King" left in Memphis if she was given the chance. I mean, after all, she could see all these people lining up and paying good, hard-earned money just to have their picture made with me.

I was smitten, but there was no way anything could come of it. I was married, she was practically engaged, plus she thought I was a "redneck rassler." Those were some pretty big mountains to climb, and I only had ten days to do it in; after that the Fair would be over and so would be any chance of winning Paula. The pressure was on, so I pulled out all the stops. I was saying and doing anything and everything that I thought might change her opinion of me.

I can tell you I spent more time talking to Paula during that Fair than I did taking pictures. One night after the Fair closed for the day, I persuaded Paula to let me take her home. She reminded me she had a boyfriend so all I got from her was a little peck on the cheek, but the ice was broken! That little kiss from her was like winning the world championship to me. After the Fair I called her a lot and we finally started seeing each other.

Well, it wasn't long till she found out I was married and that was it. She didn't want to be the one to break up anyone's marriage and she said I should try and work it out with my wife. I told her I was pretty sure I was going to get a divorce anyway and she said we possibly could get together when that was all done. But I kept on trying to see her every chance I could. Finally, one night I invited her to come see me sing with Jimmy Hart and his band, the Gentrys, at a nightclub in Memphis. She came and she was sitting out in the audience and I was up on the stage singing and all of a sudden, her boyfriend walked in. I guess he had had his suspicions, but it didn't take him long to realize what was going on. He confronted Paula and told her she was going to have to choose. He left the club and told her that if she wasn't at his house by 10 P.M., they were finished. Me and the Gentrys finished singing at midnight and Paula was still in the audience.

Paula's boyfriend was Dean Nichopoulos, and as I said, his dad was Dr. "Nick," Elvis's personal physician. Dean also worked for Elvis and so he and Paula were often part of Elvis's entourage. That also meant that Paula got to hang out at Graceland a lot. She'd go with the group, dubbed by Elvis as the Memphis Mafia, when they went to watch movies after-hours at the Malco Theater. She has some great memories of being around the other King, like the time Elvis sang a song just to her once in his den. And another time Elvis sent his personal jet, the *Lisa Marie,* from California all the way to Memphis just to fly Paula out to Palm Springs. She was the only person on the plane. She said Elvis was a very sweet and a very funny man.

Not much later, my wife Kay and I went to a ballgame in Cleveland. That night after the game, we were lying in bed in a motel. I loved Kay, but I was no longer "in love" with her. I was in love with Paula. I really didn't know any other way to do what I wanted to do. And I just blurted out, "You know, I've been thinking about divorce."

She said, "What?"

"It's just not the life I had anticipated. Not the life I wanted."

Kay was relieved to come back to her family and friends in Memphis. I stayed on in Nashville. I bought her a house and paid the note and gave her money. I'd see Brian and Kevin basically every weekend. Honestly, it probably worked out better for everybody. Kay married again and just a couple of years ago had another baby.

At the time, I never told Kay about Paula. After Kay and I got divorced, I took an apartment in Memphis. One day I took Brian and Kevin over to the apartment. They were somewhere around six or seven years old. Paula came over and we hung out together. When he got home, Kevin said I'd taken them over to my house. Kay said, "No, your dad doesn't have a house here." Kevin says, "Yes, he does. And a young woman came over there too." Kevin was smart enough to lead his mother all the way across town to the apartment.

I was out at the time and when I came back, Kay had come over and smashed the hanging plants on the patio and tore up the lawn chairs and generally trashed the outside. I called her and she said, "You didn't tell me you had a girlfriend all this time." I said, "I didn't have a girlfriend *all* this time." She had never wanted me back or anything but she wanted me to know she knew what was going on. I guess I was lucky, she could have left a boiling rabbit on my stove. But Kay and I stayed on pretty good terms. She did a really good job with Brian and Kevin. Raising two kids is pretty hard work.

When I was married to Kay, no one knew about it. But Paula and I had a big, high-profile marriage in Memphis, so that was a little harder to keep quiet. In 1982, we were married by Shelby County Mayor Bill Morris in the Continental Ballroom of the Peabody Hotel. I'd wrestled, and lost to, Dutch Mantel for the Southern Title in the afternoon and we got married in the evening. All the Memphis television stations covered our wedding on the news. The lead to the story on Channel Five said, "The King loses his title, but wins a bride!" Not long after Paula and I got married, we moved to Memphis.

Paula was sort of like Lucy on *I Love Lucy*, always hinting at the fact that she'd like to be in the spotlight. So, I finally gave her a segment of her own on my TV show. She started doing "Paula's Picks" on the *Jerry Lawler Show*. Paula loves the NFL so she picked the winners of the upcoming football games each week. Her picks weren't very scientific, she'd pick the Minnesota Vikings because she liked their purple uniforms. She's a huge Pittsburgh Steelers fan so she'd always pick the Steelers to win, and she'd always pick against the Browns just to antagonize me. When we met Terry Bradshaw he looked at me, and he looked at Paula and said, "King, you overmarried." Paula loved him even more than ever after that.

Paula

For the Picks, I started by filming Paula at home; that way she could mess up or make mistakes and we could keep doing it over and nobody would know. When she got a little more confident, a crew from Channel Five came to film her and eventually she went to the studio. Paula really liked being on TV and she did really look great on the show. So much that she was constantly asking the station's general manager, Ron Klayman, for her own show. She was relentless. Once I got stuck in Texas in a big storm and Paula had to host the show herself. She said it was the worst show ever and after that, anytime Paula mentioned her own show to the station manager, he'd invite her up to his office to view that show.

Wrestling was the centerpiece of the show, and I'd have a different wrestler on there every week, but we had all sorts of other entertainers come on as guests as well. I had some really heavy hitters on my show. Muhammad Ali was on talking about how he got his entire boxing persona, or "shtick," from watching the wrestler Gorgeous George. Garth Brooks was on talking about playing against me in a softball game. Al Gore was on talking about bringing the NFL to Memphis. Warren Moon, the then quarterback for the Oilers, was on and I think he was just there trying to hit on Paula. One of my favorite shows was when I had Mickey Mantle on the show. He was a really neat guy and he wrote me a nice letter afterward thanking me for having him on. But my favorite shows of all were when I had players from the Cleveland Browns on my show. Paula and I were doing the show right when we were getting divorced and we'd always be getting digs in at each other. If the show had been on four more weeks, it would have lasted five years.

Paula never wanted to try to wrestle, but she did like to be involved in other ways. We put her hair up in a match once with Bill Dundee. I had already wrestled and beaten Bill with his wife's hair at stake and we shaved her bald. I had to assure Paula that there was no chance she was going to get her head shaved. We went on a working vacation to Hawaii in 1985. That, incidentally, was the last real vacation I went on. Paula worked as my valet or manager. In the first match at the Aloha Stadium, I was wrestling this guy who was the promoter. Paula didn't know that and she was shouting at him from the corner. "He's old, Jerry, he's fat, he shouldn't even be in the ring!" and so on. When it was over I said, "What were you doing? He's the guy paying us."

In another match in the islands, Paula again worked as my manager. I was working with Plowboy Frazier. As a rib, and to let Paula get a taste of the action, I asked Plowboy if he could safely give her a big leg-drop. He said, "I won't even touch her, neighbor." Paula was outside the ring on the apron and she hit Plowboy with her high-heeled shoe. He hauls her into the ring and gives her the leg-drop.

When you're lying there and this guy who weighs nearly five hundred pounds jumps up and you can see his butt coming right for your face, it's a scary thing. There's quite a bit of trust involved. Plowboy did the leg-drop and he didn't really have perfect control over every bit of his legs, which were as thick as most people. He landed, with a little bit of force, but most wrestlers would have thought nothing of it. Paula thought her nose was broken! She was pretty much in shock. She was trying to cry, but couldn't. She was making a funny little hooting sound with her hands over her face. I got scared and thought she really was hurt.

The promoter was The Rock's grandmother, Leah Miavia. Her husband, Peter, had been the big wrestling legend out there and she had taken over from him when he died. Leah thought Paula's nose was broken too. She jumped up from her seat ringside and came up to the ring and helped her up. Paula took her hands away and realized her nose was fine. She did split her lip open. That was the last time she ever came into the ring with me.

Right before Elvis died, I'd talked to his father, Vernon. The contact came through an unlikely route.

After Sam got killed, I looked for a replacement. But Sam was irreplaceable. We had such chemistry and we knew each other so well. We tried guys like Private Diamond, who was involved in "Lawler's Army," which we started when I was not only wrestling but I was in everybody's corner too. We were trying to transfer my heat onto all the other heels we had because they didn't have much heat of their own.

In Evansville, Indiana, we wrestled every week at the Municipal Auditorium, which was sponsored by a veterans' organization. I had gone to an army surplus store and bought a uniform and a load of medals for Lawler's Army and these veterans got really upset. They almost made us shut down wrestling. They told me where each medal was actually from and there was no way I should be wearing them in the ring and stuff. Anyway, after all that, and a spell with Danny Davis, I took Mickey Poole as a manager and a valet. He'd do anything. He drove everywhere. He got the bags and all that. Mickey was an extremely goofy individual. I think he'd been left out in the sun too long.

We were making a video one time. I think it was for a Ken Patera match. Patera was billed as the world's strongest man, so the video was about how tough and mean I was. I took a basketball and dribbled with it. I said I was going to take my opponent and put him in a head-lock. I took the basketball and grabbed it and squeezed. Mickey was behind me out of sight and took an ice pick and stuck it into the valve so the ball went flat and it looked like I'd squashed the basketball.

The last thing I was going to do on the video was hold my fist up to the camera. I figured there must be some way stuntmen used to set themselves on fire. Something that burned real quick, but not real hot. I wanted to set my fist on fire. Great scientist that I am, I thought I'd give petroleum jelly a go. I figured it would protect my skin from the flame. But of course I tried it on Mickey first.

We got ready to go. I told him to let me know as soon as it got hot. I was holding a wet towel to throw over his fist. "Okay, Jerry." He held his fist up and I applied the Vaseline and squirted the lighter fluid on. I told Mickey I was holding the wet towel. He lights his hand and his face contorts like you see in the movies. He screamed and turned to me and knocked the towel out of my hand. I grabbed the towel and put out the flame. Mickey said, all out of breath, "Don't do it, Jerry, don't do it, Jerry. Fire burns." We had to come up with a new idea.

Another time we were out in some backwoods place at a National Guard Armory doing a match. Mickey was in my corner and we were the big heels. We got the folks very riled up and after the match, a few of them came after us. I got back to the dressing room, and Larry was there standing guard but Mickey got surrounded. I had to go out and rescue him and bring him 'round the back to the car. We had to make a getaway with the locals chasing after us. So I guess he could be an effective manager, even though he wasn't much use in a fight.

One day we were talking and Mickey told me his brother was the president of the Elvis Presley International Fan Club. I said, "Yeah, Mickey, I'm an astronaut too." But he said, "No, really. All the fan clubs are under him and he hangs out at Graceland all the time. He knows everybody, talks to Elvis all the time." I told him what I wanted to do.

I got him all geeked up. I said that Elvis was into karate. What if we had this big karate versus wrestling match at the Coliseum? Mickey said, "I guarantee Elvis would love that. I'll get my brother to talk to him." I thought he was just a goof, his brother's no more

At the gates to Graceland.

president of the fan club than I am. I said go ahead.

Next day, Mickey said he'd talked to his brother and his brother was going to talk to Elvis's uncle, Vester Presley, who was the main guard at Graceland. At this point, when he was still alive, Elvis was not that big a deal. (Terrible as it sounds, dying was the best career move he ever made.) He was looked on as a recluse in Memphis.

But still, this was Elvis. Mickey told me that Elvis's dad, Vernon, was going to call me. Now Mickey is the guy who let me set his hand on fire just to see if it would hurt, so I'm really waiting on the call. I was living in Hendersonville, near Nashville, at the time. I get home one night and Kay said that somebody had called the house looking for me and his name was Vernon Presley. I said, "Really?" She said he sounded like an old man with a real southern voice and I said well, he would be an old man with a real southern voice. She said he'd call back tomorrow.

I was going to Evansville, Indiana, the next day. I had to leave around three o'clock. I got back and Kay said he'd called again. He said he'd call the next morning at ten o'clock. I'm sitting there by the phone. Sure enough, Vernon Presley called. "Jerry . . ."

I was in double shock. For one, here was Vernon Presley on the phone. And that also meant Mickey's brother Eddie really was the president of the Elvis Presley Fan Club. Vernon had talked with Elvis about the idea. He said Elvis would like to do it. But he said Elvis was not really in very good shape. He's starting to work out because he's got a tour coming up. When he comes off the tour, Vernon said he'd call me back and we'd figure out all the details. He said it would be a lot of fun. I said cool. I bet it was three weeks later that Elvis died.

Elvis was really big into karate; he worked out with this karate champion called Bill Wallace who taught martial arts at Memphis State and he co-owned the Memphis Karate Institute. He was a wrestling fan too. A guy called Mr. Coffee who worked at the Ellis Auditorium for forty years used to let Elvis in to watch the wrestling from the stage. Vester Presley came every Monday night to the Coliseum for a long time and he used to bring Lisa Marie to the matches when she was four or five years old.

It would have been great to have set up a program with Elvis. But by the time we were talking about it, it was too late. By 1977, Elvis was doing so many drugs. I guess he told Dr. Nichopoulos, give me this stuff, or I'll buy a drugstore. Dr. Nick would give him placebos and stuff but he also prescribed thousands of narcotic and amphetamine pills for him in 1977 alone. His license got suspended for a while.

There were all these stories about Elvis just before he died. At night he had to wear diapers. He had a long flashlight and before he got on one of his planes to go anywhere, he'd get on the plane with the flashlight and look around. People who knew him said Elvis was as nice a guy as you'd want to meet but he was still real country, as country as you could be. And he had the most magnificent complexion. Smooth as anything.

Jimmy Hart, Jimmy Valiant

16

After the split, it was really just a matter of months before Nick Gulas's business went south. At first, Jerry and I really didn't want the whole territory. We were content with the Memphis end of it, so that's what happened. Nick continued to operate that other end and tried to come in and run some shows in Memphis. But after a while, the wrestlers wanted to work our end. They could make three times the money working with us than they could with Nick.

Jerry Jarrett ran our office and his mother, Christine, helped. At first, she stayed working for Nick. She was so loyal to Nick and had worked for him for so many years, she loved him like a brother. She stayed on until they found somebody to take her place and then she came over and worked for me and Jerry. At first, Jerry pretty much did all the booking.

When I became involved in the ownership and promoting end of wrestling, I got a crash course in the business elements of it. Before cable TV, wrestling was a regionalized enterprise. There really wasn't a need for contracts and everything was basically done on a verbal contract and a handshake. It was simple. A wrestler would send out pictures and tapes and make calls to a region he was interested in going to. Say I wanted to go to the Carolinas. I'd get Jim Crockett's details and I'd send him some pictures and tapes. Then I'd give him a call and say I'd like to come and work your territory. I'll be available such and such dates, can you use me? They'd say yes or no.

I had experience of that side of it, of course, but I started to learn about the booking. We'd find a guy and say, "We want you April 1 in Memphis." We'd give him a booking sheet that said which town he was going to wrestle in on what date and time in which building. Everybody was expected to show up for their match and every week they'd get their paycheck. The wrestler was responsible for his own transportation, his own lodging, his own meals. They worked as independent contractors. They weren't employees.

You wouldn't say, "How much money am I going to make?" We got paid according to the attendance of the crowds. All the wrestlers got a percentage of the gate. Your pay was pretty much based on your performance. If you got over, if people liked you and wanted to see you, you could make money. If no one wanted to see you, you weren't going to make very much money. It wasn't until much later, when there were real national stars, that wrestlers started using agents or managers. Real managers, not Mickey Poole types who worked your corner. The first guys to use agents may have been Bret Hart or Jesse Ventura. When wrestling started being seen all over the world, the wrestlers realized they were as big a star as an NFL player or a baseball player and everyone got some representation.

If you didn't like it where you were wrestling because you weren't making any money or you felt like moving on, you'd go to the promoter and tell him you had another spot and you gave two weeks' notice, which was the understanding. You knew during that last two weeks that you were there, you'd get beat every night. You'd

have to put somebody else over. That was just the understanding. The office could do the same thing. If they got
tired of you or they couldn't think what to do with you,
you'd get two weeks' notice from the office. If you got
your notice, you were fired.

The mid- to late seventies to the early eighties were, by
and large, a boom time for wrestling in our area. Sometimes things were so hot, we'd be putting on live shows in
fourteen towns a week, which meant running shows in
two towns every night. Some Saturdays we would broadcast a live TV show from three different towns, and do an
event from a fourth venue that same night. We were
working our butts off traveling everyplace, but everything was drawing fantastically well. At this point in
time I was only a 20 or 25 percent partner. Jerry was getting 75 percent. But I was still doing well, making main-
event wrestler money but also the share of the profit. I
was doing really well, not even thinking about the fact
that Jerry Jarrett was doing unbelievably well.

There were some great performers around and I was
involved in some epic feuds. I probably had more
matches with Bill Dundee than with anyone. He was a
babyface about as much as I was. There was a real
rivalry between the two of us because we both thought
we were pretty good. It was an ego thing, I guess. He
was always trying to knock me off my perch. He did
some booking too like I did and we also had every kind
of match imaginable. We had hair matches for his hair,
my hair, his wife's hair; car matches where he won my
car and he smashed the windshield. We had a loser-
leaves-town match in 1985 and I lost and that was when
I went on vacation to Hawaii. Everything worked with
Bill Dundee.

But when he was in his prime, there wasn't a better
showman in the business anywhere than Jimmy Valiant.

Jimmy was nothing great as far as the wrestling was concerned but he gave a fantastic interview and he had the look. In short, he was great. It's much better to have it that way 'round. I've seen so many more charismatic guys who are great showmen but crappy wrestlers make money than great wrestlers with no charisma.

Dusty Rhodes might be the best example of what charisma means in this business. He had as much as or more charisma than any wrestler you're likely to come across. At the same time—I don't know if he'd agree with this—but Dusty was always a big, heavy guy. He wasn't very athletic-looking or even that great a wrestler. But he was one of the best interviews in the business, if not the best. He could just talk the people into the arena.

Anyway, Jimmy Valiant took Memphis by storm. Everyone talked about Handsome Jimmy, the Boy from New York City. That was his theme song. Then he started calling himself "Handsome Jimbo from Mempho." Other people started calling Memphis "Mempho." He called me Kingfish and people started doing that too. He looked amazing: long blond hair and a big mustache. When he went to WCW later, he became "The Boogie-Woogie Man." They changed his entrance and his music and he did a crazy dance routine when he came to the ring.

I did a retirement program in 1977. The angle was that I was retiring to go into music. While I was retired, Valiant came in and won my title. After five or six weeks off we booked a concert at the Coliseum along with the wrestling show. This was going to be my big musical debut. We had the local stars, the Gentrys, as the band and the McCarver Sisters were going to sing backup. The McCarver Sisters, Kerrie, Sherrie, and Dee-Dee, were a legit singing group. They were real young. (Kerrie McCarver later married Jerry Lee Lewis. It was announced in 2002 they were getting divorced.)

We didn't tell anyone what we were going to do. The McCarver Sisters were excited to be singing and their dad was there filming the whole thing. The stage was set up for the band and everything. They had some wrestling matches and then an intermission to add anticipation for the big music show. We were introduced and the Gentrys played the intro to a song. I'm getting ready to sing and all of a sudden, from way offstage, comes Jimmy Valiant like a maniac, wielding a guitar that he smashed over my head. I go down, bleeding, and there's chaos. The McCarver Sisters are screaming and their dad's running around. He actually threatened to sue us afterward.

That was the start of a great feud with Handsome Jimmy that went on for a long time, maybe sixteen weeks, and sold a lot of tickets all over the territory. I think Jimmy got suspended for his antics at the concert. Of course, I came out of retirement and I was more popular than ever. We then built up to a big hair-versus-hair match. Jimmy had the long blond hair. At this time, he had a ton of heat. People figured that Jimmy was going to get his locks cut off because I'd never lost one of these matches. The Coliseum was sold out.

I went out to the ring ready for the match and the spotlight went over to the back of the ring. Here comes Handsome Jimmy in his street clothes. And he's on crutches with a big bandage on his ankle. As soon as they see him, people started booing, figuring they were fixed to get screwed. He comes into the ring. "Brother," he said, "as much as I would love to have this match and shave Kingfish Lawler's head, when I was getting on the airplane leaving the Big Apple, New York City, there was a patch of ice and I slipped and sprained my ankle real bad. Look, I got a doctor's note right here."

He took a piece of paper and gave it to Lance Russell.

"Read it, brother, read it to the people." Lance reads the thing. "To whom it may concern, this is to verify that Jimmy Valiant is under my care with a severely sprained ankle he received this morning. Under no circumstances will he be allowed to compete in a wrestling match until my office has given him clearance." Crap like that.

I got up to say it was a bunch of bull but Jimmy said, "No, brother, it's true. I don't know what to say." He was hobbling around. We milk it for five minutes. I say, "Crutches or no crutches, Valiant, people came here to see you get your head shaved and by God, they're going to see it." I turn to get the fans to cheer that idea and Valiant takes one of his crutches, hits me over the head, and knocks me down and out. He starts hitting me with the crutch, dancing around the ring to show his ankle is fine. He hammers me a few times and reaches into his pocket and pulls out a big pair of scissors. "Right, brother, they're going to see a head shaving." He starts hacking away at my hair and people are hot because they haven't seen a match yet.

My idea for the finish was that when Valiant cut a little bit of my hair, Bill Dundee was going to rush to the ring and chase Valiant back. I'd be carried back to the dressing room unconscious and Dundee was going to challenge Valiant. "You may have knocked Lawler out, but I'm here," he'd say. We weren't going to say anything about hair-versus-hair. They'd have a five-minute match with Dundee pounding Valiant all over the ring, get the people up in the air until Valiant, after selling all that time, would do something to screw Dundee. He'd get the scissors out and start cutting his hair. The referees would come in and pull Valiant off and that would be it. Because Valiant had screwed both me and Dundee, we didn't think people would want to see either of us have our heads shaved.

Bill Dundee

Well, they pull me out of the ring and in comes Bill Dundee. But he doesn't make a speech or anything and just starts going after Valiant. Valiant takes his boot off right away, hits Dundee, and covers him—one-two-three. Then he goes for Dundee's hair. I think people felt cheated out of a match rather than out of a head shaving.

We were sitting in the locker room when someone told us the crowd was going nuts. They kicked out some windows and the doors to the Coliseum. Someone set fire to some chairs. It was a pretty ugly scene. As a result we had to suspend Valiant. Or, rather, Valiant had to go home. We always made sure the angles with Jimmy had some kind of enormous payoff because he'd be out of the territory awhile.

So I'd use my big finale on Jimmy Valiant. When I was ready to end the program with somebody, I would throw fire at them. I'd be down on the mat and it looked like I was really out. All of a sudden, out of nowhere would come this fireball in the guy's face and they'd have to be carried out and they'd be out of commission

awhile. That's what we did with Handsome Jimmy. I threw the fire and it really looked impressive, a very vicious, fireball in his face. I had flash paper, which will burn big and bright but so fast that it doesn't do any real damage. It always singes your hair but it won't leave a mark. I think it's made by soaking paper in nitric and sulfuric acids.

About three weeks later I wrestled Harley Race in the ninety-minute championship match. We hadn't as much as mentioned Valiant's name all that time. Then Valiant ran on in his street clothes and busted a Coke bottle on my head and cut my shoulder. Glass went all over the ring. The fans went nuts and the police had trouble controlling the crowd. People wanted to kill Jimmy Valiant. Some young girl ran out of the audience and jumped over the railing and into the ring. She was going after Jimmy. She ran across the ring. I have no idea why, but she was barefoot and as she ran across the ring, she cut her feet up on the glass. She jumped on Jimmy before the police could go in and get her.

Jimmy Valiant has a lot of tattoos. He used to look at the scars he put on my shoulder and my chest and say, "Kingfish, brother. There's your tattoos you'll always have from Handsome Jimmy." Jimmy has a tattoo somewhere on him I drew a picture for.

I once whizzed Jimmy to go to Japan with me. He hated it. I went to Japan three times. The most I would go for was seven or ten days. One time I went over there right at the end of a three-week tour. Everyone else was homesick and ready to leave. They brought me in for the last week, just for the big shows. One guy was so mad, he quit right there and then and went right home. They paid for Paula to come, which was unheard of. I was adding so many conditions because I really wanted them to say no, but they agreed to all of them. That really made the other guys hot.

The first night we were there, Antonio Inoki, the wrestler, who was hugely popular there, the biggest deal in the business, had Paula come sit with him at ringside. He wasn't wrestling that night. Inoki took a big shine to Paula. Everywhere he went, there were photographers all over him. Next morning, on the front page of the main sports paper, there was a picture of Inoki and Paula with the headline "Who is this mystery woman?"

The wrestlers were huge in Japan. Every place was always sold out. Kids waited all night in eight feet of snow outside the hotel in Sapporo just on the chance of seeing someone. They'd buy special cards with a space for your autograph. I learned to write my name in Japanese and they thought that was the greatest thing.

Everyone took their shoes off on the way into the arena. Tiger Jeet Singh would come out in his turban waving a sword. He put on a good show. He'd walk through the crowd whacking people with the sword. One night, the whole crowd stampeded, trying to get away from Tiger. Paula was stuck out there with Jimmy's wife, Big Momma, and she thought she was going to get trampled by 10,000 people in their socks. Paula also got caught in an earthquake in Tokyo when I was off wrestling somewhere. It made her hotel sway but I didn't feel it where I was so I didn't believe her at first.

When we were there, fewer people spoke English than is the case now. When we were coming in from the airport, the driver was insane and we almost had four wrecks. I thought the worst thing would be to end up in the hospital. Sure enough, the first match I had, I jumped down from the top rope onto the floor and hit my foot so bad I thought I broke it. I went to the hospital and couldn't make them understand what was wrong at all. The next day, I was trying to get some Epsom salts to soak my foot. I found a pharmacy and the guy had no idea. "Epersom sauce," it sounded like. So I drew a throbbing foot, I drew a bucket, I drew a pack of Epsom salts. I drew the foot going in the bucket. He said, "No got." There's nothing to soak your foot in in Japan.

Back in Memphis, Jimmy was over so big. But he decided to move away from the territory completely and our crowds went down to nothing. So we called him up and said, "Jimmy, what would it take to bring you back?" He said, "What if you bought me a house." He and Big Momma came to town and picked out a house. Jerry Jarrett bought the house for them and they stayed about six weeks.

One day Jimmy said, "Kingfish, let me talk to you for a minute," and he called me over. He took my hand and turned it over and put the keys to the house in my hand. He moved off and left Jerry Jarrett and me holding the house we'd just bought and we had to resell it. Thing was, the whole house was black. It had black furnishings, a black tub, black floors, everything. We eventually unloaded the house on someone who bought the place because it had been Jimmy Valiant's house.

Jimmy stayed in the business all these years and he's still on some of the local cards I wrestle on. Jimmy Valiant is about sixty years old. He lives in Virginia, where he runs a wrestling school, Boogie's Wrestling Camp. Jimmy will find somebody to drive him to the matches. When somebody books Handsome Jimmy, they also book one of his students.

Just recently, I was talking to Jerry Jarrett about Jimmy and Jerry remembered this guy he booked as an Evangelist. The evangelism business is very much like the wrestling business. You have a bunch of Evangelists. You have your main-event Evangelists, your semifinal

Evangelists, your middle-of-the card Evangelists, and your opening-match Evangelists. Jimmy Swaggart was a main-event guy until he screwed up. You also have your ultimate guys like Billy Graham.

There was a guy who worked as a warm-up guy for Jimmy Swaggart. He'd go out and basically work the crowd. He could do this great Evangelist rap so we booked him as a wrestling manager. We called him Reverend Ernest Angel, after Brother Ernest Angley, who was a main-event Evangelist on television. Our guy had a book that he'd use as a weapon and he'd hit people over the head with it. He called it his "Good Book." He'd say, "You will feel the power of the Good Book."

I said to Jerry that he's got to bring Jimmy Valiant in as Moses. Get him a long white robe, one of those big staffs, and two big tablets for the Ten Commandments. I guess Moses didn't have a tattoo 'round his forehead like Jimmy does but a laurel wreath or something could take

The King and Jeff Jarrett show the Moondogs the meaning of hardcore.

care of that. He's got the white hair, he'd be perfect. Jerry
Jarrett said that's great, but I wish I could find Brother
Ernest, and I said I had his phone number, I just used
him a couple of weeks ago. He said he'll get Brother
Ernest to be the manager and have him bring in Moses.
That's the kind of stuff you try. Who knows what will
click with people. Most of the people won't know it's
Jimmy Valiant.

People still talk about some of those matches with
Jimmy Valiant from the seventies. Another famous match
was the concession stand brawl in Tupelo in 1978. A local
promoter named Herman Sheffield and his wife Jean put
matches on every Friday night in a renovated warehouse
and they ran a concession stand in the back of the arena.
We had an idea. We talked to Herman and Jean and said
we wanted to tear up the concession stand. What? They
said the stuff cost money. We said we'd pay for anything
that got damaged or broke. They relented and said okay,
but whatever you do, just watch out for the popcorn
machine.

The match was Bill Dundee and myself against Larry
Latham and Wayne Ferris, who later was the Honky
Tonk Man. They were the Blond Bombers. I think they
had been the champs and we won the belts from them.
After the match, they grabbed the belts and we contin-
ued the brawl, first in the ring and then out the back.
The TV cameras were in a loft above the ring and Lance
Russell was commentating. He said we were still fight-
ing but that they'd run out of time. He said so long from
Tupelo and the camera went dark but you could still
hear the fighting.

Then you heard Lance tell the cameraman, "Randy,
bring the camera, they're having a hell of a fight down
here." The camera goes back on and there's the concession stand being smashed to pieces. We threw gallon jars
of mustard at each other and they splattered over the

wall; we knocked down the tables. Of course, I jammed someone's head in the popcorn machine and broke the glass, which got us in trouble. We demolished the place. It started a program that lasted almost a year. People are always talking about that. It was a forerunner of the hardcore matches.

Larry Latham was later one of the Moondogs who we had some crazy, wild battles with in the 1990s and made a lot of money. We actually re-created the Tupelo concession stand battle with those guys in Kennett, Missouri. We did basically the same thing: tore up the whole concession stand and pretty much the whole armory. Larry Latham was Moondog Spot in that rumble and he'd also been in the original brawl in Tupelo as one of the Blond Bombers. He had about four other Moondog partners. It was one of those gimmicks that fans really bought into. They acted real crazy. They had these huge cow bones they gnawed on as they came into the ring and they used them as weapons. They had wild long blond hair and beards, cutoff blue jeans with ropes for belts. They were fun. Every match with them was a hardcore match.

Larry's Blond Bomber partner, Wayne Ferris, is my first cousin. Our mothers are sisters. We were never really close. They lived about sixty or seventy miles away and we'd visit a couple of times a year. I had a few cousins who got into the business after I did. I helped them out a bit, booked them up pretty good. Wayne always did okay. When Vince was taking over everybody, Wayne left our territory and went with Vince, which I always saw as deserting his home territory and leaving a sinking ship. I could have left, but the territory would have died.

Wayne became the Honky Tonk Man and did really well. He got married and bought himself a big house. But he knocks me a lot. I don't know why he does it, and I never really talked to him about it. He used to go on the Internet and knock me. I wrote him an e-mail about it once. I asked him what his problem was. He said, "Man, it's business. I'm trying to work a big angle. Answer me back and knock me. We'll have the first-ever Internet angle." I never did answer him.

Austin Idol

he King of wrestling has recorded at the same studio where the king of rock 'n' roll got his start: Sun Studio, right here on Union Avenue in Memphis. Music is a big part of life in Memphis. What Nashville is to country music, Memphis is to the blues. If you take a walk down historic Beale Street any night of the week, you can hear great music. Perhaps B. B. King will be playing in his club. Or there might be someone at the Orpheum Theater right nearby. The last performance I saw there was Barry Manilow, which was on a Sunday night when the Indians were on the ESPN game. Not my first choice of what I wanted to be doing that night, but Joni really wanted to go.

In the seventies, Jim Blake wanted to take advantage of my popularity and make a real record. Not like the deal with the McCarver Sisters. I told Blake I'd never done any singing but he said not to worry, he'd get a bunch of musicians and find a song that I'd just basically have to talk my way through. So he comes up with a song called "Bad News," which John D. Loudermilk wrote and which Johnny Cash had recorded in 1964. I was the big heel in town and the words lent themselves to my character.

At the time I was doing a lot of trash talk on TV, talking like Elvis and insulting everyone around Memphis. I was pretty well hated. We sold around 20,000 copies of

"Bad News" at the matches. It was a 45 (a vinyl record, for our younger readers, this was even before eight-tracks) and people used to buy them and break them. Blake would tell people to buy two and break 'em, they'd feel twice as good. More amazing is the fact that as many people kept the singles as broke them. "Bad News" used to infuriate people. It was great.

To make the record, Blake had got this kind of all-star band together and we met at the Ardent recording studios in Memphis. He used Jim Dickinson, who played piano for the Rolling Stones on "Sticky Fingers" and with Ry Cooder on "Paris, Texas" and "Streets of Fire." He could play anything. Blake introduced me to someone else. That was Jimmy Hart, who was going to do backup vocals.

When I'd been in high school, the big local band was the Gentrys. They were a bunch of guys who were a couple of years ahead of me at Treadwell High. In 1965, they got to be a major deal. They went on the *Ted Mack Amateur Hour* and won it five or six weeks in a row. Then they got a recording contract and their song "Keep on Dancin'" got to number four on the Billboard charts. It was a huge hit. Jimmy Hart was one of the Gentrys. I told him I'd gone to Treadwell High and had been a big fan. Now the roles were reversed. He was a big wrestling fan and he was now telling people he went to high school with me.

Blake had pretty much assembled a bunch of stoners for the recording and I'd never been around this kind of stuff. Jimmy was like me in that he never drank, never smoked, and never did any kind of drugs, so we migrated toward one another at the recording session. He told me he was still doing the Gentrys all these years later using a bunch of other guys. He invited me to see them play at the Levee Lounge on Winchester. Jimmy said they'd work up some stuff if I wanted to sing with them. I went over and we sang a couple of songs. At one time he'd had a huge hit but he was still chasing the second one, playing in little clubs. I knew the second hit wasn't going to come. I felt a bit sorry for Jimmy in that respect because I knew he wasn't making a lot of money.

We made another record and the second one was the one we did at Sun Studio. Sam Phillips, who discovered Elvis, had sons called Knox and Jerry, and Knox was a big wrestling fan and a big Lawler fan. We cut "Cadillac Man," which was a remake of an early Sun record. We got free studio time and the musicians played for nothing because they wanted to be part of it. Jim Blake says the only guy he ever paid was Fred Ford, the blues saxophonist.

I really loved performing and I went looking for another band, after Jimmy Hart and I split up. I had the good fortune of hooking up with a talented musician, Tom Nunnery. Tom and his brothers—Mark and Richard—are longtime Memphis musicians; they had formed the Nunnery Brothers Band. We recorded an album together, and the featured single got some airplay on Memphis radio stations. It was called "World's Greatest Wrestler." We also performed in several of the Beale Street nightclubs, as well as at the Memphis Music Festival. As a matter of fact, Tom is working on a new song for us to record right now; it's called "Puppies!"

Jimmy Hart and I started hanging out some and he came to the matches at the Mid-South Coliseum. Jimmy was very charismatic and energetic so I talked to him about getting involved with wrestling in some capacity. He was ecstatic. I started using him as my manager and he was a natural, just perfect. And he's stayed in the business all this time and has done really well from it. He went from managing me to working with Hulk Hogan. So I am wholly responsible for the Mouth of the South being in professional wrestling.

* * *

Jimmy had been managing me about a year when I broke my leg. I was playing touch football with a bunch of guys over on the field at Treadwell High School. We'd start playing touch football but it would always degenerate into tackle after a while. I got my leg broken in a game. It was a bad break, both bones were broken and it hurt like crazy. For some reason, I thought it would be six to eight weeks and I'd be back. I figured I needed some time off anyway and it wouldn't be such a bad thing to rest up.

Jerry Jarrett was really upset with me for risking injury playing football and our relationship went sour for a while. He got mad when I played other sports anyway and this really pissed him off. The next week, he had Jimmy Hart go out on TV and say, "What do you do with a race-horse that breaks its leg? Shoot 'em." There was a mus-cled-up guy named Paul Ellering and he took my crown and put it on his head saying, "This is the new King." Needless to say, that didn't sit so well with me either.

I was completely wrong about the six to eight weeks. The leg didn't heal right and it needed two surgeries to correct it. It was a year before I was able to go back to wrestling. I did work a little over the summer as a commentator. I had a feud with Killer Karl Krupp that ended up with us having a match. My leg was in a cast from my upper thigh to my ankle and for the match, they made Killer Karl Krupp wear a cast too. My brief return may have helped attendance, but it didn't do my leg any good and I just had to let it heal in its own sweet time.

I had no income the whole time I was out and I was almost broke by the time the year was up. The closer I got to coming back, Jerry Jarrett got friendlier. The crowds had got pretty small. When I did come back, there was some natural heat. People knew I'd brought Jimmy Hart in and there was animosity against him for seeming to turn

Eddie Gilbert just thinks he's got me.

his back on me. We had a feud that's lasted pretty much to this day. People thought we just hated each other.

The heat would transfer to any wrestler Jimmy Hart brought in. He developed this team called the "First Family," which had Randy Savage and Rick Rude and Eddie Gilbert, Lanny Poffo, Kamala, King Kong Bundy. The idea was that he was trying to find someone to get rid of me. I wasn't mad at Jimmy at all but we had a long run with that angle.

Jimmy Hart and I are still at it. I remember we were going to have a big confrontation on Channel Five in 2001. Jimmy said his piece to the camera and the audience in the studio and I was just about to come out and respond when the network cut in to announce that George Bush had nominated Colin Powell to be Secretary of State. In the best showbiz tradition, the show went on, and we entertained the studio audience.

Breaking my leg in 1980 was the worst injury I've ever had and it had nothing to do with wrestling. I have

been, touch wood, lucky in the ring, though I have witnessed some terrible things happen, the most horrible
being the tragic death of Owen Hart.

The worst injury I ever got wasn't even painful. I got
kicked in the stomach by Austin Idol in a routine sort of
way and didn't think anything of it. I had to fly somewhere and I was in a stall in the bathroom at Nashville
airport when I passed out. Someone found me lying there
and I was taken to the hospital. I lost a lot of blood and
needed to be stitched up and given blood pretty urgently.
The strange thing about it was that it didn't hurt at all.

The next worst one absolutely hurt like hell. About
ten years ago a young wrestler called Todd Champion
really dislocated my hip. He was green as a gourd. He
was a big, nice-looking guy—about six-six and two
eighty-five—but he couldn't work a lick. I was working
with him in Louisville, Kentucky, one night. He had me
lying down in the ring. He grabbed both my feet and
pulled my legs apart. If you do this what should happen
is either you reach through and stomp the guy in the
stomach or get the referee to look the other way and do a
knee-drop in the groin. These are about the only two
things you can do.

This was when I was a heel and he was looking out,
talking to the crowd. "What should I do?" he was saying.
All of a sudden, with no notice he jumps way up in the
air and throws his legs out and lands inside mine. My
legs were stretched straight out. Something had to give
and one of my hips popped completely out of its joint. It
felt like I'd been shot. I think that's the only time when I
got injured and couldn't finish the match. I had to be
carried out of the ring on a stretcher. I cussed Champion
like a dog. What an idiot. I fired the guy. I had to go to
the hospital and then get someone to drive me all the
way from Louisville back to Memphis.

Other than my broken leg, I've been very lucky. There

was an incident with Jos LeDuc I'll come to later. I pulled a rotator cuff wrestling in Trinidad quite recently. As we'll see, that's all I pulled down there. I broke a couple of bones in my hand. I rebroke the small bone in my leg, the same one I broke before, but wrestling this time, in a match with Brad Armstrong. I didn't miss a day with that. I went to the hospital, they put a cast on, I went home and took it off and wrestled the next day. It hurt like crazy but I had a football game to play in that Sunday, a league championship game. I wasn't going to let that keep me from playing. I couldn't very well play football and miss wrestling shows, so I just had to go and do it all.

When I was coming back from my broken leg, my first match was scheduled against the "Dream Machine" Troy Graham. He just died in March 2002 (his name was Troy R. Thompson Jr., and he was just forty-seven). I rigged up this elaborate entrance. I think that down in Memphis, we were the first to do these elaborate entrances.

I'd been to see Kiss, and their show blew me away. It was the greatest piece of entertainment I'd ever seen. They had one flat stage and a second platform a little higher and the big Kiss logo overhead. There was nothing else on the stage at all. When the concert started, the houselights went out. Four spotlights hit the stage. The crowd started going crazy. Right where the spots were shining, smoke billows up out of the floor. After thirty seconds or so, you see these four mics rising up out of the floor. Then the band appeared up from the floor and the drum kit came up with them.

I wanted to try to duplicate that. I knew we had a spotlight and the stage. There was a portable stage at the Coliseum about six feet high. I went to this place that sold fire extinguishers. I bought two big old CO_2 jobs. I got a guy with a forklift at the Coliseum and we rigged this up under the stage. We made an opening and put the forklift under. I stood on a little platform on the forklift and there were two guys with the fire extinguishers. It worked out really well. People hadn't seen me in about a year.

Jimmy Hart and the Dream Machine went out. The lights went out. Boom, one spotlight comes on. The guys shot the fire extinguishers and it looked great. I went up on the forklift with my fist up. The place went crazy. When I got into the ring, Jerry Calhoun, the referee, came over. I said, "How was that entrance?" Jerry made this little noise that we used at the time to show big-time approval. It was so good, he came in his pants. We had a turn-away crowd that night. The first time I went back to the Louisville Gardens there was an ice storm and still 4,500 people showed up. And in Evansville, the crowd was backed up to the bathrooms where people propped open stall doors to get a view. That began another boom period for us.

As for entrances, I used to come in on a white horse. I came in on a camel once. I was carried in on a sedan chair with three guys on either side wearing these hooded robes. My brother Larry was one of the bearers and he says the fans were kicking them in the shins real hard all the way down the aisle. That was a match with Valiant, and characteristically, he attacked me while I was still in the chair. I was once lowered down from the top of the Coliseum. I put the harness on and there was one guy up there with me, a rigging guy, a somewhat shaggy-looking individual, who tied the rope around his waist and over the catwalk and lowered me down about twelve stories by hand. In the light of what happened to Owen Hart, that doesn't seem such a good idea in retrospect.

One night there was an eight-man tag match. Me, Dundee, and the Fabulous Ones—Stan Lane and Steve

Keirn, were partners. We were pretty much the top guys and it was the first time we were all together. We had a big sellout crowd, 11,500 people. Jerry Jarrett was so cheap you'd almost have to have a sellout before he'd use spotlights and stuff like that. They cost an extra two hundred dollars or something for the lights and the operators. But he sprang for them that night.

This night, the bad guys came out first. The faces all had their separate entrances. The Fabulous Ones were in their sequined tuxedoes and their top hats. We had made videos with them riding in limos to the song "Sharp Dressed Man," so they drove up in a limousine as far as the car could go to the back of ringside. The car stops and the Fabs get out and are escorted to the ring by the police. Their music stops and Bill Dundee's starts. It was, appropriately enough as it turned out, "Wipeout." Dundee was going on his motorcycle, which was a dirt bike. Curtain goes up and off he goes. I was waiting on my big white horse.

Dundee's gone and my music starts. The music from *2001* or "The Eye of the Tiger" or something. It starts up and off I go on the horse. People are screaming and yelling. Then I see a policeman coming back the other way. He's got this girl in his arms, passed out. I thought, *Oh my God,* this is going over so big, girls are fainting! Then there's another girl being carried out, and she's apparently unconscious too.

I step off the horse and get up into the ring. Dundee's got this funny look on his face. I said, "Man, this really got over. Girls are passing out down here!" "No, mate," he says. "When I came up on my bike, spotlight hit me in the f-ing eyes and I couldn't see a thing. Took out the whole frickin' front row." I look down and his bike is lying on its side in the front row. People weren't so sue-crazy then and I think we promised the couple of people who got hurt tickets to the shows for a year and we paid their doctor bills. Someone gets a hangnail today and they call a lawyer.

Despite what happened to my leg in 1980, I carried on playing football. Since high school I've played football in winter and softball in summer. I play with Robert

Reed, who I've known since we were kids and a bunch of neighborhood guys. My old neighbor Mike Mashburn was on the softball team for years. It's touch football, and this year they changed it to flag football so I hope I'm not going to bust anything again. We play about fifteen softball games and about ten football games. I think people in this business are really competitive and once you get in here it's not really competitive at all, so you're always looking for an outlet. Wrestling is competitive in a different way.

Andre and "the midget"

chapter 18

I am often asked what was the best angle I ever ran, or what was the best program I ever worked. I have no doubt: it was the long deal I had with Andy Kaufman from 1981 to 1983. People who aren't even vaguely wrestling fans might recollect the matches Andy had with women or the one with me in the Mid-South Coliseum in 1982. And if people don't remember that, they probably know something about the famous fight we had on David Letterman's TV show.

For the longest time, I respected the deal Andy and I made not to talk about how all of that all came to be. But there were other people involved and one of them, Andy's friend and cowriter Bob Zmuda, decided to tell what had happened. He wrote a book called *Andy Kaufman Revealed* and was a co-executive producer on the movie about Andy, *Man on the Moon,* that came out in 1999. In the book, Zmuda says he decided to come clean because Universal Studios was going to disclose it in the movie. Bob later told me in private that he figured, "What the heck? It's been fifteen years and it's time I made a buck or two off Andy!" Whatever the reason, the cover was blown and the whole affair was revealed to be a huge work. So now it's my turn to give my side of the events.

I have to thank the wrestling reporter Bill Apter for

sending Andy my way in the first place. I'd known Bill for a while. Bill is a short Jewish guy with an incredible sense of humor. He does an amazing Jerry Lewis impersonation and often when you talk to Bill the character bleeds over into his personality. At the time, he was a photographer and magazine editor in New York for G. C. London Publishing, a company that produced several wrestling magazines. I knew early on that placing my name in these wrestling publications was the best way of getting national publicity. As a matter of fact, when you lived in Memphis, Tennessee, it was the only way of getting national publicity. This was before there was cable TV, so it paid to be in good with the writers.

I'd get stories from time to time, but what I really wanted was to get on the cover of one of these magazines. I was like the rock band Dr. Hook and the Medicine Show, who, next to the Beatles, are my favorite musical group of all time, when they sang about being on the "Cover of the *Rolling Stone*." I wanted to feel "the thrill that'll getcha', when you get your pitcha' on the cover of the *Rolling Stone*." Except I wanted my picture on the cover of *Pro Wrestling Illustrated*, or *Wrestling Superstars*.

As a matter of fact, that was part of my motivation for an empty arena match I had with Terry Funk in 1981, which was one of the best-known matches we ever put on. Terry Funk came to town several weeks in a row and he and I had knockdown, drag-out battles that only Terry Funk was famous for. We wrestled each other week in and week out for almost two months and somehow Terry kept coming up with the short end of the stick. Looking back, it may have had something to do with the fact that I was part owner of the wrestling company, but nonetheless, Terry lost most of those matches.

To keep our program going, Terry complained that he couldn't get a fair shake. He said everybody in Memphis was prejudiced against him. He moaned that it started as soon as he got off the plane in my town. Cabdrivers would take him on the scenic route from the airport to the Coliseum and charge him an arm and a leg; hotels would give him the worst rooms. The announcers were biased, the referees were in Lawler's pocket, and the fans were just plain bad. He said the only way we could have a match on an even playing field was to have no fans, and no referees. There'd be no one at all, just one cameraman and one announcer. So Funk handed a folded piece of paper to our TV announcers, Lance Russell and Dave Brown. On the paper Terry had written a secret day, time, and place for our match to take place.

We had the match at the Mid-South Coliseum. Imagine this. It was a Monday afternoon before our regular Monday night matches, so the ring and seats were already set up, but the fans hadn't started arriving yet. When the one camera that was allowed to be there started rolling, there was Terry Funk standing in the middle of the ring in front of 11,500 empty chairs. Funk bellowed at the one announcer in attendance, "Where's Lawler? Is he chicken? Is he not gonna show up?" His voice echoed through the massive empty arena. "I knew Lawler was yellow!" the lonely Funk continued. "He don't want to face me without all his friends around to help him!"

The camera panned to the left, and there at the back of the Coliseum, I stood. I remember later thinking how stupid I looked standing there in full "King" regalia—tights, crown, cape—with no fans in the building. Why did I wear the crown and cape? Anyway, when Funk saw me he crowed, "Well, looky who's here all by himself! The King, with no one to hide behind! Well, get in here, Lawler, and take your whipping like a man!"

Neither of us really knew what we should do to start such a match, there was no referee and no timekeeper to ring the bell, so we just locked up and went at it as if we were in front of thousands of screaming fans. We fought in the ring and out of it into the chairs. I had been in matches where I got very little reaction from the crowd but never had I wrestled to absolutely no reaction . . . well, maybe that first match I had in West Memphis, against the Executioners, but you've already heard that story. Funk and I tumbled into the empty chairs at ringside and took turns seeing who could bowl over the most seats with our bodies. It was a really weird feeling wrestling in complete silence, almost embarrassing. We both began making exaggerated noises when we hit or kicked each other just so that there would be some kind of sound to the match.

Terry got the upper hand while we fought on the floor

and then he threw me back into the ring. He picked up the wooden ring steps and smashed them into pieces. He pulled off a piece of wood that was shaped like a long knife and came at me, jabbing. I blocked his hand and we struggled and the piece of wood appeared to poke into his eye. The next instant, blood was pouring down his face, through his fingers. He cried, "Somebody help me, somebody help me." And I said, "There's nobody here!"

"I need help! My eye! My eye! Lawler, my eye!"

That's how the match ended. Terry Funk, on his knees in the ring, blood streaming from his eye and him crying out for help that wasn't there. I thought afterward that we could have done so much more with the match. It could have been really hardcore. It certainly could have been longer, but as I said before, I really felt silly wrestling in front of no fans, and so what seemed like an eternity while we were doing it turned out to be a very short match in reality.

Funk was gone for a couple of weeks. He was always a goofy sort of guy. Well, not really goofy, but you never knew what to expect from Terry because he would do almost anything. Not many wrestlers would "blade" themselves that close to their eye so as to make it appear the blood was actually coming from the eye itself. He did an interview down in Texas and sent it to us to show in Memphis to set up the big return match between the two of us. I didn't have time to preview the interview before our live TV show that Saturday morning, so I watched it live with the fans.

There was Funk, wearing a big eye patch. Supposedly, his eye had been pretty much put out. "Lawler, you tried to blind me. The doctor said I may lose my eye." I watched the interview on camera standing next to our announcer, Lance Russell. I saw that Funk's eye was all covered up with, of all things, black electrical tape! It went all the way 'round his head. I thought to myself,

"How can anyone watching this believe he is really injured when he has electrical tape wrapped around his head?" The only thing I could think to say when Funk's interview ended was tell the truth. I told Lance Russell I hoped I never had to go to the doctor in Texas if they put electrical tape on a wound.

We drew big crowds on the return match, despite the electrical tape. Terry's brother, Dory Funk Jr., was booking in Florida. He took the videotape of the match and showed it down there and we had return matches all over Florida. Terry was probably more popular in Florida than I was because I had very seldom wrestled there. So to ensure that he would be the heel in our matches, he did a television interview in which he said he wanted to know what it felt like to be a Floridian. He took two quarts of thirty-weight motor oil and poured them over his head as he talked about greasy Floridians. The oil ran down and he smeared it all over his body. There was motor oil in his eyes and in his mouth as he spoke. He then poured a big bucket of dirt and sand over his head and body to illustrate how dirty and grimy he thought Floridians were.

As I stood there watching Terry make this interview I thought, "Now that is dedication. That is going above and beyond the call of duty to help an angle draw money." I really thought, "Of all the things he's lost, I bet he misses his mind the most!" But it did draw money. Everywhere that interview aired the Florida fans turned out in droves to see Terry Funk get punished for making fun of them. I know the interview lasted about three minutes, but Funk had to spend nearly two hours in a hot shower trying to clean himself up afterward.

Anyway, beforehand, I had told Bill Apter about the "Empty Arena" program and as far as I knew, this had never been done in wrestling. I said if this doesn't get me on the cover of the magazine, nothing will. But the magazine publisher, Stanley Weston, who was yet another wrestling person who died in 2002, told Apter that it wouldn't sell magazines. Their main points of sale were Atlanta, New York, and the mid-Atlantic region and I wasn't well-known enough in those areas. In the eyes of the wrestling publishers, we were doing a lot of weird stuff down in Memphis, but the rest of the country wouldn't be interested in it. The publishing office was on Long Island, and people in that area were used to seeing wrestlers like "Superstar" Billy Graham or Bruno Sammartino on the cover. So I got a spread on the empty arena match, but not a cover.

I finally did get a cover story in the magazine, but when I did, it got me into trouble with the NWA. I met Vince McMahon Sr. at a National Wrestling Alliance convention, the annual meeting of all the promoters I mentioned before. It was always in places like Las Vegas, Lake Tahoe, or Reno. Like most conventions, it was more or less a vacation or getaway for the promoters and a chance to visit with each other, take care of a little business, but mostly, to get away from their wives and do a little gambling. The main business concern at this particular meeting was that TV stations were starting to charge wrestling companies for their shows. In the past, it had been a barter. Wrestling promoters made the show; the station would air it. Now the stations were starting to realize that we wouldn't be in business without the show, so why not make promoters pay for the airtime too? This was a major corporate problem and it put a lot of promoters out of business.

But the promoter from the northeast had something he wanted to bring to the attention of his colleagues. This was something he thought more important than any TV contract. Vince McMahon Sr. stood up at the meeting and said, "I'll tell you what a big problem with the business is. It's things like this here." He held up a copy of *Wrestling Superstars* magazine and on the cover there was a headline, "The Night a Midget Beat Andre the Giant." I was sitting in the room at the time and I kind of slunk down a little in my seat. That was because the midget the article was referring to was me.

You had to book Andre the Giant through the World Wide Wrestling Federation. You could call Vince Sr. and ask for Andre for three days or a week or whatever. To get him, you'd have to guarantee Andre a certain amount and you had to pay the company an extra booking fee. We had Andre wrestle against me in Memphis, Evansville, and Louisville. When we were wrestling in Louisville, there was a photographer who took pictures of the pair of us in action. They were great. The size difference looked amazing; Andre looked colossal and I looked like, well, a midget. Of course, I am not a small guy but Andre was listed as seven-four and weighed more than five hundred pounds. He was significantly bigger than Paul Wight, the Big Show, which is saying something.

I sent Bill Apter the pictures of me and Andre. I used to send him pictures all the time to try to get in the magazine. He said the Andre pictures were great and he asked if I minded him calling me a midget in the story. He also said what he wanted to title the story. At the time, you couldn't beat Andre the Giant. He wanted to say that Andre had been thrown out of the ring and couldn't get back in and got counted out. But the whole deal was great to me because I finally made it on the cover of the magazine.

I didn't think anything more about it until Vincent J. McMahon Sr. held the magazine up and said, "Here's what's wrong with the business today, stories like this." He was angry. "No one's ever beaten Andre. He's one of the biggest attractions in this business and he needs to be protected. We go out of our way to make sure none of this ever happens and then someone sends in pictures and writes stories. Not only did someone beat Andre the

Giant, a midget beat Andre the Giant!" At this point Mr. McMahon's face was starting to turn red; he was boiling. My face was turning red as well, from embarrassment. I slunk a little farther down in my chair.

Terry Funk, who loved this kind of thing, thought it was really funny. At these meetings Terry was like the mischievous kid in school who didn't want to get called on by his teacher, so he'd sit in the back of the class. He was sitting back there looking at me and he shouted out, "Well, who was the little bastard who beat Andre the Giant, Vince?"

"Jerry Lawler, that's who it was," Vince yelled back. It wasn't a secret, but Funk made sure that everyone in the room knew I was there. So I had to stand up and explain how this came about. I said I hadn't called anybody to say I'd beaten Andre the Giant. I said Bill Apter was a friend of mine. Vince McMahon said, "That's what I'm talking about. These magazine writers don't check with anybody. They're writing this stuff that's not good for the business." That was really my only dealing with Vince McMahon Sr.

Bill Apter had got a number of furious calls from Vince McMahon Sr. over the story. Vince said the story had killed Andre the Giant's career. I spoke with Bill and we had a bit of a disagreement about the story. We both thought the other had come up with the line that I'd beaten Andre. Bill and I didn't call each other for a while after that. The magazine made amends with another cover of Andre; this time he was posed and the headline was "Why Andre the Giant Is Wrestling's Only Undefeated Superstar." That satisfied Mr. McMahon.

Andre the Giant was a big deal and a huge drawing card all around. We used to have him for a week at a time and he'd work all our main towns: Memphis, Nashville, Evansville, Louisville. A lot of the guys have different opinions of what Andre was like. If he liked you, he was fine. If he didn't like you, he didn't mind letting you know it and he wouldn't have anything to do with you. Plowboy Frazier told me one day, "You know what, neighbor? That Andre the Giant, he don't like me." I said, "Aw, Frazier, what makes you think that?" And Plowboy said, "He told me."

Andre knew Jerry Jarrett and I owned the territory so when he came in, he was basically working for us, although he wound up working with me in the matches. He was always very respectful and he would call me "boss," a term he used for people he liked. He'd greet me, "Hey, boss." He was real easygoing. He'd let you do anything you wanted in a match. Other than beat him. If he liked you, he would sell like crazy and he could make you look like a million dollars. You had to work to get him off his feet, but once you did, man, it looked good. You could choke him, pull his hair, punch, kick, everything. He would stay down and sell until it was time for the big comeback.

But if he didn't like you, he'd make you look like crap, and there wasn't anything anyone could do about it. It was all about strength and he had that in spades. One of the things I remember most about Andre was that every night after his match he would drink two cases of beer. Not two six-packs, Two cases! Forty-eight beers, every night! And I recall those beer bottles looked so tiny in his huge hands.

A little while after we had our little problem with Andre, Bill hooked me up with Andy Kaufman. Andy had been a huge wrestling fan growing up on Long Island in New York. He idolized "Nature Boy" Buddy Rogers and saw him wrestle Bruno Sammartino at Madison Square Garden. It fascinated Andy that somebody in show business would intentionally go out and make people dislike them and still be popular and make money. That influenced his whole career. He didn't really want to be a comedian or be funny. Andy really hated sitcoms like *Taxi* with the canned laughter. He thought comedians did sitcoms. The main reason he took the gig was because he thought he would get to do specials on ABC. The other actors on the show, like Judd Hirsch, Tony Danza, and Jeff Conaway, resented him a bit because he got preferential treatment. Andy didn't really have to rehearse. He got special billing, all sorts of stuff.

Above all, Andy wanted to entertain. He liked to elicit a response. He didn't care if it was laughter, and most times he would rather it not be laughter. He loved it when he could make people mad. Before he wrestled, he created Tony Clifton, the Lounge Lizard, his alter ego, who could go out on stage and who people would hate. To become Tony Clifton, Andy had to go through hours of applying makeup and a costume so that no one in the audience would know Tony was actually Andy. That was before he went into wrestling and for Andy, the wrestling was perfect. Rather than having to masquerade as Tony Clifton, he could play himself.

Andy used to go to the matches at Madison Square Garden and he was buzzing around Vince McMahon Sr. Andy had been doing his "Intergender Wrestling Champion" gimmick, where he went against women from the audience. He'd been doing it at comedy clubs and on *Saturday Night Live*.

Andy said his intergender matches weren't being appreciated by comedy fans as he wanted them to be. He said he wanted to wrestle in front of real fans. Real wrestling fans! His dream was to wrestle as a bad guy and feel the reaction. Andy really wanted to ask Vince McMahon if there was any way he could come into the ring and challenge the women in the audience at one of Mr. McMahon's shows at Madison Square Garden.

Bill Apter knew that Andy Kaufman wanted to get into pro wrestling. Bill used to go to the Garden and he rented a photo studio near there and took pictures of the wrestlers. One time Bill told Curt Hennig he wanted to take his picture and Andy was standing nearby and he said, "Can I come?" Next month, he came up and took pictures with Hennig and Eddie Gilbert and so on. Andy started hanging out with Bill at his apartment at Kew Gardens in Queens and they talked about wrestling, Buddy Rogers especially. Andy was saying he wanted to be Buddy Rogers, he wanted to get into the wrestling. He asked Bill if he thought he could talk to Vince McMahon Sr. Bill said, "No." He said McMahon was a traditional wrestling promoter. He just won't go for it.

Andy may well have asked Vince McMahon Sr. about it but he didn't get anywhere. Vince Sr. would just have been too skeptical of having a TV actor come in and wrestle. He would have thought the fans would think his wrestlers were acting as well. God forbid! Of course, his son, Vince McMahon Jr., went that route himself beginning with Cyndi Lauper working at the first *WrestleMania*, but that was some way down the road.

Bill Apter said to Andy, "But I do know a friend in Memphis, Tennessee." He said they wrestled at the Mid-South Coliseum in Memphis, often in front of 11,500 people. They have a TV show with big ratings, the whole thing. Andy had no idea there was a company down in Tennessee that promoted wrestling. Bill thought Andy would get over great. He assured Andy that I'd be interested. He thought we'd love the idea because we did stuff that was a little more out of the ordinary than other promotions.

This was about one o'clock in the morning and Bill called me. "I'm here in my apartment with Andy Kaufman."

"Andy Kaufman? The guy from *Taxi*?"

"He wants to talk to you."

"Andy Kaufman wants to talk to me?" So Bill put Andy on the phone and we talked awhile. Then Bill came back on and I told him it sounded great. Was I interested? Hell, yes!

I've always been grateful to Bill for the introduction. At one point, Bill told me he had been saving to buy his first-ever car in New York. I couldn't comprehend a grown man with a job having never owned a car, but he explained how in New York City everyone took cabs and there was no place to even park a car where he lived even if he owned one. But now he was going to go ahead and make the historic purchase. He was five hundred dollars away from having enough cash to buy the car. I wrote a check for five hundred dollars and sent it to Bill and said go get your car, congratulations. He never forgot that and he really helped me. I gave Bill the money because I liked him and he was my friend and it turned out to be the best money I ever invested. Bill called me a couple of years ago and said his daughter Hailey was getting bat mitz-vahed and asked me to draw a couple of pictures. He offered to pay, but I was happy to do it and I drew four panels for Hailey. I did it for Bill and for Andy.

chapter 19

Andy Kaufman came down to Memphis in the summer of 1981 and we met and talked about what we might do together. Originally, the idea was that he was just going to wrestle women. After we did that for a couple of weeks, and it went well, I tried to insinuate myself into the deal.

When Andy traveled to Memphis in October to have his Intergender matches, it was totally legit. He simply asked for volunteers from the audience and went in and wrestled them. We had no idea who these girls were. About twenty of them came down to the ring and volunteered to wrestle Andy and we actually let the audience decide by their applause which four would get the shot at him. Each girl got a three-minute-time-limit match with Andy. We put some stuff on the line for the matches. He said, "What if I offered to shave my head if she beats me?" I said, "What if she does beat you?" He didn't care about that. Then he said, "I'll tell everybody, if she beats me, she'll get to marry me." It was classic.

He came back in November and wrestled some more women. There were four of them on the card again. The first three Andy handled with ease. The last one, Foxy, nearly beat him. Foxy was a short but stocky black woman in her early thirties. She weighed as much as, if not more than, Andy and she had a low center of gravity. Andy claimed he was tired after beating the first three women, but I think Foxy was legitimately tough.

Andy had dominated the first three girls much to the chagrin of the fans, but when the bell sounded to start his match with Foxy, she rushed across the ring, grabbed Andy, picked him up, and actually body-slammed him! The roof nearly came off the Coliseum. Foxy caught Andy completely by surprise and she had him on the ropes. I mean he was really hanging on to the ropes for dear life as Foxy was trying to pull him back to the center of the ring. She almost pulled off the thermal underwear he wore in the ring. The crowd went wild.

As a matter of fact, Andy wasn't able to beat Foxy. She lasted the entire three-minute time limit and the match was declared a draw. When it was over, I told him it was great. He agreed but I could tell he was sort of sad because he thought that was it, that this was his last appearance in front of a wrestling crowd. Andy had loved it. But I was looking at the sellout crowd of 11,500 people. We struggled to get crowds anything near that size at the time, so we were ecstatic. I immediately said to Andy, "I don't know what your schedule is like, but if you could come back . . . What if I were to take this Foxy chick out on TV and show people how close she came to beating you. I could say I was going to take her under my wing and teach her a few holds. With me in her corner, she could beat you." He said he could see it. It would be great. Jerry Jarrett didn't know what would be an appropriate payoff for a Hollywood TV star to work on one of our shows. I don't know if Andy even thought he was going to get paid at all. We wrote him a check for two thousand dollars and he seemed almost embarrassed to accept it.

To set up the program, we made some interviews of

Andy knocking women. He said they're inferior, they belong in the kitchen, and things like that. Andy's deal was that he said if there ever was a woman who could beat him in the ring, "She would be worthy of my hand in marriage. I'm telling you this right now, Foxy, if you can beat me, Andy Kaufman from Hollywood, I will marry you right there in the middle of that ring, and give you five thousand dollars."

A week later, Foxy and I came out on the set to make her interview. She was precious, a hundred percent real. The week before the show, her house had burned down. It was true, it wasn't a work at all. Foxy came on TV and told this heartfelt story. She said she heard what Andy said and that I'd taught her some moves. She said she thought she could beat Andy Kaufman. "And, Lord knows, my house burned down last week and I need the money so bad. But I tell you this right now. I would not marry Andy Kaufman if he were the last man on earth."

I think we put in a thousand extra seats and raised prices and we still turned people away on the night. Andy came out with his bathrobe on over his union suit as usual. Andy had been to Libertyland, the amusement park next to the Coliseum, and bought a pair of blue plastic sunglasses that said "Andy" on the side. I still have them.

Now it was possible that Foxy could have beaten Andy and she did give him a good run for his money. I was worried because we hadn't actually gone over the match like you would with a couple of guys. There was certainly no finish that was predetermined. Foxy came out full of spit and vinegar and she was very strong. She was tossing him all over the ring. Andy knew not to ever let someone get him on his back. If he was thrown, he'd immediately get over on his knees or elbows to avoid getting pinned.

Foxy was exerting a ton of energy, but she had no stamina. After three or four minutes, she was blown up. Her tongue was hanging out like a red necktie and she was struggling to catch her breath. Also, there were 12,500 people watching and she'd never been in this kind of situation. She was nervous and cotton-mouthed. After about eight minutes, when she was completely spent, Andy picked her up, turned her over, and the referee counted her out. She just lay there. Andy was prancing around the ring, goose-stepping, doing his impression of the famous "Buddy Rogers strut," showing off because he'd pinned Foxy.

Andy decided to rub it in. He looked back at Foxy and went over and started kicking her, real hard. He got down and grabbed her by the hair and started hitting her head on the mat, "I told you, I told you!" I was in Foxy's corner watching while Andy pounded her head on the mat. I'd gone out on TV before and said, "This is my girl, I'm going to show her how to beat Andy." All of a sudden, this "Jer-ry, Jer-ry" chant starts. They wanted me to get in there and do something.

This is where the ad lib part started. I went into the ring and reached out and grabbed Andy in a working kind of way. I basically reached down and pulled Andy up off of Foxy, but when I did, Andy flew halfway across the ring as if he'd been shot out of a cannon. I went to console Foxy and looked over at Andy. He took the microphone. "You can't put your hands on me," he said. "You're a wrestler. I'm a movie star. A TV star. I'll sue you for everything you're worth. I didn't come here to wrestle you, I came here to wrestle her. Don't you touch me." People were booing like crazy.

I really didn't know what to think. I didn't know if Andy was serious or what, but I do know the fans wanted me to cream him. What took place at the end of that match was one of the great things that developed between Andy and me. It was totally extemporized and we had no plans for anything past that. At the time, all I wanted was to get the "rub" off Andy wrestling women.

We got back to the locker room and he was eager to know what I thought. "How was that? How was that? Was it good?" I said it was great. It *was* great. He was very happy, but I'm sure that, again, he thought that was the end of it. I called Andy into my little private room I used at the Mid-South Coliseum. I said, "Andy, you've got the most heat of anybody we've ever had here in Memphis. The fans want to kill you." He said, "I know it, I love it." His face was lit up like a little kid's at Christmas. He said it was so much more fun than anything else he did. He actually said he would quit everything he was doing in Hollywood if he could stay involved with wrestling.

This may sound selfish, but I knew I could cash in on Andy's enthusiasm. I was already getting the rub in Memphis from working with a big network TV star, but I thought it could go national. Once again, I said, "I don't know what your schedule is like, but we're here every Monday night. I think we could get a lot of national publicity, Andy, if you agreed to wrestle me." This was a time when nobody got national publicity for wrestling. He said, "What would we do? I can't wrestle you!" I said, "It doesn't matter, we can do *anything*. That isn't important. Believe me, you can wrestle me. We can come up with something that's not that physical. The fact that you'd actually wrestle a man is going to be huge news." So that was the next thing. Andy Kaufman was going to wrestle a man for the first time, and it was going to be the King on his home turf.

So that was set. You could see Andy's mind working again. He said he loved not to let anyone in on what he was doing. I think Andy was actually orgasmic when he could pull the wool over everyone's eyes. He used his family as his barometer. If he could ever fool them, then he knew he'd done it because they expected everything he did to be a hoax. He said he would love to keep the fact that this match was going to be set up quiet. That's why he decided he wasn't going to tell anyone he was doing the wrestling until they found out. He wanted everyone he knew to think this was on the up-and-up. I agreed I wouldn't even tell anybody in the wrestling business.

Andy came over to my house and we talked over different scenarios. He was a very humble guy. Even though Andy was a few months older than me, he always referred to me as Mr. Lawler. I finally had to tell him, "Mr. Lawler was my father, I'm Jerry." He'd never tell me, "Let's do something this way," he had so much respect for wrestling. He'd ask a lot of questions, "How would they react if we did this?" We bounced ideas off each other and we concocted a series of interviews we'd play for four or five weeks before we had him on TV live. It was a few months before he would come back to Memphis and take me on, and these interviews would serve to keep our feud going.

There was a long buildup to the match that went on at the Mid-South Coliseum on April 5, 1982. Andy went on David Letterman's show a number of times to promote it. We both made videos and attacked each other. Andy was filmed by a swimming pool wrestling some very large woman down to the ground. He said, "You may be bigger than me, Lawler, but I've wrestled women who are twice as big as me and I've mopped the floor with them, and that's what I'm going to do with you, Mr. Lawler!" I made somewhat unconventional wrestling interviews where I laid out what I wanted to do to Kaufman, and I acknowledged the fact that he was not a real wrestler:

I make my living, I put my food on the table by wrestling, and it's a very serious sport to me. And I don't like anyone like you coming around making fun of it, or thinking that they can do it just coming in off the street. So I'm going to show you just how serious it is, so don't expect any mercy from me, Andy Kaufman. Because when you climb in that ring, I'm going to consider you a professional wrestler and I'm going to burst your bubble about being a wrestler and it'll be the last time you ever want to wrestle, it'll be the last time you ever want to step in the ring, and it'll be the last time you ever fantasize about being a wrestler. Andy Kaufman, you're going to get hurt, son.

I think the fact that my interviews were more serious, and not the typical yelling and screaming that one had come to expect from wrestlers, helped convince people that this thing between Andy and me was indeed real. Our regular sportscaster on the five o'clock news, "Big" Jack Eaton, interviewed me one day about the match and asked me if I was going to really hurt Andy Kaufman. I told him sternly, "I think I have to hurt him." He knew I meant I had to prove something to the world as far as the integrity of wrestling went. That someone, even if he was a big Hollywood star, couldn't just walk in off the street and have a match with a real wrestler and not get hurt.

Finally the time for the big match had arrived. Andy Kaufman, the Intergender Champion, was going to climb into the ring and do battle with a member of his own sex. The Mid-South Coliseum was completely sold out, had been for days. In the back, I was trying my best to kayfabe the other wrestlers, but I really wanted to get together with Andy and go over what we were going to do one more time. I sent Jimmy Hart to Andy's locker room to tell him to sneak over to my dressing room. Jimmy came back a few minutes later and said, "He can't come, he's meditating." He's meditating? Then I remembered this was one of the things that infuriated Andy's costars on *Taxi*. While they were rehearsing or were ready to do a scene, Andy would be in his dressing room, with a "Do not disturb" sign on his door, communing with himself. He did not finish up and come out of his dressing room for our match until I was in the ring.

When we got into the ring, it looked like the enormous mismatch that it indeed was. Andy was listed at a hundred sixty pounds, which looked generous, and I was officially seventy pounds more than that, but I must have outweighed him by a hundred. He had his usual goofy thermal underwear and gym shorts outfit on. He started out by backing way off me. He wouldn't come within ten feet of me and he was content to make monkey imitations. Andy put a foot through the rope if I got too close, or stepped out of the ring entirely and stood on the apron, preening himself. This was actually a way of adding time to our match. We didn't really have an entire match laid out and the things we did have laid out were not going to take that long to do, so the "walking and talking," as it's known as in the business, was not a bad thing.

Of course this incensed a lot of the fans, which was the point. Eventually, I'd had enough and I got out of the ring myself. I went over to the commentary position, took the microphone from our announcer, Lance Russell, and said, "I want to ask you something: did you come down here to wrestle or to act like an ass?" I told Andy he could have a free headlock. I went back into the ring, put my hands behind my back, and bowed down so he could apply the hold. Andy came up to me real slow and cautious like and put his weak headlock on. Bob

Zmuda, Andy's cornerman for the match, was jumping up and down outside the ring and made like I was being squeezed by Hulk Hogan.

After a moment, Andy pretended to gain confidence. He got comfortable being in control with his headlock. He started yelling insults to the fans at ringside and told them, "I told you I could beat the King!" I let Andy maintain his headlock on me and run his mouth for a couple of minutes until I felt the crowd was at a fever pitch. Then I simply raised my right hand and held up one finger to signify to the crowd that I was just biding my time and letting Andy get overconfident. The crowd responded. They knew immediately what my signal meant. Andy just looked confused when he heard the cheer go up from the crowd, while he was supposedly in command.

Then the match really started. I picked Andy high up into the air while he still had his headlock and dropped him backward in a big side suplex. He was bent in half when he hit and he stayed down.

I milked this awhile and, seemingly in response to the crowd, dragged Andy back into the middle of the ring. Piledriver time. The piledriver is a move in which you put your opponent's head between your legs, then lift him by his waist, upside down. Then you fall or sit back, dropping the other guy headfirst into the mat. I picked Andy up and his thin legs waggled in the air as I got him set. BAM! It was a beauty, and Andy was lying with his legs splayed out over the ropes. It looked as if Andy's neck surely must have been snapped from the force of the piledriver he'd just received. Piledrivers were officially illegal in our territory, so I was automatically DQ'ed, at six minutes and fifty seconds. But the crowd wanted more. So far, this was a two-move match to them, and even though poor Andy was lying motionless in the ring, they weren't satisfied.

"Do that to me one more time . . ." So I picked him up and did it again.

Andy sold it great. He was limp, and to all appearances he was unconscious. Now since this was the main event and the last match of the night, there needed to be some sort of closure to the match so that the crowd knew it was time to go home. But Andy just continued to lay there, and as long as wrestlers were still in the ring, the crowd wasn't going to leave because they thought they might miss something. I guess I had just assumed that Andy would know enough to sell the piledrivers sufficiently and then let someone help him to his feet and then walk back to the locker room.

Not Andy. Fifteen minutes had gone by and Andy was still lying in the ring being ministered to by Bob Zmuda, his manager, George Shapiro, and his current girlfriend, whose name I didn't know, who'd accompanied him to the matches. I was walking around the ring, smiling to the fans and basking in the afterglow of my big moral victory. But I was trying to send a message to Andy that enough was enough. He had played up the piledrivers long enough and it was now time to leave the ring. I told my manager, Danny Davis, to tell referee Jerry Calhoun to go over and tell Andy to get up and be helped back to the locker room.

I watched as Calhoun leaned over Andy's body and told him what I said. I could see Andy telling Calhoun something, but he was trying not to move his lips so as not to appear conscious. Then Jerry Calhoun came over to me and said, "Andy wants an ambulance!"

"An ambulance?" I choked. We hadn't mentioned anything about an ambulance. Not that I was against calling an ambulance, but we'd done a couple of angles before where to really make it seem serious we had called an ambulance, and by the time you took the person to the emergency room you'd run up a five-hundred-dollar bill.

One of my very first publicity photos, long before I even dreamed of being the King. COURTESY JERRY LAWLER

My first wife, Kay, and our sons, Brian and Kevin. COURTESY JERRY LAWLER

The very first Lawler's Army softball team, undefeated and we owed our success to our tailor. COURTESY JERRY LAWLER

Moondog makes it look easy in this steel cage match. COURTESY JERRY LAWLER

Sometimes you just have to make your point totally clear. A chair does help. COURTESY JERRY LAWLER

Trying to bring down Plowboy. COURTESY JERRY LAWLER

Obviously, "the greatest" guest I had on the *Jerry Lawler Show*–
Muhammad Ali. COURTESY JERRY LAWLER

I managed to get through to Bret Hart, there is only one king.

Here I am with Jimmy Valiant, one of the premier wrestlers of any age.

Wrestling has taken me many places. Stacy and I were thrilled to be invited to the White House. COURTESY JERRY LAWLER

A plain case of when it is good to be the king. I officiate in a highly
competitive wet tee-shirt contest.

There are some parts of my job that are just beyond wonderful.

Oh, the horrors. Oh, the humanity. I plead with Mae Young—enough, no more.

Here I am laying out how it *really* is for Vince.

I've appeared at countless openings, but this was my favorite, for my brother Larry's store. COURTESY JERRY LAWLER

The best commentator in any sport venture, Jim Ross.

So I told Calhoun to go back over and tell Andy that it was too expensive and he needed to just go ahead and slowly get to his feet. Once again, Jerry Calhoun bent over Andy's prone body and delivered my message. Again, I could see Andy, like a bad ventriloquist, mouth something to Calhoun. Then Calhoun came over to me and said, "Andy says he'll pay for the ambulance."

So Andy was taken to St. Francis Hospital, where he spent the next three days in traction. He wore a neck brace for months afterward. I kept a copy of *Ringside Wrestling News* for June 1983 and it said that the final assessment of Andy was that he'd suffered "serious muscle strain, considerable abrasions on the top of the head, and a sprained cervical spine." Even the Memphis *Commercial Appeal* reported that Andy had suffered "compressed vertebrae." As I said, when you give someone a piledriver, you hold their head up in your legs, but you do it in a way as to make sure their head doesn't hit the mat, but Andy went down like he really was badly hurt. Piledrivers can go wrong, of course, but I'd done these two perfectly.

So when I spoke to him, I assumed he was fine, that he wasn't injured at all, but I asked anyway. I said, "Is everything all right?"

"Yeah, yeah." I said, "Didn't hurt you with the piledriver?" And he replied, "Yeah." I said, "Yeah? What do you mean?" Andy meekly replied, "Oh, yeah, it really hurt. I landed right on my head." I couldn't believe it. Was Andy trying to fool me as well? So I asked, "But not hard enough to go to the hospital?"

"Ah, no. But I felt it good."

If someone goes to the hospital and says they have a neck injury, they don't mess around. No one had any reason not to think Andy wasn't hurt.

Jimmy Hart and Andy Kaufman vow to destroy the King.

20

The next day we knew the world pretty much DID think Andy was hurt. The publicity was tremendous! It was in every newspaper around the country, even *The New York Times*. It was on every newscast. "Hollywood TV star hospitalized by pro wrestler!" Photos of me delivering the devastating piledriver on Andy were all over the media. It was better than either Andy or I could have expected.

Another thing I didn't anticipate was the reaction our match got in the wrestling world. Andy and me had both kept the pact we had made not to tell anyone that our match was a work, so there were some very big names in wrestling who actually thought that what happened between Andy and me was a "shoot," or a genuine fight. After the word went out in the media about what I had done to Andy, I got several calls from wrestlers and promoters around the country congratulating me for "sticking up for the business," and putting that "punk" Kaufman in his place. I even received the first, and only, telegram I have ever gotten in my life. It was from longtime Houston promoter Paul Boesch, praising me for piledriving the detractor! It was embarrassing to have to lie to my fellow wrestlers, but Andy and I had a deal.

When Andy came out of the hospital he admitted

publicly he was no match for the King. "He's a sea-soned champion and I'm just an Intergender wrestler, a man from Hollywood." He went on *Saturday Night Live* and, sitting there looking very uncomfortable in his neck brace, he apologized to wrestlers and promoters for making fun of the sport. Andy apologized to the women and the fans he'd insulted. But he didn't apologize to me.

I saw Andy once more in Memphis before we went on Letterman. He was on the show once by himself and he was saying consistently that he was retired from wrestling. His one experience of wrestling a man, after being undefeated against hundreds of women, had been enough. Then, on July 28, 1982, we were booked on the Letterman show together.

Once we were in New York, the show had separate meetings with Andy and me. We both met with Robert Morton, the Letterman producer. He and I talked a little about the background, about the stuff Andy and I had done, which, of course, they thought was all legit. They went over what they wanted me to do. I was going to come out first, then Andy. They would show footage of Andy harassing me and of me piledriving Andy in Memphis. Then Dave would talk to the two of us.

The producer said to me, "I would like for you to be a little bit adversarial during the first segment." "Okay," I said. "But how adversarial?"

"Just argue a little bit back and forth." Then Dave was going to take a break. During the second segment, Andy would apologize to me for making fun of wrestling. After Andy did that, I would apologize to him for hurting his neck. Then Andy would get up and sing, "What the World Needs Now Is Love, Sweet Love." And that would be the end of things. Okay, cool. I was due at the theater at five o'clock.

I went back to the hotel and Andy called me. He said,

"Did they tell you what they want us to do?" I said, "Yep."

"What do you think?" he wanted to know. I said, "It should be funny. I don't know if it's going to be very memorable. It's pretty much going to bring closure to our deal."

"I know. I don't like that." His mind was obviously working away. "I don't know," I said. "What're you gonna do?" Andy said, "I don't know. I wish there was something else we could do."

"Well, what?" Then Andy asked, "What would happen if I apologized but you wouldn't accept my apology and you slugged me?" I started laughing. "Let me think, since the show is taped, if I slugged you and we didn't do what they asked us to do, one; they probably wouldn't air it. Two; they'd probably have me arrested."

"Yeah, you're probably right," Andy agreed. "But man, wouldn't it be great?" I said, "Yeah, it would certainly keep our stuff alive." So he added, "Just think about it." And that was basically the way it was left.

We went out on Letterman, and what happened was pretty much ad-libbed. Neither one of us really knew what the other was going to do. Andy, still in his neck brace, started off somewhat conciliatory, but I was angry. This guy had come down to Memphis and insulted me and the fans. I got some good zingers in. I said Andy was a wimp, "When Andy was born, his father wanted a boy and his mother wanted a girl—and they were both satisfied." Then Andy started on his "I'm a big star from Hollywood" deal. Now he was wanting an apology from me. I'm getting madder. "Is that a neck brace or a flea collar he's wearing?" I asked. Then Dave took the first break.

During the commercial breaks they would turn off all the lights in the studio and it would be really quiet and dark for about two minutes. I assumed they did that so as not to have Dave overheat from all those lights. As soon as they went to break, Andy got up from his chair and walked away from Dave and me. About that time, Dave leaned over to me and whispered, "Do you know Dick the Bruiser?" Now this was the first time Dave had said a word to me other than the on-air stuff, and I was surprised at the question. Nonetheless, I answered that, yes, I knew Dick the Bruiser and had even wrestled him a couple of times. Then Dave said that he had done some ring announcing for Dick the Bruiser's wrestling organization back in Indianapolis when he first started in TV. That was neat to find that even David Letterman had a wrestling connection.

The show was going along pretty much without any intervention from Dave Letterman. He did stop us to ask whether our match in Memphis was rigged and whether we were really friends. "No way," I said. "I couldn't warm up to this guy if we were cremated together." Andy called me a redneck and went on about suing me. This was the second segment and as far as Dave knew, Andy and I were supposed to be apologizing to each other and getting ready for Andy to sing.

I could tell from the look on Dave's face that he sensed something was not going right. I guess he thought he would take another break and get things reset, so now Letterman is trying to go to commercial but Andy and I are still going at it. I didn't know what was going to happen between Andy and me at that point, neither did Andy, and neither did Dave. I only knew that when Dave took that second break, Andy and my segments were over and we were going to be out of there.

Suddenly I hear Paul Shaffer and his band start to play the music that meant commercial break, so I stood up, looked down at Andy, and hauled off and slapped the taste out of his mouth! The slap was so hard that it actually knocked Andy over backward and out of his chair. I didn't pull it at all. I figured I wouldn't do any permanent damage, like a broken jaw or anything, with just a slap, so I really laid it in.

After the slap, a complete hush came over the studio. Paul Shaffer and the band abruptly stopped playing. Dave was in shock. I was in shock. I was thinking to myself, "Did I just slap Andy Kaufman out of his chair on network TV?" I know Andy was in shock, and a little dazed, because just like everyone else in that studio, he had no idea that was coming. Even I didn't know that was coming. I just did it because that's what I felt Andy wanted me to do.

Now Andy was lying on the studio floor. An NBC security guard rushed over and helped Andy to his feet, and then Andy staggered toward the studio door. Then another security guard asked me to go back to the green room. It was now mysteriously empty. When I left the green room to go out onto the set to do the interview, there must have been twenty people in there, whoever was waiting to go on the show and the people they brought with them and assorted hangers-on.

I sat down and wondered if I was going to be arrested or what was going to happen. I could hear a lot of commotion outside; it was like someone had been assassinated or something. I sat there by myself for what seemed like an eternity, but it was actually about fifteen minutes. Then, a young man stuck his head in the door, as if he were sticking his head into a lion's mouth, and said, "Mr. Lawler, would you mind coming back out on the set?" I breathed a sigh of relief because at that moment, I knew that what we had done up to that point was going to air, but more importantly, I wasn't going to jail.

I walked back out onto the set to a chorus of boos from the studio audience. I sometimes think Jerry Springer may have been in that studio audience that day and saw me and said to himself, "Hey, I think they've got something there." Anyway, as I sat back down beside Dave, Andy was still pacing back and forth over by the studio door. We were seconds away from starting to tape again and Dave asked Andy if he were going to come back and join us on the set. Andy shook his head and said, "No, because if I do, I'll say words you can't use on TV!"

The director counted us down . . . three . . . two . . . one . . . and we were on the air again. Dave was classic with his first response. "Well folks, Jerry's here, Andy's here, and some nights I wish Tom Snyder [who did the show before Dave] were still here." Dave then started to thank me for being on the show, but before he could get the words out of his mouth, here comes Andy. He starts ranting away with a whole load of language that would never make it on the air. "I am sick of this bullshit!" he started and went downhill from there. He apologized again to his fans but me, I was a "fuckin' asshole."

Once again, you could tell by the look on his face, Dave was in shock. He wouldn't even look at Andy or me, he just stared straight ahead while shuffling some papers in his hands. Andy, meanwhile, is banging on Dave's desk and cussing a blue streak. Every time Andy would hit Dave's desk, Dave would flinch. Whenever I watch the tape I get the biggest kick out of watching Dave's expressions and reactions. It's easy to tell he knows he has lost complete control of his own show.

To be honest, I was right there with Dave. I thought Andy was out of control as well; I thought he'd really lost it. I felt certain that what he was doing and saying now could never be shown on television and I figured it was jeopardizing what we had already accomplished. So I tried to send a message to Andy with my body language. I just slouched back in my chair in disgust, crossed my legs, and tried to look totally uninterested in what Andy was doing to make him realize I didn't approve. Since it was bleeped out by the network censors, I don't believe anyone has ever heard the actual words Andy used during his tirade. So for those of you who would like to know, here is how I remember what Andy yelled at me on that show:

> I am sick of this bullshit! You are full of bullshit, my friend. I will sue you for everything you have. I will sue your ass! You're a motherfuckin' asshole, as far as I'm concerned. You hear me? A fuckin' asshole! Fuck you! I will get you for this! I am sorry, I am sorry to use those words on television. I apologize to all my fans. I'm sorry. I'm sorry. But you, you're a fuckin' asshole! You're a fuckin asshole! You hear me? A fuckin' asshole!!

Wow! I'm still a little shocked every time I recall exactly what Andy said. When he had finished his cussing, he grabbed Dave's cup of coffee and threw it at me and then turned and ran out of the studio. Once again, Dave's response was classic. He said, "I think you can use some of those words on TV. But what you can't do, is throw coffee. I've said it over and over again!" With that I was whisked off the set and right down the elevator and back to the hotel. No one said another word to me other than the security guard asking me to autograph a wrestling magazine while we were in the elevator. Paula was with me and she later said she thought I was sure to be arrested. She'd had no idea any of that was going to happen either.

After the show Bill Apter called the *New York Post* and sold pictures of the show to them for seventy-five dollars and they were on the front page the next day. I'm sure David Letterman and the people at NBC were upset with Andy and me for what we did on the show, but they couldn't have been upset with the publicity it got. It was huge news all over the place, strangely mirroring the time when I made the front page again after allegedly beating up Jim Carrey. It was a tremendously well-kept secret that this whole thing was a work.

That started a long run of a wrestling feud between me and Andy. He loved it so much. It was his favorite thing to do. We must have worked together thirty or forty times. He came back on our TV show in Memphis and put a bounty out on me. "Any wrestler who will piledrive Lawler and injure him like he did me gets five thousand dollars from me! I want that hick Lawler to lay in a hospital bed and suffer like he made me do, and I want him in there for at least a week!" It was an easy program. He united with Jimmy Hart and they looked for revenge. Anyone we brought in to wrestle me would automatically have Andy's heat.

My connection with Jesse Ventura came about through Andy Kaufman. Jesse worked for Verne Gagne in the AWA through Minneapolis and the northwest. We or, as it appeared, Andy, brought in Jesse and other guys like Ken Patera and we came up with multiple combinations of rematches.

In January 1983, I wrestled AWA World Champion Nick Bockwinkel and actually had him pinned. The way Bockwinkel avoided losing was that his foot was on the ropes. They announced an immediate rematch. Jimmy Hart had been interfering every week, so I'd used fire on him and he was thought to be really badly burned up. We said he was going to be at ringside for the rematch with Bockwinkel. There's a shop called "Trick or Treat" in Memphis where they sell costumes and Halloween masks that had a great Invisible Man mask that looks like bandages. I got one of those. So the Invisible Man is there at ringside and I'm wrestling Bockwinkel when suddenly, here comes Jimmy Hart, no bandages or anything. I'm stunned: What's this? Who's this other guy?

Bockwinkel takes advantage and pins me. The masked man is unveiled and it's Andy.

The following week, we used Andy and Jimmy Hart against me. We had it that Andy and Jimmy got into it because I'd beaten the crap out of both of them. On TV the following Saturday they confronted each other and each blamed the other for their miserable showing. Their argument finally degenerated into a "fight," or I should say, "nonfight." Both Andy and Jimmy were flailing away at each other like a couple of girls and neither one ever landed a punch. It's still my favorite Andy Kaufman segment to watch.

So finally Andy asked me to be his partner against Jimmy Hart and one of the Assassins. Andy comes out and has a check for ten thousand dollars for me. He says he hates Jimmy Hart ten times more than he ever hated me, asks me to be his partner, and offers me the check. I said I would be his partner but I didn't want the money. There was one condition, however. After the match, once we've taken care of Jimmy Hart, Andy would hang up his wrestling tights for good. He'd say good-bye to wrestling. He promised he would.

He and I were supposed to be wrestling together. I'm in there against one of the Assassins with my back to Andy, who was still in our corner. Andy reaches into his pocket and pours something into his hand. He comes into the ring and taps me on the shoulder. I turn around and he throws powder in my face. I'm blinded, and one of the Assassins gives me a big piledriver. Andy runs across the ring and jumps into the waiting arms of Jimmy Hart and the two conspirators savor their sweet revenge. But everyone knows that in wrestling, right must eventually prevail, so Andy had to come back.

He kept coming back and coming back. We almost booked him on a weekly basis after a while, return match after return match. We had to come up with ways

to keep the interest up and that was difficult to do. The first matches were turnaway, sellout crowds. It dwindled somewhat. We ended up with Andy in boxing matches. Instead of 11,500 people in the Mid-South Coliseum, there were 6,000. It almost got to the point where I was going to have to tell Andy, "Er, thanks, I think we've had our run." But then he got sick.

I remember, Andy was doing an interview on my show and he was coughing uncontrollably. He couldn't really make it through the interview and afterward, he apologized for not being able to finish it properly. Then he told me he'd been diagnosed with lung cancer. Like a lot of people he told, I thought he was kidding at first but it only took a couple of minutes for him to convince me.

I think Andy lasted five months from the time he was diagnosed to the time he died, which was May 16, 1984. He was only thirty-five. He was the neatest guy. He wasn't a weird nut, he was brilliant. He was so respectful of wrestling. He was all "sir," this and "yes, ma'am." He loved everything about the squared circle, it was one of the most fun things he ever did. He was great for wrestling and I really miss the guy.

After Andy died, Lynn Margulies, his girlfriend, was going through his things. She found all the checks we'd written him for his matches. He never cashed them.

chapter 21

Some years later, I saw in a magazine there were plans afoot to make a movie about Andy Kaufman. Jimmy Hart, who was with the WCW at the time, confirmed it. He called me up and said there was indeed a movie in the works about Andy. And then he said, "I hear they're going to have Disco Inferno play you." I said, "What?" Well, that was what he'd heard. I called my Hollywood contact, Larry Burton, and asked him to find out who was going to do the movie. I told him that Jimmy Hart had heard they were going to have this goof Disco Inferno play the King. It was an outrage. Larry said he'd check it out.

I found out that Bob Zmuda was involved in the plans for the movie. I didn't have any way of getting in touch with him, but I knew he was the founder of Comic Relief. I just got on the telephone, dialed 411, and asked for the offices of Comic Relief. After several calls, I got through to his office. I said who I was and that I was the guy who'd wrestled Andy and had met Bob the night he came down to do the match in Memphis. I said I wanted to talk to him about the movie.

The day after I called him, Bob Zmuda called me back. He said he'd been trying to get in touch with me. They wanted me to help as a consultant on the movie and they were interested in my thoughts on who they could get to play me. I said, "Well, here's a thought. What about me playing me?"

I sent them tapes and all sorts of stuff that I had. I wasn't exactly short of material. Larry Burton also got involved. He had contemporary pictures of me and also ones of me when I had wrestled Andy. They looked pretty similar. He sent these out to the casting people. The executive producer, Michael Hausman, came to a show at the Meadowlands and we met him and the casting director. We talked and they said they thought I'd be great in the role of myself. They wanted me to meet Milos Forman, the director. He liked me too so they offered me the part of Jerry Lawler. I didn't do an audition or anything like that. I don't know what they would have done

Jeff Conaway

to make me prove I'd make a convincing Jerry Lawler.

Larry Burton tried to help by negotiating my pay for the movie. A lot of people who liked Andy worked for scale. The movie was full of people playing themselves. David Letterman, Judd Hirsch, Jeff Conaway, and the people on *Taxi* worked for relative peanuts. But Larry was holding out on my behalf like I was a big superstar. As the negotiations dragged out, I got really mad with him because I thought he was going to lose me the part. I think he was equally mad at me and felt I was getting 80 percent of his salary. But, finally, when most of the stars got less than $10,000, he got me $75,000 to do the movie. I've probably gotten another $15–$20,000 in residuals since.

Larry Burton is one of the guys I wound up selling the Memphis wrestling to. He's been involved in show business a long time and he knows a lot of people in Hollywood. He knew Jeff Conaway from *Taxi* because they'd made a movie together, a swimsuit epic called *Bikini Summer 2*. I told Larry I heard that movie was so bad when it played at the drive-in, people asked for their gas money back. That's when he told me there never had been a *Bikini Summer*. This was their way of making people think they were watching the sequel to a hit. It must have helped because the movie made a lot of money. Anyway, Jeff was pretty hot at Larry for getting me that kind of fee. But Larry came through for me there.

Larry once arranged for Stacy to meet Jeff Conaway because her favorite movie was *Grease*. Kenickie, who Jeff played, was her favorite character in the movie. Actually, her favorite movies were *Grease* and *Gone With the Wind*, but even Larry Burton couldn't pull off a meeting with Clark Gable. We were in Hollywood and Larry set it up so Jeff was sitting at a table in a restaurant when Stacy and I came in with Larry. Stacy had no idea who she was about to meet. Needless to say, she was speechless. We had dinner and afterward, Stacy got a kiss, but no "Hicky from Kenickie."

Before I went out to Los Angeles, I went to Cozy Corner, picked up some barbecued cornish hens, and took them out to the shoot. The first day I got there, they were filming the *Taxi* scenes. Milos Forman and Danny DeVito were there on the set, which was the actual set of *Taxi*. I told them I had brought a present from Memphis. Cozy Corner barbecue. They knocked everything off a table they were using in the scene and opened that bag up and started eating and they were like two little kids at Christmastime. It was like they hadn't eaten in years. Danny DeVito knew about Memphis from *The Rainmaker* and Milos Forman had made *The People vs. Larry Flynt* there. I couldn't have brought them anything they would have enjoyed more. From that moment on, Milos, Danny, and I were fast friends.

They may have got a lot of the people involved in Andy's life to play themselves, but they didn't use the Mid-South Coliseum for the scene of the match between me and Andy. They used the old Olympic Auditorium in Los Angeles, which looks nothing like the Coliseum. The movie people seemed to want to make the Tennessee crowd into a bunch of real hicks. They must have had three thousand extras there. It's amazing, they had to feed all those people and they'd made costumes for everyone. Unfortunately.

Well, I got ready in the trailer and walked onto the set. If there were three thousand people there, three-quarters of them must have had bib overalls and straw hats on. Like our crowds were made up entirely of Depression-era farmers. The wardrobe guy was there with a big smile on his face. "Well, what do you think? Does this look like the Mid-South Coliseum?" I said, calmly, "I've been wrestling in the Mid-South Coliseum every Monday night for twenty years, and I don't think I ever remember seeing anyone once wearing a straw hat at a match." He said, "Really?" He turns around and gets a megaphone. "Everybody. Lose the straw hats." And they put the hats under the seats. As far as Hollywood was concerned, in Memphis, everyone's a hayseed.

They had sent me a script of the whole thing, sure. But I didn't read it. Actually, I didn't even read my part. Remember when I said I don't like to rehearse? So I got there the day of filming and I had no clue what to do, what I was going to say, what kind of scene I was going to do. Nothing. I got the feeling they assumed I was an actor like the others. At least they treated me like one.

Right away I was introduced to my "personal assistant," a person who was going to be at my beck and call throughout the shooting. My assistant was a very pretty young lady named Jade. She introduced herself and said, "Mr. Lawler, I'll be working with you during the filming, and if there is anything at all I can do for you, just let me know . . . my name's Jade Jagger." Holy crap! This was Jade Jagger! Mick Jagger's daughter! Mick Jagger, of the Rolling Stones . . . and she was my personal assistant! Already, making movies was cool! Jade handed me my call sheet. The call sheet said the limo would pick me up at such and such a time and take me to an address that was not on the lot but turned out to be an office building. Makeup was at this time and filming would be at that time. Filming was to be of scenes X and Y. But I was completely clueless.

When it was time to get dressed for the first scene, I saw that wardrobe had this big old rodeo belt buckle out for me to go with a goofy-looking western shirt. The damn buckle was nearly as big as a WWE Championship belt! I told them I'd never worn a belt like that in my life nor would I ever wear one. I also assured them that I didn't own a homemade fur coat, and that just because I was from Memphis, my school fight song was not "Dueling

Banjos." They got rid of the belt buckle, but somehow, the shirt stayed.

The first scene I did was actually one of the last ones in the movie. It's the one where Andy's manager is telling him he just got voted off *Saturday Night Live*. He said he didn't think Andy and I should ever work together again. We were handed single pages from the script. Little pieces of paper with the lines we were going to do that day on them. We looked at those for few minutes and it was time to go. "Places everybody." Oh my gosh . . . that was it for rehearsal!

I sat at this little desk. Then Jim Carrey came and sat down next to me, real close. His leg was touching mine. They asked us to get in a little tighter for the shot so we're jammed right together and two feet in front of us was Danny DeVito. Now I don't get intimidated or nervous very easy. I just go with the flow and try to not think too seriously about what's going on. But here, all of a sudden, this feeling came over me. This is freakin' Jim Carrey, maybe the biggest star in Hollywood, and I'm sitting here right on top of him. And right there is freakin' Danny DeVito, another one of the biggest stars in Hollywood . . . And I'm going to do a scene with these two guys!

I started to get really intimidated for a second but then I thought, how cool is this! So I went the other way and started to get a little cocky, yeah, that's right, it's Jim Carrey— Danny DeVito—King!

Someone says, "Places," and I see a few people scurrying around behind the cameras. Then you hear, "Quiet" and suddenly, you could hear a pin drop. Then, finally, "Action." Jim is looking at a copy of *Variety*. The headline was about Andy being voted off *Saturday Night Live*.

The way the reveal was going to work was that the camera had, to that point, only shown Danny and Jim. The camera would shoot from behind Danny and there I was sitting next to Jim, which would be the first time in the movie that it would be clear we had been working together on this thing. Jim was saying this is bad, and Danny said, "It pains me to say this, but I don't think you two guys should ever work together again." The camera comes out showing me and my line is "I'm sorry, George, we just thought it was funny." (George being George Shapiro, Andy's manager, who Danny DeVito was playing.) Jim looks at me and says, "You don't have to be sorry, Jerry. You were terrific." Now the final movie

Danny DeVito

version was different, but what we shot had Jim talk about this being a shining moment, and then he was going to say, "But I think George is right, maybe we shouldn't work together anymore."

That was the setup. Danny DeVito nailed his lines. Right on cue, the camera panned out and there I was, with "Sorry George, we just thought it was funny." Jim then says his line perfectly up to the part he was supposed to say "But I think George is right." He stopped. There was silence. He just sat there staring at me. He'd obviously forgotten his line. So after a few seconds of nothing, I said, "Do you think maybe . . ." I started to tell him his line. Not a good idea.

There must have been fifty people in the room and there was dead silence. Jim was staring at me, his eyes wide open. I think everyone else there was pretty bug-eyed also. He stood up and walked about twenty feet to the back of the room. Now, all eyes were on him. He goes to the corner and squats down facing the wall and then he starts screaming at the top of his lungs. "EEEAAAR-RRGGGHHH!" About four times. "EEEAAARRRGGG-HHH!" I turn to look at Danny DeVito and he puts his hand out as if to say, it's okay. I knew enough not to say anything. "EEEAAAARRRGGGHHH!"

When Jim was done screaming, he stayed down for twenty seconds or so. Then he stands up and composes himself and comes walking back over. He pulls his chair over nice and gentle and sits back down. He looked at me very calmly and said, "You were right, and I'm professional enough to admit that I was wrong." He looked at someone else and said, "Now can we hurry up and get this scene shot because I am very uncomfortable sitting next to this man." That was my first day of filming.

Afterward, everyone said I was good and not to mind Jim. That's just the way he is, he's a little eccentric. Good guy, just a little high-strung. But after that, it was like he was trying to provoke me. I'd be standing somewhere and Andy/Jim would run up behind me and push me. I'd turn around and he'd run off like a little kid. Obviously he was trying to be Andy. After a while, it started to piss me off. One time he did it and he actually stuck a piece of paper on my back. I was walking around the set for a while with a sign on my back that said "Hulk Hogan Wannabe."

On the lot, when it was just me and him and Stacy, we did pictures and stuff, but if anyone else came around, he wanted to be really adversarial. And once filming started, Jim never came out of character to talk to me about Andy. For some reason, he acted as though he thought Andy and I were really enemies. That's why it got so annoying later on when he did that crap about spitting on me. I wound up telling Milos Forman, "Has this guy even read the script? [Which was good, coming from me.] Did he realize Andy and I were friends?" Andy never did any of the kind of stunts Carrey was pulling.

We were filming the scene with Jim and me in the Mid-South Coliseum. The deal was that I'd be about to do the suplex on Jim and they'd cut and get a stunt double in so Jim Carrey wouldn't get hurt. I know Jim wanted to get suplexed and piledriven himself, because before shooting started on the movie, I got a conference call one day at one in the morning. On the phone was Jim Carrey, Danny DeVito, and some insurance guy for Universal Studios. Jim was trying to talk them into letting him do his own stunts for the movie. He wanted me to assure Danny and the insurance guy that I could give Jim a suplex and a piledriver without him being hurt. Of course I couldn't give them an ironclad guarantee that Jim wouldn't get hurt, so they opted for a stunt double to take the suplex and piledriver.

We filmed that scene for many hours. It started with my entrance to the ring, then Andy/Jim's. We did our verbal abuse of one another and then we started the match. Andy/Jim got the headlock on me and then I lifted him high in the air, and the director yells, "Cut!" I gently set Jim down and the stunt double comes in and grabs me in a headlock. I lift the stunt double high in the air and hold him there. The director yells, "Action!" And I drop the poor stunt double backward on his head with a big side suplex. "Cut!" Jim comes in and lays down where the stunt double had landed. "Action!" I go over and lift the limp body of Jim up and prepare him for the piledriver. I stick his head between my legs and lift him up for the piledriver. "Cut!" Very carefully, I set Jim/Andy down and then pick up the stunt double. Once again, the director yells, "Action!" And, once again, the poor stunt double gets dropped on his head.

After repeating this probably ten or twelve times during the day we were almost ready to wrap. Everyone, including the more than 3,000 extras in the audience, was tired and ready to call it a day, but Milos Forman wanted one more take to make sure he had everything he needed. While they were adjusting lights and fixing actors' makeup, I was just standing in one corner of the ring by myself. Suddenly, Bob Zmuda walks over to me from where he had been standing with Jim. He sort of looks around to make sure no one is looking at us or listening to us, and then, under his breath, he whispers to me, "Listen, on this last take, Jim wants you to do something for him. When you pick him up for the suplex, and when the director says, 'Cut,' Jim wants you to go ahead and suplex him and then turn around and pick him up and give him the piledriver. The cameras will be rolling, they'll have it on film, and there'll be nothing they can do about it." With that, Zmuda turns around and walks back over to where Jim is standing.

Now, I'm standing there with what I felt was the weight of the world suddenly on my shoulders. Jim Carrey wants me to do him a favor and go against the wishes of Universal Studios and the director, Milos Forman. A million things were going through my mind. First, I'm thinking, "The only reason Jim wants me to piledrive him is so that he can claim he's hurt and go to the hospital like Andy did." Second, I'm thinking, "If I piledrive him, and he claims to be hurt, the movie people are going to look at me and say, What the hell did you do that for, Lawler?" I could get kicked off the movie or worse yet, sued by Universal Studios.

So, just as someone yelled "Places!" Milos Forman walked by the ring. I bent down and said, "Milos, Jim just sent word over here that on this take he wants me to go ahead and really suplex him and really piledrive him." Milos looked at me in disbelief, and said, "Oh Jerry, I'm so glad you told me that." Then he turned to the audience and crew and yelled, "That's a wrap, ladies and gentlemen! Thank you all very much!" I looked over at Jim Carrey and he was glaring at me. He knew immediately I had told and spoiled his plan. He was furious!

As the crowd started to file out of the building, Jim sprinted to the center of the ring and grabbed the ring mike. "Listen! Let me tell you people something! I wanted to take the suplex and I wanted to take the piledriver, but Jerry Lawler is so afraid of the movie studios that he won't do it. He went and told . . ." And at that point, someone cut the power to his microphone. Carrey's standing there yelling into a dead mike and nobody's hearing a word. Now he was really mad. His face turned a bright red and the veins were popping out on the side of his neck. He threw the microphone on the floor and screamed at the top of his lungs, "I HAVE WORKED ON BROADWAY AND I DO NOT NEED A MICROPHONE TO BE HEARD!!"

The executive producer of the movie, sensing Carrey was having a meltdown, came over and tugged on my tights, and motioned for me to just get out of the ring and let Jim throw his temper tantrum. But as I started through the ropes, Carrey came over to me. Looked me straight in the eyes. And then he spit right in my face! Not just a little spit, but a big wad of spit! Spit went on my cheek, in my eye, and on my mouth! As soon as he spit, there was this pause for just a second. I know I couldn't believe what he had just done and I think suddenly, HE couldn't believe what he'd just done. Then the realization hit us both! I snapped, and he ran! He ran across the ring and tried to slide out under the bottom rope, but I caught him. I caught him from behind with my arm around his neck in what's known in wrestling as a "reverse chin lock." Suffice to say, he wasn't going anywhere.

Now the reality was setting in on the people around the outside of the ring. "Hey, these guys are serious!" Carrey had a bodyguard assigned to him on the set. He was this huge black guy who had to weigh at least three hundred fifty pounds. He saw Jim's legs dangling out of the ring as Carrey was flailing around in my grip, so he grabs Jim by his ankles and starts to pull with all his might. I got Carrey by the head and neck so the effect was like he was on a rack being stretched from both ends! This whole confrontation probably lasted no more than fifteen seconds before I came to my senses and said to myself, "I can't beat up Jim Carrey right here in front of 3,000 people," so I let him go. When I did, the bodyguard yanked Jim out of the ring with such force that Jim fell straight to the concrete floor. A huge crowd gathered around him and he was still lying on the floor when I left the arena and went back to my trailer.

I think this was all a big plot of Jim's to try to provoke me into piledriving him so he could be like Andy. So he could say he had to be sent to the hospital at the hands of Jerry Lawler. When it came to it, he didn't get a piledriver but he got the chokehold that stretched his neck. That probably hurt him worse than a piledriver would have. So he did go to the hospital and he had to have X-rays.

There was a big hurricane hitting Florida at the time, yet this was the lead story in Los Angeles for a day. Next day, when we arrived at the set, there had to be at least twenty different news crews there. There was a van with a great big extension gimmick and a stills cameraman sitting in a chair on top so he could shoot into the lot, which was closed off. People were on top of buildings looking in. It was crazy. History was repeating itself but this time, at least on my part, it wasn't a work.

As far as the other actors were concerned, I didn't have much interaction with Courtney Love, who played Lynn Margulies in the movie. She didn't seem like that pleasant a person to be around. I remember her as a woman who smoked one cigarette after another, and who had extremely pale, white skin. Everyone else was pretty cool. Milos Forman and Michael Hausman were very nice. I still get a Christmas card every year from Michael. Danny DeVito was the best, a real regular guy. Except he's very short, so he's like half a regular guy. He's one of those guys that when you meet him, he's even shorter than you imagined he would be. He might be the only guy I could beat in a slam-dunk contest. He was shorter than Stacy and she's five feet tall.

I thought Jim Carrey played Andy very well. The physical resemblance was amazing, but the script wasn't so good. When I got to meet the guys who wrote the screenplay, they looked like a couple of kids. They were probably ten when Andy died. There was no way they could know what Andy was really like. It would have been better to show Andy as a normal guy with all the weirdness put on. They made him seem like a really strange person and he was not that way at all. As far as wrestling was concerned, he was just like one of the boys. When he went in front of the camera, he went into character. It wasn't strange revisiting the whole thing; it was kind of cool.

ARTWORK BY
KING JERRY LAWLER ©87

22

Jerry Jarrett and I put up a big sign in our office to remind us of the Golden Rule of booking wrestling matches: "Personal issues draw money," in case we were thinking of deviating from that path. The well-crafted feud means so much more than the belts or the championships. People need to think there's something between the two guys in the ring. It adds so much if they believe there's some real animosity there. Over the years, we've thought up literally thousands of personal issues as angles. Beat up some guy's kid, run over people in cars, shave the wife's head.

Jackie Fargo was involved with one of the best gimmicks I've ever seen, and that was his brother who went by the name of "Roughouse." Roughouse wasn't a very big guy but he had the greatest gimmick in the world. Jackie was living in Memphis, but Roughouse lived in North Carolina where he just worked as a referee. He also worked for Cannon, the company that makes towels. Twice a year he'd get a week's vacation and he'd come to Memphis.

They built a story that Jackie's brother had been committed and was in a mental institution. With a nod to the forces of political correctness, Jackie called his brother "Roughouse." When Roughouse's vacation was coming up, they'd work a deal where two guys would destroy Jackie and have him beat down. Jackie would go on TV that week and say, "You guys have done it now, I'm going to have to call in my brother Roughouse. I don't like to do this. Ain't a pretty sight, and no one can control him but me. It's only a day pass, but Monday night, I'm bringing in Roughouse."

The imagination of the thing. People could visualize Jackie going to North Carolina, checking his crazy brother out in a straitjacket. The two days a year that Roughouse was in the house would always sell out. The night of the match, here would come Jackie and out would come Roughouse, half a foot shorter than Jackie, not a good body or anything but acting completely crazy. He'd go after the referee, he'd go after the announcers. He'd punch the wrestlers, bite 'em, kick 'em. People would be deathly afraid of him and this would all put him over huge.

The first time I met Roughouse, I was like the rest of the fans. I thought he really was in a mental institution. We had a trip to Dyersburg one Tuesday and I was planning to ride with Jackie. I met Jackie down at the Southern Frontier, forgetting that Roughouse had wrestled the night before. So I'm riding with Jackie and Roughouse. I started to get in the front seat and Jackie said, "Nah kid, get in the back." The door opened and here comes Roughouse to join me.

I thought I was sitting next to a certified lunatic. I was trying not to look at him but I'd glance over and he'd be staring at me. I'd never been 'round anyone that chewed tobacco. Roughouse was using a foul-smelling spit cup. Grossest thing I'd ever seen. That was until he swallowed the tobacco juice. Had me a nervous wreck. We stopped on the way and I went and got a bag of potato chips. He grabbed the bag from me and smushed the chips inside into little crumbs.

* * *

Don Fargo, the Fargo brother who wasn't, was a real nut too. Had his body tattooed and piercings in very unusual places. He did a match in Pensacola one night where he told the other wrestler, "Pull my tights down." If you're going to back-drop somebody, and they leap over you and reach up and they move to pull you back over in a sunset flip, you can pull their tights down halfway through if you want. Don got this guy to do it and he stopped, got out of the ring, and walked back to the dressing room just like that. People went crazy.

The WWE has to be very careful. It is a publicly traded company that operates on network and cable TV with worldwide advertisers. So they can't be too offensive with the programming. They have to skirt the edges of stuff. Like Goldust and his infatuation with Booker T. Wrestling used to be full of mean-looking guys like Al Greene. Big, rawboned, country guys. There were more guys with the demeanor of Brock Lesnar. He doesn't have a gimmick. He really is a big, mean-looking individual.

They kind of blur the line between good and bad up in the WWE. And they switch a lot. Usually guys don't want to be stuck being one thing. The bad guys want to be cool, so it's hip to like them, and the good guys want to be tough badasses. But I think if you try to please everybody, you wind up pleasing nobody. So when guys are trying to be cool bad guys or hardass good guys, instead of getting over with everybody, they don't get over with anybody. Triple H tries to be too tough to be a really good guy. The secret of a good face is to have people sort of feel sorry for them, for them to be in jeopardy. You can't imagine Hunter in jeopardy at all. If he's knocked down, you don't worry about him. Get up, you look like you can push a mountain over.

* * *

There was a guy in Memphis we set up like Brock Lesnar. He was the Mongolian Stomper, whose real name was Archie Gouldie. He was from up around Knoxville, Tennessee, which is way Outer Mongolia. He was a really good-and-scary-looking heel. We never let him talk. When we first brought him in he had a manager, Bearcat Wright. Bearcat did some good heel promos. Like Brock Lesnar, we just let him squash people. Something happened to Bearcat and we switched the Stomper to another manager, Sonny King, and the Stomper kept winning.

Then something happened to Sonny King and someone had the bright idea of letting the Stomper do his own interview. Biggest mistake we ever made. We said we were actually going to hear from the Mongolian Stomper today. When he spoke, of course, the Mongolian Stomper had a real southern accent. "Let me tell you sumpthin', Jerry Lawler." We had to say he wasn't from Outer Mongolia after all, but from the Mongolian Deep South.

I always worked well with the killer-type heels. You'd have them squash a bunch of people and then go against me and squash me too. Then they'd be made. Then we'd go backward. Instead of having someone beat everybody and have me beat them, we'd have someone beat everybody and beat me too and then work returns until I worked my way back up to the blowup, the do-or-die finale. I'd then come out on top and stay there while we're building the next monster heel from underneath.

One of the toughest guys we ever had in our territory was Jos LeDuc. (Michel Pigeon was his name.) He was an unbelievably strong guy. He once pulled a bus clean 'round the Coliseum. Another time, he leaned up against a wall and a car drove up and parked a little in front of him. He put his feet on the fender and locked his legs. They started up the car and put it in drive and they put the gas on as much as they could 'til the tires started smoking. He was unreal.

One time, Jos picked me up and held me over his head. What he was supposed to do was pressslam me over the rope and onto the announcers' table, which was about ten feet from the ring. Everything went fine until he threw me. I only went nine feet and hit the oak table sideways and bounced off onto the floor. I severed a muscle in my thigh and had to have surgery. As soon as I hit the table, I knew something was wrong. The promoter Eddie Marlin rushed over. He said, "Don't move, don't get up. That looked great!" I said, "Don't worry, Eddie, I *can't* get up."

Jos played a Canadian lumberjack with a flannel shirt and everything. He carried an ax into the ring with him. He also had a scar on his face that just added to the whole look. What solidified his reputation to the Mid-South fans was one interview he did. "Let me tell you something, Jerry Lawler. I am a lumberjack. When we promise we're going to do something, we take an oath." (Except he didn't say "oath," he said "oat.") "We take an oat' that we're going to do something, we put a scar on our body. So every day, when we see the scar on our body, it reminds us of our oat'." Lance Russell was standing there mouthing, "Oat'?" Jos says, "Jerry Lawler, I'm going to take an oat'. I'm goin' to put you out of wrestling. I'm going to end your career. And I'm goin' to put a scar on my body to remind me of the oat'." He rolls up his sleeve and takes the ax and starts sawing at his arm. He really did scar himself up. "Look at this, Jerry Lawler." This was on live TV. People talked about that forever. He was a legit tough guy.

A friend of mine once bought a blue light and put it on the dashboard of his car. He pulled guys over all the time and got Jos LeDuc one night. He drove past him and pulled over and waited for him to go by. Then he went up behind him and hit the blue light but Jos wouldn't pull over for an age. Finally he pulled over. He got out of the car and this guy said, "Turn around, face the car, put your hands on top of your head." The ribber started patting Jos down, but then he goosed him in the butt. Jos sees who it is and got so mad he wanted to fight. "You son of a bitch. Fricking blue light came on, threw a whole bag of dope out the window."

Jos also died recently, in 1999. He was visiting his son in Atlanta, fell in the shower and hurt himself and got an infection. He went to the hospital and got pneumonia and died. He'd had a lot of trouble with diabetes. He was only fifty-five.

So the trick with booking was a combination of good programs, set up by a smart angle, and believable characters, or guys with a clever gimmick. There was a great program we set up in the eighties with Austin Idol that had an unusual, and unusually painful, shoot element to it. Austin Idol's real name was Dennis McCord. He was a big, good-looking guy. He was just getting started when he was involved in the plane crash that killed "King" Bobby Shane. Austin got his legs broken and he was badly messed up but he made it all the way back to wrestle. He hated flying after the crash, which you can understand, and he didn't like to travel at all. He preferred to spend time with his family.

We used Austin a lot in Memphis. He was one of the biggest stars we ever had there. He was like Bill Dundee in that we had him as my partner, we had him as my opponent. We did all sorts of things with him. He wasn't the greatest worker of all as far as his in-ring ability was concerned, but it was more than good enough to get by. His great strength was his interviews. He was great on

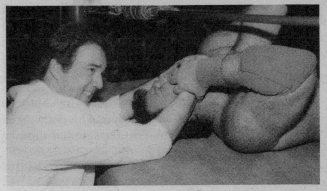

Typical of Paul Heyman's managing style, not trusting his guy to win clean.

the stick. "Universal Heartthrob" was what he called himself. From Las Vegas, Nevada. The Ladies' Pet, the Men's Regret.

Austin and I were scheduled for a hair-against-hair match. Paul Heyman was working as Paul E. Dangerously, the manager, and Tommy Rich was going to be Austin's surprise partner. We stuck Tommy Rich under the ring about five hours before the match. He was there an hour before the show started when the door opened so no one would see him. The show lasted two and a half hours, then the cage went up and our match started and Tommy Rich came up from nowhere, out from under the ring. He got into the cage and no one could help me. I was in the ring not only with Austin Idol but with Tommy Rich too.

They did the number where they each took one of my legs and pulled me into the post. I got posted. It looked like it wrecked me. Well, the truth of the matter was that I was scheduled to have a vasectomy reversal the following morning. We had cameras at the hospital, filming me going into surgery to have my testicles worked on. It was a real short operation but we did the angle to play off it, to utilize the operation. I had to be off a couple of weeks anyway. It turned out to be one of our hottest angles ever. It looked great when they ran me into the post. I kind of turned my ass up when they did it so it hit my butt, more or less, but I got a big bruise.

When I came back, I could go through partner after partner to try to find the right combination to beat these guys. I used Dundee and Bam Bam Bigelow and all sorts of guys. If I'd have come back with Bam Bam the first week and beaten the guys, it would have killed their heat. To keep the program alive, I got screwed, or my partner was screwed every week. It always drew well when you brought someone in from outside Memphis. They loved to see someone new. As for the vasectomy reversal, all I need say is that I still have two children, Brian and Kevin.

I can't possibly list all the guys we created. As well as being my manager, we went through I don't know how many gimmicks with Danny Davis. Danny now owns Ohio Valley Wrestling (OVW), which is a developmental league for the WWE that Jim Cornette works with. He went through I don't know how many gimmicks in our territory. He wrestled with a mask a lot. He was with the Nightmares, the Galaxians. I repackaged people all the time. Vince does it too. If you see someone use something that isn't working, you'd try something different. You'd pick up on fads. When video games got hot, we got guys to try to look like something from Galaxian, which was a big deal at the time.

Another wrestler whose gimmick we started was Sid Vicious. I think Sid was trained by Tojo Yamamoto. Sid's a huge guy who came from West Memphis, Arkansas, I believe. He was green but big and good so you'd try to come up with a gimmick that would keep them within their limitations. He was just getting started, learning how to work. I could carry raw guys like that to a passable match. If you put him with a guy just as inexperienced as he, then you'd have a terrible match more than likely. With somebody who knows as little as they do, it'd be horrible.

After I watched the movie *Road Warrior* I came up with the Humongous gimmick for Sid Vicious. I had someone wrestle as Leatherface from *The Texas Chainsaw Massacre*, Freddy from *Friday the 13th*, Frankenstein, Werewolves, Draculas, Mummies, Darth Vaders, every kind of character.

The first Leatherface was Tex Slazenger, who was another guy we used with every kind of gimmick. I set him on fire one night and I had to help put it out or he was going to get badly burned. He had a butcher apron and a chainsaw (with no blade). The mask was great and he looked just like the character in the movie. He had all the moves down. I'd have the program and work toward finishing them off with the fire that meant I'd come out on top without actually having to beat the person.

Leatherface had got me a few weeks in a row and it was time to burn him. But I thought it wouldn't be that big a deal because he had the mask on. I worked it so that Leatherface's manager had a bulb that would squirt the flammable liquid. He had it hidden in a towel. Leatherface beat me down and beat me down in a corner. The manager jumped up on the apron and screamed for Leatherface to come over and get a weapon to use on me. While he's going over, I'm getting my lighter and my flash paper ready. As the manager hands the weapon over, he squeezed lighter fluid all over his apron. It took just a second.

As he walks over to me with the weapon raised, I threw the fire paper and the apron burst into flames like a grill going off. The fire went all over the front of the guy and over his back. He was hopping up and down. I jumped up and tripped him up and rolled him 'round on the mat. Burned a big hole through his apron but fortunately not through his jeans or anything. Tex later went up to the WWE as one of the Godwinns, the hillbilly family.

We invented Kamala, the Ugandan Giant, in the early eighties. We were at the Coliseum one night and this big black guy comes walking in the door. Big. He came up to me and said, "Hey, Jerry. My name is Sugar Bear Harris." "Hey, Sugar Bear." (His real name was James.) He said he wanted to work with us. I asked him if anyone had seen him come in. They hadn't. I took him back to the dressing room to see Jerry Jarrett. I said this is Sugar Bear Harris from Senatobia, Mississippi. I remember that for some reason we were looking for a cannibal gimmick at the time. We told Sugar Bear to go out the back door and make sure no one saw him. Jerry Jarrett told him to come to his house in Nashville the next day.

We finished the matches and next day, I went over to Jerry Jarrett's house. Sugar Bear showed up in his

Kamala

beat-up pickup truck. He lived in this little town twenty-five or thirty miles from Memphis and he'd done some wrestling. We told him our idea. There was a feature on Uganda in a *National Geographic* magazine that took our eye. We said we'd call him "Kamala, the Ugandan Giant." (He was "Kimala" in Memphis, and then "Kamala" later on in the WWE.) Jerry had a big African tribal mask on his wall that he'd had for years, together with a couple of spears. We took the mask and put it on Kamala. I found this painting by Frank Frazetta of a guy and a girl all scared surrounded by these cannibals. The face of one cannibal had a big star painted on the top of his head and jagged teeth going up one side and lines on the other. Big earrings and a ring through the nose. The absolute stereotype of a cannibal.

So we put this all together. Sugar Bear had his trunks and we tied a piece of leopard skin cloth around his waist. I painted his face and stars on his chest and a big yellow crescent moon on his belly and a couple of red lines. He had some bracelets over his arms and one of Jerry's wife's big hoop earrings pressed in his nose. It was like something out of a movie. Jerry had a little lake out back of his house. Part of it was like a little swamp. We threw some dry ice out there and filmed Kamala. We put some drums on the tape and wrote a voice-over about him. He was this cannibal who had been brought over to America by J.J. Dillon, who was a wrestling manager in Atlanta.

We didn't want to use anyone out of Memphis. The story was J.J. was on safari when he got attacked by these guys. He captured one and brought him to the United States. He was a wild, crazy man. I think J.J. may have added something about Kamala having been a bodyguard for Idi Amin at one time. I'd never seen Sugar Bear Harris wrestle but he'd never made a dime wrestling as Sugar Bear Harris. We told him to never do anything resembling a real wrestling move. He was going against me and I said he should just do chops. He should stay in motion and act like he didn't know where he was, like he'd never seen a building like this or this many people.

I said I'd start real leery of him and try and stay clear of him and he should look at me like I was his next meal. When I fought back he should look real surprised because no one had ever stood up to him before. Then he should catch me with these vicious chops, as hard as he wanted. I wouldn't complain. The worst thing would be if he hit me with a phony chop.

We went through this story line and I was hoping and praying that he could pull it off. We had no rehearsal and we'd never seen him in the ring when we booked the match. Well, he couldn't have been better. It was fantastic. I was convinced the guy had never seen a crowd before. He was perfect. One time he jumped out of the ring and went toward the crowd and people jumped out of their seats and started to run. J.J. Dillon was supposed to be the only person who could control him, so he'd go get him back into the ring. He'd catch me and beat me down with the chop. He'd knock me down and beat his chest and slap his stomach. He'd start biting. I cut my head so blood started flowing everywhere. It was made. People thought this guy was for real. This was before anyone knew anything about AIDS, so he'd have blood all over his mouth, he'd rub his stomach and stuff. Every week he'd beat me.

Kamala went on to the World Wrestling Federation and had a huge run with Hulk Hogan. He made nothing but money with that gimmick. He ended up buying a house and two eighteen-wheeler trucks. When he stopped wrestling, he fulfilled his dream, which was to drive his own eighteen-wheeler rig. The Rock was talking about him on a show with Kane. Hogan said to Rock that he was worried about Kane because he's a big, scary guy. He'd been drafted by *Raw* and Hogan and Rock were *SmackDown!* Rock said, "I know he's a big and scary guy, but you've been against a lot of big and scary guys. This guy's no Andre the Giant. This guy's no Kamala!" And The Rock slapped his stomach.

Another good idea was the Rock 'n' Roll Express, Rick Morton and Robert Gibson, who were two young kids wrestling in our area. We had these other two guys, Steve Keirn and Stan Lane, who were the Fabulous Ones. We started doing music videos with our wrestlers, which few promotions had really done before. We used them to get people over. Taking the most popular songs of the day, we'd add some wrestling footage and shots of the guys getting into a Corvette or with girls. A two-minute video got some guys over much better than a fifteen-minute match or an interview. The Fabulous Ones went out to ZZ Top songs like "Sharp Dressed Man" and "Legs." They were about as successful a team as we had for a while. They were as hot as could be. At intermission, they sold a lot of pictures. In the mid-eighties, if you had a thousand-dollar week, you were doing well. Those guys were selling fifteen hundred dollars worth of pictures a week and probably another fifteen hundred in wrestling payoffs.

I told Jerry I wanted to try and dress up Rick Morton and Robert Gibson like Van Halen, with long hair and bandanas and so on. I bought thirty bandannas at a flea market and some shirts I cut holes in. I told the guys to put on the stuff and they were embarrassed to go out. They thought they looked stupid. We put them out to "Rock and Roll All Nite," the Kiss song. And they were a hit. They're still doing a version of Rock 'n' Roll Express today.

Nick Bockwinkel

23

For years, we worked with the NWA and used their champion in our territory, probably more consistently than any other promotion. But the program was getting old. People knew the title wasn't going to change hands. Jerry kept lobbying the NWA because he wanted them to do a title switch, even for a week or two, but they'd only change it every year or so, and never with us. So they never agreed to have the King as NWA champ. Finally Jerry quit doing business with them and started to recognize the AWA, which was Verne Gagne's territory in the Midwest.

Nick Bockwinkel was their champion. He was great. Nick epitomized what you'd think a wrestling champion should be; like Lou Thesz, he was very classy and well spoken. He looked good and was always dressed to the nines. He had Bobby "The Brain" Heenan as his manager. Between them, they made some of the best interviews you've ever heard. I don't know how many matches I had with Nick. And like the NWA days, the people would feel I was the better wrestler, but the champ would manage to hold on to the belt, often because Bobby Heenan would interfere in all sorts of ways. The title switched from Bockwinkel to Curt Hennig, and, finally, in May 1988, we did a title switch to me in Memphis. We got a huge pop for that at the

Mid-South Coliseum. I defended the title against other territories' champions until I was "stripped" of the belt the following year.

I think the Mid-South Coliseum was only louder on the night I beat Curt Hennig, and that had nothing to do with any championship. Rick Rood was given a huge push by Jerry Jarrett as "Ravishing Rick Rude." He looked great and he also did a terrific interview. He used to come into the ring to the song "Smooth Operator." However, my fondest memory of Rick Rude was of his valet, Angel. Rick was one of the first guys we used who had a female valet with him and Angel was the best-looking valet I've ever seen. She didn't stay in the business long, but long enough to make a big impression on the King. She was as cute as could be.

She had interfered several weeks in a row. We'd never really done anything like this before, but I came up with a special finish. I wondered what would happen if I gave Angel a piledriver. Now this is the Deep South where men are supposed to be Southern Gentlemen. This is no way to treat a lady. We had to make sure she was so mean and bad and involved in the match that by the time I got to her, the crowd had to really want to see her get what was coming to her. But at the same time, we didn't want to turn people off.

I had the match with Rick. She had this little shorts outfit on. Every chance she got, she pulled my hair, scratched my eyes, choked me. Rick would knock me over to his corner and she'd be there, hitting me. When the time came, I pulled my strap down, made the big comeback on Rick, and knocked him around. He fell out of the ring and she came running in and jumped up on my back. She's pulling my hair and scratching me and the people are going crazy. So I flip her over my head so she's standing there facing me. We stand there a second face-to-face and she's open-mouthed. "Oh my gosh, what have I got myself into here." You see that look in the WWE when one of the Divas gets stuck in the ring with someone they shouldn't be there with.

So I spun Angel over and held her up for the piledriver. The Coliseum erupted. They wanted to see her piledriven so bad. I was holding her there, making the most of the move. Then, I happened to look down. It was the greatest view I'd ever seen in my life. She wasn't wearing any panties. Oh my God. I milked that out forever, playing to the crowd. People must have been wondering if I was ever going to give it to her. The piledriver. I finally did the move, but man, I hated to.

In 1988, Jerry went down to Texas and started a partnership with the Von Erich family. They operated World-Class Championship Wrestling and we changed our name from the CWA to the United States Wrestling Association. Jerry spent more time down there than I did, partly because I didn't want to go back and forth to Dallas all the time. Actually, I hate to travel. There's still an occasional sight you see, but usually it's not worth the trip.

The biggest potential hazard of traveling, after the actual journey, is the hotel. I've stayed in so many terrible hotel rooms. Hotel rooms with bloody sheets. Rooms so small and dirty you'd call the front desk and ask them to send up a room. I stayed in a hotel recently in Pennsylvania after a show and it reminded me right away of the place in *The Shining*. When I got up to my room and turned on the TV, what was on? *The Shining*. I swear to God. I called some of the guys and asked them if they wanted to come over and play some cards. We played a couple of hours and ordered pizzas. It was real hot, so we had the windows open and for a while you could forget about ax-wielding maniacs. The guys left and I went to bed. I woke up and I had a funny feeling I was not alone. And I wasn't. The whole room was full of pigeons. There must have been thirty of them, eating up the pizza crumbs. Freaked the heck out of me. Things like that don't happen at home.

I did go down and work some with the Von Erichs in Texas. I was over about as much as you can be in Memphis, and the Von Erichs were the same in Dallas, except there was a whole family of them. They used to wrestle in front of huge crowds at Texas Stadium. The dad's name was Jack Adkisson, who was a major athlete in his own right and a wrestling champion. He was pres-

A perfect fit: the title belt.

ident of the NWA at one point. He wrestled as Fritz Von Erich and his first gimmick not that long after the war was as an old Nazi, which was brave. Or foolish. He had six sons, five of whom met tragic ends. First, a young son, Jack Jr., was electrocuted in 1959. He was only seven.

Then there were the five boys who were in the business. David was the eldest, and he was probably the best worker of any of them. He died of an infection that was probably brought on by an overdose in Japan in 1984. He was twenty-five. Then Michael overdosed in 1987, aged twenty-three, and Chris shot himself in 1991 at twenty-one. They were all wrestlers. Kerry was the second best of all of them, and then Kevin. Kerry made it to WWE and was doing really well. He was Intercontinental champion for a while.

Kerry had a drug problem, which got worse when he lost a foot in a motorbike accident in 1986 and got hooked on painkillers. He'd gotten arrested and it looked as though he was going to have to do some jail time because he had apparently tried to forge a prescription. Then, he was arrested on drug possession charges. After that was when he shot himself. That was 1993. He was only thirty-three. That family had such an absolutely terrible time. Fritz died in 1997 and you can't help thinking his heart was broken by then.

I wrestled Kerry Von Erich at something called *SuperClash 3* in 1988 in Chicago, which was a big Pay-Per-View where they were going to unify the World Class and the AWA titles. There was some question about who was going to win. After waiting all those years to get a shot at winning the title, now Verne Gagne was lobbying for me to keep it. The idea they came up with was for the match to be stopped because of excess juice.

Kerry and I met before the match. Kerry was a big guy with these impressive muscles. Absolutely mountainous biceps. Kerry had a blade taped to his finger, which was exposed like half an inch. He was going to cut his head at some point in the match. Kerry was a bit distant, shall we say, and he wasn't paying attention while Verne was going over the match. He started scratching under his arm. Which would have been fine if he hadn't used the finger that had the razor blade taped to it. He sliced his bicep open. His muscles were so big it was as if his skin

Kerry Von Erich

was stretched out over them. There was blood like you'd opened a fire hydrant and we had to try and staunch it.

Everyone worked on Kerry and we put a robe on him as he went to the ring. Underneath the robe, something was wrapped real tight 'round his arm. The bell rang and I had to go in right away and make it look like he hurt his arm because he was already bleeding so much. I attacked him before he even got his robe off. I jumped on him, pushed him up against the corner, and hit his arm on the metal part of the turnbuckle to make it look like I cut his arm.

I was worried about the match but we still went about forty minutes. He cut his head as planned and with his injured arm as well, that was as bloody a match as I've ever had. There was so much blood, the ring looked like a hog had been stuck in it. It was a gruesome sight, but I thought it turned out really well even though it was unusual to have a match of that magnitude stopped and awarded to somebody. Even though Kerry had me in his claw hold, the referee stopped the match because of the blood and awarded me both titles.

Later, I had a match with Kerry at the Sportatorium in Dallas. Toward the end, Kerry would be kind of messed up in some of his matches. He was down on his knees and I was standing behind him with a front facelock on him. While I was holding him I was yelling stuff at the crowd, getting heat. Without saying anything to give me a warning, he jumps to his feet. The top of his head hit me under the chin and I bit all the way through my lip.

After we started the USWA, I would wrestle for that championship too. I wrestled guys like the Snowman (in a match refereed by boxer Leon Spinks), Terry Funk, Austin Idol, Eric Embry, Kamala, and Eddie Gilbert. I did a great, though nearly fatal, work with Eddie. We did it in the parking lot of the TV station in Memphis. What we did was have me get run over there one morning by Eddie Gilbert. It was all filmed and we were going to use it as an angle to work off. But when he ran into me, he was going a little faster than he might have, and I flew up and hit the windshield. It broke and I flew over the top of the car. Eddie's brother, Doug Gilbert, was in the car and he said he thought I'd been killed.

Right across the street is a police station, which we must have forgotten. Well, someone called the police and they came over to see what was going on. I was actually hurt, I had dislocated my hip and had to go to the emergency room. It still bothers me every now and then and it will pop out sometimes after I take a big bump. The police came to the emergency room and said, "We understand you were involved in a hit-and-run." I had to try to explain that it wasn't a real accident and that I didn't want to press any charges or anything like that. I said I'd had these guys do it, which must have sounded a little odd, and I said I wasn't hurt even if I was.

We did a lot of stuff in the car park at Channel Five, knocking out windows and running people down, staging fights. Because the police station is right there, they could see everything that took place. As a result, we had a lot of interaction with the police. On another occasion, we were about ten minutes away from doing a TV interview with Billy Travis, one of our top heels, when in walk the police. I said, "Guys, is there any way that we could wait until we've done the TV show? We're going live in about five minutes." The cops said they'd like to help, but they couldn't. They wanted to ask him a few questions and they couldn't take a chance on him leaving.

That made me hot. So I said, "If you got to get him, you got to get him, but we're going to film you." They said, "No, we don't want to be on camera," but I said we couldn't help it, we were going to be on live in about three minutes. "If you can't wait till after the show to talk to him, we're going to have the cameras rolling." I told Billy to act like it's a work and that's what it will look like on TV. So we went on air and filmed the cops putting cuffs on Billy. He's saying, "I can't believe it, I can't believe it!" He said one of our babyfaces was having him arrested, it was a setup and everything. He was filmed actually being arrested but everyone thought it was one of our angles. When he got out, we used it as part of the story line the next week. He was hot at this guy for having him thrown in jail.

The booker doesn't often get an angle presented to him like that. Booking is difficult and the booker has a lot of responsibility. He decides what the matches were going to be, what the TV was going to be. He's responsible for coming up with all the ideas for every wrestler. You take the week's calendar out. Okay, Memphis, Monday night opening match is going to be X versus Y. You have to decide what the card was going to be that night, and Louisville on Tuesday and Evansville on Wednesday. You hire whoever you wanted to wrestle, people you think you work well with. Then, if it doesn't work out, you fire them. You send all the wrestlers a booking sheet. By Saturday you have to have the whole TV show written out and have told everyone what the angles are and what to say for the interviews. Everything is timed out perfectly. The booker does everything except the bookkeeping.

Another job a booker would have is to decide on the finish. The match itself could be ad-libbed, but the finish would have to make sense in terms of what you were trying to do with a particular wrestler. People said I always won the matches but the truth was, you'd go on a "program" with somebody. Your top guys are always involved in programs and angles. The booker would sit down and ask about the program you were having with

someone and they'd think up some ideas to keep it going
as long as it would draw. Everything was based on the
crowds. Sometimes you'd have what you thought was a
great angle. You'd sit and write all the details of it for
weeks or even months. Then you'd shoot the angle and
it would be a big flop and you'd just cut it off right there.
If it doesn't draw right off the bat, it's not going to.

I've looked back over some of my booking books, the
diaries I used to keep track of the schedule. I must have
wrestled in every town with more than eleven people in
it in and around the Mid-South. French Lick, Indiana,
where Larry Bird is from. Fort Knox, Kentucky, where
they keep the gold. Oolitic, Indiana. I've no idea what
goes on there. Eminence, Kentucky—an appropriate
place for the King. I wrestled in Glasgow, Paris, and
Stuttgart. No, not in Europe. Glasgow, Kentucky; Paris,
Tennessee; and Stuttgart, Arkansas. And Lebanon, in
Kentucky. I said I didn't like to travel.

We had just about every kind of match you can think
of, plus many that you couldn't. We had a million loser-
leaves-town   matches,   then   loser-never-wrestles-in-
Lexington again; loser-leaves-CWA; loser-eats-dog food.
We had pole matches, pole versus bull whip matches
and mask versus mask; hair versus hair; hair versus belt;
belt versus limo. Then someone's hair will be dyed
green. Or Idol's hair versus Rude wearing a dress.
Dundee's belt and Cadillac against Lawler's hair. We had
scaffold matches; cage matches; barefoot; lumberjack;
stretcher; hospital elimination; strap and bunkhouse
matches. A lot of Texas death matches; plus Texas bull
rope matches; Tennessee street brawls; Bluegrass brawls;
back-alley brawls; and at least one Australian football
match. There were no-time, no-DQ, no-stopping
matches; no-ref matches; coward waves the flag; I-quit
matches; diapered; powdered and diapered; *Star Wars;*
biker roulette; four-pole roulette matches; and explosive

matches galore. The most redundant were the "anything goes" matches, because anything went in most of them.

When we first got into business together, Jerry was doing all the booking. After a while, Jerry said he was getting burned out. He said why don't we do a deal where I'll book for six months, then you book for six months? No matter what's going on, at the end of six months, we'll switch. So we started doing that.

I had certain guys and people I liked to work with and use and Jerry had his. Often, we had totally different ideas about it. When my six months came to an end and Jerry took over, he'd fire the people I had working for me and have somebody else come in. But people expected that, their whole future in a territory depended on the booker liking your work.

I was not only booking, I was wrestling every night. His six months, Jerry does the booking and comes to the towns and I'm there wrestling. My six months, I'm doing the booking and wrestling too and Jerry's got a six-month vacation. He's just doing the books back home. So, at the TV one day, we had a sort of a showdown like he had with Nick Gulas. I was all disgruntled. "You know what, Jerry, I've been thinking. No hard feelings, but I've been thinking about going in business for myself." I was doing all this work and getting 20 percent of the money. He'd just built this huge house in Hendersonville. It had a ballroom in it that seated five hundred people. I was just getting by. I could have gotten TV away from him because I was the known person. He was the business guy in the back. The wrestlers were loyal to me too. He panicked. He said he'd been meaning to talk to me. He said our business should be fifty-fifty. If we were equal partners, would I stay? This was in the eighties, right toward the end of the big run. I stayed.

Wrestling has always gone in cycles. It will enjoy a great period of huge popularity. Then it gets overex-

My long-standing rival, Austin Idol.

posed and will go into a little decline. But it's always
there. You're just doing business, then someone or something will happen and you get a new generation of fans
and it will become real popular again. It's always done
that. It was big in the seventies and then it went flat. In
the mid-eighties it was huge again and then it went flat
again.

That was the time wrestling got on cable. At first, it did really well but then, as always happens, the good idea overproliferated. ESPN put wrestling on every afternoon. WTBS had it on Saturday and Sunday. WGN had it on Saturday and Sunday. And there were local shows and syndicated shows. In Memphis at one time, counting our show, there were about nineteen hours of wrestling on a week. It was oversaturated and interest got diminished for a while. It went into a lull and a lot of the territories fell by the wayside. The only person who was doing well was Vince, and he had a down period in the early nineties. But after that, the company took off and this is the longest sustained run of success that I've ever seen. And the King is delighted to be a part of it.

24

What's it like to be the King these days? As far as the business is concerned, in addition to my announcing duties, I still wrestle for the WWE like the 2002 European Tour where I teamed with Trish Stratus to go against Mr. Perfect and Molly Holly in Germany, Scotland, and England. Those London PPV's are not shown here but they are available on tape or DVD. In the U.K., they get all our TV shows on Sky, the satellite channel. The main event was *Insurrextion,* which had Undertaker versus Triple H and Steve Austin against the Big Show. The crowd was terrific. The venue had sold out in twenty-one minutes. The German show drew ten thousand people and they don't even get WWE TV. I think they decided *Raw* and *SmackDown!* were too violent. All they got is *Metal* and *Jakked.*

I mostly stay in ring shape by wrestling at various independent shows around the country. The independents were always the lifeblood of wrestling and they remain so to this day. The WWE doesn't visit the neighborhood that often. In the mid-South, the big show might come to Nashville three times a year and Memphis and Louisville twice, but fans who can't get to these events or who don't necessarily want to spend the big money can often see live wrestling right in their hometowns. Like the show I did last spring in Tompkinsville, Kentucky, a little town about a hundred miles northeast of Nashville. And when I say "little," I mean little. I think they're considering putting a mirror at one end of town to make it look bigger.

Local independent shows haven't changed much since I started in the business. I even see a lot of the same people I used to work with thirty years ago. Like Sarah Lee, who scared the heck out of me with Cora Combs back during the Nixon administration when I thought one of them was going to sit on my face in the ring. That was in the pre-King days, and as long as he's got a face, girls will always have a place to sit. Sarah's worked the doors and sold tickets at these local shows for fifteen years. She was a women's world champion back in the day; she'll show up in a huge thunderstorm to a show in Tompkinsville, Kentucky, because she can't stay away. She says, "Once you get wrestling in your blood, it never gets out."

Sarah is married to a wrestler called Corsica Joe, who is from the island of Corsica. He was in a tag team with Corsica Jean, who might even have been Joe's real brother. They came to work for Nick Gulas years ago and stayed on in America. Nick probably didn't give them enough money to get back to Europe. Sarah said that Joe's eighty-two now and they've been married forty-three years. It's kind of sad to me that the younger guys wrestling today have no idea of Sarah and Joe's history and the trails these two blazed for us all many years ago.

That Tompkinsville show in the local National Guard Armory last spring was a typical local event. The promoter was Bert Prentice, who puts on matches in Kentucky, Tennessee, and Southern Illinois for his USA Wrestling company. I like working for Bert. Bert's been in the business forever, mostly as a promoter. He did have a stint as a manager called Chris Love. We've been friends for years and Bert uses me a lot and reckons he's booked me at least a thousand times over the years.

That night, he put together his usual mixture of veterans and young guys. I was headliner against Big Bully Douglas. He is probably typical of most of the independent headliners. Big Bully Douglas looks sort of impressive: big and bald. He is a decent-enough worker and he can have a good match, but there's something missing. It's probably that intangible factor we call charisma. Somehow, you just know that Big Bully Douglas is never going to make it to the WWE. Headlining shows in towns like Tompkinsville is about as far as he's going to go in this business. But don't tell Bully that. I'm sure that in his own mind, he's just a phone call away from headlining *WrestleMania XIX* against The Rock or Triple H.

Bert also had young wrestlers like David Flair, Chris Harris, Leviathan, Air Paris and older guys like Larry Zbyszko, Terry Taylor, and even Handsome Jimmy Valiant, the Boogie-Woogie Man, the man who should be Moses. There was a camera taping for the local TV with Jim Cornette and Scot Douglas doing the commentary.

As I mentioned, there was a terrible storm that night. A police officer said a tornado had touched down nearby and the TV stations were telling people not to go out. The cops seemed happy enough to stand there and watch Joni, who was working my corner. She was wearing an outfit that would certainly have caused a scandal had she been a resident of this little town. Let me just say her puppies were definitely pointers.

I guess about two hundred fifty people showed up in the rain, including a lot of young kids. And the great thing is, the enthusiasm is the same from these two hundred fifty fans as it would be from twenty-five hundred. The same elements are there for every show. There'll be a couple of raffles and competitions and guys will be selling

When Joni walked in, I could see she had qualifications to be the King's valet.

videos, pictures, and T-shirts and signing autographs. A wrestler's wife runs the concessions stand where you can get a hot dog for a buck. Or fifty cents if you wait 'til the end of the night.

Thanks to the weather, Bert must have lost his butt that night. He has to give guarantees to a lot of the wrestlers. Even if he pays most of them not much more than gas money, I would guess he was out at least a couple of grand. Promoting is always a crapshoot. I can't say how many times it's happened. You establish a program, and work the angle for weeks, write great interviews, and have everything set up beautifully for the show and the weatherman would say, "We're looking at snow flurries tonight" and the whole thing's down the toilet. Bert has a different attitude than I did when I was running shows. He says he looks at the month, not the night. Not me. I always looked at the night.

Joni and I got to the Armory a little late. We'd driven up from Memphis to Nashville where a limo picked us up and drove the hundred miles out into Kentucky. We got changed in the major's office and watched the storm coverage on the Weather Channel for a couple of minutes. Then we went out and signed pictures and took Polaroids with a few fans before my match. One of the things you miss about independent shows once you get to the WWE is the close contact with the fans. Here, you get to actually meet the people and talk with them. I try and measure the line of people. If there's not many waiting, I'll write, "To my friend Billy, best wishes, King Jerry Lawler." But once you do that for one person, you have to personalize everybody's picture. If there's a lot of people, I write, "To Stephen, King Jerry Lawler." A whole lot of people, and I just write "King Jerry Lawler." On this night, not only could I personalize every picture but I could write a few puppies comments too.

As usual, I met my opponent in the ring. We can ad-lib the moves and sort out the finish during a hold. Big Bully Douglas had this little fat guy in his corner, Ernest T, who works some of the local shows. He was dressed like a homeless leprechaun and he annoyed the heck out of me that night. He was never in the right place at the right time and he was taking away from the match. Several times I fell right in front of him where he could take a cheap shot—try to choke me or hit me, but he wouldn't do anything.

The interference is supposed to happen when the referee isn't looking but the one time he did do something, it was right in front of both the referee and Joni. It forced Joni to slap him and you want to save that to the end. I'd also told him, "When I pull my strap down, jump up on the ring like you're trying to get in, and I'll nail you. Then Joni'll hold you by your legs and keep you from making the save." He never got up on the apron so I yelled at him, "Don't you remember any f-ing thing?" I must have been mad because I never cuss. I just turned away and finished off Big Bully Douglas with a trademark King-size piledriver.

I always feel people get their money's worth with wrestling whether it's the WWE or a Bert Prentice promotion. The Tompkinsville show was four hours long and admission was eleven dollars. The wrestlers hang out afterward and sign stuff for fans. They're always polite and happy to say "hi" because they know who helps pay the rent. In Tompkinsville, a young man named Stephen Pennington from Moss, Tennessee, ten going on eleven, won a picture with the King. His dad says he knows every wrestler's name. He knows their momma's names. Stephen had his Polaroid taken and he looked like he won the Powerball jackpot, he was that happy. No one can begrudge a young fan like that a minute or two of time.

The following night was a better one for Bert Prentice. He put on the "Sixth Annual Tojo Yamamoto Memorial" at the Nashville Fairgrounds. There's something wrong with Bert's math because Tojo died ten years ago. In the early nineties, Tojo wasn't wrestling anymore and he'd become a manager. He was always a loner—Jerry Jarrett was really his only friend. He didn't really socialize and he lived in the same boardinghouse in Nashville he'd been in for years. There's a couple of versions of what happened to Tojo, one about his health, another about his personal life. Anyway, he went down to his basement, and shot himself. I just looked it up; it was February 19, 1992. Tojo was sixty-five years old when he died.

In the early seventies, I bought a house from Tojo Yamamoto on Old Hickory Lane in Nashville. He'd never moved into it. He'd always lived in apartments. Someone had talked him into buying the house and he immediately regretted it. Jerry told me Tojo had bought a house he didn't want so I bought it from him. I liked it; it was on the lake and had a boat dock, an acre of land, a pool. I lived there for seven years. On the walls of Kevin's bedroom, I drew Sesame Street characters all over. Of course, he thought that meant it was okay for him to draw on the walls too. One night I came home from wrestling and found that he'd scribbled his version of Bert and Ernie all over the house.

The morning of the Fairgrounds event, I watched the local Nashville TV show where Bert was plugging his Tojo Memorial. He showed a lot of old footage of Tojo chopping people. It brought back fond memories to see Tojo and a lot of my old friends on TV. I smiled as I watched wrestler after wrestler succumb to Tojo's "Oriental Claw." But my heart sank when he said there were going to be fifteen matches that night. Joni and I were driving back to Memphis afterward, and I didn't figure we'd be getting home much before four in the morning.

There's not a lot to do on days on the road like this when you're just waiting for the evening to roll around. I often go shopping. Steve Lombardi, the Brooklyn Brawler, told me, "King, you shop more than any man I've ever known in my life!" Most men hate to go to malls, but I love it. As soon as I arrive in any city, the first thing I seek out is the mall. Traveling with the WWE, I've been to a zillion of them. I went to the biggest one there is, the Mall of America in Minnesota, which was so crowded, there were even people in the piano and organ store. I've shopped malls so crummy that the "Gap" was just an empty space between two stores. I enjoy shopping for clothes and electronic gizmos, and I can spend a couple of hours in a bookstore any day. I used to really like to shop for Stacy. I'd always come back from the mall with something neat to surprise her with.

That day in Nashville, Joni and I spent some time walking around a big mall near where I used to live in Hendersonville. I was excited to find a restaurant on the strip that combined a Church's and a White Castle so I could get a bunch of burgers with my fried chicken for lunch. You only have these in certain parts of the country. White Castle hamburgers, and Krystal's too, are tiny little burgers with meat so thin you could read the newspaper through them. But man, they're good! White Castle says, "Take home a sackful" and I have, many times.

I have never worked out regularly. I hate to do it. I've bought some memberships to gyms but I haven't been. If I'm bigger than I used to be, it's not muscle. I never was real muscular. I was listed somewhere at two hundred seventy-seven. I did get up to about two fifty, which was the heaviest I ever was, so I knew I needed to lose weight. But I started to do the no-carbohydrate thing to lose weight.

I used to drink about twelve regular Cokes a day. Every now and then I'd try a diet drink. I remember Pepsi One, when that came out. There was such a to-do about how that would taste like a regular drink. I couldn't wait. First day it was on sale, I was wrestling in Alabama. I went to a store to look for it and I found it and bought a big bottle of it. Tasted like a diet drink to me.

The doctor said it wasn't going to work if I kept drinking all these sodas. There's forty carbs in each one. He told me to just try the no-carb deal. He said, "You can do anything for a week." He said that by the end of that time, I'd be used to it. So I made my mind up and I did get used to it. Some people claim that after they get used to diet drinks, they can't stand the regular, but I can stand the diet.

It's almost impossible to eat healthily on the road or to follow a diet. I'd stop at McDonald's after a match and get two double cheeseburgers, large fries, and a large Coke. Paula liked to cook. After the wrestling on Monday, I'd get home at midnight and she'd have made fried chicken, milk gravy, biscuits. She mastered everything except chocolate pie, which she could never get to stick. I called it "cup-of-pie." You could drink it.

When I started to diet, I would religiously take the

bun off the hamburger, then I started taking half the bun off. But on the strict no-carb diet, which I followed really closely, I lost thirty pounds in a month. Diligently, I drank a gallon of distilled water a day. I think that helps clean out the system. I took a lot of different kinds of supplements. One of them is like a laxative. The average person, I was told, has about ten or fifteen pounds of waste in their bodies. You eat something, it stays with you about three days. See you later. You eat corn, it really is see you later. My doctor says corn has no nutritional value whatsoever.

When we got to the Fairgrounds, it turned out that there weren't going to be fifteen matches, but near enough. The climax to the evening was billed as a twenty-five-man Battle Royal for the Tojo Cup with the winner getting twenty-five hundred dollars. I was also teamed up with Brian Christopher against David Flair and Jim Cornette in the last match before the Battle Royal.

Every time I'm in a Battle Royal where the promoter advertises a large cash prize to the winner, I'm reminded of the time Austin Idol was presented a check for five thousand dollars for winning a Battle Royal somewhere in the Carolinas. The promoters usually make these checks out to "Kay Fabe" or Santa Claus. They mark them "void" or don't sign them. Something that will render the check useless because these large cash prizes weren't real, they were just for show. But on this occasion, the promoter had written five thousand dollars, left the payee blank, and signed the thing! So the next day, Austin made the check out to himself and cashed it. When the promoter found out, he lost it, but Austin went home richer by five thousand dollars and basking in the glow of a major win for the boys over a promoter.

The previous night in Tompkinsville, I'd given an

idea to Bert Prentice. He said he wanted to do something in our tag match that would switch David Flair to a babyface. Bert was originally going to have me win the Battle Royal and he was going to do the deal where Leviathan comes in and turns on his partner, David Flair, during our tag match. I suggested he let our tag match go as planned but he should let David win the Battle Royal and have Leviathan turn on him then. I don't know if he really liked it or not, but Bert said it would be great. It puts me over and that's important to him.

With so many matches that night, there were a lot of wrestlers in the backstage area. Wrestlers spend a lot of time under the stands of arenas. In the WWE, everyone gets to use a dressing room, of course. Everything is looked after. There's a commissary with the good protein and carbs athletes need. Each venue has a production office with phone lines, faxes, and computer stations. There's even a masseuse on hand in case anyone needs a rubdown. The masseuse asked me one time if I wanted a wax job. I didn't really know what it was but I said sure. I went into the room. I was only wearing a little cloth. She reached under it and grabbed hold of my gimmick, put it on the table, and hit it with a mallet. The wax flew out my ears. That's a wax job.

Where was I? Right, at the Fairgrounds, the King gets to use a bathroom to change in but the rest of the guys share a couple of spaces. They're walking around and getting changed, loosening up and stretching their hamstrings, oiling themselves down. They might check over their match with their opponent and shoot the breeze about how they're being used in their matches. When you get all these characters with their different gimmicks assembled in one area, it sometimes looks like the bar scene from *Star Wars*.

I've used the comparison before, but independent

wrestling is like AAA baseball. There are guys on their way up to the majors, guys on the way back down, and career minor-leaguers. A lot of these guys who wrestle for Bert have other jobs and wrestle for the fun of it pretty much. But you can bet every one of the young and ambitious wrestlers is thinking, "Man, if Vince McMahon ever saw me, I'd be bigger than The Rock." You need that kind of self-confidence. If you don't have it, you're probably not going to make it anyway.

As I mentioned before, Jim Cornette helps run OVW, a developmental territory in Louisville, like the one we used to have in Memphis. He describes himself as the matchmaker. It's an AAA affiliate of the WWE. Jim says in the last three years Ohio Valley Wrestling has worked with about forty developmental contract guys, wrestlers like Brock Lesnar, Randy Orton, and Rico. I think their deal is they get something like seven hundred fifty dollars a week, which is a gift. WWE wrestlers also go down there for rehab assignments, again, like the minors. The Big Show rehabbed there, and Mark Henry and Chris Benoit. The WWE doesn't really need to have anyone under contract because there's nowhere else for anyone to go. It's like getting paid to go to college.

Anyway, David Batista, a powerful wrestler then called Leviathan, threw me clear out of the ring during the Battle Royal at the Fairgrounds. He flipped me like a cheese omelet. I went right over in midair as I flew out of the ring and onto the concrete floor. There's no padding at ringside like in the WWE. Bert can't afford it. I landed with all my weight on the heel of one foot. I had a bone bruise that hurt like crazy for a couple of weeks. The angle we decided on for the match worked out well. The challenges were laid down and the following Saturday night back at the Fairgrounds, I was going to team up with David Flair against Jim Cornette and Leviathan.

After the show had finished and everyone had left the arena, the four of us did some interviews Bert would show on his TV show the morning of the next show. David Flair seemed a little intimidated doing interviews with me and it was about take fifteen or sixteen before he felt at ease enough to finish a usable interview. We didn't get to leave until one in the morning, almost two hours after the show finished. Even then, there were a couple of fans who'd waited all that time in the rain in the parking lot to get the King's autograph. I was right; we got back home to Memphis around 4 A.M.

Thirty-two hours later, I was in Albany, New York, for *Raw*. My heel hurt pretty bad but the most strenuous thing I had to do all evening was stand up to get a better view of the Divas' paddle match between Terri and Trish. Two beautiful girls in thongs trying to climb a pole with a paddle attached to the top of it. The rule is, first girl to get the paddle gets to use it on the backside of her opponent. What a match. Did I mention, I love the WWE. And congratulations to Terri's parents; she's obviously well reared. And speaking of rears, earlier in the night, Terri had once again gotten on to me about receiving erotic e-mail. She claims I once told her to type in a certain web address on her computer. She said, "First thing I see is . . . I don't even know what it was." Must have been a bunch of rear ends and gimmicks. She took it off her computer immediately, but she's been getting this e-mail ever since.

That night in Albany was when Steve Austin pretended to sign with both Vince McMahon and his *SmackDown!* show and Ric Flair and *Raw*. But it was an April Fools' joke. In true rattlesnake fashion, he knocked both co-owners on their asses. Stone Cold toasted the crowd with Bud from the top rope with McMahon and Flair lying in the ring. The 12,000 fans were going wild as Steve banged his cans. By that point the only way anyone else was going to get a drink was to ask Steve for one of his because the Pepsi Center ran out of beer.

The first leg of my flight home left so early the next day, I didn't even bother going to bed after the show. I hung out in the hotel bar with some of the wrestlers for a while and checked my e-mail back in my room until it was time to leave for the airport. I always thought it was a blessing that I've never needed that much sleep.

25

The WWE is clearly the biggest deal in pro wrestling. But it wasn't always that way. Back when the NWA was in operation, there were dozens of territories that I've talked about. Vincent J. McMahon, Vince's dad, ran one, the World Wide Wrestling Federation, for twenty years starting in 1963. Vincent Sr.'s dad, Jess McMahon, was a boxing and wrestling promoter in New York, so Vince is a third-generation wrestling guy. I'm not just saying this because he's my boss, but Vince revolutionized wrestling when he started centralizing it. What he really did was take it over.

In 1982, Vince Jr. bought out his dad and the following year he started showing World Wrestling Federation wrestling on the USA TV network. That cable exposure meant that many local promotions had to compete with a national power and they didn't have the money or talent to do it. I said in a previous chapter that there was overexposure in the late eighties, but that came after this initial burst. Vince started signing all the top stars and buying out other promotions. In 1984, for example, he purchased Georgia championship wrestling and then shut down the company. But soon, he didn't have to buy the territories, he could just roll over them.

A lot of people had said that Vince's dad would never have done what Junior did. He was more of a traditionalist and a mild, easygoing kind of guy. He probably wouldn't have let Vince buy all the territories, mostly because of the alliance that he'd been part of. That was the business as he knew it and he wouldn't have wanted to be the guy to change that. But he died in 1984. Anyway, Vince was looking out for the World Wrestling Federation and his expansion plans caused the other territories to pretty much fall by the wayside.

What Vince did was sign up nearly all the good wrestlers. It was easy to do because all the guys wanted to get on cable. They knew they'd be seen all over the country rather than just on regional TV. That was where the big money was going to be. So from the AWA in Minneapolis, for example, he hired Bobby Heenan, he hired Hulk Hogan, he hired Jesse Ventura, he hired Gene Okerlund, all the top guys. Then he went right back into Minneapolis with those guys and all of his wrestlers too and promoted shows. Fans would see the guys they were used to seeing, plus all these other stars. The World Wrestling Federation was the big deal and what was left looked like a bunch of yokels. This happened all over the country.

We were able to hold on in Memphis because I had ownership and I was also the top guy, the star of the territory. That was pretty much the only reason why our territory was able to withstand the pressure. Had Handsome Jimmy been the top guy, for example, and he had no ownership and no real reason to stay and he went with Vince and Vince came back in and promoted the territory, we would have gone under too. But I was the anchor and because I was over as much as I was, I could pretty much make new talent by having them work with me. If I went to work for Vince, that would have left us without a main-event star in the area. Namely, me. Also it would mean that I would lose my own company. That was a lifelong investment I was going to stick with.

We felt like we were in the Alamo sometimes, fending off the World Wrestling Federation. They were taking a lot of the good wrestlers from the territory and we were fighting to survive. My son Kevin was a big World Wrestling Federation fan. He wanted all sorts of their toys. I told him they were fixing so that I wouldn't be able to afford to get him any toys. I'd go on our TV and knock the World Wrestling Federation, saying they were a bunch of steroid freaks and so on.

I actually sued Vince McMahon one time. They were going to run some shows in Memphis and Nashville. Then they went out and got Harley Race, who had been a world champion, and put a crown and robe on him and called him "King Harley Race." When they came to Memphis and Nashville, they advertised events with "the King" without mentioning his name. Well, I'd been the King around those parts for years. If someone saw a sign advertising World Wrestling Federation wrestling with "the King," they'd probably assume I was involved. So I sued. It never went to court, but I won out. It got pretty heavy. In Nashville, the sheriff went down and held up the entire proceeds from their event. They stopped saying they had wrestling with "the King." Just like Vince was looking out for his company, Jerry and I were looking out for ours. Every now and then, Vince reminds me that he still owes me one for that lawsuit.

Finally, I don't remember exactly how it came about, they offered both Jerry Jarrett and me a job. What had always been the case was, you had to go to work for Vince McMahon and the World Wrestling Federation exclusively. But they offered a deal to Jerry and me where we could work for them and still have our own territory. It was a situation that would be beneficial to everybody. Vince realized it would be bad if all the smaller territories went out of business. There would be no training ground. He didn't really have a place where he could bring young talent along. Everybody who was going on his TV shows needed to be seasoned, well-trained entertainers. He looked at our territory as a training ground and a place to bring up people.

That's how Jerry and I went to work for Vince. Jerry went as a booker and I went as a wrestler. I was always thought of as a real good worker but I was known as a good or a better interviewer than I was a worker. I was wrestling but I immediately started doing *The King's Court* every week. Of which, more in a minute. We also kept our territory going and Vince started sending some of his talent down to help us. It was a good working agreement. We would stay in business for ourselves and work for Vince.

We started doing some crossovers. Bret Hart wrestled Jeff Jarrett, who was a USWA champion, and I appeared at the *Royal Rumble*. Papa Shango had been with us in Memphis and with the World Wrestling Federation and he won the USWA title in May 1993. Even Vince McMahon himself came down to Memphis and worked one of our shows at the Mid-South Coliseum. Then they had Bret Hart win *King of the Ring,* after which I attacked Bret before he could be crowned. I was determined to be the only King. Bret Hart and I had a long feud.

I did not have a totally smooth transition. There was some heat on me. When you've been the booker, you've had the power to hire and fire, which means you've got these guys' lives pretty much in your hands. It's like a football coach. The best thing you can do is not to let it get personal. You have to make the best decisions that are going to put the most fans in the seats. You can't worry about things from that point. I understand why Vince was like he was with me. It has to be business. The worst thing you can do is try to be one of the boys. Ninety-nine times out of a hundred, someone will try to take advantage of that.

As I mentioned, I seldom liked the guys Jerry used and he usually hated the guys I used. Subsequently, everyone knew that when I took over the booking, they'd have to look for somewhere else to go. Jerry was using Mike Miller and when I got to book, I called him in. I said, "Mike, I'm going to be changing talent as you know and I've got some new guys so I'm going to have to give you two weeks' notice." He said, "Man, is there any possible way I could stay a couple more months? I've got something opening up and I don't have anywhere to go until then." I said, "I wish I could, but I've got these guys coming in already. I hate to say it." That was that. He stayed the two weeks and left and went to Florida and a few days later he got killed in a car wreck down there. I've thought a million times, would that have changed if I'd found something else for him to do? Would he be alive today?

Another reason wrestlers are like football coaches is that you're hired to get fired. Everyone will eventually be fired. A lot of people had built up animosity toward me and toward Jerry Jarrett. I was easygoing as far as rules were concerned. If you were late, I didn't scream because I was late a lot myself. If you were late a minute for Jerry, he'd rant and rage. I was last-minute on everything, which they liked, and I was a good payoff man. I believe I always paid the guys better than most, including Jerry. But we both got some heat. Everyone who ever put on a pair of trunks and got into a ring thinks that they'd be bigger than The Rock if they got a chance. Why are the promoters so stupid that they can't see I should be the main event? Not Undertaker. Not The Rock. If you don't have self-confidence, you're not going to make it in this kind of business. That means that over the years, when you cut some of these guys loose or don't book them, it creates hard feelings.

That was a lesson Jerry Jarrett and I had learned the hard way about twenty years before when Jerry was doing the booking in Memphis for Nick Gulas and Roy Welch. One day, we're at the TV studio. Jerry and I were wrestling a

singles match when all hell broke loose. We had to get
the story later because at the time, we didn't have a clue
what was going on.

There was an older wrestler named Mario Galento.
He had long black hair and a mustache plus a reputation
as a mean guy. He only had vision in one eye. He'd been
a star in Memphis years before but he was by this time a
bitter old guy that people didn't use that much. And
Jerry wouldn't use him at all.

For the TV show, we dressed in the women's and men's
bathrooms and went out to wrestle. Without any warning,
here comes Mario Galento running out of the men's room,
across the studio, and he rolls into the ring. I knew there
were some hard feelings between this guy and Jerry, so this
was a shoot. This was legit. He thinks he's going to make a
name for himself running in on a live TV match and
attacking Jerry Jarrett, which is what he proceeded to do.

It looked really stupid, but I had to go help the guy
who'd just been my opponent two seconds before. I
pulled Galento off Jerry and Jerry started pummeling
him, punching and kicking him. We get him out of the
ring and he runs out of the studio. I had to try and fix the
fact that I'd just had to help Jerry Jarrett. So I jumped out
of the ring and went over to Lance Russell and grabbed
the microphone. I said, "Let that be a lesson to everybody. I don't need any help beating this punk. [Meaning
Jerry Jarrett.] This punk is mine, and nobody's going to
beat him up except me. Anyone with any other ideas,
you'll have to go through me first."

I went back into the ring and Jerry and I start up our
match again. We get ready for the finish because we want
to go find out what just happened. But before we could,
here comes Mario Galento running through the door
again. He'd gone back to the dressing room and into my
bag. Most guys would carry a gun in their bag in those
days but I never did. What I did have was a policeman's

nightstick or billy club. And here he comes back into the ring carrying it. He goes after Jerry Jarrett again and I grab his arm before he can hit Jerry. Jerry takes the billy club out of Galento's hand and WHAM! hits him right across the eye with it. He was split from his eye to his hairline and blood started spurting out all over the ring.

Mario Galento gets out of the ring again and heads for the exit but Jerry follows him and catches up. He hits Galento like he's banging in a nail. He was busted wide open and blood was everywhere. This was taking place on camera. I pulled Jerry back and the guy slumps down. By the time we finished our match, Mario Galento was on his way to a hospital.

Jerry finds the promoter Roy Welch and starts shouting at him. What the hell was that all about? Later, it turned out that Mario swore that Roy Welch, who was getting a little old for this, told him to jump into the ring to work an angle. But more than likely, it was just Galento trying to beat up Jerry Jarrett on live TV. Galento had to have a hundred thirty-five stitches and the word went out that he was going to kill me and Jerry Jarrett. He was saying he was just coming in to work an angle and these guys tried to put out the one good eye he had left.

About three months later, Jim White, Sam Bass, and I were booked in Batesville, Mississippi, a town about sixty-five miles from Memphis. We were in a little bitty dressing area. The door opened out and you could see the ring. Jim and I were in single matches, which was unusual, and I was due to wrestle some local kid. There was a guy called Dick West who used to work for Jerry Lee Lewis who was buddies with Erich Von Brauner who trained the guy I was wrestling. Dick West came into the dressing room and started to tell some tale. Anyway, he closed the door to get on with his story as I was going out to wrestle.

The local kid and I started our match. I do a couple of moves and this guy goes down. But rather than come back to lock up, he gets out of the ring. He stands down on the floor, looking back up at me. I remember walking over to the ropes above where he was standing and saying, "Come on, you punk, get back in the ring." As I'm looking down at him, all of a sudden, BAM! I feel something hit me on the side of my head. It almost knocked me over and I could tell I was busted open. I still have the scar. I turned and there was this guy with a big slapjack—a leather handle with two big pieces of metal sewn in. I was really woozy from being hit. I saw this guy, and then across the ring, I saw Mario Galento with his long black hair. He's crawling into the ring and he has a big, long straight razor. Open.

When I saw him and that razor, I was snapped back to reality pretty fast. As he came across the ring, I bailed out and grabbed a metal chair and threw it toward the ring where he was coming at me. I ran over to the exit and pulled the door open to where Sam and Jim were hanging out. "Freaking Mario Galento's out there with a straight razor!" Fortunately, Jim carried a gun, a big one like a .357 Magnum. He went to his bag and picked it up. Right then, Galento's coming through the door. Just in time, Jim raised his arm and pointed the gun right in Galento's face.

The Chief of Police and Sheriff of Batesville were all at the match. They see this stuff going on: razors and guns and the like. The local law enforcement comes over and someone says, "I don't know what's going on, but you're all under arrest." We all went down to the station. We told our side of the story and they let everybody go.

That was the last time I saw Mario Galento, but he was still going 'round saying he was going to get me and Jerry Jarrett. Jerry and his wife, Deborah, were living out in this big house in the country. They were pretty scared to walk past their windows at night. They didn't know what he was planning on doing.

But we never heard any more from him. When Jackie Fargo heard about it, he called Mario Galento. They had obviously worked together for years in Memphis. Jackie cussed the guy and said if he ever even looked at this kid again, meaning me, "I'll find you and I'll pull the one fucking eye you got left out of your head." At some point, Mario Galento moved out of the area and he died a few years back.

So I knew about hard feelings. I had the scar to prove it. And pretty much everyone who was in the World Wrestling Federation in 1992 had worked for me in Memphis at some point in time. A lot of these guys thought, "Ah, here's Lawler. He's back on our terms now. He's one of the boys." Well, what happened was, first week I get up to the World Wrestling Federation, some-one took a dump in my crown. It's not the straight razor, but it's still a rib with a lot of heat attached. I never even saw it. Jimmy Hart came to me and told me and I thought, well, I'm not even going to put it over. I'm not going to let them know I know, so I'm not going to go look. I left it right there for someone to take as a souvenir.

Next day, I went to Vince McMahon. I said, "Vince, I don't think my being here is going to work out." I told him what happened and said I didn't need that. There were obviously some hard feelings and I'd rather go back to what I was doing. Nobody ever crapped in my crown in Memphis. He said it would never happen again and promised he'd put a stop to it. I guess he put the word out because nothing like that ever did happen again.

Up here at the WWE, if you get cut it's like the end of the world because there's not really anywhere else to go. People have contracts, usually for three years. But you can wipe your rear end on contracts. They're made to be bro-ken. They're built with the WWE in mind. You can't get out of them so easily, but they can. They can fire anybody at any time for any reason. As I later found out myself.

chapter 26

I guess my whole life, I've been a huge mark for TV. When I was a kid, TV was the biggest thing in the world as far as I was concerned, and has been extremely influential. One of the main reasons I started to draw was a TV show called *Learn to Draw* with John Nagy. I'd watch that show and draw and draw and I found that I loved doing it. He made it look so easy. I remember he looked almost like a Beatnik with a little goatee. I finally got a John Nagy Learn to Draw kit and I learned more from that than from my two years at Memphis State.

There was also a show called *Winky Dink*. You could send off and get a piece of clear plastic that you were supposed to put over your TV screen. Then the idea was that you drew on that plastic. We couldn't afford to pay attention, much less buy a piece of plastic for me to draw on, so I drew right on the TV screen, which got me in trouble of course. I watched all kinds of shows, especially Saturday morning TV with the cartoons. Anytime they would show any monster movies, I loved that too. I only watched stuff like Andy Griffith later when it was in syndication. A lot of times, I was forced to watch shows that my parents wanted to see because we only had one TV. I hated Lawrence Welk and another one was *Sing Along with Mitch*. Good grief.

My dad loved *Maverick* and we'd watch that every week. There were two Mavericks. James Garner was the cool Maverick, Bret; then he had a brother Bart—Jack Kelly, who I couldn't stand. You didn't know from week to week who was going to be featured. I liked *Gunsmoke* and *The Lone Ranger* and everyone in our family loved *Amos 'n' Andy,* which was on TV for a couple of years after being a radio show forever. Probably my favorite shows were *Superman*, and then *Batman* when that came out. I was always fascinated with superheroes, probably because of the art in the comic books.

All this helped to explain why I thought it was so great when I first got to go on TV even though I was getting slaughtered every week as the job guy. Eventually, I got to be the featured wrestler in the area and I was on TV all the time, doing interviews and wrestling. When we were on Channel Thirteen, everything down at the Coliseum was shot on film, not videotape. The tape we ended up with was two inches wide and the cassettes were huge. They were also real expensive. We would tape our live shows and the next week, we'd just use the same tape. So we don't have copies of most of that stuff on Channel Thirteen. Wrestling nostalgia wasn't really a big deal until the eighties and nineties when the baby boomers grew up. We had no idea that a tape of a match from the seventies might be worth something one day.

One of the things that I was always known for in Memphis was my interviews. I was voted in different magazines as one of the top interviews in the business. When I started with the WWE as a wrestler, they were looking for commentators even then. Vince asked me about it. I told him I'd never done it and I didn't think I could. But Vince said he'd give me a segment of the show every week where I'd do an interview. That was the beginning of *The King's Court.*

During a commercial they would roll out a big red carpet in the ring and bring this huge throne out, together with some other royal paraphernalia. My music would play and I'd introduce *The King's Court*. I'd say that the peons in the crowd should be on their hands and knees kissing my royal feet. I'd bring out a wrestler and interview him. This was in 1993. Eventually, I was doing the *Court* rather than having a match. I'd have a match at house shows or a PPV but *King's Court* was my spot.

I was a heel interviewer. I'd get a good guy and insult the heck out of him and degrade the hicks and rednecks in the crowd and talk up a bad guy. I asked someone in Alabama if their mom and dad got divorced would they still be brother and sister. They were so dumb they thought the Gaza Strip was a topless club. I said I'd rather play naked Twister with the Golden Girls than live in Canada. I even wore a Baltimore Ravens jersey to *SummerSlam* in Cleveland in 1996, which was guaranteed to incite the Browns fans. (I really hated doing that.)

We had some celebrities on *The King's Court*. On one episode, I snatched poor Tiny Tim's ukelele and smashed it up. Tiny Tim was wearing a truly horrible

Tiny Tim

suit. He looked like an unmade bed. I asked him where he got it from, "Did the man at the carnival guess your weight wrong?"

Once I was told there was a guy out in the crowd who had his girlfriend with him. He wanted to propose to her on live TV. Not necessarily a good idea. She knew nothing about it. They get word back to Vince and he says, "Cool." He asked what I thought: what would be better, have the guy in the ring, or the girl in the ring? I said it would be much better to have the girl out there. It was very off-the-cuff and I was trying to think of some different things to make it fun.

I went out and said, "We have a very special occasion here tonight." We got the girl to come up to the ring. I said that her boyfriend had something he wanted to ask her. He said, "I want to ask you if you'll marry me." She was all, "Oh my gosh!" I said, "Don't answer yet, we're live on TV. Before you answer, I want to make sure you both know what you're doing here." I told the guy I didn't know how much he knew about the girl, but I'd heard some things. I started ripping off these one-liners. She's had more hands on her than a doorknob, she's been on more mens' laps than a napkin. This and that. She was humiliated. Then I turned and went after him. I said to the girl, look at his ex-girlfriend, she's been around more than a carousel. Anyway, she finally accepted, though she was nearly in tears. I told her now she'd said yes, she should remember a few things. Love your husband, respect your husband, but try to get everything in your name. I got backstage and everyone said they thought it was funny.

Next day, a lawyer came calling. The woman wanted to sue me. Whoops. She didn't do it in the end but we didn't do any more live-audience-participation things without getting a release first. Let this be a lesson to people. If the King wants to put you on live TV, run a mile. I'm sure this couple when they're old and gray will not be getting out a tape of how Grandpa proposed to Grandma on television.

I've insulted all sorts of people for the WWE. John Wayne Bobbitt. That was a classic. He was an easy target. He'd start to say something and I'd say, "Hold it, John, I don't want to cut you off, but let me say this." I was talking about TV clips and cutaways. And that I was glad they found what his wife had cut off and thrown out the window because I didn't want to see that on the side of a milk carton. Five minutes of that. He must have felt about one inch tall when he left, but he should be used to that.

At the time, there was just the one show, Monday night *Raw* on USA. Then there was another show on USA and Bobby Heenan was on that and Vince was doing the play-by-play. Vince had me come and be on to see what it was like. I'd never done it before but it was fun because Bobby was like me with the one-liners and funny stuff and he was the bad guy too. Bobby and I would tee off on Vince as he was trying to do the play-by-play. I told Vince he was so cheap he wouldn't tip a canoe. He'd given so many people a piece of his mind, he'd run out. I said he thought Snoop Doggy Dogg belongs to Charlie Brown.

For some reason, Vince wanted us to say that he wore a hairpiece. I have no idea why. Sometimes on camera he'd make sure he was caught trying to fix it. I'd say, "Vince, this one actually looks real, it's even got imitation dandruff. The last hairpiece, the chin strap was a dead giveaway." I said, "I knew Lee made press-on nails. I didn't know they made press-on hair." I ribbed Vince about people telling him how great he was. "His head was in danger of getting so big, his toupee wouldn't fit." During a match, Mankind pulled out some of his own locks and I said, "Look McMahon, there's some extra hair for your toupee." I said his toupee used to get up and move around on its own when the lights went down for a match.

Vince and I had fun together. He and I were talking about Sunny, who was at the time the most popular WWE Diva.

Lawler: "She once asked me out, McMahon."

McMahon: "She did, huh? Out to where?"

Lawler: "Well, I was in her room."

My opportunities increased after WCW took Bobby Heenan. WCW came about when Jim Crockett sold his promotions to Ted Turner's WTBS in 1988. WCW went out on cable; it was national and it became huge. I always thought the main difference between Vince and the WCW was that Vince is a master at creating talent and making it. No one at WCW ever had that knack like Vince does. They realized they had trouble creating stars so they thought they'd try to buy some. When guys' contracts would come up with Vince, WCW would offer an insane amount of money. They lured Bobby "the Brain" Heenan, the number one commentator; they lured "Mean" Gene Okerlund, who was a main-ring announcer. Hulk Hogan, Scott Hall, and Kevin Nash all took the big bucks. I never really blamed them, and later on it worked out better for me that they did.

I remember that Randy Savage took Heenan's place doing color. We were there all day preparing. WCW's show *Nitro* was on the same night but it came on an hour before *Raw*. Then our first hour went head-to-head with their second hour and then we were on for an hour on our own. It was a couple of hours before we went on and someone said, "Anyone seen Randy Savage?" They wanted to go over the show. I hadn't seen him. Vince hadn't seen him.

An hour before our show was starting, I hear someone finally found Randy. They ran over to Vince and said, "I know where Randy is, he's on *Nitro* right now." Savage had bolted to the competition, and that left no one to do the show but Vince and me. I don't think I ever got the chance to thank Randy for that.

From 1995 to 1997 Vince and I worked with Jim Ross and since 1997 it's been just J.R. and me. Now J.R. has a very big job with a lot of duties. He's in charge of talent relations, which means he's responsible for hiring and firing people. As far as the boys are concerned, he's a very powerful person. He books the live events, helps the TV production. He wears a lot more hats than just his Resistol cowboy hat.

J.R. is the best at what he does, the play-by-play. He's a fan and he has the bedrock wrestling knowledge. Maybe, if I really took a long time to prepare, I might be able to do it. But J.R. does play-by-play like I do color. It's natural to him. His sincerity makes you believe what he's telling you. We have a natural rapport that was there immediately. The chemistry worked right away and worked ever since. Most people will say that we might be the best broadcasting team there's ever been in wrestling. When I left for the nine months, no one fought harder to get me back than J.R. He quite frankly told me that he struggled without me. He said it was hard for him to get used to somebody else. J.R. and I don't have to work at it, but it was work for him to do it with anybody else. He has fun when we work together.

When they started the brand extension gimmick, Vince and the writers wanted the two shows to be as equal as possible. Their concern was that the show that has J.R. and the King will be viewed as the "A" show and the other will be the "B" show. They decided to split us up. Leave me and Michael Cole on *SmackDown!* and put somebody else with J.R. on *Raw*. J.R. lobbied against that. But they were going to do it anyway. Then TNN stepped in and said look, they'd lost The Rock. Don't take the King too. They basically demanded that J.R. and I stay together.

J.R. often tees it up for me to hit out. Often I'll ask him to say something to set me up and I won't say what the punch line is. I was dogging out Molly Holly one night and he said, "What is it with you, King? You don't like to watch Molly Holly wrestle?"

"No, I don't care about watching her wrestle, but I'd like to see her box!" J.R. said, real gnarly, "You'd like to see her box . . ." Then we were talking about Molly Holly again and J.R. and I were speculating about her waistline. "Maybe those are just love handles," says J.R. I said, "Love handles? I always thought a woman's love handles were her ears," and he said, "Her ears, listen to you."

There was a real exciting lingerie match between Terri and Trish on *Raw* from Dallas. The King was watching these two Divas go at each other. Terri, who was wearing a shoelace G-string and a tiny bra, put a couple of good moves on Trish. "Terri's showing a lot of confidence," says J.R. "Terri's showing a lot of everything," says the King, gratefully. It's always easy to get up for a match when the puppies are on display. At one climactic point, J.R. stood up and looked down at me and said, "Come on, stand up, King. Aren't you excited?" I said, "Oh, I'm excited. That's why I can't stand up!"

I hate to admit it, but I did not originate the term "puppies." It was a fumble I picked up and ran in for a touchdown. The ball was loose and I jammed it in with two hands. It was like I started calling myself the King, just by innocently saying. "You've been the King around here, I'm going to knock you off your throne." I picked it up and went with it and it worked.

I was doing commentary one night and I think Debra was valeting for Jeff Jarrett. She and Jeff had a confrontation in the ring one day with the Road Dogg, who had a feud going with Jeff Jarrett. In some kind of way, just in a quick interview, Road Dogg said to Debra, "Show me those puppies." He said it one time, but I picked up on it. "Yeah, show me those puppies!" That's how it started out. It's grown and grown. They have T-shirts saying, "Show Me Your Puppies" with little paw prints on them. Debra told me she was working with Jeff in 1998, so this was just 1999.

So what does the King appreciate in a woman? First and foremost, it's the puppies, of course. Jerry's a little different from the King in that regard. Jerry has always been a sucker for a pretty face. The puppies are not, if truth be told, the be-all and end-all for Jerry. I also love a nice little derriere. That's more of the end-all. The thing about the WWE is that all the Divas have a pretty face, but some of them have more powerful puppies than others.

But I have bought many sets of puppies. I've actually personally purchased seven puppies. What I mean by that is that I've paid for three-and-a-half boob jobs. One girl had enough money for half the operation and I gave her the rest. Later, she came to me and said, "You know, one of these belongs to you." The King is, of course, all about the puppies. Then Stacy Keibler came along with her long legs and the King became a leg man too. Reminds me of the old Rodney Dangerfield line. "I guess I'm an ass man because everywhere I go people say, 'Hey, you're an ass, man.'"

The strange thing about the commentating is that I'm not really that crazy about doing it. But it's always come easy for me. I somehow have a knack for saying what most of the male fans are thinking, and that seems to work. I don't put a great deal of effort into it but I can do it. I know in my mind what needs to be said to get the match over and to get the wrestlers over. I'm on television every week and I still am a big mark for TV. There are certainly much worse ways to make a living.

Of course I was also involved in the XFL deal in 2001. I think that if the powers that be in the entertainment world had left that alone and allowed Vince to do what he had envisioned, I still think it could have made it. It wasn't going to be a huge success the first season, but had it been given another season with Vince doing what he wanted to do, which was to add more entertainment surrounding the sport, I think it would have gone. It just needed some time to develop. The problem was, it was immediately compared with the NFL and described as being competitive with the NFL. That's never what was intended. It was supposed to be an alternative to the NFL. Dick Ebersol wanted the XFL to be the NFL for NBC. It had to be completely serious. But that wasn't what Vince wanted and Ebersol won out.

Vince McMahon admitted to Bob Costas in an HBO interview that he lost a lot of money on the XFL, in the order of tens of millions of dollars. But Vince said he was actually delivering the eighteen-to-thirty-four-year-old males that NBC and the advertisers were desperate to attract. I knew after the very first week that it wasn't going to fly. They said don't mention the cheerleaders,

Arnold Schwarzenegger and Michael Cole

don't shoot the cheerleaders. I realized then they were going to try to take on the NFL and that was never going to work. The football wasn't good enough.

I had all sorts of lines. Some I got to use; some I didn't. "When I'm around the cheerleaders, I like to use the terms 'tight end' and 'wide receiver.' We heard that the cheerleaders will be encouraged to date the players. I think cheerleaders dating the announcers should be mandatory." I poked little digs at the football. I said the players were paid so little I saw one guy putting a Big Mac on layaway. I said that some of the best players admitted they're only giving a hundred and nine percent. One I got in trouble for was "These guys have to stay in motels that not only leave the light on for you, they leave some hair in your shower and a little stain in the middle of your sheets."

I did one game in Memphis. First they teamed me with J.R. Then they moved him up with Jesse Ventura and I had Matt Vasgersian, who had been with the governor. Vince McMahon said they'd like to put Vasgersian with me and Jim Ross with Jesse because they weren't happy with the emotion those guys brought to the game. I think they felt that Matt could learn from me and they thought that Jim Ross would raise Jesse Ventura's enthusiasm level. I think the one they really wanted to move was Jesse Ventura, but they were paying him too much money.

The XFL always drew decent live gates but the TV ratings were bad. The games were fun and people had a good time. There were some good players who later got on NFL rosters. When the players started, they'd only had four weeks of practice and then they were thrown out there. And everyone was comparing them to NFL veterans who'd played together for years, and no one could understand why the play wasn't as good as the NFL. It was difficult to get anything going. The Memphis team was called the Maniax. There was a big protest from mental health groups about "Maniax," who said it was a bad connotation for people with mental illness. People in New York complained about the "Hitmen" name for their team because of the idea of organized crime.

I remember reading a review in *USA Today* that gave me an F for the commentary. The reviewer said, "Jerry Lawler reached an all-time low by saying we're in the land of milk and honeys." I called the *Commercial Appeal* in Memphis about that. They printed my comment. "If that guy thinks that was an all-time low," I said, "he doesn't know me very well."

27

I met Stacy Carter at my alma mater, Treadwell High School. I was on a field there with my softball team practicing for a Sunday afternoon game. One of the players on my team was dating Stacy's mother. Her family was originally from West Memphis, Arkansas. Stacy's parents had got divorced and her mother moved to Memphis. Stacy and her little brother and sister stayed with her father, who was a police-man. When she graduated from high school she moved over to Memphis to stay with her mother. I'd seen her mother, Cathy, a few times with this guy on my team, "Dink" Golden, but I didn't even know she had a daughter.

That day, we'd finished playing ball and we were walking off the field. Stacy was sitting there with her mother. She was two months away from turning nineteen. She was not a raving beauty, by any means. She was too young for that. She hadn't grown into her beauty yet. But I could see it. Stacy had an angelic little face. She seemed so innocent. I guess it was just one of those things. Paula and I had fallen into that situation where she wanted to have kids and we couldn't and it was really affecting her. I wasn't really out looking for anything. It was chance. It was a similar situation to when I'd met Paula. When somebody goes off from the arrangement they're in, they're usually not leaving something they're completely happy with. You're obviously not that content with what you have if you're willing to up and leave it.

I wouldn't say it was love at first sight, but there was definitely an infatuation at first sight. When I first met Stacy, I didn't give a thought of leaving Paula. I was thinking about a fling. Stacy's attention was flattering to me. In this business, you want to still prove that you appeal to as many people as you can. It felt good that I did appeal to her, especially as she didn't watch wrestling or even like it.

We would play a ball game out of town every week. A lot of the guys would bring wives or girlfriends, but Paula very seldom came with me. The next week, I said to Stacy that she should come with her mom to the ball game. We'd take about four cars and I'd have several of the guys ride with me. Once we played the ball game, I asked her to ride back with me. I let everybody off in Memphis and took her back to her mom's apartment. I asked her for a good-bye kiss, and it was on from there.

Passion in a relationship is an amazing thing. I don't even know how to describe it really. It's wonderful. It's kind of a mixture of the greatest pleasure you can imagine and the most intense pain you can feel. It hurts so bad to be away from that person for even a minute, but then it is the most wonderful feeling when you are with them. Stacy and I had a passionate relationship. I couldn't be around her enough. I wanted to be with her, in every sense of the word, every minute of the day.

Looking back, all of my relationships started out that way. But the reality of most—no, I think all—relationships is that passion is impossible to sustain forever. I know the passion went out of my relationship with my first wife Kay. I don't know how or why. It's not something you want to happen; it just happens. Certainly having babies so soon had a lot to do with that situation. It was very hard on Kay and I'm sure I wasn't as understanding as I could have been.

Paula was a different story. She and I had a very passionate relationship for many years. I just think that time took its toll on us. That and the fact that I guess I'm just a pretty lousy husband. When that passion starts to wane, somehow my eye starts to wander.

Paula was disappointed and sad, but we've stayed friends over the years. She is a great person and maybe more beautiful today than when I first met her. She waited for a few years before she married again. She bought two very nice houses, one in Germantown and the other in Cordova, Tennessee. Paula never had any kids but now she is married to a really nice guy named Larry and he has a son from a previous marriage. She was married briefly to a guy before Larry. I think she said his name was Satan. I see her from time to time and she is doing great. I'm glad that Paula's doing well and is happy because I've always had feelings of guilt about leaving her.

Stacy was working as a bank teller in Memphis when I met her. There was a guy named Mike George who had a photography studio. He was doing wrestling pictures for us. I helped Stacy get a job with him. Then she opened up her own hair salon for a time. After Paula and I split up, Stacy moved in.

I never even thought about involving Stacy in the WWE until all the Divas stuff started. In 1996–97 the girl thing was busting open and starting to get really hot. We were in a little rut in Memphis. It was very difficult to get any female talent down there but I thought it would be good to have a pretty face on the show in some capacity. I didn't have to look too far from home to find one of those.

I had to drag Stacy kicking and screaming to the television studio. She was begging me not to make her do it. When she first went out on TV she was crying, wiping away tears right as the camera went to her. She worked as a roving interviewer, like the sideline reporter at a football game. She was our Melissa Stark. Stacy was there when the show opened with Lance and Dave and she'd interview a couple of guys during the program. I think secretly she enjoyed it. She seemed a natural from day one. She appeared at ease on stage.

The first person Stacy interviewed was Jackie Fargo. She was going to do it over the phone with Jackie from his home in North Carolina. I called Jackie to ask him if it was okay for us to have an interview with him. He said, "Sure, son, who's doing it, Dave Brown?" When I told him about Stacy working the interview, there was a pause. Then he said, "You put Stacy in this business? You're making a big mistake. You're going to regret it." I said she'd be fine but Jackie didn't let up. He said it had nothing to do with Stacy being an interviewer, she could do that easy. But he said if I put Stacy in wrestling, "Mark my words . . . Maybe not right away, but eventually, you will lose her. She will leave you." I laughed, but Jackie was serious. He said if she gets into wrestling and finds she could make it without me, she'd leave.

As far as the WWE was concerned, never once did I use any influence or ask anybody to get Stacy a job or suggest to anybody that she should even be considered. The truth is that someone at the office saw her on the Memphis TV show. They were increasing their roster of Divas. Originally, they were hiring people just for their looks. There was one particular good-looking girl they used. They called everyone who was going to be involved in a certain match to a meeting to go over the finish. They told her that when her wrestler gets knocked out of the ring, she should get up on the apron and distract the referee. That would give her wrestler time to get some sort of foreign object. He can hit his opponent and you get down and the ref will turn 'round and count the guy out.

The match is live on *Raw* and it comes time for the finish. They knock the guy out of the ring and the girl never does anything. She just stands there. So the ref has to stand there too twiddling his thumbs and the whole thing is messed up. Meanwhile, Vince is blowing a gasket in the control room. After, he asks the girl what happened, why hadn't she got up on the apron like they told her to? She looked at Vince and said, "I don't know what the apron of the ring is." I understand that Vince asked why they were using girls who didn't have a clue about the wrestling business. They looked for girls who'd at least been around the ring a little. So they thought of Stacy. She's been with me for years so she'd at least know what the ring apron is. And so they called her. She was a natural.

Stacy's persona was basically left up to the creative types at the WWE. They went for a while without being able to figure what to do with her. She was Stacy and she was my valet. In 1999, Debra was valeting for Jeff Jarrett and they brought Stacy in to valet for Debra. That was when she was Miss Kitty. Then there was the deal where Chyna beat Jeff Jarrett at *No Mercy* in Cleveland for the Intercontinental championship as Jeff was on his way out of the WWE. Then Stacy became a sidekick for Chyna. She wore a black wig and was like a Mini-Me for Chyna. She wore the same outfit as Chyna every night. There was Chyna, and there was Chynette.

Then Stacy started going in some matches. In the most famous one, *Armageddon* in Fort Lauderdale in 1999, she was in an evening gown match in a swimming pool with Ivory, Jacqueline, and B.B. It was almost like a Battle Royal. When the girl was stripped down to her bra and panties, she was eliminated. The last person left would win the WWE women's championship. Now the truth of the matter was that Stacy didn't wear any underwear. That got around and they made an angle out of it. Actually, that was what first caught my eye about Stacy when I saw her at that ball game in Memphis. I realized she wasn't wearing any underwear. I knew she was a girl after my own heart because I've never worn any underwear either.

In the buildup for this match at *Armageddon,* they interviewed Stacy on TV. They told her that someone was eliminated when they were stripped down to their bra and panties and Stacy told Chyna, "I can't be in that match." "Why not?" She said, "I don't wear any underwear." And that was the end of the spot. They built the whole match up on that.

Of course, they can't show any nudity on a Pay-Per-View broadcast. What they decided to do was to have Stacy be the last one left so she wouldn't have to strip down to nothing. But she said, "If I get stripped down, I get stripped down. But I don't wear underwear . . ." The idea was that she'd be the last one left and they'd tear off her dress, and she would actually be wearing a bra and panties. I thought that was a bad idea and I said as much. It would have killed the angle. Why after all this buildup would you make a liar out of Stacy? To me, that would put tremendous heat on everybody. People are going to be mad and upset. Why even bother to promise something like that if you're not going to hand it to them.

I suggested something different. Stacy wins and she's in her bra and panties. She takes the mike and says, "They made me wear a bra and panties for this match. The WWE made me put underwear on. But now the match is over. And I'm not wearing these anymore." Sergeant Slaughter would be standing right there with a towel. Stacy would turn her back to the crowd and undo her bra. Just as she's fixing to turn around, Sergeant Slaughter would put the towel 'round her. It would save face for everyone. Stacy would try to show her puppies but she wouldn't be able to. Then she could start a campaign: "The Right to Nudity!" Another campaign, "The Right to Censor," said that this kind of thing was the downfall of civilization and so on.

The powers that be finally agreed that it would work. Somewhere, there was a miscommunication. Someone forgot to figure out which camera angle to use. There are cameras everywhere at WWE events so this would have to be handled carefully. When Stacy pulled her bra off, obviously the camera behind her was supposed to be running. Instead the camera right in front of Stacy was on. So there on live TV, BOOM! Topless! Puppies! This was the first nudity on the WWE. It was huge news and caused a lot of problems. If you're planning to do something like that, you have to let the FCC or someone know because it's a different rating. It was an honest mistake, but the WWE had to explain to the cable companies that this wasn't in the script and it wasn't supposed to have happened.

Of course the fans had no problem with it at all. It was tremendous publicity and I think it helped sell a lot of Pay-Per-Views. We did a PPV in London where they asked if Stacy would mind having her top come off. There was an arm-wrestling match that I refereed between Stacy and Terri Runnels and they both just had bikinis on. They looked fantastic. I refereed the match. I kept stalling, saying I had to check them over, and I was rubbing Stacy's leg. Terri said I had to check Stacy because she had some sort of oily substance on her, something slick, so I rubbed her legs again. "No, feels fine." That kept happening.

Moolah and Mae Young were in the corners and when Terri just about had Stacy's arm down, Moolah took a big glass of water and spat it in Terri's eyes. So Stacy won. She stood with her arms raised and Terri came up behind her. Stacy's bikini top had a bow in it and Terri undid it. More puppies! I had to go over and reach around and cover her puppies with my hands. People went crazy.

She did it that time and also in a pudding match. Stacy did a bunch of stuff up to the time she got fired. By 2000, she was The Kat, which meant she could have a "kat fight" with Terri at *WrestleMania* in Anaheim, with Val Venis as the referee.

chapter 28

The WWE did a lot more of this overtly sexy stuff as time went on. The King says there's nothing wrong with sex on TV . . . unless you fall off. They also pushed the envelope a bit as far as language was concerned and recently they went the kind of *Fear Factor* route when they had Tommy Dreamer eating his own hair and drinking out of a urinal and stuff like that. Since I've been up there, I've been involved in some crazy angles. As far as I'm concerned, there's not much that's off-limits. You can say pretty much anything on *Raw*, especially in the second hour, except for certain words, of course.

I do have to say that I am not a huge fan of having women wrestle in the WWE as it's set up today. I am, of course, a huge fan of women and I am a huge fan of the WWE Divas. The King is their biggest supporter. I guess Vince Russo, the former writer, was the champion of bringing more sex into the show when he was with the WWE the first time. Vince McMahon is game for anything, so they added more and it worked. He also went for more bad language but that loses its shock value the second it is overused, which it was. First, Stone Cold Steve Austin was allowed to cuss. That was his character. Then, some of the other wrestlers went into business for themselves, thinking, "If it works for Steve Austin, it'll work for me." Next thing you know, everybody was cussing all over the broadcast. Vince had to actually send out word: nobody cusses, except Stone Cold. That may seem like preferential treatment, but it was also good business. If one person does something, that makes them unique; if everyone starts doing it, there's nothing special about it.

Back to the Divas. Bring 'em on. But as far as the Divas' wrestling is concerned, I don't like it so much. Like the King, I appreciate a lovely woman. I love to see them and I love to see them up close, scantily clad, walking up to the ring. It's a real turn-on for me and I'm sure it is for most of those eighteen- to thirty-four-year-old guys the advertisers want to be watching. But once they get into the ring and start wrestling, I think it's a big turnoff. At a show, the crowd will be chanting for puppies and then the women start beating each other up.

Most of them are hired because of their bodies, their looks, their charisma and personalities. And they have

Two of my favorite Divas, Trish and Terri.

One of those days I would've paid Vince to work.

all of that in abundance. I guess they figure they can
teach them the wrestling later if they need to. Fit Finley
works with the girls almost daily. They're excited to learn
wrestling moves. Trish Stratus is a perfect example.
When she first started with the WWE, she didn't know a
wristlock from a wristwatch. Now she adds one new

Torie Wilson and Stacy Keibler, oh yeah, and Chuck and Billy.

move every match she has and she's got a pretty good repertoire now. She names the moves too. The Chick Kick. The Stratusfaction. But the King gets all the Stratusfaction he needs watching Trish in a swimsuit, not getting thrown 'round the ring.

Originally, women wrestlers were wrestlers who happened to be women. They didn't look like Divas. My first encounter with women wrestlers was one of the more embarrassing episodes of my career. Soon after I started working for Nick Gulas and Roy Welch, Jackie Fargo set up the match with Cora Combs and Sarah Lee. I mentioned before I'd never been in a mixed tag match. I rode into town, Kennett, Missouri, with Jackie. All the way up there from Memphis, he was saying, "Man, Cora Combs and Sarah Lee; they're two of the wildest women I've ever met in my life. Be careful." I was extremely green. I'd been brought up to respect women, but Jackie told them I was scared to death and that they should really have some fun with me.

I went into the dressing room with Jackie and he said, "Where are you going?" I said, "To the dressing room." He said, "No, no. When you're in a mixed tag match, you dress with the women. You've got to come out of the same dressing room as your partner." I said I couldn't do that, but he said I had to. I think they were already dressed, thank God, but they were in there. It was a small officer's room in the National Guard Armory. I was looking around, wondering where I was going to put my tights on. We were the second match and I didn't have that long. Surely they were going to go out and let me get dressed . . . They never did. They just sat there.

Finally they asked me when I was going to get dressed. I said I was waiting for them to leave and they said they couldn't go out where all the people were. "Just go ahead and get dressed. It's not like we haven't seen it before."

"Well, you never seen *me* before."

"Seen one, seen 'em all. Or are you different? You hung like a hamster? Couldn't break a Cheerio with it? Go on, we won't laugh." I took my shirt off, my shoes off, my socks. They finally said they'd turn their backs. I got my tights on in record time.

Then they wanted to go over the match. We'd start with the guys. Then he'd go and tag Sarah Lee. "You go to tag Cora, and Sarah'll come up and pull your tights down. She'll cover you up with her hands, don't worry," Jackie said with a straight face. "Later in the match, the guy'll bodyslam you and Sarah'll come and sit on your face." I said, "Sit on my face?" "Yeah. Great high spot. People'll go crazy."

I was just a rookie so I didn't think of saying no. So I went out and thought they were going to abuse me but we just had the match without any of that kind of stuff. After, they thought it was the funniest thing. That was one more step in the learning process. I've pulled that same rib myself I don't know how many times since. I spoke with Jackie Fargo about that night recently and he remembered it a bit differently. He swears he saw Sarah Lee sit on my face.

Some of the best, most fun stuff I did in WWE concerned Moolah and Mae Young, who were of a similar vintage to Cora and Sarah. The Fabulous Moolah first won the women's title in the fifties. Mae Young was riding with me one night not too long ago. We were going across the bridge to Jonesboro, Arkansas, to work a show there. She looked over at the Peabody Hotel and said, "I wrestled in Memphis and was staying at the Peabody Hotel the night World War II broke out." I almost swerved off the road when I heard that. She said her goal was to wrestle on her hundredth birthday. She's well over eighty now and I'll bet she makes it.

Before the WWE stuff, Moolah and Mae Young were living in North Carolina and they weren't doing much in the business. Moolah had a training camp for girl wrestlers but that had tapered off a bit. We were running an angle in Memphis in which I was working against Shawn Stasiak. I had a friend named Terri Filipetti who worked in production at the WWE. She had confided in me that she would love to do something on camera, but she didn't have the nerve to say anything to anyone.

She's a very pretty girl with a great personality and she's not married. Stacy and I were living together, but when I was on the road, Terri and I would travel together. We had some things in common and we were both only on the road two days a week with the TV people. The main thing was she was originally from Cleveland. She was a big sports fan, Indians and Browns; she played softball and volleyball. I secretly wanted to play ball with her myself.

I asked Terri, what if I worked you into our program down in Memphis? Would you come down there and do some stuff? I said that someone at WWE watches our show every week and they know what we're doing. They take ideas from what we do. She said she'd love to. I'd just started using Stacy as my valet. We had Shawn Stasiak get infatuated with Stacy. He was doing everything he could to win her affection. I told Terri we'd bring her in as Stasiak's sister. Shawn had got Stacy in the ring and out comes Terri and we introduce her as Stasiak's sister. She dogged the South and said Stacy was trailer trash and so on. Everyone started booing. I came out and confronted her and she was belligerent back.

My little program I laid out was that I would say in response that down in the South we pride ourselves on being southern gentlemen. I grabbed her and kissed her. She fought at first and then stopped fighting and then her arms go around me and she's into it. So Stacy's looking on and Shawn Stasiak tries to grab her and Stacy gets hold of Terri and they get into a big catfight. We make the match: me and Stacy against Shawn Stasiak and Terri. It went really well. As a matter of fact, Stacy accused me of coming up with the scenario just so I could kiss Terri. Guilty as charged.

Terri loved the deal. She planned to come back the next week. But in the middle of the week, she phones me and says that Shane McMahon called her in. She said that I was right, they do watch the TV up at WWE HQ. Shane said that she couldn't go down there and do that. They didn't want her in front of the camera. Terri said Shane mentioned something about insurance.

That was that, but we had the match booked. This was the big angle, the main event. We couldn't just throw another girl in there, saying Shawn Stasiak had another sister. Everyone knew that Shawn's father Stan had passed away. He was WWE World Champion at one time. I was thinking, I'm not going to be able to bring his sister in, but what if we brought his mother in. I thought of Moolah, but everyone would know her. I called Moolah and told her I needed someone to be Shawn Stasiak's mother. She said Mae Young would be perfect.

Mae Young comes to our TV the next Saturday morning and Shawn Stasiak comes out and says, "Now you've done it. My sister blabbed the whole thing to my mom and, I'm just going to let her tell you herself. Ladies and gentlemen, my mom." Out comes this old lady looking like a mummy. She got real animated like an old crow. It was a great promo. "Son, I didn't raise you to associate with this kind of trash. These people down here are hillbillies and bumpkins. That Stacy wears a potato sack for a dress." Stacy said, "Hold it, I've had all I'm going to take from you, you blue-haired old bat." Mae Young said "Whaaat!" and she jumped on Stacy. They had a big catfight, Stacy and this eighty-year-old woman. People were going crazy in the studio. The director said it was the funniest, most entertaining show he'd ever seen.

So the tag match was me and Stacy against Shawn Stasiak and Mae Young. It was a classic. Eighty-year-old Mae Young took all kinds of bumps and she looked like she was dying. This went over so well, the WWE called

Moolah and Mae Young and asked them to come up. They put them out and I got to do every ancient old-people joke under the sun. They were the waitresses at the Last Supper. When God said, "Let there be light," Mae Young threw the switch. Mae Young is so old, Joseph and Mary were voted cutest couple at her prom. Moolah's birth certificate was in hieroglyphics. The last time Moolah and Mae went on a double date, it was with Fred Flintstone and Barney Rubble. We had a long run with them. They loved it and thanked me and said it revived their careers. They were just at *WrestleMania X8* in 2002 signing autographs.

Mae Young had a thing on the show when she got pregnant with Mark Henry's baby at eighty. Mark Henry, the Olympic weight lifter, was in love with her. They came out in the ring and were all lovey-dovey and I said, "This all started with a game of spin the bottle of Mylanta." They were going to have her give birth to a hot-water bottle. There'd be doctors going, "Push, push, breathe, breathe," and the hot-water bottle would come out. And she'd say, "I was wondering where that went."

At the production meeting that morning, Vince was going over that part of the show, but he said Mae Young was going to give birth to a douche bag and all the women in the room were offended. They said it was going to turn off all the women watching. They talked him out of it, even though no one was going to say "douche bag" on the air. They sat there and wondered what she could give birth to. Somehow, someone came up with an idea that I think was one of the worst they've ever had and just didn't make any sense. So on the air, she gave birth to a hand, a big old rubber hand. Everybody said, "A hand?" And, boom, they cut to something else. The only thing I could think to come up with was "Hey J.R., I think that hand was wearing an Oklahoma class ring."

They put Mae Young into a wheelchair and had the Dudleys power-bomb her off the stage, through a table. She was absolutely indestructible. Like the Terminator, you couldn't kill her. And I think they really tried.

We had a bikini contest—"Miss *Royal Rumble*" in Madison Square Garden. I was the emcee and a judge. The Divas came out in robes. They dropped the robes and paraded around the ring in their bikinis. I talked about each of the girls and how great they looked. I made a bubble-wrap bathing suit for Stacy for that. I bought bubble wrap and used a bikini as a pattern and cut out shapes. When we told Vince, he said, "Er, I better see that first." We took the first version in to Vince. It was great, but you could see right through it. Vince said we better put another layer of bubble wrap on it. We wound up having to triple the bubble wrap, which cut down the effect somewhat, but it still got over.

I said it was up to the judges to decide who would be "Miss *Royal Rumble*" when Mae Young's music started. "Wait a minute," I said. "There's one more contestant." Mae Young came on in a robe, which she drops. She was in an old one-piece. I'm going, "Oh, no, Mae, please, get out of here." Then they started playing "The Stripper." The crowd's growing wild and she's acting like she's going to take her bathing suit off. "Please no, don't."

They had made these fake latex boobs, long and wrinkled and hanging down. They got the idea from the wrinkly woman in *There's Something About Mary*. It looked very realistic. She takes her suit down and 17,000 people went nuts. I acted like I'd fainted. Mark Henry came out and put a towel 'round Mae and took her back inside. Mae and Moolah were a lot of fun to work with. If Mae Young does wrestle on her hundredth birthday, I want to be commentating on the match.

I also enjoyed myself in the long feud I had with Bret Hart. As I mentioned, they had a *King of the Ring* tournament as soon as I got to the WWE. Of course, my point was that there was only one *King of the Ring*, namely myself. You could have any sort of tournament you wanted and that wouldn't change. Whoever had the audacity to call themselves *King of the Ring* would have to face the wrath of the real King. I promised I'd be there to crown the fake king. They had a big throne set up, a magnificent crown and scepter and a robe. Bret Hart won and as he ascended the podium and was getting ready to be crowned, I came out and attacked. I hit him on the head with the scepter, ripped his robe off, smashed the throne on him, and stomped on his crown. Well, actually, my crown. Since it was my idea to destroy the set, I volunteered one of my crowns to get stomped.

On *The King's Corner*, I was always telling people to kiss my royal feet and Bret Hart and I set up a "Kiss My Foot" match for the old Spectrum in Philadelphia in 1995. The match wouldn't end until one guy was made to kiss his opponent's feet. We built that up for weeks. I went out to this place in Toronto called Medieval Times. It was perfect for my gimmick. The place looked like a castle, complete with knights and horses and stables and

all. We told the fans that it was actually my home.

I did a series of interviews about how I was getting ready for this match while Hart was in the gym. I said, "You see these horses? You see these stables, you see these stalls? Cameraman, zoom in on this." We didn't have real horse manure, but it looked very authentic and I was walking in it barefoot. I sat down and put my feet up to the camera. I said, "I'm not going to wash my feet. I'm not going to bathe between now and the time we have that match, Bret Hart. I want my feet to be rancid. I want there to be calluses, corns, every foot rot there is. That's what you deserve to kiss."

The mark of a good worker is to convincingly say he's going to do something when in reality he knows he's not going to have to do it. I knew Bret Hart wasn't going to kiss my feet. I knew I was going to have to kiss his, and I wondered how we were going to do that.

We had the match. I came out and got the upper hand. While he was down I pulled my boot off and there was this horrible-looking sock on. I cut holes in it and spray-painted it brown and green to make it look old and filthy. I pulled it off and Vince McMahon, who was doing commentary, said, "The stench is horrible. It's putrid." He acted like he was going to throw up. I was about to put my foot in Bret's face when he grabbed my ankle and flipped me on my back. Bret then beat me down and got me in the sharpshooter. I was knocked out. He took his boot off and stuck his toes into my mouth. I don't remember them having any particular taste. He took his foot out, but he realized I hadn't woken up. He grabbed me and held me up and stuck my own foot into my mouth. He won the match.

I went into the back and they sent word back that Vince loved it. He wanted me to go to the bathroom. They were going to do an interview with Bret and then

they wanted to get a shot of me about to be sick. I always wanted to go a bit further. I jammed a load of crackers into my mouth and drank a big slug of Coke. All I was supposed to do was look like I was going to be sick. They said they were coming to me, "three, two, one." And I went BLURRGGGHHH all over the mirror and everywhere. It looked extremely realistic. They all thought I really vomited on live TV.

Then I said that the whole ordeal affected me so
much I had to go to my dentist to have some work done
on my mouth. We introduced a new character, Dr. Isaac
Yankem, who was my personal dentist. It was a classic.
Isaac Yankem is Glenn Jacobs, who is now Kane. He was
real big with a dental smock and a metal disk on his
head. They made up his teeth to be rotten. When I introduced him, I said Isaac Yankem is so tough, he could
floss his teeth with barbed wire. I said here is a man who
is so dedicated to his profession that he has let his own
teeth become an example of what can happen to you
children if you don't practice good dental hygiene. He is
a living, walking, breathing example of terrible dental
hygiene.

We told the good doctor about Bret Hart and what he
did. They rented a dental office and filmed Dr. Yankem
pulling some kid's teeth, with no Novocain or anything.
We wound up wrestling Bret Hart in a PPV match.
During that match I was put into a cage that was lifted
and suspended twenty feet over the stage. They put a
microphone into the cage and I had an earpiece listening
to Vince McMahon doing the commentary. For a long
time the WWE was aiming its programming toward
younger viewers. They had to be very careful what they
showed. For a long time they would never show blood.

For about fifteen years I've had a deviated septum,
probably from a hit I took at some time or another. I've no
idea which, because I've never had a broken nose.
Anyway, on one side the nasal passage is much narrower
than the other. I'd have some trouble with breathing so I'd
use a nasal spray. It's strong stuff and when it wears off,
the membranes over a period of time swell a little. You
feel like you have to use it to open the passage up. The
doctor said I could go and have the surgery done. Robert
Reed had it done last year and apparently it's painful.
They break your nose and reset it and I never wanted to

Dr. Yankem

do it. I get a scab on the inside of the nasal passage and sometimes it feels like it's closing up. It feels like it's huge but when I pick it out it's tiny. When I do that, it bleeds for a few minutes. It's been that way for fifteen years.

My mind was working. While I was up there in the

cage, I'm screaming to Vince, "Don't raise me up, I'm scared of heights." I reached up and got my finger up there and picked the scab. Blood started trickling over my lip and down my chin. I said, "Vince, I can't stand heights, I've got a nosebleed." The camera gets a close-up of the blood. Apparently that was the first time there was blood on WWE since it was on national network TV. Vince didn't know how it happened. You could hear his voice change, "King, you're alright. You're alright King, you'll be okay. Don't worry, we'll get you down." After the match, I didn't tell anyone the whole story. Everyone thought my nose started bleeding from the height. It was a huge deal to have the blood back on the TV and soon after that they started letting guys bleed again.

After that we had another great run with Bret bringing his parents, Stu and Helen Hart, to *Raw*. Helen Hart died in November 2001 and Stu must be nearly ninety. But on this occasion, they were sitting up in the balcony. Bret was wrestling Bam Bam Bigelow in the ring and I made my way up the balcony and started interviewing the Harts. The commentary was going out to the crowd. I was doing all the old jokes. "Hey, Stu, I heard you wrestled when the Dead Sea was only sick. I heard Stu goes to the dentist twice a year. Once for each tooth. Stu and Helen never miss any big fights. They still got their ticket stubs from the David versus Goliath. They were nudists once, until they got thrown out of the Garden of Eden. They visited an antique store and the store kept them." And so on. They were great sports.

Bret Hart forgets about who he's wrestling. He wants to get up there and get at me. We had a long run following the insults of his parents. We had another match he was going to dedicate to his mother. I said, "Don't think I don't have feelings, don't think that I'm not a proud son. I'm going to dedicate this match to my mother too. I'm going to have my mother at ringside too. As a matter of fact, I want to introduce my mother right now." They open up the curtains and there comes this beautiful twenty-five-year-old model. She comes down and I say, "Hi, Mom." We added all sorts of spice-ups like that to the angles.

Perhaps the hands-down worst taste event I was involved in was the mauling of Mad Dog Vachon in Omaha, Nebraska, in 1996 that Diesel and Shawn Michaels were also part of. Mad Dog Vachon had been a big draw for Verne Gagne in the AWA in the Minneapolis area. I knew that Mad Dog had lost his leg when he was hit by a car after he finished wrestling, so he wore an artificial one. We were doing a show and they planned to honor Mad Dog in Omaha, which was his hometown. They were going to give him a plaque or something.

J.R. and I were doing the commentary on the cere-mony. Vince McMahon loves to rib and I'm sure Vince thinks they're hilarious but some of them are pretty mean-spirited. Whenever we go to J.R.'s home state of Oklahoma—J.R.'s real proud and he plays the Sooners fight song—Vince will invariably think of something to humiliate J.R. Last time we were there, Vince made J.R. kiss his bare butt right in the ring. One time he made Pat Patterson, the longtime WWE agent, get his pants pulled off and be shown wearing underwear with a huge skid mark on national TV. Anything to really humiliate you.

I like to take a page out of Vince's book every now and then when it comes to J.R. I have a whole sheet full of Oklahoma/country lines to use. I've said that Jim Ross was the best commentator in the country. Too bad he came to the city. I say, do directions to your house include, "Turn off paved road?" Is it hot down in your neck of the woods? I'll bet you have to feed your chick-ens ice to keep them from laying hard-boiled eggs. I'll bet your cows are giving evaporated milk . . . and so on.

Back in Omaha, Mad Dog and the other wrestler were in the ring about to get their honor. Vince will often sit at the gorilla position—the backstage area that is the control center for what goes on in the ring—and talk into our earpieces. He'll remind J.R. and me of stuff to say or suggest things. That night I hear, "King, this is Vince, can you hear me?" I couldn't say anything because we were on the air so I look into the little camera that's on us and I nod my head slightly so he could see it on his monitor. And Vince says, "I want you to go in the ring. I want you to grab Mad Dog. I want you to knock him down and pull his artificial leg off." I look into the camera and shake my head from side to side with my eyes open, imploring, as if to say, "Don't make me do that." And he says, "Yes, yes. Go do it, go do it." So what're you gonna do?

I'm on the headset and I'd been playing the heel. I'd said stuff to J.R., "You know, I've had about as much of this as I can take." I'd been knocking Mad Dog anyway. "This is a wrestling show. We don't have time for these old dinosaurs being trotted out to get some plaque. Who cares? And who ever heard of Mad Dog Vachon any-

way?" That kind of shtick. Then Vince tells me to go out there. "I've had it with this," I said, and I take off my headset and head for the ring.

Of course, none of the people in the ring knows that this is a work. I get in there and I shove Mad Dog up against the ropes. I immediately feel sorry for him because he has to grab hold of the ropes to stop himself from falling down. I reach down and under his pants leg and start yanking. But I feel hair and I realize I'm pulling on the wrong leg. I hate it when that happens. So I go for the other leg and pull and it pops off like a plunger. I hold it up like the Stanley Cup and throw it down, cheering.

Poor old Mad Dog has no idea what is going on and the crowd is a bit perplexed too. Funny way to show your appreciation to a guy. I go back to the commentary position and put the headset on and Vince is laughing hard. J.R. says to me, "King, what's with you? That's disgusting." I say, "I don't care. He can't sue me, he doesn't have a leg to stand on." Then Vince says, "King, King, go back and get the leg and hit him over the head with it." I shook my head again and he says, "Yes, yes, do it, do it. Hit him with his own leg."

So I say to J.R., "You know, I'm not through with this idiot." Off comes the headset again, back I go into the ring. I grab the leg and start to swing it at him. I think I hit him with it. He's covering up and someone takes the leg away from me. I jump out, go back to the table thinking sure this is over with. J.R. is even more outraged. "You are deplorable. I can't believe you'd do something like that." Meanwhile Vince is dying. "King! You gotta go back up there! Beat him up!"

So I have to go back. "J.R., I'm not done. Watch this." In I go again, but by this point, Mad Dog is hot. It's like he's being humiliated. So as I went to get the leg, he hit me so hard on the head with it that I saw stars. It felt like it was made out of concrete. Now Mad Dog is swinging his leg like he's Sammy Sosa and the crowd's going wild. I go back to the desk and look at the camera. Nuh-huh. That's it. Vince was rolling on the floor. The rib turned out to be as much on me as on Mad Dog. After the show, he went and smartened Mad Dog up to it and told him what we'd done. He thought it was a great rib and Mad Dog laughed, but I know it embarrassed him and hurt his feelings. But what could he do, so he went along with it. I didn't come around to see Mad Dog afterward, but at least Vince told him he'd sent me in to do what I did.

chapter 29

In 1996, we stopped wrestling at the Mid-South Coliseum. We were the last weekly tenant there. We were the last main tenant period. In our twenty-two years in the place, we'd dealt with four managers and never had a problem with any of them. Except the last one. Beth Wade. She came in when we were right in the middle of a promotion with a guy named the Snowman. He was an outsider who wanted in. He asked for a match and we wouldn't give him one and he'd then gone all around town telling people that we wouldn't use him because he was black. It was nothing to do with that. We just didn't think he was a very good wrestler. He was out there though, in the neighborhoods, talking it up. You'd hear people say, "Hey, Snowman challenged you, why won't you let him wrestle?"

Finally I called him. "You've been saying you want to work with us. I'm going to give you a shot." He said great. I said the way we'd do it was to make it look like he still didn't work for us. I wanted him to bust in on the TV show and then bust in on the matches at the Coliseum too. I said don't use the dressing room or anything. Just disrupt the show. It worked. People really bought it and believed he was breaking into a show. Unfortunately, Beth Wade had just started that week. She'd come from Kalamazoo, Michigan.

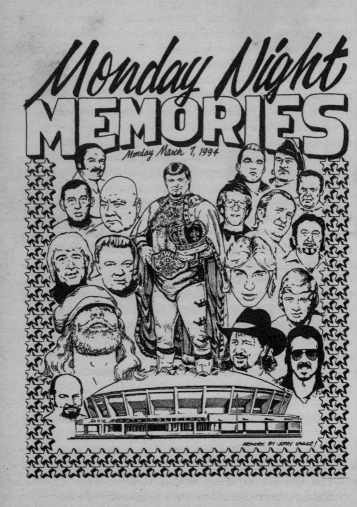

Monday Night
MEMORIES

Monday March 7, 1994

ARTWORK BY JERRY LAWLER!

It was always an unwritten rule to avoid any kind of racial situation, especially in Memphis where over half our audience was black. But with the Snowman, I decided to intentionally capitalize on that. Snowman was well-known in the black neighborhoods and that's where he pled his case. So when Snowman came through the crowd with no security, his entourage grew as he came toward the ring. He came up and threatened me near the ring. It was very realistic. I think that scared Beth Wade as she envisioned some sort of nasty racial situation. Even though there was no trouble, we felt she set out to get us out of there. It appeared to us that rent increases and security raises and larger parking fees were added to price us right out of there.

We wrestled at the Mid-South Coliseum for twenty-two years. A sellout there was 11,500 and over the years, we probably averaged around six or seven thousand fans each week. That's amazing—twenty-four, twenty-five thousand people a month. New York City didn't draw that many people when they had wrestling at Madison Square Garden once a month. So Memphis became known as the wrestling capital of the country. It could outdraw any other city, admittedly because most cities didn't promote on a weekly basis. But it still maintained its ability to draw fans every week.

In the program for the last night's matches, we printed a tribute to the place:

Mid-South Coliseum June 19, 1971–June 17, 1996

Tonight marks the end of an era. . . . The last USWA wrestling matches to be presented at the Mid-South Coliseum. Starting Monday, July 1, the matches will move to the 200,000-square-foot building known as "The Big One" located at Hollywood and I-240. Wrestling first moved to the Coliseum nearly twenty years ago to the day, June 19, 1971, from the old Ellis Auditorium downtown. During that span Monday Night Wrestling enjoyed success like no other wrestling in any other city and like no other sport in Memphis. During the late 70s and early 80s, crowds for Monday Night Wrestling averaged more than 8,000 fans a week. With the influx of cable TV and the overexposure of wrestling shows in the late 80s, crowds dropped to around 4,000 a week. In the last few years a hockey team moved into the Coliseum and that led to ice being left on the floor for nearly a four-month period and the wrestling fans having to view the matches through Plexiglas barriers that were not taken down after hockey games, and more stringent security that included frisking fans with metal detectors. Subsequently, promoters decided to look for a more "fan friendly" facility and now they have found one. So tonight will be the last time USWA wrestlers like Jeff Jarrett, Brian Christopher, the Moondogs, Tommy Rich, and Doug Gilbert will walk down the aisle and climb into the Coliseum ring. It will bring back memories of all the great wrestling stars that have passed through Memphis or even started their careers here. . . . Like the Fabulous Ones, Jackie Fargo, Sputnik Monroe, the Road Warriors, Jimmy Hart, Ultimate Warrior, Undertaker, and the list goes on and on and on. But of all the great stars to ever grace the Coliseum, tonight will mean the most to Jerry "the King" Lawler. . . . The King has spent his entire career wrestling almost every single Monday night at the Coliseum. More people have come to see the King at the Coliseum than any other entertainer or sporting event in the Coliseum's history. He still holds the consecutive sellout record at the Coliseum and at times the Coliseum has been referred to as "The House That Lawler Built."

"I'm sad to see the Coliseum go," Lawler said, "But it's the fans that make Monday Night Wrestling, not the building, so I'm glad to see that we are moving to a place that will be better for the fans!"

The last card at the Mid-South Coliseum had at the top,

Jeff Jarrett w/Frank Morrell vs.
"Too Sexy" Brian Christopher.

Jerry Lawler w/Scott Bowden vs.
Cyber Punk, Fire w/Lance Russell

If you look closely, the opening match was,
Flex Kavana & Bart Sawyer vs.
The Punisher & Tony Falk.

In case you don't know your recent wrestling history, Flex Kavana was what The Rock called himself before he called himself The Rock.

The Rock was one of the many, many great wrestlers who came through the Mid-South Coliseum on their way to fame and riches with the WWE. I remember working with Rock's father, Rocky Johnson. We bought Rocky into Memphis. In 1976, Muhammad Ali had fought Paula's friend Antonio Inoki in a big crossover promotion. They fought in Japan and at Shea Stadium. Chuck Wepner fought Andre the Giant and they broadcast it live on

Last meet at the Mid-South.

closed-circuit TV. These were big boxing versus wrestling extravaganzas. For his bout, Ali cut a lot of promos saying how boxers were superior to wrestlers. He was going to prove it to the world. There's a long tradition of wrestlers taking on boxers. Buddy Rogers had a fight with Jersey Joe Walcott once in Montreal. After Jersey Joe retired from boxing, he wound up refereeing matches. He even refereed a match of mine at the Coliseum.

In Memphis, we wanted to capitalize on Ali's publicity. Rocky Johnson had trained as a boxer. We said he was a sparring partner of George Foreman's and Foreman had just had a championship fight with Ali. We brought Rocky Johnson to Memphis as a boxer. No one had heard of him as a wrestler. I challenged him to a wrestling-versus-boxing match as well.

It was always hard for us to get any coverage in the *Memphis Commercial Appeal,* which is the big local newspaper. The sports department never covered wrestling properly and they didn't have a sports entertainment department. We could have a turnaway crowd of 11,500 fans at the Coliseum and they'd barely print the results. For this match, we sent out a press release and some pictures of Rocky with George Foreman. The papers ate it up. They thought the boxer was going to come in and kick the crap out of the phony wrestler. We got a huge buildup.   .

When we did the match, we did it in rounds. He boxed and I wrestled. We did a return match too. I won the matches—it was a wrestling show after all. He put me over. Then Rocky started wrestling. He got over in a big way himself. As I said, a lot of our fans were black and they loved him. I was the big heel and we had a long run. Rocky came in when we were still working with Nick Gulas and he made the switch with Jerry Jarrett and me when we broke away. That was a tremendous help to us because he was the top guy among African-American fans.

When The Rock got ready to wrestle, the WWE signed him to a developmental contract. His dad said let them send you to Memphis. Go down there and work with the King and the guys down there. He said it would be a great education. Some of the first matches he had were with me in Memphis and in all The Rock was down with us about six months. He and Brian became good friends. I felt proud that myself and our Memphis territory helped with Rock's success. We coached him on his interviews. He's a great wrestler, but on the stick, on the mike, he's as good as or better than everybody. I think he got a chance to learn that right in Memphis.

As soon as we saw Terry Boulder—who would become Hollywood Hulk Hogan—we knew right away he had tremendous potential. He had a great look with the blond hair. We made the first video of the Hulk. Michael St. John was the voice. It started at his feet and we went up his body, "Legs like tree trunks . . ." He'd wrestled as

"The Super Destroyer" in Florida and then he came to Memphis where Jimmy Hart became his manager. Problem was, he brought this other guy with him called Dizzy, who was supposedly his brother. He was really Brutus Beefcake. (Or Ed Leslie, whichever you prefer.) He was awful at the time. Jerry couldn't stand him he was so bad.

Terry had no money. Jerry Jarrett and I cosigned on a car for him. He'd been there a few months and he left, mainly because we wouldn't use the other guy. He went to Vince Sr. and worked with Andre the Giant as a heel. It was then that he became the Hulk, and the rest is *Hulkamania*. Come to think of it, I don't know if Hogan ever paid us back for the car . . .

Remember Steve Austin? He came through Memphis too. When he was there, he wasn't a main-event guy at all. This was the era of Stunning Steve Austin with the long blond hair. Stunning Steve Austin wasn't there yet as far as being a star. He went down to WCW and he languished. They didn't do that much with him. He left and went to Vince, who saw something different. Steve may have come up with the name, but Vince molded the character and made a Superstar out of a guy that everybody else had seen as a midcard guy.

When Undertaker was in Memphis, he spent most of his time as Mark Calloway, the Master of Pain. He was a young, tall, skinny guy living in Nashville. The Master of Pain was really just a name rather than any kind of gimmick. He came and worked for us for quite a long time. He was managed by the Illustrious Ronnie P. Gossett, or Fat Albert, as we called him affectionately. Mark went basically from us to the WWE and they put that gimmick on him and made him a Superstar.

Speaking for myself, I liked the deadman deal with

Undertaker better than the biker image. I don't think someone is really looked on anymore as being cool because they ride a motorcycle. But as the deadman, he was genuinely very menacing, scary almost. Now, he looks like a normal guy with a few tattoos who rides a motorcycle.

'Taker was in Memphis for a while. He wrestled all

over the territory in all sorts of matches. I've got a photograph of him after he lost a tar-and-feather match and we
were pouring the gunk on him. He and I wrestled in a
water park on a day when it was about a hundred and
seven degrees and the ring was in the full glare of the sun.
Mark was managed that day by three-hundred-fifty-
pound Ronnie P. Gossett. It was so hot, Gossett was sweating Crisco at ringside. The ring was set up right on the
edge of this huge wave pool. To win the match you had to
throw the other guy out of the ring and into the pool and
neither of us could wait to get out of that frying pan of a
ring and lose the match. I also found a note I made years
ago in a booking book of a match that was "Bill Dundee &
two midgets versus Pain," and it's probably just as well I
don't really remember what that was all about.

Kurt Angle was down for several months when he first
came in. Shawn Stasiak, Shawn Michaels, Glenn Jacobs.
The Godfather is a guy who they've repackaged several
times trying different things. When he was Papa Shango,
I helped with the design of the makeup. I painted his
face the first couple of times. He was a witch doctor,
who was a voodoo-type guy. He worked for us a few
times in Memphis. They took him off TV for a while and
brought him back as the Godfather.

I saw Glenn Jacobs (Kane) in Nashville when we were
getting ready for *Judgment Day*. His arm was recovering
from surgery pretty well, though he had a big medical
contraption fitted over his elbow. He'd been worked on
by the famous Dr. Andrews in Birmingham, who's the
guy who fixes the arms of all the baseball pitchers. He
did Bo Jackson's hip replacement. When you see Glenn
you're reminded why he has to wear that scary mask in
the ring. Without it, he's such a nice-looking, soft-spo-
ken guy.

Kurt Angle

Kane has come a long way from his turn as Dr. Isaac Yankem. He wrestled as the Unabomber out of Knoxville for a time and as the Christmas Creature for us. My son Kevin thought that up. Kevin was the first guy to use Glenn really. Christmas Creature appeared at a Christmas show in Missouri, which is where Glenn grew up. He wore a full green body suit with tinsel wrapped 'round him. I think Glenn's mom made the outfit. Kevin Nash and Scott Hall were working for WWE as Diesel and Razor Ramon. They quit and went to WCW but Vince owned the names and he brought Glenn in as the new Diesel. The new Razor Ramon looked a bit like Scott actually. They just used the same names, same outfits, everything. It didn't work. I guess the WWE was trying to prove that they owned these characters, but the fans didn't buy the replacements.

The last Mid-South Coliseum program mentioned Ultimate Warrior. He was one of the guys I had feuds with in my early years in the WWE. Another was Rowdy

Roddy Piper, who I had a Pay-Per-View match with in 1994. He had been gone making movies like *They Live* and he made a big comeback. It evolved out of me knocking his acting ability in the movie. I said things like, "I've seen better film on teeth. State prisons are showing his movie in lieu of capital punishment. Instead of their thumbs, Siskel and Ebert rated that movie with their middle fingers." I think Piper took some of these comments personally because that was one of the stiffest matches I was ever in. By "stiff," I mean he barely pulled his punches.

In some wrestling angles, art imitates life. It's best if the story lines are reality-based and the fans really know that. Jake "the Snake" Roberts was one of the most promising wrestling stars to come along in a long time. He had a huge fan base and unlimited potential, but unfortunately, he also had a substance-abuse problem. That problem was widely known, not only among the wrestlers but the fans as well. When Jake returned to the World Wrestling Federation, after trying to clean himself up, he came with his reputation. It was decided that I, as the heel, would zero in on Jake's personal problems and through that develop a personal issue between the two of us and work that into a major feud. I began to lambaste Jake on the broadcast by saying things like:

"Vince said Jake called from Atlanta [this must have been in 1996], and I asked if there was a drinking contest at the Olympics."

"When most people get drunk they see snakes; when snakes get drunk, they see Jake."

"His favorite drink is his next one."

"He thinks Beethoven's Fifth is a bottle."

"Unlike Clinton, Jake always inhaled."

"Every time he walks by a liquor store, his nose lights up."

"The only reason he doesn't drink and drive is because he's afraid he might hit a bump and spill his drink."

"Jake the Snake's two best friends are Jim Beam and Jack Daniels."

And so on. The angle with Bret Hart was a reality-based angle in that I was making fun of his parents being old and, in reality, they *were* old and they were really his parents. It was a real, personal issue; it wasn't just a match about who's going to win a belt or a championship. Again, it was something fans could relate to. I know how mad I'd be if someone came along and made fun of my parents. The same with friends of Jake. In every case, it's been cleared with the other wrestler. Jake knew what was happening. This stuff is fair game. It's not only fair game, it's good business.

Vince has laid his whole family out there as fair game. He looks on it as two worlds: the real world and the WWE world. It's acting, entertainment, showbiz. A lot of the angles with the family are reality-based, but they haven't been through the kind of substance-abuse problems to be made fun of. His children have been poor little rich kids, princesses, and snobs. He's done all kinds of story lines with his family. He had his wife "drugged" so he could have illicit affairs. Of course, life can imitate art. Triple H was with Chyna and the story line evolved that Triple H got married to Stephanie and they got involved.

I had a short-lived feud with Ultimate Warrior. Some company in California had just released an Ultimate Warrior comic book. This was right down my alley. I had always wanted to be a comic-book artist. So I knocked the artwork in his comic book. I did a really nice portrait of Ultimate Warrior, had it framed and everything, to

prove that he should have come to me, the best artist there was. Eventually we called him out to the ring and I was going to bury the hatchet by giving him the portrait. He knocked me and wouldn't accept the gift. As he turned to leave, I busted the portrait over his head.

Problem was, the big, tough Ultimate Warrior was scared of the glass breaking over his head. He was afraid he might get cut. I told him I was going to hit him with the back side of the picture, not the glass. It was just a piece of cardboard. The glass will break out, away from him. I assured him I'd done it several times before on Memphis TV and no one had ever been cut. So we're going out live on TV on *Raw* and I'm standing there with the picture and here comes Ultimate Warrior out to the ring . . . and he's wearing a frickin' baseball cap! He looked so stupid with his hair up under the cap. It didn't even really look like him. Never once had anyone seen the Ultimate Warrior wearing a baseball cap. It was an instant "angle alert." You could tell something was coming that involved him getting hit on the head. As far as I was concerned, that killed our angle.

* * *

Randy Savage is another guy who spent a long time down in the Mid-South. Randy has had a great career in wrestling and beyond. He was in the *Spider-Man* movie, for God's sake. Randy had everything it took to be a successful wrestler. He did a great interview and he was a very good worker to boot. He and I had some epic matches. Personal issues draw, remember? Well, the program with Randy Savage had some genuine heat on his part.

When he first started, Randy tried to work in Memphis. What he told me later was that I was doing the booking at the time and apparently I was not overly impressed with Randy for some reason. He must have been right, because I don't even remember him. Needless to say, he didn't last there very long and was asked to leave. He wound up with his dad up in Lexington, Kentucky, running an outlaw promotion called the IWA. Lexington was considered part of our territory. They found a venue in Lexington they ran every other week and they did other little towns in between. They started doing shows featuring Randy and his brother Lanny Poffo and some wrestlers 'round there who we never used. They got their show on a local TV station, a small, low-power station. It was an outlaw operation meaning they weren't the longtime, recognized promotion.

They tried to legitimize themselves. They'd go out on their show and challenge all the guys on our show. They wouldn't talk about their own matches; Savage would just rip into me. "I went to Jerry Lawler's house in Memphis and I threw a rock through the window and he was too scared to come out." Stuff like that. What you'd usually do would be to just ignore the opposition, but they were making a big deal out of attacking us.

They were in business a couple of years, but even then they were just treading water. It got to a point where they were going to go belly-up. Randy's dad, Angelo Poffo, called Jerry Jarrett and said they were on the verge of going under. He asked if there was any possibility of running a couple of joint shows 'round the area to make it look like their promotion was going against our promotion. It would put us over, and then they'd be gone. That was worked out. It was set up like a real grudge: the two companies against each other. We sold out Rupp Arena with me against Randy Savage. I think I had Jimmy Hart in my corner. Randy Savage had his dad in his corner. Because the two promotions were at war, we had two of everything. Lance Russell was at ringside with their announcer. We had one of our referees and one of theirs.

Randy and I had a loser-leaves-town match. The people couldn't figure it out. That's when you win out, is when the people want to know what's going to happen, but they can't know. They have to show up to the event to find out. They thought there was no way Randy Savage and his dad could leave town because Lexington was their home. Jerry Lawler's been the King since 1974, so he's not going to leave town. What's going to happen? Savage actually did leave, and went straight to the WWE. And that was the best thing that could have ever happened to him. He went on to make a ton of money and snapped into many Slim Jims.

Paul Heyman also worked in Memphis. I guess we never really got along that well. Paul managed guys like Austin Idol and Tommy Rich and we had a big problem about a match we were trying to put together. We had Austin and Tommy booked to do a scaffold match in Louisville. Scaffolding was erected over the ring and a narrow catwalk was erected fifteen feet over the ring. But when it came to the crunch, Paul said he couldn't get up on the scaffold. He was afraid of heights. I thought he was kidding, that it was a rib of some kind, but he really wouldn't get up there. But to do what he did in the ECW—Extreme Championship Wrestling—to build a company right up from nothing shows that he's a smart guy and a good promoter. I accidentally broke Paul's jaw once with a punch in a match in Blytheville, Arkansas, and he to this day swears I did it on purpose.

If you've been around awhile like I have, and you've worked a lot with most of the guys both when they were on their way up and once they'd made it up there, you establish a trust. I've had as much experience as anyone in the WWE and more than most. That means that guys will sometimes come to me for advice or to vent a little. Like Shawn Stasiak, whom I've known and liked for years, who approached the King outside the production office in the back of the Civic Center in Hartford. He said, "They're beating me to death and just squashing me. How can this be good for me?" I tried to explain to him, "Shawn, you're working for somebody. Just the same as if you took a job at McDonald's and they tell you to make french fries. You don't say no, I'm going to make pizza. You make french fries. You do what they tell you. It's the same in any job. Do what they tell you, be the best employee you can be, and that's the way you're going to get ahead.

"In wrestling, they can beat you and squash you every night of the week for a year, and all of a sudden you'll beat someone on a show that you're not supposed to beat, and you're made. The fans will forget every bit of the stuff that went before." I said, "Remember when William Regal was out there having to kiss Vince McMahon's butt?" Shawn said he didn't. But Regal's now the guy who knocks people out with brass knuckles. Next week it will be something else. "Right now," I said, "they're building Brock Lesnar, and you're just a piece of meat they're feeding him this week. It'll be someone else next week." Shawn used to call himself "Meat," come to think of it.

Most wrestlers, except the ones like Kurt Angle who are put over right away, worry about where they stand in the pecking order. The young ones resent the older ones and the older ones try to hold back time. It's like watching a pride of lions on the Discovery Channel. The big old lion is sitting there and the young lions are looking at him. One of the young lions finally gets up and says, "Okay, I'm going to try your ass."

Anyway, I told Shawn, "The reason you're there is that you did such a good job of getting beat up over in England. I guarantee they said, 'Shawn did such a good job over there, let's do it here.' That's in your favor. They're not trying to squash you and beat you down; you did so well, they want you to do it again." A lot of guys think it's their time. It ain't. First off, it isn't their job to think. Their time will come. Unfortunately, Shawn Stasiak is a worrier. Someday, they'll be feeding him guys and he'll be beating them in five minutes, and he'll say, "Don't you think I should beat them in four minutes?"

30

There's something I mentioned earlier that a lot of people find hard to believe. The fact that in my life, I have never tasted any type of alcoholic beverage. No beer, no whiskey, no wine, nothing. Not even a sip. Nor have I ever smoked. I've never even had a cigarette, of any kind, in my mouth. And no drugs either, ever. Not even the proverbial "experiment."

So that pretty much only leaves one vice. SEX! Now that, I can't say I've never tried. As a matter of fact, I've probably made up for the lack of all the other vices with the amount of sex that I have partaken in. But you have to admit, sex is great! Probably the most fun you can have without laughing. The worst sex I ever had was wonderful. A lot of people get uptight about sex or act offended if someone talks about it, but let's face it. Sex is what makes the world go 'round. Why, without sex, you wouldn't even be here!

If you're a guy reading this, you probably have realized, as I have, that everything we do in life we do to get sex. Think about it. I know the first time I thought about what I wanted to do in life was when I saw girls going crazy over that disc jockey, Scott Shannon. Those girls looked like they wanted to have sex with the guy, so I wanted to be a disc jockey. Then later on,

when I interviewed wrestlers on my radio show, I saw the girls that those wrestlers had with them. I knew those girls were having sex with those wrestlers, so I wanted to be a wrestler. After I got to be a wrestler, I found out there were a lot of girls out there who wanted to have sex with wrestlers. It was a good thing, and too much of a good thing . . . can be wonderful!

Rock music is probably the most well-known occupation for having "groupies." Girls who love to have sex with musicians. But every occupation has its own form of groupie. Think about it. There are girls who are turned on by men in uniforms. Servicemen, policemen, and firemen all have groupies. My attorney buddy, Joe Barton, told me there are girls out there who love to bed lawyers. We know that politicians have groupies, just ask Bill Clinton. Athletes have groupies by the thousands. Girls who love football players. Girls who love baseball players. And didn't basketball player Wilt Chamberlain say he had slept with something like 20,000 women?

I once went to the FedEx/St. Jude Golf Tournament in Memphis, and while I was there, I decided that golfers may have the best-looking groupies of all. I'm sure the golfers don't call them groupies. Nor do the lawyers or politicians call them groupies. I'm certain that each occupation has its own special term for such girls. A rodeo rider once told me that the girls who follow them around are referred to as "buckle bunnies." In wrestling, the girls have affectionately been known as "arena rats," or more recently, as "ring rats." I know that doesn't sound very flattering, and I really don't know how that term came to be, that's just what the girls were called when I started in the business and are still called that to this day.

During the mid-seventies, promoter James E. Barnett, who owned the Atlanta territory, used to call all the boys together in the locker room for a weekly "arena rat report." About an hour before the matches would start on Friday nights in Atlanta, Jim Barnett would take great pleasure in listening to one wrestler after another tell of their encounters with arena rats during the previous week. I never really understood why he was so interested, because he was openly gay.

I have arena rat stories by the hundreds, maybe thousands, but of course, I can't put them all in this book. One reason I can't is, if I did, this book would be thicker than the New York City phone book. The second reason is, most of them are unprintable! I really don't know exactly how to write about my sexual adventures tastefully. I know I talked with Jim Ross about the subject, and he told me the sex stuff had to be in the book. It's what people would expect. I asked him how to word those stories, and the only advice he could give me was, "Well, I don't think it can read like 'Letters to *Penthouse*.'"

One fan wrote to me and suggested that I talk about all the hot WWE Divas that I have "banged." Boy, would I love to talk about that. Unfortunately, the list of WWE Divas that the King has been with is pretty short. As a matter of fact, it's only one, The Kat, and I was married to her. That's not to say that I haven't "lusted in my heart," as former President Jimmy Carter once called it, when I look at some of the Divas. Of course, The Kat was my favorite, and to me the sexiest Diva of all time, and I was so lucky to get to make love to her for many years.

With Sunny and Missy Hyatt's endowments, where else would the King be found?

But next to The Kat, I have some other favorites that I have certainly fantasized about.

Before I joined the WWE in 1993, one of the hottest women I knew in wrestling was Missy Hyatt. She had it all. A great face, a great body, and she was incredibly sexy. I always thought I might have had a chance to make it with Missy, but I never really tried. She married Eddie Gilbert and she and I have been good friends ever since. Missy has a sexually explicit web site. I think you can see all of Missy Hyatt and then some. She called me not too long ago and asked if I would pass along an offer to Stacy of $10,000 if she would pose nude on the site. Stacy declined.

After Missy was Sunny. Tammy Lynn Sytch is her real name, but in the WWE, she was Sunny. Would I have liked to have done it with Sunny? Duh! I actually thought I was going to get to one time before she got into the business. I was booking Memphis and I met her and her boyfriend Chris Candido at a show I worked in New

Jersey for Dennis Coralluzzo. Eddie Gilbert was on that show as well and he knew a little bit about Chris and Tammy. Eddie said that if I brought Chris down to Memphis to work, chances were he would bring Tammy with him. He also said that they hadn't been going together all that long and that he didn't think Tammy was all that serious about Chris. He figured that if we could get her down to Memphis, and away from Chris for a while, we could both hook up with her.

To make a long story short, I booked Chris in Memphis, he brought Tammy, but we never hooked up. Once she was in the WWE she did come to my hotel room one night and let me take a photo of the nice little Superman tattoo she has right at the top of her butt crack!

Believe it or not, as I am writing this, I have just finished working matches two nights in a row on independent shows in Massachusetts. Both nights I worked against Chris Candido and Tammy. In those matches we worked in "high spots," in which I got to kiss Tammy and then put her head between my legs, pull her skirt up to expose the little thong she was wearing underneath, and then give her a piledriver. It was still a great sight to see Tammy's bare butt, and have it actually be that close to my face as I held her upside down. I can report her little Superman tattoo is still as cute as ever.

As I said, The Kat was my all-time favorite WWE Diva, but to me, there is one who has always run a close second. Terri Runnells! God, she is sexy! Beautiful face and the best body of any Diva ever . . . bar none. I know everyone thinks I am a "puppy" man, but the truth is, the thing I love most on a woman's body is her butt! I've said it before but it bears repeating. And Terri has the most beautiful butt I think I have ever seen in my life. It's perfect.

One of my fondest memories of any backstage skit I have ever done with the WWE was one in which Terri was standing at the top of a ladder, and for some reason,

I was at the bottom looking up her skirt. There was no way to shoot that scene except just the way I described it. I intentionally flubbed my lines a few times so we had to reshoot it over and over again. Man, what a beautiful sight! Have I ever hooked up with Terri? No, but I'd give my right arm to, and that's my drawing hand!

All the WWE Divas are special in their own right. They are all beautiful, but not all have appealed to me in the sense that I thought I would like to have a meaningful one-night stand with them. But there are some who do appeal to me that way. Without going into details, let me just say that two more Divas I would love to have as queens in my king-sized bed are Trish Stratus and Stacy Keibler. I once said about Trish on *Raw,* that she "has a Sunday school face, and a Saturday night body." And of Stacy Keibler, I said, "My favorite team in the WWE is Stacy's right leg and her left leg." What I wanted to say, after that, was "I'm all for unity, but that's one team I'd like to see separated!" Once again, with these two Divas . . . have not, but would love to.

Well, enough about sex I would like to have. What about sex I have had? When it comes to sex, you name it and I've probably tried it. I have always believed that you can "make love," and you can "have sex." They are both wonderful in my book. I have also subscribed to the theory that "eatin' ain't cheatin'," and I have said that I thought "ménage à trois" was a French term for "Kodak moment." Since I have been in the wrestling business I have had the pleasure of knowing many girls who thought the King was something special. Let me see if I can recall a few of them.

This one girl was great. All she wanted to do was have sex; all kinds of sex; everything to do with sex. I don't know if I've ever met a genuine nymphomaniac, but she had to be as close as they come.

One time we were having a wrestling show up in

Dyersburg, Tennessee, which is about eighty-five miles north of Memphis. It was usually about a two-hour drive that could get pretty boring after you'd made it a number of times. She rode with me and on that particular night there wasn't much traffic so we got into town a little early. There was a little dumpy motel by the side of the road. The kind of motel where they'd steal *your* towels.

We thought it would be better to do some "parallel parking" in the motel rather than doing it in the car like we usually did, so I checked in. I pull up in front of the room, which was the corner room closest to Highway 51. We go in and engage in a little "box springs bingo." I remember there were a couple of things memorable about that. One involved a packet of Sprees getting lost, but I can't write about that. The other was what happened afterward.

As we were lying there, suddenly we could hear some people talking right outside the room. Then, we could hear more people talking. I said, "What the heck's going on?" My friend gets up off the bed and walks over to the door. She looks out the peephole and says, "There's about fifteen people standing outside our room." I came over to look and sure enough, there's all kinds of people just standing there, by the door and around my car, and more pulling up.

I didn't know what was going on. I got on the phone and called the front desk. "Have you got any idea why there's all these people standing in front of my room?" "Oh yes, Mr. Lawler. I called the radio station and said I had Jerry 'the King' Lawler staying at my motel." I said "What?" I pull off for a little roadside fun, and all of a sudden, I'm making a personal appearance.

My friend got dressed and walked out of the room by herself. I told her to get into the car, drive away, and come back in about fifteen minutes to get me. The fans outside asked where I was and she played dumb. "Jerry

Lawler? Who? I don't know what you're talking about, I'm staying in this room by myself." Then she left, and, fortunately, so did most of the fans.

When she returned in fifteen minutes, there were still four people waiting outside. I just figured, what the heck, and walked out of the room and got into the car. I signed an autograph for each of them before we drove off. One guy winked as I signed his piece of paper. He knew.

Every state has its yearly beauty pageant that leads up to the Miss America contest. Well, I knew about the various Miss pageants but I didn't know some states also have a Mrs. contest. A beauty pageant for married women in the state. I did a personal appearance for a charity at a bowling alley and the reigning Mrs. State—I can't name—was appearing there as well. She was really hot-looking. The promotion was that money was raised by fans paying to bowl with celebrity partners. We wound up bowling against one another. Me and a partner and her and a partner. We beat them real bad.

After, she wanted some pictures. She suggested that since we'd beaten them so badly, she should literally bow down to the King. She got down on her hands and knees and grabs hold of my legs while the cameraman starts taking pictures. She had her hands all over my legs and was coming on strong. It was almost embarrassing (notice I said, almost). Finally I said, "You're Mrs. State. That means you're married. What would your husband say about you doing that?" She said, "I don't think he'd mind, but you can ask him yourself, that's him taking our picture!"

She and her husband had a pretty special relationship. He traveled a lot and when he was out of town, he didn't like for her to be lonely. I took care of that situation for him a few times. Come to think of it, that's probably why my mother had told me never to go bowling. "Anything done in an alley can't be good."

One time, I did a personal appearance at the grand opening of a huge Fred's Dollar Store just outside of Memphis. They picked me up in a limousine. I sat there doing the appearance, signing autographs. There were so many fans in line for signatures that I knew the appearance was going to go overtime. I was signing as fast as I could, and it got to the point that I was barely looking up at each person in line. Suddenly, someone drops a piece of paper in front of me that already had something written on it. It read, "I'm having a party in my mouth, would you like to come?" I look up and there is this incredible-looking girl standing there. Long, light-brown hair, and the most fantastic set of puppies ever! Not only was she beautiful, but she had a friend with her! They were both really knockouts.

She said, "What time do you get finished with this autograph session?" I said, "Another hour." She said, "Okay, we're gonna wait for you." I had no idea what she had in mind. I finished the autographs and she said, "Right. Follow us." I said, "I can't, I'm in a limousine with a driver and everything." She said, "Oh. That's even better."

The three of us piled into the back of the limo and off we went. I had the driver take us to Audubon Park. He pulls over into a little secluded area, and these two girls get down to business. You know how some people are said to be very "anal retentive"? Well, let's just say these girls were very "oral." Both, at the same time. When it was done, they got out of the limo, got back into their car, and drove off. They'd come and gone, as it were.

I looked up front and the limo driver's hat was on sideways. His face was covered with sweat, and the rearview mirror was twisted all askew. He said, "Uh huh. Mr. Lawler, you *is* the King!" I laughed and said, "What are you talking about?" He said, "If I had two girls do that to me, I'd mess up the upholstery on the roof of this car in about ten seconds. You lasted nearly an hour. You really is the King."

Another time, I'm signing for a long line at a jewelry store in a mall in Memphis. I'm signing and signing. I hold my hand out and the next person says, "I don't want an autograph. I want you." It was my friend again, the girl who just couldn't get enough. There was a line of people right out the door. She said, "Don't you think you need a five-minute break? Isn't your hand getting sore?" So I told the guy in charge, "I'm getting a little writer's cramp. I'm going to take five minutes."

We went out the back of the store, but there was someone working in every room. So we went out of the back of the store, and there was a long hallway with all the back doors of the stores. There was a stairwell leading to the second floor and she said, "This will do!" Anyone could have come walking down those stairs or up that hall, so I made it fast and furious. I was fast, and she was furious! And five minutes later, I was back signing autographs.

The memories are flooding back. I could sit here and write about this stuff all night long. But as we speak, there's a girl knocking on my hotel room door. I guess I've got to get up and let her out.

chapter 31

I met Larry Burton in 1993. At the time, I didn't quite figure out what his actual job was, and I still haven't to this day. We were in Detroit doing *SummerSlam*. Before the show, a guy comes walking up to me and says, "Jerry Lawler, right?" This was Larry Burton. He was with the Major League Baseball umpire Rocky Roe. He said he'd been wanting to meet me. He asked if I remembered back in 1982 when I was doing that stuff with Andy Kaufman? Of course. There were some interviews Andy sent me where he wrestled a heavyset girl down to the ground, right? They'd been filmed in front of a swimming pool. He said, "I filmed those interviews in my backyard. That was my swimming pool." He said that he and Andy and everybody on *Taxi* had been friends and Larry went on to help me out when we made *Man on the Moon*.

Larry and I found that we had a lot of stuff in common. We knew a lot of the same people, had the same interests. For one, his wife was from Amherst, Ohio, which was where my family had lived years before when we were in Ohio. And he'd lived up in Cleveland and was a huge Indians and Browns fan.

Larry was some kind of big wheel out in Hollywood. It was 1995. We were out in L.A. for a show. He picked me up in this Mercedes convertible, which was like a

$150,000 car, and we cruised around. He was dropping all these names. I thought he had to be full of hot air. There was no way he could know all these people. He asked me where I wanted to go—movie studios, TV studios. Whatever I wanted. The O.J. thing was the big story at the time, the biggest story there'd been for years it seemed, and I said I wanted to go see Nicole Simpson's house.

We drove over there and the whole block was cordoned off. The only people who could go in were the people who lived there. The house itself was taped up. We pulled up near the police cars stationed there and Larry got out and went over to talk to the officers. He called me over and introduced me to the cops, who, it turned out, were wrestling fans. They explained that everything was blocked off and you couldn't even drive by the house. But these two guys took us over to the house and let us walk down the walkway and onto the grounds. They'd just cleaned up the bloodstains but everything was still marked off. It was a really weird, eerie feeling. One of the policemen gave me a piece of the crime scene tape as a souvenir.

Then Larry asked where I wanted to go next. "Movie studio, I guess." He said we should go over to Disney and see his friend Mitch Ackerman over there. We drive over to Disney. It's got statues of the seven dwarfs on the gates and stuff. The guard looks out and says, "Hey, Larry, how're you doin'?" We walk in and he's telling these really off-color jokes to the receptionists. They all knew him.

We went up to this Mitch Ackerman's office. It was even neater than the D.C. Comics guy's office I saw one time. This one was about twenty feet square, full of Disney memorabilia. He was talking to me about the wrestling. He took us to the set of *Home Improvement* and we met Tim Allen and the cast. Then we went to another set and back up to Mitch's office.

I was wrestling the next day and I had forgotten to bring my crown. It was no big deal but Larry asked Mitch, "You all got any crowns around here?" He got on the phone. Five minutes later a guy comes in with a box. Remember the movie *Darby O'Gill and the Little People*? It was made in 1959, about the King of the Leprechauns. Sean Connery was in it. Anyway, this was the crown from the movie. This was a piece of movie history. Mitch wanted to lend it to me but I said I couldn't take it— what if something happened to it? And I never told him about the curse of Lawler's crown.

Then we went over to Burbank. It was the same thing at NBC Studios. "Hey, Larry." Jay Leno was filming his show. A limousine pulled up and eight or ten Dalmatians on a big leash get out of the limo and are taken into the studio. Larry takes me into the back and they're ready to tape the show. He's talking about baseball with Branford Marsalis. Then we went into the green room. I felt all out of place but Larry seemed to know everyone who worked there. There wasn't a lot of space in the room and there was another guy in the room sitting pretty near to me. Larry kept looking at him, I had no idea who he was. Larry leaned over and looked again. Finally, he said to the guy, "Are you with the band?" And the guy said, "I'm Kenny Loggins." About a minute later he got up and sat somewhere else.

The first guest was Richard Simmons, who had all the Dalmatians with him. Jay Leno said he really appreciated Richard coming on at the last minute because he knew Richard had a tough choice to make. Today was his mother's birthday. He could have spent time with his mother or he could have come on the show and he chose the show. Jay said he'd try to make it up to Richard's mom. He would call her from the show and everyone in the studio would sing "Happy Birthday." Leno picked up the phone and dialed and got Mrs. Simmons. There was a little small talk. Leno said they would take a break but she should hang on because they were going to get everyone in the studio to sing "Happy Birthday."

They went to commercial. The table in front of us in the green room had this phone on it with rows of lights to show which lines were in use. Larry says that that was the phone that was on the air right then. I said no it wasn't. But he said that one light on the phone was the line with Richard's mom on. I said it couldn't be, so he said, "Watch this." He pushed the button and the light went off. They went right back on the air and Jay says, "We've got Mrs. Simmons here," and picks up the phone. "Hello. Hello. Well, Richard, we lost your mom." We jumped up and took off and Leno had to redial Richard's mom.

Larry Burton calls me the Teflon King. I've actually been sued a lot but I've never lost a case. Once, I was coming up on an intersection in Memphis and the light started to go green-to-yellow. I speeded up because I was already through but someone in a van turned right in front of me on the yellow light. I slammed on the brakes but I hit the van and spun it 'round in a big circle and it hit another car that was waiting at the light. It stopped right in the middle of the intersection.

My door was jammed, so I got out on the other side. I went around. The second car was barely swiped so everyone was okay. But the back door of the van was open. The van was full of plumbing tools and they'd shot out of the back all over the intersection. I looked in the van, but there was nobody in it. I walked around the side. The whole door was sitting in the intersection, and there was a little old man sitting on the door, dazed. I went over to him and said everything was okay. I started to help him up but he howled so I left him sitting, reassuring him. The ambulance came and picked him up.

I didn't hear anything more until the lawyers called. The guy's name was Russell Salt. He was seventy-four years old and had thirteen kids. He was still working as a plumber. He had a broken back and was suing me for $300,000 and his wife was suing me for $100,000 for loss of consortium. (Loss of consortium means that due to the injury, he wasn't able to have sex with his wife. Sex with his wife at seventy-four? If the guy wasn't suing me, he would have been my new hero.)

It was at that point that I learned a lot more about insurance than I ever knew or wanted to know. I'd always had the cheapest you could get. My insurance company called me up and said my maximum coverage was ten thousand dollars. So I would be responsible for the other $290,000 plus the other $100,000. But they were going to supply a lawyer. His name was Ralph Holt. I went downtown to talk to him. He was a little bitty short guy with big glasses. The most dapper man you've ever seen. He had on a huge amount of jewelry— a big Rolex with diamonds all 'round it, big diamond rings on both hands, and a studded tie clip. He was a cocky guy, but friendly also. He said, "Well, Jerry. I offered the guy the whole ten thousand dollars but he wants to be a hard-ass. He won't accept. He wants to go to court. This could be a tough case." They kept trying to settle.

Finally it came to trial. I was worried because this could ruin me. I went to the lawyer's office in the morning and Ralph was sitting around, all happy. I was thinking, man, how can he be so happy, my whole life is on the line here. Then I realized it didn't mean anything to him, it was just another day at the office. He asked me if I was ready to go and he stands up and walks over to his drawer, takes off his diamond rings, and puts them in the drawer. He took off his Rolex and put on an old Timex. He took out a silver ring with some turquoise in it and put that on. I asked him what he was doing. "One of the first rules of being a lawyer. Don't ever wear any fancy jewelry in court."

It had been something like a year since the wreck and they bring in old Russell in a wheelchair looking like he'd just been hit in the parking lot. I get on the stand and tell my version of the story and then it's his turn. They had a blackboard with the intersection drawn on it and two magnetic cars. His lawyer asked him to come up and position the cars exactly as they were. Someone had to come and give him a walker. He hobbled slowly across to the blackboard. I was looking at the jury, thinking I was sunk. He moves the cars and limps back and sits down. The lawyer talks to him another ten minutes and then he says he's moved the cars and he hates to do it, but could Mr. Salt come up and show the position of the cars again? So he limped up again.

Russell said I must have been going so fast he never saw me. His lawyer tells the jury he wants to talk to them about the pain and suffering of his client. They were asking for even more money on top of the $400,000. His back was broken and has not healed properly and probably never would. He said Mr. Salt will probably never know another pain-free day. "What is a pain-free day worth?" He said, "How do you put a price on a pain-free day? My parents sent me to the finest law school that money could buy and that's the one thing they couldn't teach me. Ladies and gentlemen, you have to decide. We want you to grant that amount to Mr. Salt."

At that point, I wanted to shoot myself. I was dead. My little bantam rooster strutted out in front of the jury. He said, "Ladies and gentlemen of the jury. I didn't have rich parents to send me to the finest law school. I had to work my way through school. I probably didn't get to go to as good a law school as my friend. But the one thing I did learn, was that when you fail to see that which is there, you are guilty of negligence. Mr. Lawler was obviously there, because they collided. Mr. Salt testified he failed to see Mr. Lawler. All I want to say is, when you fail to see that which is there, you are guilty of negligence. Thank you." That was it. He went and sat down and gave me a little wink. The jury went out and I was sweating bullets. But they came back in about fifteen minutes, in no time. "We find both parties guilty of contributory negligence," said the foreman. They awarded no damages. He got zero. He didn't even get the $10,000 we offered.

What else? I won't go into details but in 1996 I got involved in a lawsuit that cost me a lot of time and a lot more money. It was a nightmare that only got resolved in 2002. When it was all over, I was out about a million dollars.

And, I once got sued in Louisville, Kentucky, by a woman who said I spit on her at a wrestling match. That went all the way to a jury trial, but I won. When I was driving all over the area, I'd get two or three tickets a week. Brian says that when he was sixteen, he and I went down to the DMV to get his first license. You had to take a parent with you to fill out the paperwork. When I gave my information, the clerk says, "Did you know your license has been revoked for three years?" Instead of Brian taking the test and getting his license, I had to reapply for mine.

Once I got my license suspended for doing 120 but I still had to drive. I was coming home from Louisville going to my apartment in Nashville. I was just getting home at two o'clock in the morning when I got pulled over. The officer came to my window and asked for my license. I said I must have left it at home. He asked if I knew how fast I was going? I said I didn't. He asked where I lived. I said it was right nearby. The officer said he and his partner would follow me over to my apartment and check on the license. He went back to his car and I sat there for a minute.

I thought it over. I got out of the car and walked back to the patrol car looking real sheepish. I said I didn't really have my license back at the apartment, it was suspended. One of the officers looked at the other and sort of said, "Nuh, nuh, nuh." They said they were supposed to take me downtown, impound my car, and lock me up. But that was a lot of paperwork for them and they were just about to get off duty. "We'll tell you what we're going to do. We're going to follow you back to your apartment. You're going to park your car. If we see you out here in the streets driving, you will go directly to jail. You will not pass 'Go.'" They followed me to the apartment and let me go. Next day, I drove on right up the avenue. I had to. Needless to say, I would advise none of my readers to behave like this.

Of course, there is never a good time for any of these things to happen, but probably the worst piece of timing occurred in 1999 when I was running for mayor of Memphis. I got arrested and indicted when a security guard said I ran over her foot at the airport. The charge was reckless endangerment. So right then, there were at least a couple of possibilities for major change in my life. I could become mayor, or I could be sent to jail for two years, which was the possible sentence, or both. The incident happened six or eight months before. I thought it was over and done with. But it got brought up right in the middle of the race. Nothing came of it in the end. I am pleased to say—like Larry Burton said—nothing sticks to Teflon.

I got to be involved in the mayoral deal in a strange way. Jesse Ventura had been elected governor of Minnesota in November 1998 and *Time* magazine was running a story about wrestlers going into politics. Bob Backlund ran for Congress in 1999 also. Anyway, I was asked if there was any chance of me running for governor of Tennessee. I said there wasn't really because Don Sundquist had just been reelected. If anything, I'd run for mayor of Memphis, the election was in 1999.

What I didn't say was "I'm thinking of running for mayor of Memphis." Until the article came out in *Time* magazine, there was as much chance of my running for public office as there was of me joining the priesthood. But the press in Memphis picked up my comments and the radio stations started calling up. People were telling me it was actually a good idea. It snowballed from there to my actually running and doing better than a bunch of lifelong politicians. It was weird. Jesse Ventura said something about politics being dirtier than wrestling; well, even before I got into the race a well-to-do businessman in Memphis came to my house and asked me not to run. If I didn't run he would finance my campaign if I would wait and run four years later. He needed the mayor to be reelected this time.

If you do something like run for mayor, your whole life gets put under a microscope. A lot of people start looking at you and what you get up to who'd never had the slightest interest before. Now I've never made a dime from my web site. It's caused me more trouble than it's ever been worth—I don't know why it's still there. I don't really do that much with it; I just take pictures and stick them up. It was up when I was running for mayor but I hadn't thought about it in a long time. There were all these typical wrestling pictures and there were also some very revealing photos of Stacy. I had to file qualifying petitions at the Election Commission, to officially get into the race. There was a crowd of supporters down there cheering me on. Next day, the web site was on the front page of the papers in Memphis. They mentioned

the pictures of Stacy and said this could be our new first lady. And this guy could be mayor of Memphis.

I was one of no less than twenty-one people who ran. The incumbent was Mayor Willie Herenton, who spent something like $825,000 on his campaign. Then there was Joe Ford, part of the powerful local family that includes Congressman Harold Ford and Harold Ford Jr. and Senator John Ford. Joe Ford was president of the city council. He spent $530,000. Then you had Pete Sisson, the Republican Party's candidate, who was once Shelby County commissioner. He was a lifelong politician and he spent a lot of money too. There was also former city council member, Mary Rose McCormick, who had been in politics all her life. Then there was Shep Wilbun, a black candidate who was on the school board. I thought out of all the candidates, he made the most sense. He should have won. There were a bunch of other people who didn't have any money to spend who ran. So there were really six live political people, and me.

In the end, it was neat. I had no political experience whatsoever and I was making it up as I went along. I was working full-time for the WWE so I wasn't even in town half the time. Every now and then I'd go out and do some campaigning out of a Winnebago that was my HQ. But I did go to some town meetings and tried to persuade people that I would take the job seriously should I win. Sometimes, I sounded like a real politician.

"Mine is a campaign of convenience," I said. "What I'm going to tell the people is, 'The campaign is in your neighborhood.'" And, "I say it is time to run Memphis like a business, where the taxpayers are the customers and the customers are always right."

I hired a couple of political consultants. A man and his wife who lived in St. Louis. I paid them a certain amount of money. If I'd won, I'd have to pay them a whole lot more money. They studied Memphis and sent me these different outlines and proposals. I put my own ideas to them. Between us, we came up with a seven-point plan of action: safer streets; educational excellence; a cleaner community; attracting new business; get traffic moving; lessen the property tax burden; and more parks for families.

In the end, Herenton polled 74,896 votes, 46 percent. Joe Ford finished in second place, with 41,161 votes, or 25 percent. I was third with 19,092 votes, 12 percent; and Pete Sisson finished fourth, with 18,012 votes, or 11 percent. Seeing as I spent exactly $24,583, got indicted in the middle of the campaign, and spent half of it out of the city, I did pretty well. Old Mayor Chandler was right:

70 percent of whites voted for white candidates, 30 percent for Herenton. None for Ford. No significant numbers of black people voted for white candidates. I tried to talk about that during the campaign. Memphis is probably one of the most racially divided cities anywhere in the country. It's never really going to change until people will admit that. No one will talk about it. No one will say we're a racially divided city, say let's try to do something about it.

The biggest interest in my career at the WWE came in the year after Stacy got released. I was getting 60,000 hits a day on my web site. Some people seemed to think it was an overreaction on my part when I quit the WWE after Stacy was let go, but I can't imagine that any man would think his job is more important than his relationship with his wife. Or if a woman and her husband were working at the same place and all of a sudden, for no apparent reason, they decided to fire her husband, and if they made her go and tell him he was fired and then expected her to stay and two hours later do her job like nothing's happened, I can't believe she wouldn't walk out the building. I know I did.

"Well, King, I want to thank you for everything you've done for us. . . . You've gone above and beyond the call of duty and really helped us tremendously. . . . GOOD-BYE."

With those few words from Vince McMahon, my nine-year ride with the World Wrestling Federation came to an end. We were in Tucson, Arizona. It was Tuesday, February 27, 2001, around 5:30 P.M., barely two hours before we were scheduled to start taping *SmackDown!*, which was going to air on Thursday night on the UPN Network. Vince had a protein bar in his left hand that he'd been munching on the whole time Stacy and I sat and tried to talk with him, and with his right hand he reached out and shook my hand. I looked into his eyes. I guess I was hoping to see some kind of indication that what was taking place was a joke, or a prank, or a rib. But I didn't detect any humor in Vince's eyes, or compassion. All I saw was the straight-ahead corporate stare of a company head who'd just made another business decision. One of hundreds of decisions Vince is called on to make every day as the owner of the world's most popular wrestling/sports/entertainment company.

But this decision hit me like a ton of bricks. This decision meant the World Wrestling Federation didn't want to be associated with my wife, Stacy, or me, anymore. Our services were no longer needed. I still can't describe what I was really feeling as Stacy and I walked out of Vince's office and away from the company. Was I mad at Vince? I guess not. I mean I didn't want to punch him or anything. I think hurt and disappointed would more accurately describe my feelings.

Heck, just a week earlier, Vince had walked up to me and said, "King, I know you're going to love the segment I'm doing on the show with Trish Stratus tonight, because you and I are cut from the same cloth." Cut from the same cloth! I remember feeling proud when Vince said that to me. I felt he meant we thought alike. That we had a lot in common. And I felt we did as well. We'd been in the wrestling business about the same number of years. We'd both owned wrestling companies and had hundreds of wrestlers working for us. We'd spent many hours together in the broadcast booths and in front of the camera. Why, I'd even had the honor of making Vince McMahon's first "blade," the specially adapted razor blade that Vince used to cut his forehead and bleed on TV for the first time in his life.

But all of a sudden, in the blink of an eye, we had nothing in common. We no longer thought alike at all. I would never have thought to do what Vince had just done.

Vince had presided over a production meeting with the television crew at 2 P.M. that day. During that meeting he read a format for the show that included four segments featuring my wife, Stacy, or The Kat, with the group of wrestlers called "Right to Censor." Just thirty minutes later, at 2:30 P.M., Vince called Jim Ross, Vice President and Head of Talent Relations, and told him that he had suddenly decided not to go any further with the Kat/Right to Censor story line and as a matter of fact, he wanted J.R. to give Kat her release from the company . . . effective immediately. He was firing one of the prettiest and most popular Divas, instantly, without warning, and for no apparent reason, right in the middle of a featured story line.

Vince also said he thought I would be upset, but he didn't think I would leave the company along with Stacy, just because she was being fired. He and I surely weren't thinking alike anymore. It was strange in the fact that Vince and I had never had a cross word. Every single time I had ever been around Vince, other than this day, he had been as nice and as friendly to me as he could possibly be. Sometimes some of the production people would tell me stories of Vince going on a tirade and lambasting people when he was provoked. But I had never witnessed it. As a matter of fact, I was with the company for several years before I even heard Vince utter a swear word.

I knew Vince had a cold side. He's a workaholic. He works seven days a week—at least. And usually, workaholics feel that everyone should think like they think and want to work twenty-four, seven as well. There's nothing more important to him in the entire world than the WWE. I think a long time ago Vince realized it's almost impossible to have true friends who work for you in your company. You can be friendly, but not real friends. No matter who it is. The buck stops with Vince, he's the boss, and he looks at everybody else as an employee. He can't afford to let it get personal. In that respect, everybody's vulnerable. Everyone could go at a moment's notice. You never know with Vince. No one's going to get bigger than the show.

The Rock has probably gotten to a point where he could go on his own without the wrestling. But there's still the chance he could turn out the same as Sable. It seemed to me like she may have felt she was bigger than the company. She was so big and so hot. She was in *Playboy* magazine and on all these TV shows. They wanted her in Hollywood. But she quickly found out that the only reason they wanted her was because she was a big star in the WWE. I think The Rock would find the same thing. Rock has become a megastar. He has a ton of talent and a ton of charisma. But he would have never got a chance to show that to the world were it not for the WWE. And all those millions and millions of The Rock's fans became his fans because they were WWE fans first. Even with his movies, if The Rock quit wrestling completely, I don't think his popularity would last that long. He's The Rock from WWE. Even in his movies, he's The Rock from WWE. I just think that if he was no longer with the WWE, The Rock character would lose a lot of its appeal. I don't think his skills are honed enough so that he could make it on acting alone yet. He needs the WWE fan base.

One other example of Vince making cold, hard business decisions came in 1994. J.R. had a bout of Bell's palsy. Bell's palsy is a condition brought on by stress that results in the same symptoms as a facial stroke. You suffer paralysis of part of your face. But unlike a stroke, where the effects are permanent, with Bell's palsy the damage usually improves greatly after a period of time. When the Bell's palsy hit J.R. it affected his face and slurred his speech a little. Vince called him in and said they were going in a different direction and J.R. wasn't included in the plans. He was gone, simple as that. J.R. said he felt it was because, with the palsy, Vince was not comfortable with the way J.R. looked and sounded on TV anymore.

J.R. and I weren't real big buddies at that time, I just didn't know him well enough yet, but he'd call me from time to time. One day, he said he was better and if the opportunity ever arose, he'd appreciate it if I'd put in a word for him with Vince. "No problem," I said.

Next night, Vince and I were standing by the curtain, waiting to go out for the show. Suddenly a stagehand said there was going to be about a three- or four-minute delay before we could go out, so there was no one there except Vince and me. I took the opportunity and told Vince that J.R. called me and said he'd really like to come back if there was a chance. He said he appreciated it. The next week, we were in Stamford getting ready to do some voice-overs. They needed something voiced-over for a montage clip and it wasn't right for me to do or for Vince either. I said, "You know who'd be perfect? J.R." Vince agreed, "Yes, he would."

The next week, they hired him back. It was good timing; I'm not trying to take the credit. Vince is all business. When he thought J.R. couldn't do it, he just cut him loose. When he needed the guy, he hired him back. Strictly business.

I was really amazed at the reaction from the fans when Stacy and I left. It was a major story on the Internet and in almost all of the newspapers around the country. I think one of the reasons there was such interest was because it was somewhat of a mystery. No one really knew the real reason for Stacy's dismissal and it made for a tremendous amount of speculation, and Lord knows wrestling fans love to speculate about things on the Internet. Another reason it was big news is that not only was I gone from the World Wrestling Federation, I was gone from the XFL as well. The *New York Daily News* published the story with this headline: LAWLER QUITS XFL IN KAT FIGHT.

I wrote pretty regular updates on my web site and I was getting well over a thousand e-mails a day at one point. The emotion and outpouring of support from the fans was really overwhelming. My web site gave me a vehicle to have my voice heard by the fans and to let them know what was going on with Stacy and me. People e-mailed me that they had called Titan Towers, WWE HQ, and complained. Fans e-mailed me that they had started a petition to get Stacy and me back. E-mails came in from people who said they weren't going to watch the WWE until we returned.

Many people e-mailed me and asked how they could contact the powers that be and let them know how displeased they were that Stacy and I were no longer there. That's when I figured, "Here's an opportunity." I often wonder why opportunity only knocks once, but the postman always rings twice. Anyway, this was one knock I shouldn't have answered. I knew everyone's e-mail address at the WWE. What an opportunity to let the fans voice their opinions straight to the people who mattered. So, like an idiot, I posted the e-mail addresses of the creative team, including the senior writer, Bruce Prichard, on my web site and told the fans they could vent their frustrations right to the source.

That's when it really hit the fan. Because not only did their e-mail addresses appear on my web site, which was getting about a hundred thousand hits a day. My updates, along with their addresses, were being reprinted on some of the biggest wrestling web sites in the nation. They all carried my updates and between them, they got close to a million hits a day. So, you can imagine what happened. The computers at the WWE headquarters were deluged with e-mails. So many, in fact, that the system shut down. And these weren't just any ordinary e-mails. These were vicious, venomous, hate-filled, threatening types of e-mails.

J.R. told me later that some fans even e-mailed him and said that they hoped he'd get Bell's palsy again. Now this was certainly not what I had intended when I posted the addresses, but that's what happened. And it had the exact opposite effect on the WWE that I had hoped it would. I had buried myself with the writers and Bruce Prichard and I knew it was going to be a long time, if ever, before anyone in the WWE wanted to hear my name again.

There were, however, some people who wanted to hear from the King, and they all seemed to work at radio stations. I got calls from what felt like every station in the country and they all wanted the same thing. They wanted me to come on and blast the WWE. They wanted sour grapes. They wanted me to dog out Vince. That wasn't what I wanted to do. I did want the company to know that there were a lot of fans out there who wanted the King and Stacy back in the company. But I wasn't going to beg, and I wasn't going to bad-mouth anyone. So I talked to every DJ on every station who would listen. But no matter how hard I tried not to ruffle any feathers and say the right thing, somehow, someway, something would always get turned around or misquoted.

I appeared on the highest rated show in Chicago, *Mancow*, on March 7 and talked about my departure. I said I'd always thought that Vince and I were good friends, but the Vince who coldly shook my hand and ended the relationship was probably the real Vince. This is probably the reason he became so successful. The claim that Stacy had been fired for an attitude problem was "a cop-out." I always tried to keep things on a pretty light note. When Mancow asked me what I was going to do now that I was unemployed, I said I had enough money to last me the rest of my life—provided I never wanted to buy anything.

Stacy and I were booked on an independent show somewhere in Wisconsin for a promoter named Rockin' Randy. He got us lined up to do some radio to promote the event. Once again, we went on Mancow Muller's radio show in Chicago, in April this time, to promote Randy's wrestling matches. We talked for a short time about the upcoming matches and then the topic switched to the WWE. I got myself in a certain amount of trouble even though the show is designed to be a chaotic sort of yukfest. Mancow is the star of the show and he's a very talented guy. It's 6 A.M. and he's bouncing off the walls like Tom Arnold after a caffeine overdose. He's got a pretty weather girl in the studio, a pretty traffic girl in the studio, and two comedic sidekicks to pick up any slack.

The questions started coming like a machine gun. He asked if I hated Vince McMahon and I said no. Then he asked if I heard Vince McMahon had been killed in a car crash, would I cry. I said I wouldn't want to see that happen to anyone, but I don't think I'd actually cry. Then he immediately switched tack. Stephanie McMahon is hot, do you think she's wild in the sack? So I say the first thing that comes into my mind, "Well that's what Bruce Prichard told me." Then right away, he says something about Paul Heyman, who had replaced me, and how he sucks. He got everyone chanting, "He sucks," in the studio and I finally said, "Okay, he sucks."

Well, right away, it was being posted on the Internet that I wanted Vince to die in a car crash, that Stephanie McMahon was sleeping with Bruce Prichard, and that I thought Paul Heyman sucked. Well, no, I didn't want Vince to die, and the thing about Bruce saying he'd heard that Stephanie was a wild child was something he really told me he had "heard," not experienced. And no, I didn't think Paul Heyman sucked, because, the truth was, I hadn't watched the show with him on it yet. So I couldn't know if he sucked or not. But things get taken out of context and the Internet means they're around the world in an instant.

Every single interview started with the same question: "Why did they fire The Kat?" The problem was, we didn't know the answer. We knew what the official statement was, but I felt in my gut that there was much more to it than that.

When Jim Ross called me into his office that day in Tucson, he swore, as did Bruce Prichard, that he had just gotten the word from Vince to give Stacy her release, and that he knew nothing about it beforehand, and the only reason Vince gave him was that "creative" was unhappy with her "attitude." I asked J.R. what Vince meant by that, but he didn't know. J.R. said he was totally in the dark on the situation and that it was as big a surprise to him as it was to me.

J.R. said that telling me this was one of the hardest things he's ever had to do, and he said he didn't know how to tell Stacy. That's when J.R. asked me if I could tell her. I thought, "This is a hell of a note. They're firing my wife, but they want me to tell her she's fired!" So that's when I told J.R., "Yeah, I'll tell her. I'll tell her while we're on our way back to Memphis, because if she's fired, then I'm leaving too."

When I knocked on the door to the ladies' locker room, I don't even remember which Diva answered, but I asked for Stacy, and in a moment she was peeking around the corner of the door just half-dressed. As far as she knew she was just a couple of hours away from one of her biggest roles to date on *SmackDown!*, and she was getting ready early. I think she could tell from my face that something was wrong. I just said, "Baby, get dressed and get your things, we're leaving." She looked at me like I was kidding, and said, "Why, what's wrong?" I believe she thought that I had been told we had a death in the family or there was some kind of emergency or something. "Tell me what's wrong, why are we leaving?" I just said, "J.R. just told me that Vince is giving you your release so I told them I'm leaving too, so get your things and let's go." Stacy was stunned. She just looked at me and said, "Why?"

When Stacy had her belongings together, we took them out, along with my bag, and put them into our rental car. We got into the car and I started it up, but then I turned the engine off, and said, "Let's go talk to Vince." We went back into the arena and up to Vince's office. It was a very small office that day. At each show, a different room is chosen to be Vince's office and usually they are pretty nice and spacious. This one was not much bigger than a broom closet. When I looked in, Vince was sitting there, eating that protein bar, and talking on the phone. I said, "Vince, can we talk to you for a second?"

He motioned for us to come in and sit down while he finished his phone conversation. The room was so small that when I sat down, my knee was actually touching Vince's. I was pretty sure that whoever he was talking to on the phone was informing him that I was leaving along with Stacy. When he got off the phone, Stacy asked Vince what she had done that was so bad that she was being fired for it. That's when the mystery began.

Vince said he really didn't know what she had done, that it was a talent relations issue. Well, J.R. is the head of talent relations, and he had just sworn to me that he had no idea what the reason for firing Stacy was. I said to Vince, "Jim Ross said someone was unhappy with her attitude. If that was the case, shouldn't someone have come to us and said, 'Stacy, there's a problem we need to talk to you about and get straightened out'?" Vince said, "Yes, someone should have come to Stacy and talked to her about that." I pointed out, "Well, no one did. No one has said anything to either of us about any kind of problem." He said, "Well, they should have." That's when I knew that Stacy's attitude wasn't the real reason she was being fired.

Stacy and Chyna had been really close friends up until Chyna got featured in *Playboy* magazine. Then, for one reason or another, they drifted apart and I wondered if Chyna may have been upset with the sudden "push" the Kat was getting with the "Right to Censor" angle. We both thought that could have been the reason Stacy was fired.

One of the people from the office who was instrumental in getting Chyna hooked up with *Playboy* had asked Stacy if she would be interested in posing for the magazine. When Stacy said she would, the person set up a meeting with Hugh Hefner. Stacy and I went to the Playboy mansion and met Hefner. He spent a few minutes with us and said to Stacy, "We have a great relationship with the WWE, and as far as I'm concerned, you'd be perfect to be the next Diva to be in our magazine." Stacy was really excited, but somehow word got back to the company that Stacy and I had gone out there on our own and met with Hugh Hefner behind their back. Like I knew Hugh Hefner and could just call up and say, "Hef, this is the King . . . I want you to put Stacy in *Playboy*." We never really got that misunderstanding straightened out and Stacy and I thought that may have been the reason she was fired.

Another item that was going around was that Stacy was fired because there was a photograph going 'round of her kissing Chyna. Like some sort of lesbian pictures or something. The truth was, there was a picture on the Internet of Stacy and Chyna with their faces close together and their lips puckered. The picture was taken by me and had actually been on my own web site for more than a year and they were mugging for the camera, not kissing.

I really had no idea what had gone wrong. I wrote a heartfelt letter to Vince and said I wished the whole thing hadn't happened, but at no point did I beg for my job back. Anyway, I didn't hear a word back from Vince. For a long time, I didn't hear anything from anyone. The only communication was through lawyers. It was an ugly situation.

It wasn't that we lacked for anything to do. We did a lot of local shows around Tennessee and Kentucky for

Our last appearance

Bert Prentice. We hooked up with a guy out of New York, named Michael O'Brien, who had promoted shows throughout New England and he booked us on a ton of independent shows. Bobby Mintz from Tri Star Promotions in Houston booked us on a lot of sports card shows to sign autographs with other sports stars. We were staying very busy, and actually making about the same money as we had been making with the company, but I could tell the firing had had a major effect on Stacy. She wasn't the same.

chapter 33

Well, if I thought my life changed in February 2001 when the World Wrestling Federation fired my wife, and I quit my job in protest, that absolutely paled in comparison to what happened on July 1, 2001. That was the day Stacy told me she was leaving me. Many of the old sayings applied: "You're always the last to know." "You can't see the forest for the trees." Whatever. I sure didn't see it coming.

If someone had asked me just one day earlier, I would have told them they couldn't find a better couple than Stacy and me. I thought we were happily married and completely in love. I know I was. Unfortunately for me, apparently Stacy wasn't. She told me later in a twenty-page letter that she had not been happy for the past two years. TWO YEARS!??! How the hell do you stay with someone and act as if everything is fine, if you're not happy for two years? But that's what Stacy said she did. I really can't remember which day goes down in history as the worst day of my life, the day Stacy actually left me, or the day she told me she was going to leave.

I was in Cleveland, Ohio, appearing at the National Sportscard Convention. It was one of the biggest, no, *the* biggest, event of its kind in the country. Some huge names in sports, past and present, were there for three days to sign autographs for the fans. I was thrilled just to be a part of it. I can't begin to list all the great athletes that were on hand at that convention. Muhammad Ali, Willie Mays, Jim Brown, Magic Johnson, Joe Namath, to name a few. Oh, and of course, me.

There were tables set next to each other from one end of the convention center to the other. Each sports star had his own table to sit behind and the fans would queue up in line in front of each table to wait for their autographs. There were some other celebrities appearing that were not actually from the world of sports. As a matter of fact, I was sitting next to a movie star of sorts. My table was next to one of the last living Munchkins from the classic movie *The Wizard of Oz*. He was the neatest little guy with an unmistakable voice.

I was having such a good time at the convention, I was like a fan myself. I never dreamed what dark days lay ahead. The convention was memorable for two reasons. The first was that while I was there, the call I had been waiting for from the WWE finally came. Kevin Dunn is the guy who is pretty much the head of WWE television. Other than the actual story lines and wrestlers, Kevin decides what goes on WWE programming. His official title is Executive Producer of WWE Television and he decides who the announcers are on *Raw* and *SmackDown!* He is the man who called me while I was in Cleveland. It was the call I had hoped would come for the past four months. It meant the WWE was asking Stacy and me to come back to work. I thought Kevin had wanted me back on the shows all along, but this had been one decision that was out of his control. He said that there were still some in the company who were against my coming back, but they had been overruled. He wouldn't, however, tell me who wanted me back and who didn't want me back. I really didn't care, as long as we were coming back.

The one thing I was really excited about was that I was going to get to call Stacy and tell her we had our jobs back again. I couldn't wait to hear how excited she was going to be. Kevin and I pretty much had everything set. This was on a Friday, and we were supposed to be at the TV show the following Monday. Stacy was at our condominium in Fort Myers, Florida. She had been there for over a week. Stacy's father and stepmother were visiting from Texas and had been staying down there for several days. I couldn't wait to call her and tell her the news. Needless to say, she was happy but still a little apprehensive, as if the news were too good to be true. How right she was.

My good friend Frank Derry was helping me at the card show in Cleveland. I had painted a cover for his publication *Indians Ink*. It was a painting of then-Cleveland outfielder Kenny Lofton. Frank had gotten Kenny to sign a hundred issues of the paper and I had signed and numbered them as well. Frank had them for sale at my table at the convention. It was great that he was there, because I had to spend a lot of time away from the table while I was on the phone with the WWE, and Frank explained to the fans where I was and what I was doing.

The next day, Saturday, things started to go downhill. Frank and I got to the convention center at around 10 A.M. I knew this was going to be the biggest day of the show, and the fans were already lined up at everyone's tables. Muhammad Ali was there. Willie Mays was there. *The Wizard of Oz* Munchkin next to me was in rare form. He actually got up and sang, and did a little dance for some of the fans. Then my cell phone rang.

It was Kevin Dunn again. He said Vince wanted me to understand one thing before I agreed to come back: that right now, the writers didn't really have anything in mind for Stacy to do, so she would just be brought back for this one show and then have to wait until they could come up with a story line for her. It was a little change in the plans, but nothing major. I assumed that she would be back under contract like she was before we left and since she had been used sparingly in the past, that waiting for a new story line would be something she was used to. I told Kevin I would call Stacy and then call him back. Sure enough, Stacy said that she was used to that so it wasn't really a big deal. I called Kevin back to tell him that would be OK, but by the time I got back to him, things had changed again . . . for the worse.

In the next phone call, Kevin said that Vince had called him back and said that Stacy wasn't going to be under contract, that she was only going to be used on the one show and that was it. So in reality, Stacy wasn't getting her job back, it was just me. I called Jim Ross and had a long talk with him. His advice to me was that I should go ahead and come back. Once I was in place, I would have a better chance of getting Stacy reinstated. He said he felt confident that Stacy would eventually be given her job back if I was working at the WWE.

I hung up and called Stacy. I knew this was going to be a big blow to her and it was, I could hear it in her voice. She said, "They only want you back, and you need to go. Go ahead and tell them you'll come back." I told her what J.R. said. About my working for her return from the inside. I knew she didn't think it would work, but she said okay anyway.

So there it was. I come back to work as an announcer, Stacy comes back for the one show and then goes home to wait for me to try to get her job back. It was not really what we wanted, but we were taking it. I called Kevin Dunn back to tell him that it was a deal, and believe it or not, things had changed again. This time, Kevin said,

"King, here's the deal, and I don't think you'll take it. . . ." I knew then that something was badly wrong. Kevin said Vince had decided that they were not going to have Stacy back on television at all, not even the one show, and that it was just me. No Stacy, take it or leave it. I told him I'd leave it. I wasn't going back without my wife. I felt if I had done that, there would have been no reason for my leaving in the first place.

Now I had to call Stacy back and tell her that neither of us was going back. We were back to square one, and it had been an emotional roller-coaster ride for me, but even more so for Stacy.

I finished the day signing autographs and trying to smile for photographs, but my heart wasn't really in it. I kept thinking about Stacy and how she must be feeling about what went on that day. When I got back to my hotel, I was going to get cleaned up and Frank and I were going to go to Jacob's Field and watch the Indians play. That was the original plan, before the day got so screwed up. Once I was in my room, I called Stacy, but there was no answer on the condo phone. So I tried her cell phone. Same thing, no answer.

I immediately got worried. It wasn't like Stacy to be out of phone contact. I knew her parents had left a couple days before, so Stacy was in Florida by herself. With all the bad news she had absorbed in the day, I was really concerned for her safety. She had been visibly depressed for the last four months, then to get her hopes up that day and then have them dashed, I was worried. I called again, first the condo phone; then her cell phone. No answer to either. I called again, and again, and again. Frank and I decided not to go to the ball game. Instead, I just sat in my hotel room and dialed the phone trying to reach Stacy.

Finally, I called the police in Fort Myers and asked to have an officer go by and check our condo. About thirty minutes later, the police called me back and said they had gone to our condo and no one was there. Stacy's car wasn't there either. I knew she had a reservation on AirTran Airlines to return home to Memphis on Sunday. Frank suggested that maybe she decided to go home a day early and that she was en route. That's why she couldn't answer her phone, perhaps. That made sense. I was hoping that was the case. Maybe I could check with AirTran and find out.

I called and got someone who agreed to check Stacy's itinerary. Thank goodness, Frank was right. Stacy had changed her reservation. She had left Florida a day early. But then the agent said something that didn't make sense. He said that Stacy had left Fort Myers early that day, connected through Atlanta, and then she was flying to another city . . . not Memphis. She was not flying into Memphis until the next day, Sunday. WHAT??? Something was definitely not right. Why wasn't she flying straight from Florida to Memphis? The agent said she was due to land in Memphis on Sunday at around 6 P.M.

My mind was a blur. I tried to figure out where she was and what she was doing, but couldn't. I tried to call her every fifteen minutes all night long, but her cell phone was turned off. I tried to call her sister in Memphis to see if she knew where Stacy was but all I got was her answering machine, all night long.

Finally, at around ten the next morning, Stacy answered her phone. The first words out of my mouth were "Stacy, where are you?" She sounded fine. She said she was fine too and that she had decided to fly home early. When she landed, her sister had picked her up at the airport and asked if she wanted to go with her and some friends up to the Tennessee River, about a hundred miles from Memphis, and go water skiing. She said she decided to go and that her cell phone didn't have reception up there. Strangely enough, it was working now, and she said they were leaving to drive back at around four and that she would be back in Memphis at around 6 P.M. The same time the agent had said she would be landing in Memphis on AirTran.

I wanted to believe Stacy, but something told me she was lying to me. I talked to her for a while and had her describe what all she had done on the trip and who all was with her even down to what the weather was like. She told a convincing story. They had been water skiing, she was with her sister Suzanne and her friends, and the weather was hot and sunny. I told Stacy that I had one more day at the convention and that I would see her tomorrow morning.

As soon as I got off the phone with Stacy, I called Continental Airlines. I booked a flight from Cleveland to Memphis that landed at around 5 P.M. I called my buddy Frank and told him I wasn't going to be able to finish the convention, that I had to fly on back to Memphis on business. All the way home on that flight I was hoping that the AirTran agent had been mistaken, but I had my doubts. My flight landed right on time. I went straight to the AirTran ticket counter and asked about the flight that Stacy was supposed to be on. The agent working the counter knew who I was so I told him that I thought my wife was supposed to be on that flight but that she may have missed it, was there any way he could check and see if she was indeed on that flight. He looked down at his computer, typed in a few letters, and then looked up at me and said, "Yes, Mr. Lawler, your wife is on that flight." I felt like someone had just knocked the wind out of me. Stacy wasn't at the Tennessee River, she wasn't water skiing. And she sure wasn't with her sister.

I walked down to the AirTran gate that the flight was coming in at to wait for her plane to land. Then I decided I didn't want to confront her there at the airport, so I went and sat in a little restaurant next to the gate, where I couldn't be seen. I sat there and prayed that Stacy wouldn't get off that plane. I sat there for what seemed to be an eternity, and finally the plane landed. "Don't let her come off that plane, please, Lord." First a businessman, then another man, then a woman with her child, and then . . . Stacy. She had on a T-shirt and jogging pants, she looked like she hadn't done her hair that day, and she looked tired. She walked right past the restaurant I was sitting in and got on the moving walkway to go toward baggage claim.

I waited until she went down the escalator to get her luggage and then I went outside and walked downstairs to where I could see the drive in front of baggage pickup. There was Stacy's car, a Sebring convertible with the top down. Stacy's sister Suzanne was behind the wheel waiting to pick up Stacy. After a few minutes, Stacy came out with her bags and got into the car with her sister and they drove off. I went back into the airport and got my own bag and sat down and waited and tried to figure out what to do next. I waited for about thirty minutes and then I called home. Stacy answered. I asked her what time she had gotten home from the river. She said that she and her sister had just gotten home and that it had been a long drive and that she was tired. She sounded perfectly normal, like everything was fine. That's when I told her that I had left Cleveland early and that I had just landed in Memphis and that I would be home in about twenty minutes. She sounded surprised.

I took a taxi home and when I got there, Stacy's sister was still there. I asked her how the water-skiing trip was and she said they had had a lot of fun. I knew she was in on it too, but I didn't know exactly what it was. Suzanne left after I'd been home about thirty minutes. Now it was time to confront Stacy.

I had envisioned in my mind how this conversation

would go about a hundred times over the past few hours. I know this may sound weird, but I actually wanted to be making love to Stacy when I told her I knew where she'd been. I somehow thought that it would let her know that I was going to forgive her for what she had done, no matter what it was. I asked her to come into the bedroom and we sat down on the bed. I don't know if she suspected that I knew anything or not, but before I could ask her anything, she started to cry. I tried to get her to tell me what she was crying about but she couldn't. I really didn't know, but I thought maybe it was guilt feelings she was having. I was wrong. Finally, I said, "Stacy, I'm going to ask you a question, and all I want is a one word answer. Not, what, or how do you know, or anything except one word." She looked at me and nodded, and I said, "Who were you with last night? I know you weren't at the Tennessee River with your sister. I know you left Florida and went somewhere other than here. I saw you come in at the airport today, I was there and watched you. Now, who were you with last night?"

Looking back now, I really wish I'd never asked her that question. I wish I'd never heard the answer. I would give anything if I could go back in time and handle the whole situation differently. I wish I hadn't caught her at the airport. In fact, I wish I hadn't even known she wasn't where she said she was. Maybe if I hadn't confronted her. Maybe if she didn't feel backed into a corner. Maybe she wouldn't have told me what she told me next.

"I want to leave . . . I want a divorce." Those words coming out of Stacy's mouth hit me harder than I'd ever been hit by any wrestler. They floored me. This was my little angel who I'd been with, and loved more than anything in the world, for the past twelve years, telling me she wanted out. I didn't know what to do or what to say. My head was whirling. I knew she wasn't joking, this was real. But why? Stacy was already crying, then I started crying. She said she wasn't happy. That she wanted to find out who she was and what she wanted out of life. She said that she had been with me since she was nineteen years old and that I had made all the decisions in her life. She said she felt that I was controlling her and that she just wanted to be out on her own.

I tried to reason with her. I told Stacy I didn't realize she felt that way, but that I could certainly change anything she didn't like if she would stay and try to work things out. But her mind was made up. She was leaving me. I asked her if it was another man and she assured me that was not the case. She just wanted to be on her own. She wanted to get a divorce and move to Florida and live by herself. I couldn't talk her out of it, so I tried to compromise. I said, "Let's not rush into a divorce. Why don't you go down to our condo in Florida and stay there as long as you want, and just see what happens. Let's just call it a trial separation." I really thought that she just needed to get away for a while and once she was down there she would eventually want to come back.

That conversation took place at about eight in the evening on Sunday night, July 1, 2001. The next day I tried to act as if it had never happened. I guess I felt if I didn't mention it, maybe she would come to her senses. Monday went by rather uneventfully, with neither of us talking about Sunday. Then on Tuesday, we both worked a wrestling show in Memphis that was put on by our local television affiliate, WMC TV5. It was a pre–Fourth of July show called "The Star Spangled Celebration." Jimmy Hart was there, along with GrandMaster Sexay and a bunch of our local talent.

Stacy was in my corner as I went against Emory Hail. Jimmy Hart was in his corner. Once again, neither of us said anything to anybody about our situation. As a matter of fact, Stacy was acting as if nothing at all was wrong, so I started to feel better about things.

The next day I had to fly to Mansfield, Ohio, to appear at a monster truck show. Actually, Stacy was booked there as well, but she said she just didn't feel like going. I came back to Memphis the next day, and then on Friday we both flew to New York to work an independent show put on by our friend Elliott Pollack. Stacy wrestled on that show, which was in White Plains, New York, against Jasmine St. Claire. For people who'd never worked against each other before, they had a surprisingly good match.

The next day, we were booked to sign autographs at a place in Seaside Heights, New Jersey, then that night we were in Philadelphia for another independent show at the old ECW arena. That would be the last wrestling show Stacy worked.

All that week, things seemed so normal that I fell into a false sense of security. But on Monday, it became evident that Stacy had a plan. She informed me that her sister, Suzanne, was going to move to Florida along with her, and that they intended to leave that coming Friday! Once again the reality of it set in on me and I tried several times that week to talk her out of going, but there was nothing doing.

On Tuesday, Stacy wanted to trade her Chrysler Sebring convertible for a Jeep Cherokee. She said she would feel safer making the trip in a Jeep rather than a smaller car. I took her to the dealership that I did commercials for and introduced her to the owner, who found the car Stacy wanted. Next thing I knew, Stacy had her sister in there and she was getting a new car as well. Obviously they intended to make a fresh start of things when they got to Florida. She spent most of Wednesday packing her clothes and stuff, and on Thursday she brought a U-Haul trailer to the house.

I told Stacy I didn't think it was wise of her to try to drive and pull a trailer behind her on such a long trip, especially since she had never tried pulling a trailer before. I volunteered to drive her down there myself and then fly back, or have Jim Blake, my friend who worked at my house for us, drive her down there. She said she could handle it. She was a big girl and everything would be alright. Besides, her sister would be following along behind her if there were any problems. I didn't want to seem overly against the idea for fear that Stacy would say, "See, you're still trying to control me."

Then Friday came. The day Stacy was going to leave me. Appropriately, it was Friday the 13th, and I remember writing in my itinerary book, "Stacy left me on Friday the 13th, the unluckiest day of my life." My mind was a blur. Her Jeep was packed full of clothes and things. The U-Haul trailer was full as well. Stacy kept going back into the house and bringing out one more thing or another she had forgotten. The last thing on earth I wanted Stacy to do was leave, but I tried to appear helpful. I checked the trailer hitch to make sure it was connected right. I made sure Stacy had the right directions. I even gave Stacy and her sister a pair of walkie-talkie radios so that they could talk while they were following one another down the highway. I was so worried about Stacy trying to drive that long distance by herself, and especially pulling that trailer behind her. I remember how tiny and fragile she looked sitting behind the wheel of the Jeep with that big trailer behind it.

Tears were streaming down my face as I kissed her good-bye and watched her pull out of our driveway for the last time. I walked back into my house, and through tear-filled eyes, I looked around. Everything still looked like Stacy was there . . . but she wasn't. It was the most alone I have ever felt in my life. I remember thinking, "How could Stacy want to be alone like this?" Little did I know, she wasn't alone at all.

I found out two days later that there was a good reason she didn't want me or Blake to drive her to Florida. There was a good reason she wasn't worried about being able to handle driving that Jeep herself while pulling that big trailer behind her. It was because she didn't drive the Jeep herself. Just minutes after pulling out of my drive and leaving me standing there in tears, Stacy pulled over at some prearranged location and picked up a guy. The guy who drove her to Florida. The guy she spent the night with that night while they were on their way to Florida. The same guy she had gone to see when I caught her at the Memphis airport. How did I find out that Stacy had this guy with her on the trip to Florida? Well, they told me so themselves when I woke the two of them up at 3:30 in the morning in my and Stacy's condominium in Fort Myers.

I knew something wasn't right shortly after Stacy left our house to drive to Florida. I waited about an hour or so before I tried to call her on her cell phone. I left it that long because, one, I really couldn't talk without crying, and two, I didn't want to seem like I wasn't letting her be on her own. But when I called, Stacy had her cell phone turned off. Once again, it was like the time I was trying to reach her all night from Cleveland; her phone was off. Stacy never turned her phone off. A few hours later, she called me from a restaurant, or at least, outside of a restaurant. After that, her phone was off again.

Then late that night, she called and said that she and her sister had gotten a motel room and were very tired from driving and were going to bed. Once again, I could tell she was outside.

It was the same scenario the next day. Phone off, then a call saying how she and Suzanne were fine, then phone off again. Finally at around 5:30 in the afternoon the next day, I got a call from Stacy saying they had arrived at the condo and that they were unloading boxes. She said she would call me later. As I said earlier, I knew something wasn't right. It was just a gut feeling. When you've been with someone for more than ten years you know about certain things. You just know.

I hated to do it, but I picked up the phone and called my buddy Larry Burton. Larry lived in Boca Raton, Florida, about an hour and a half's drive from Fort Myers. I was embarrassed to ask Larry, but I didn't know what else to do. I felt I had to know. So I told Larry that Stacy had left and had arrived at our condo. And then I told him I thought she might not be alone. I asked him if he would drive up to Fort Myers and check things out. He said he and his wife, Roberta, would leave right away, drive up, and call me as soon as they got there.

The two-and-a-half hours I waited was the most excruciating time. A million things were going through my mind, and none of them was good. Finally Larry called. He said he and Roberta were parked right down the way from my condo. Larry sees Stacy's Jeep with the trailer parked in front, and he sees her sister's car as well, but he hasn't seen anyone go in or out. He asks if I want him to just go up to the door and knock and see what's going on. I told him not to do that. I asked him to just wait and watch for a while.

About an hour later, my phone rang. It was Larry. He said, "Are you sitting down?" I asked, "Why?" Larry said, "She's got a guy with her. We just saw him come out of your condo and take some boxes back in." I hadn't been sitting down, but suddenly I needed to. I actually felt like I was going to pass out. I literally got sick to my stomach. Is this what this was all about? Was all that stuff about wanting to be on her own, and finding out who she really was, just a bunch of lies? Was it really that she was just running off with another guy?

I looked down at my watch, and it was nearly 8:30. I didn't waste time calling Northwest Airlines, I just jumped into my car and drove to the airport. Since

Memphis is a hub city for Northwest, they have flights that leave late to a lot of places. By the time I got to the ticket counter it was a few minutes after nine. I asked if there were any late flights to Florida, preferably, Fort Myers. The guy behind the counter told me that the last flight to anywhere in Florida had left at around eight and the next thing wasn't until in the morning.

I had no idea what to do next. I don't think I could have gone back home and waited until the next morning. I think I would have gone crazy. Just at that moment, another agent walked up and said, "Hey, that Orlando flight is still on the ground. They've had a mechanical delay for over an hour, but it's fixed now and it's going to be taking off in about ten minutes." I asked if there was any possible way I could get on that flight. He ran my credit card, and I ran for the gate. I made the flight.

It was a little over a two-hour flight to Orlando, and Orlando was about a three-hour drive to Fort Myers. As soon as we landed, I got a rental car and headed south. I don't think the jet went much faster than I was driving that rental car. Looking back, I don't know how I even made that drive safely. Not for one minute did I concentrate or even think about driving. All I could see in my mind was Stacy with that guy. It was after midnight. I knew they had to be in bed together by now. I imagined everything they were doing to each other. My mind's eye could see them making mad, passionate love. Those kinds of thoughts tortured me that entire three-hour drive.

It was almost 3:30 in the morning when I pulled up in front of my condominium. Everything was totally dark. I put my key into the lock and turned it. Nothing happened. I realized the locks had been changed. They hadn't wasted any time. I wound up having to use my Swiss Army knife to cut through a section of the screened-in lanai and then climb up and over a wall just to get to my front door. Once again, my key didn't work. Another lock change.

I could see inside the condo and no one was up. All the lights were off. The master bedroom is upstairs with a guest bedroom downstairs. I didn't know where Stacy was, so I just started banging on the door with my fist as hard as I could. It was loud. The door had glass windows at the top of it and no curtains over them so I could see right into the condo.

After a minute or so, I saw a light come on in the guest bedroom. Then that bedroom door opened and Stacy's sister, Suzanne, stuck her head out. She immediately saw it was me standing at the front door and her eyes got as big as saucers! Like a turtle, her head shot back inside and the door closed. I banged on the door some more, and then I decided to do like you see in the movies. I'd just kick the damn door in! I backed up a couple of steps and prepared to kick that door right off its hinges. I was going to splinter that door all over the condo living room. I envisioned Clark Gable, as Rhett Butler, kicking in Scarlett's bedroom door in *Gone With the Wind*.

I reared back and . . . WHAM!! What a kick! I kicked that door so freakin' hard it knocked me backward and I almost fell down. I spun around and looked, expecting to see nothing left of the door except splinters. But to my astonishment, that damn door wasn't even fazed. Not a scratch on it! I backed up and got a running start this time. I almost gave the door a dropkick. WHAM!! Again . . . nothing! It didn't budge. That's when I said to myself, all that crap you see in the movies, it only works in the movies. Still, I was going to give it one last shot, when I saw Stacy coming down the stairs.

During one of Stacy's WWE angles, she was going to be in an "evening gown match" in which the Divas would try to rip each other's gowns off, and expose their underwear. On the shows, Stacy expressed concern because she said she doesn't wear underwear! Well, as I said before, she was telling the truth, she really didn't wear underwear, not even when she slept. As I saw her coming down the stairs she was putting on a robe. I knew she was naked underneath. I knew she had just been naked in the bed she was sleeping in. I knew she had just been naked with whoever she was sleeping with. She turned on a light, saw it was me, and unlocked the door.

I could tell she had just woken up and probably couldn't believe I was standing there. She rubbed her eyes, squinted at me, and said, "What are you doing?" I said, "What am I doing? . . . Stacy, what are YOU doing?" She just looked down at the floor. I said, "Where is he? I know you're not here alone. . . . Where is he?" Stacy said, "He's upstairs. But he's got nothing to do with this. He's got nothing to do with what's wrong between you and me."

I started up the stairs. I don't even know what I was thinking. I can understand how terrible things sometimes happen in these situations, because you are not in control of your thoughts, much less your actions. Years ago, I had a good friend who was shot and killed by a jealous ex-husband when he caught the guy in bed with his ex-wife. I knew I wasn't going to get violent. That wasn't going to accomplish anything. I just think I needed to see it for myself to convince me it was really happening.

When I got to the top of the stairs he was coming out of Stacy's and my bedroom. He, like Stacy, just looked down at the floor. I can't even remember exactly what-all was said. I just recall bits and pieces. I remember him saying that he never intended for this to happen, but that he had fallen for Stacy the first day he had met her. And something about the fact they weren't running off together, that he had just driven her down to be helpful.

But the thing I do remember, crystal clear, is Stacy sitting down at the top of the stairs, looking up at me, and saying, "I'm not in love with you anymore. I'm sorry, but I just don't love you anymore." Now, I just looked down at the floor. She couldn't make it any clearer than that. I don't know what I had thought. That maybe this guy had forced her down here against her will, and that I would come in like her knight in shining armor and take her back home and we would live happily ever after. That obviously was not the case, as much as I wanted it to be. She didn't want to be with me anymore. She didn't love me anymore.

Stacy and I went downstairs by ourselves and sat on the sofa. I asked if I could hold her in my arms one last time before I left. I was crying and I knew she felt bad for me, but she wasn't going to change her mind. I kissed her one last time, and as my mouth was pressed against her mouth, I could smell his cologne on her face. I knew I had lost her. I walked out the door and drove back to Orlando. That day, it wasn't good to be the King.

34

I can honestly say that for the few months after Stacy left, I was at the lowest point of my life. She was all I could think about. Everything I looked at in my house reminded me of her. Everywhere I would go would be someplace she and I had been together. All my friends would ask me about her, and she was all I would talk about. I tried to keep busy, taking as many independent bookings as possible, hoping that would take my mind off Stacy. It didn't.

The toughest time was at night. To crawl into the bed that she and I had shared for ten years, by myself, was a killer. I'd lie there and think about all the times that we'd made love in this bed and it was almost more than I could take. I'd pull her pillow over to me and hold it, and cry myself to sleep.

Our condo in Florida that Stacy had gone to wasn't half as big as my house in Memphis, so Stacy had not taken a lot of her stuff with her. She had left most of her personal belongings behind. In fact, when you looked around the house, it looked as if she was still there. Her closet was still full of her clothes and shoes. All her costumes, boots, and wigs she had worn in the WWE were still on the shelves. Even most of her makeup was left on the countertop on her side of our bathroom. And pictures of Stacy and me together were everywhere in the house. It was driving me crazy.

I knew I needed to get all her stuff out of my sight for my own sanity, but part of me wanted it to still be there. Like when someone dies, and the family won't touch a thing in that person's room. They leave things just the way they were when that person was alive. That's the way I was. It hurt like hell to look at her things, but it was all of her I had left. I was so miserable. I was down as low as you can get.

I was on a trip to the Northeast for an independent wrestling show: Delaware, New Hampshire, or Rhode Island, someplace I don't really remember. I was driving in a rental car by myself, thinking of Stacy . . . tears in my eyes. There was a point on the trip where I had to drive the car onto a ferry to get across some large body of water. The boat held fifty or sixty cars and was three decks tall.

I parked my car and got out and walked over to the side on the third deck. I looked over the railing and it was a long way down to the water. I just stood there staring out into the water. I thought how easy it would be to just jump over the side. I probably wouldn't survive the impact with the water, or at least it would knock me unconscious and then I would just go under. Then it wouldn't hurt anymore. All of a sudden, it was like I was in the movie *It's a Wonderful Life*. I was George Bailey, the down-on-his-luck character, played by Jimmy Stewart, who was about to end it all by jumping into a raging river. In the movie, George's guardian angel, Clarence, shows up and lets him see what the world would be like if he were not in it.

I thought about how many lives my life touches, and what the effect of what I was contemplating would be on those people. My mother, my sons, my brother, all my friends. How would they be affected if I were gone? Would they be hurt? That's when it came to me. The real reason I was thinking about doing what I was about to do. I didn't want it to stop hurting me, I wanted it to hurt Stacy. I wanted her to be sad that I was gone and to know that I wouldn't have done it had she not left me. I wanted her to feel guilty. I really think a lot of people who kill themselves do it to put somebody else on a guilt trip. The ultimate guilt trip.

That's what I was thinking. If I do that, then she'll feel bad. But then I thought, she probably wouldn't. If she still cared about me, if she still loved me, she'd still be with me. Maybe Clarence worked for me as well as he did for George Bailey, but for some reason, I decided against doing anything stupid. Well, maybe I should say, anything *that* stupid, because I did go on to do some pretty stupid things.

Right after it happened, I said on my web site:

> I am not going to say anything bad about Stacy . . . we had a great time together and it really is like the Garth Brooks song, "I could have missed the pain, but I would have had to miss the dance," and believe me, the dance with Stacy was wonderful! I hope that when this divorce is done, Stacy and I can still be friends, but that remains to be seen. Whenever lawyers get involved, things tend to get out of hand. So that is where I am today . . . trying to move forward, while waiting to be divorced . . . hoping to meet someone new to share my life with, while continuing to make appearances and wrestling dates.

That statement was part of one of my weekly updates on "Kinglawler.com." I'd sit in front of my computer and pour my heart out for all the world to read. Of course, I was also hoping Stacy was reading it as well. It was my only way of communicating my feelings to her.

Speaking of my feelings, I was on an emotional roller coaster with no brakes. I couldn't make up what was left of my mind. One minute, I was walking around, tears streaming down my face, wanting to beg her to come back. The next minute, I was cursing her name, swearing that I never wanted to see her again in my life! One day, I would e-mail her and tell her how much I missed her, the next day I would e-mail her and tell her how low-down I thought she was. As Stacy said, I became a real Jekyll and Hyde. I used the Internet to vent my frustrations. I also used the Internet to try to make Stacy jealous. (Guys, as you read this, look at it as a manual of what NOT to do to try to get your girl back.)

I got tons of e-mail from fans sympathizing with me on my ordeal; some had been in similar situations and were more than glad to offer their advice. One letter from a guy who had recently gone through what he called "the divorce from hell" included these words of wisdom, "Don't chase . . . replace!" When I read that, I thought, "He's right! That's what I'll do. I'll make Stacy think she's going to be replaced, and then she'll come running back to me."

So I went on a "talent search," so to speak. I was going to replace Stacy. I put an update on my web site that said I was looking for a valet to work with me at matches and on TV shows. "If you're a young, beautiful girl, who would like to be in the entertainment business, with the opportunity to travel and see the world, please reply!" I think it read something like that, but what probably went through most people's minds who read it was "King is seeking shallow, superficial, short-term and purely physical relationship." Actually, what it should have read was "Wanted—young, beautiful girl to be seen with the King in order to make Stacy jealous and want to come back to him," because that's what I was doing.

Well, that, and I really did want some companionship. I was unbelievably lonely without Stacy. I realized that I had gotten married to Kay when I was around twenty years old, had gone straight from her to Paula, and then, straight from Paula to Stacy. I had never really been alone my whole adult life, and I hated it. But with the new, "Don't chase, replace" attitude, I knew I wasn't going to be alone for long.

Now I did have several wrestling trips and events coming up that I could use a pretty young lady to accompany me on. Plus, I had a couple of cable network TV shows to do that I could use a valet on, not to mention our weekly Memphis wrestling TV show. So it wasn't like I was offering some bogus job to girls who were willing to be with the King.

One upcoming trip was to Trinidad, which is basically a tropical paradise. I was going down for three days to work a match against Buff Bagwell. I had never been there before, and it was going to be sort of like a paid vacation. What girl wouldn't want to fly to Trinidad, lie on the beach for a couple of days, walk out to the ring with me one night, and get paid for it all? I also had a trip coming up for thirteen days in Australia. Then two months after that, I had a two-week tour of England booked. Some lucky girl was going to get to see the world, and all she had to do was hang out with me.

Vince Russo had called me up out of the blue one day, and said he was now working for a businessman named Andrew McManus with the WWA, World Wrestling All-Stars. He said Andrew was going to promote ten wrestling events, culminating with a Pay-Per-View in Australia, and then, a couple of months later, ten shows, and another PPV in England. Vince Russo was helping Andrew round up available talent for the two tours. He told me he had already secured Bret "The Hitman" Hart; "The Chosen One," Jeff Jarrett; "Road Dogg" Jesse James; Buff Bagwell; Konnan; Disco Inferno, "The Vampire Warrior" David Heath, and his wife Luna Vachon; plus a lot of ex-WCW guys for the tour. A pretty impressive roster for a non-WWE tour.

When Vince Russo first called me I was in New York with Jerry Jarrett, Jeff Jarrett, and Scott Steiner, meeting with some wealthy investor about putting together a wrestling company that could get a show on network television. Nothing ever came of that meeting.

After I left the meeting I was walking around inside the World Trade Center when I answered my cell phone. I told Russo I didn't feel like going by myself to Australia for that long. I felt I would go crazy over there thinking about Stacy and being alone. This was one of the kinds of trips I would have loved when Stacy and I were together. We would have gone over, seen the sights, and experienced all sorts of new things together. But I was at the point, unless I had someone to share these new experiences with, they were really meaningless to me. That's when I told Russo I would go if they would buy me a companion ticket and I could find a girl to go with me so I wouldn't be by myself. Even though the round-trip airfare was close to eight thousand dollars, he agreed. The search was on!

High and low, here and there, the hunt was on. I was a man on a mission. All I had to do was find a young, beautiful girl who wanted to go with me to Trinidad, Australia, and England, and be a television star. Of course if she was open-minded and wanted to show her appreciation by bunking up with the King on these trips . . . even better! Now be honest: it shouldn't have been all that difficult to fill that job opening, should it? Free travel to exotic places, be on television, get paid five thousand dollars per trip, and maybe have sex with a celebrity . . . well, at least a guy who plays one on TV.

That's when I got a big dose of reality. It didn't take me long to come to the conclusion that when it comes to sex, all women want it . . . just not with me. I thought I'd have to beat the women off me with a stick. I thought they'd be waiting in line to go with me on these trips. I figured my web site would be flooded with female applicants wanting to be the King's next queen. NOT!

Don't get me wrong, I did get some hits on the Internet. Some girls sent bios and pictures and offered to go anywhere with me. Problem was, most of these girls looked like they'd fallen out of the ugly tree and hit every branch on the way down. Or if they looked okay, they lived so far away that it would be very difficult to coordinate travel arrangements.

I did get a response from a young girl in New York who seemed very promising. Her name was Catrina and her nickname was "Cat." How ironic. She had even sent several pictures of herself in similar poses to those that the Kat had done on my web site. The most she was wearing was a bra and panties, and in some of them, she wasn't even wearing that! She really looked great. A very athletic body, very shapely. Her puppies were not huge, they were not even big, but they looked just right on her body. I looked at the pictures and thought, "This is perfect. Replace Kat, with 'Cat.'"

I called the number she had put on her e-mail to line up a face-to-face meeting. It turned out to be the Murphy's Law phone call. What could go wrong did go wrong. First of all, Cat wasn't home. She didn't answer the phone, but her boyfriend did. He explained that he and Cat had been living together for about a year. He told me it was his idea for her to respond because he thought it would be a good way for her to earn some extra money, and to get on TV. Then he proceeded to ask me how much money she was going to get paid, how long she would have to be gone, and making sure she would have private sleeping quarters on each trip. Needless to say, I never crossed paths with that Cat.

Larry Burton was really worried about me. I think he thought I might really commit suicide, and I believe he felt partially responsible because he had been the one to tell me about Stacy being with someone in Florida. So Larry joined in the search for Stacy's replacement.

One night my phone rings and when I answered, Larry was like a little kid, he was so excited. "Jerry, I found her! Wait till you see her. She's perfect!" I said, "Whoa, you found who?"

"Your new girl! Her name's Donna. Wait till you see her. She's beautiful!" That all sounded good, but sometimes my taste and Larry's taste were not exactly the same, so I wanted to be the judge of whether she was beautiful or not. I told Larry to take some pictures of her with his digital camera, and e-mail them to me.

He took the pictures and sent them to me on the Internet. WOW! Donna *was* beautiful. Long, straight brown hair. A fantastic body, and around twenty-five years old. Larry had met Donna in Fort Lauderdale, Florida, when she walked into a bar and applied for a job as a bartender. The owner of the bar wanted to hire her on the spot, but Larry pulled her aside and said, "Before you take this job, let me tell you about an opportunity up in Memphis, Tennessee." She didn't take the job in Florida, instead she called me on the phone that night and she and I wound up talking for about three hours. After that conversation, I felt like I'd known her forever and we agreed that she'd come to Memphis and give working with me a try.

Just a few days after Donna and I talked, I had to be on two television shows that were being shot in Memphis. One was *Pop Across America*, a new talk show on TNN.

The other was *Insomniac Theater*, a really funny show on Comedy Central. Both these shows had a similar format. Each week they traveled to a different city and interviewed local personalities. Oddly enough, both shows were filming in Memphis on the same day, and both had asked me to be a guest on their show.

If the King was going to be on television, he had to have a hot-looking lady on with him. I called Donna on a Thursday and told her she needed to fly to Memphis the next day and be on these shows with me. On Friday morning, she left her home and flew to mine. I met her at the airport in Memphis at around three in the afternoon. What a pleasant surprise when I saw her in person. She was a knockout! I thought when I first saw her that she was way prettier than her pictures. She was also more petite than I had pictured her being. She was small, just like Stacy, except for her puppies . . . they were big, and they were real!

Her plane arrived in Memphis at around 3 P.M. and we were supposed to be on the set of the first show by 5:30, so she only had a very short time to get ready. We headed straight to my house and on the way I noticed she didn't bring a lot of luggage. You know how most girls overpack and take about three times more outfits than they will wear on a trip? Not Donna. She brought the bare necessities. Either she didn't plan on staying long, or she didn't own many clothes. She definitely didn't bring anything flashy enough to wear on TV, with me in my crazy King outfit. We didn't have time to go shopping, so I made a snap decision. Donna could wear one of Stacy's outfits!

I must have eaten a big bowl of stupid for breakfast that morning, because as I write this, I realize how dumb letting her wear Stacy's clothes sounds, but at the time, I thought nothing about it. As a matter of fact, I thought it was a good idea. Donna didn't seem to think too much about it either, as she tried on one costume after another from Stacy's closet.

Every one of Stacy's outfits fit Donna perfectly. Every outfit looked great on her, just as it had on Stacy. Stacy's shoes were just a little on the tight side. Donna wore a size seven, but all of Stacy's shoes were size six and a half. She finally decided on this shiny, silver-metallic-looking, skintight bodysuit. It was made out of Spandex, and it looked like she was poured into it and forgot to say, "When!"

We threw that outfit into a bag, and she picked out a pair of clear plastic heels to go with it, and we headed for the door. That's when I got my second bright idea. Donna had arrived wearing jeans and a T-shirt. I suggested she pick out something else to wear in the car on the way down to the TV show. She put on one of my favorite dresses of Stacy's. A little pink, flowery sundress that was so short it barely covered the promised land. I grabbed my digital camera and took a few shots of her in that dress standing in the kitchen, then we left.

The first show, *Pop Across America*, was being taped outside, right on the banks of the Mississippi River. The famous World War II bomber *The Memphis Belle* was in the background. My segment consisted of Donna following me onstage and standing behind me, holding my crown while I did an interview with the host. I can't remember his name, and I don't think the show is still on the air, but we talked mostly about Andy Kaufman, and then I gave a piledriver to one of the extras. I don't think Donna spoke on the show, but the host did point out how good she looked. I remember at one point in the interview, I thought Donna slapped me in the back of the head, and then I realized I had been dive-bombed by one of the huge bugs that were flying around the outdoor lights. As soon as I piledrove the guy, my segment was over. The next guest was B. B. King, but we didn't have

Donna

time to hang around and watch him. We jumped into a limo and headed across town to do *Insomniac Theater*.

Now this show was a little more to my liking. It was taped in a well-known strip club called, P.T.'s. Naked "puppies" were everywhere! The host talked to me as I sat on a couch beside Donna. In the background there were two strippers pretending to make out in a hot tub.

After the interview, I was the referee for a four-girl wrestling match in a ring full of Jell-O. The girls started out in bikinis, but by the end of the match, I was the only one with clothes on! Donna took all of this foolishness in stride and did a great job as my valet on both shows. We didn't finish taping until well after midnight and then I took Donna to a hotel not far from my house and checked her in. I had told her she was welcome to stay in one of my spare bedrooms, but she insisted on the hotel. Damn!

The next morning, I went to the hotel and picked Donna up. We went to the airport and caught a flight to Philadelphia. I was booked to wrestle in the old ECW building, for the same promotion I had worked for a month earlier. Ironically, that show, a month ago, had been the last show Stacy worked with me. Now, one month later, in the same building, in front of the same fans, it was the first show Donna worked with me.

Those ECW fans were a vocal bunch. They were also very knowledgeable when it came to wrestling. They knew from the Internet that Stacy had left me and that I was looking for a new valet. When Donna walked out with me, and got into the ring looking like a million dollars, a loud chant started. "Kat Fucked Up! Kat Fucked Up!" Donna did well at her first-ever wrestling event and seemed to like her new job. After the show, we had separate hotel rooms, but before Donna went to her room, we had a long, heart-to-heart talk. Donna was very pretty, but she was no dummy. She sensed that I was looking for more than just a coworker.

The next morning we flew back to Memphis. When we got back to my house, Larry Burton had arrived from Florida. Larry knew how bad I had been hurting, but he figured I'd be a hundred percent better if I'd just get laid. I think he assumed that would have been taken care of during the two days Donna had been with me. When I told him that nothing had gone on between Donna and me other than business, he went ballistic. He took Donna down into my den and had a long, heart-to-heart talk with her.

When they came out, Larry's face was all red and he was mad as he could be. "That's it! She's outta here! Pack your stuff, we're taking you back to the airport." Larry was livid. Donna came to me and said, "Look, it's obvious I came up here for one reason, and you guys want me here for another reason. You're a great guy and all, but I just got out of one relationship, and I'm not looking to jump back into another one. I just can't do it right now. If you want me to stay and work with you on a purely professional basis, I'll be glad to stay. If you want someone you can have more than that with, then I might as well go on back to Florida." She stayed one more day, and then went on back to Florida.

When Donna left, it had been thirty-eight days since Stacy had gone. During that time I had constantly tried to keep in touch with Stacy, either by phone or by e-mail. Sometimes she'd answer and sometimes she wouldn't. We pretty much stayed on bad terms. In one of her e-mails, she told me to get over her, to get on with my life . . . find someone new, and move on. That was about the same time the "Don't chase . . . replace" e-mail came in.

It was at that point that I pulled the dumb stunt of the century. I wrote an e-mail to Stacy saying something like "Oh, I'll get over you all right, I'll get on with my life, and as soon as our divorce is final, I'll find someone new and move on. . . . As a matter of fact, I'll give you a little preview." Then I put in the photographs of Donna. Donna wearing the silver outfit on the TV shows. Donna wearing the little pink sundress in the kitchen. And a couple more I took while we were in Philadelphia. I just knew that when Stacy saw those pictures she would think, "I'm not going to let some other girl have my things, and my life, and my husband. I'm going to go back to Memphis and get it all back!" I guess there's a good reason they say, "Men are from Mars and women are from Venus," because men and women sure don't think alike.

When Stacy read my e-mail and saw the photos of Donna, her reaction was anything but what I had expected. Actually I hadn't had any communication with Stacy for about a week. She wouldn't answer her phone or return an e-mail. It was really frustrating. But the day after I sent her the pictures of Donna, my phone rang. It was Stacy. The first words out of her mouth were "Your new girl is really pretty, what's her name?" What?! That's not what I wanted to hear. At least I didn't think it was. I wanted Stacy to be jealous, to be mad, and upset, but she was cool as a cucumber. "Oh, her name's Donna."

The small talk went on for a few minutes with me explaining how I met her and the shows we had worked and all. Then Stacy finally said the words I wanted to hear from her. She said, "Well, I've been thinking about coming back to Memphis and spending a few days with you and talking about everything." YES!!! It had worked! She's coming home for a few days to talk! I just knew that once I got her back in Memphis I could convince her to stay. She wanted to know when I would be in Memphis and when I would be out on the road wrestling. I told her I had a trip that weekend to New Jersey, but that I would be back in Memphis on Sunday. She said she would fly in on Monday. Then right before she hung up, and while I was still on cloud nine, she said, "Oh, by the way, were those my clothes Donna was wearing?"

Well, Stacy came to Memphis alright, but somehow she must have gotten her days confused. Imagine that. I know I told her I was leaving to go to New Jersey on that Thursday. And I know she had told me she would get into town on the following Monday. Somehow, right after I left Memphis on Thursday, she arrived in Memphis . . . on Thursday! When I arrived in New Jersey, all happy and everything, I got a call on my cell phone. It was my ex-wife Paula. She said, "Jerry, your bank just called me and said they couldn't get in touch with you, but to tell you that Stacy just came into the bank and cleaned out one of your bank accounts!"

Later that same day, Stacy went to my house with the police and a locksmith. My entrance music was playing and I was having to walk out to the ring in New Jersey, while I was talking on my cell phone to the police in Memphis, trying to convince them not to let Stacy into my house. What an ordeal.

I canceled an autograph-signing appearance the next day and flew back to Memphis. By the time I got home, Stacy had already hired a divorce lawyer. Her lawyer talked with my lawyer, and it was agreed that Stacy, along with her attorney, would come to the house, meet with me and my attorney, and she would be allowed to go through the house and get the rest of her things.

You can't imagine the feeling of having to be chaperoned by two lawyers as you walk around your own house with your own wife. It was awful. She didn't stay long. It was such an uncomfortable situation. She got some things here and there, and when she stopped and looked into her closet, without taking anything, I said, "What about your clothes?" She just looked at me and said, "Give them to Donna."

As I write this, it's been over a year since the divorce began. It's still not final, and sometimes I wonder if it ever will be. Stacy and I have both spent a lot of time and money with lawyers trying to get things settled, but to no avail. Her being around the other guy lasted a few months and then that was over, and now she is living by herself in Florida. At the moment she has no divorce lawyer and things are sort of at a standstill as far as that goes, and sometimes I think there may be hope of putting things back together someday. But she still insists that the other guy was not the reason she left to begin with, and that she feels she has to spread her wings and find out if she can make it on her own.

Stacy has gone to real-estate school and is now selling houses in Florida for Century 21. Her business cards read Stacy Carter, not Stacy Lawler. I guess that should tell me something. My friend Buddy Wayne and I were talking the other day, about how long it takes to get over someone you love. I told him Stacy had been gone for over a year now. He said his wife, Terri, had been gone for "ten years, three months, and thirteen days." I hope I'm not still counting the days ten years from now.

35

While I was gone from the WWE, I never really tried to do anything in particular to get my job back. I knew it was one of those things where the ball was completely in their court. I had been very close once to coming back with Stacy, but now Stacy was no longer in the picture. I felt from the conversations we had at that time that they wanted me back, but Stacy was the holdup. Now I felt that eventually they would call and open the lines of communication again.

I knew the person that I would eventually need to deal with was either Kevin Dunn, head of television, or Vince himself. In the meantime, I figured it wouldn't hurt if I called a couple of other people up there in Stamford who I thought might be against my coming back. I called Bruce Prichard to see if I could mend some of the fences I knew I'd damaged. I just hoped I hadn't busted them completely. Bruce was very gracious. We had a long talk and he wasn't upset or angry, nor did he hold any grudges. We talked about my coming back and he suggested I call Vince.

The next day, I called J.R. and we talked for a long time as well. I have always enjoyed talking to J.R. and I value his opinion. J.R.'s advice was to concentrate on the business at hand, meaning my divorce from Stacy. I

should get that done and behind me, and then I could talk to Vince about coming back. At the time, I agreed. A divorce is serious business and needs your full attention if you want to protect your own interests, which I intended to do. I had made the statement "No matter how long you're married, you never really know your wife until you meet her in court." I was about to find out how true that was.

There were times I thought I would be back and times I thought I'd never be back. I felt really good about the situation when *SmackDown!* was in Memphis. My friend Bruno Lauer—or "Harvey Whippleman" as he's known when he's a manager—called me and asked if I was going to come down to the show and see the guys. I told him I would like to, but I didn't know if I would be welcome, so I probably wouldn't go. Bruno apparently told J.R. that I would like to come down and see every-one but I felt uncomfortable about it.

Everyone had been in Nashville for *Raw* the night before and when they arrived in Memphis, I got a call from J.R. It was about one in the morning. He more or less invited me to the Pyramid to see everybody and just hang out. He said, "Everybody misses you," and it made me feel really good. But I told J.R. I didn't want it to look to Vince like I was down there begging for my job back. At WWE shows, you see guys backstage who are just hanging around. I think it's sad that these guys are there just hoping to get noticed or begging for a job, so to speak. But J.R. said he had already told Vince I might come and Vince told J.R. to tell me to come and that he had "a big hug for me!"

Once I was at the Pyramid, it was like old home week. Everyone I saw came up and put their arms around me and told me how much they missed having me there. They were saying they hoped I would be back soon. It really was a good feeling. Someone who had been in the production meeting that morning told me that Vince had said I might come to visit and he asked everyone to make me feel wel-come. Well, they did. When I went into Vince's office, I really didn't know what to expect, but as soon as he saw me, he gave me that big hug and said, "King, this is your home and whenever you get your personal problems straightened out we would love to have you back."

So I felt really good about the situation. But I still did-n't know how long the divorce would take. I still don't. This divorce could drag on for years, who knows. But now I felt secure in the fact that when that day came, that Stacy and I were actually divorced, I would be wel-comed back in the WWE.

The thing I still couldn't figure out was why my job seemed to hinge on Stacy and me being divorced. I rea-soned they thought I couldn't give my full attention to the job while I was still embroiled in legal issues with

Stacy. Even since I've been back, nobody in the WWE has tried to talk to me at all about the Stacy situation and what all really went down. I guess I'll never know exactly what their thinking was.

I was staying really busy through the months of September and October of 2001. I wrestled a lot of independent shows around the country. Pittsburgh, Pennsylvania; Savannah, Tennessee; York, Pennsylvania; and Gallup, New Mexico, to name a few. In Gallup, we wrestled in an outdoor arena setting that had been hollowed out of the desert mountains by the Good Lord himself. It was one of the most awesome places I have ever seen. Thousands of Native American fans were on hand to see the likes of Brian Christopher, Buff Bagwell, me, and Joanie Laurer, formerly known as Chyna.

It was the first time I had seen Chyna since she left the WWE and we sat down and talked about what went wrong for both of us. She told me what happened between Triple H and her, and I talked about Stacy and me. We both wound up crying and hugging each other, but she seemed to be stronger and in better shape emotionally than I was.

During September and October, I was also working with a racing team out of Lexington, Tennessee, that had put my picture and logo on two cars they owned. We had a big unveiling for the cars that got a lot of media coverage in the mid-South, then I made appearances at races in Salem, Indiana, and Du Quoin, Illinois, with the cars. I did a couple of appearances for Acclaim Video's "Legends of Wrestling" video game in New York and Las Vegas, and then it was time for the Trinidad and Australia trips.

While I was doing all this traveling, I was still trying to find some young lady to take with me to Trinidad and Australia. I was starting to feel like I had red marks all over me from where girls had been touching me with ten-foot poles. Larry Burton was still looking high and low. He went to a modeling agency in Memphis and got names of about twenty pretty young ladies and scheduled them to all come to my house for an in-person interview. The deal was, we were now looking for someone to do valet appearances in Trinidad and Australia, and to be on our local Memphis wrestling show every week. The pay was going to be five thousand dollars per trip, for a total of ten grand, not too bad.

The models started arriving at around 11:30, and by noon there were eleven lovely girls sitting in my house waiting for Larry and me to interview them. Problem was, once they'd all arrived all we could do was sit and stare at the television in disbelief. For this was September 11, and terrorists had just flown two jet airliners into the World Trade Center. We tried to talk, on and off, one by one, to the girls, but the news on TV just kept getting worse and worse. First the one plane, then the second. Then one tower collapsed, then the second. It was the most unbelievable and horrible thing I had ever witnessed on television.

Later that evening, Larry and I took one of the young ladies out to dinner. Her name was Jenni. She was very, very pretty, but she was very, very young. She had just turned twenty. I had said before, as a joke, that I'm not embarrassed to date younger women, except when I have to drop them off at school. Well, Jenni was a college student, and coincidentally, she worked at a bank right around the corner from my house. She had all the qualifications, though. She looked great. Long, dark hair. Very pretty face, and a beautiful smile. Plus, she said it was her dream to be able to travel and see the world.

I thought I had found my traveling companion. Jenni and I talked a lot the next few days trying to iron out all the details. She had some concerns. One, in order to go on these two trips it would mean she'd have to drop out of that semester of college. She wasn't that upset about school, because she knew she could start back later, but it meant the money she had already paid for school would be wasted. She was also concerned about the time she would have to take off from her job at the bank to go on the trips.

We talked about it, and she even brought her father over to my house to talk about it. I finally thought we had everything worked out, but then Jenni called me and turned me down. I really hated that. She's been turning me down ever since as well. We have stayed in touch and have even been out on a couple of occasions for lunch or a movie, and every chance I get, I rub it in about what a great time she would have had in Australia.

Now the time was short, and I was getting really desperate. I couldn't bear the thought of going out of the country by myself. I needed a girl. All my friends were telling me, "You're trying too hard. You don't find someone when you're looking for them. You find someone when you're not looking." That sounded like a crock of crap to me. What was I going to do? Just sit in my house and wait for some beautiful girl to knock on my door and say, "King, here I am!" Fat chance!

I have a friend in Hollywood who is a talent manager, named Michael Dacey. Larry Burton had told Michael about our dire situation and asked him if he could help out. Michael put out a casting call in Hollywood for me. The next thing I know, he is flooding me with photos of actresses who are applying for what they think is a job in sports entertainment television. What the heck! I didn't care. All I knew was, I suddenly had my pick of beautiful, would-be movie stars who wanted to come and work with me. Well, they really didn't care about me, they didn't even know about me, they just wanted to be TV stars. I just wanted to find out if there was any truth to all those stories I'd heard about the casting couch!

Michael must have e-mailed me at least fifty photos of Hollywood hopefuls. There were blondes, brunettes, and redheads. There were tall ones, short ones, very pretty ones, and not-so-pretty ones. All I had to do was choose one. Sounded too good to be true. Well, you know how when something sounds too good to be true, it usually is?

Larry and I were looking at the pictures together and the first one I picked out looked like she might be an exotic dancer. Larry said, "Come on . . . she's a stripper . . . she's trash!" I reminded him that "one man's trash is another man's girlfriend!" He wound up talking me out of her.

I finally settled on the one that looked like she was sweetest, shyest, and most innocent. I figured those are the ones that usually surprise you. I just knew she would be on that Hollywood "actress diet," you know, three males a day. I was betting that once I met her, she'd be anything but shy and innocent. Her name was Kelli. We spoke with her agent and arranged it so Kelli could fly to Memphis and meet me. Turned out, Kelli was just exactly what she looked like she would be . . . sweet, shy, and innocent, with emphasis on the shy. She was very pretty in person, but for the two days she was in Memphis, I don't think she said two words to me. I know she never said "Yes."

Now I'm starting to think I may have to take an inflatable date to Australia with me, but with my luck, her inflatable boyfriend would probably show up and beat me up! I NEEDED A GIRL! I felt like Austin Powers in that movie where he had lost his mojo. My self-confidence was at an all-time low. Probably, if a girl would have told me she'd go out with me, I would have told her to "think it over."

Then, the Mid-South Fair came along. It's the last week of September every year. I was going to be appearing, along with my race car, for ten straight days at this huge fair in Memphis. Thousands of women would be walking past my booth and seeing me. Plus, it was at this same fair, years earlier, that I had met my second wife, Paula. The fair would certainly be the answer to my prayers.

Ever notice how when you're single or don't have someone special in your life, all it seems like you see are happy couples? I'd never seen so many happily married people. The fair was overrun with them. Everyone that came by my booth, it was the same story; "King, can I get you to sign an autograph to me and my wife?" or, "Mr. Lawler, will you sign an autograph that I can take to my boyfriend?"

On about the third day of the fair, an old friend happened by. He was a guy I had met nearly thirty years ago when I was painting signs at Jackie Fargo's nightclub. He's a very successful businessman and he now lives in Phoenix. He was in town visiting family and he said he didn't know why he came to the fair by himself, but that he just "felt drawn there."

I hadn't seen him in probably fifteen years, so we had a lot of catching up to do. We talked and talked, and I told him about my recent breakup with Stacy, and how hard I was taking it. He then related a similar situation he had lived through with his ex-wife. He told me that when his wife left him he was devastated. He spent hundreds of thousands of dollars trying to buy her back, but to no avail. He was to the point that he was an emotional wreck and about to be hospitalized. It sounded really familiar.

My friend said he came to the realization that he was not going to let her do that to him. He went out, started dating and having fun, and found someone else. He's been happily married now for more than ten years. He told me that after his ex-wife sensed he was over her, she came around and told him she was moving out of town and that she thought they might spend one last night together, "for old times' sake." He said it was his greatest triumph when he was able to tell her he wasn't interested. I told him that all sounded good, but if Stacy asked me to spend one last night with her, no way in hell would I turn that down!

We went out to a couple of clubs on Beale Street and he started introducing me to women left and right. He said, "All you have to do is get your confidence back. Why, you're the King! You're Jerry Lawler! Any girl would want to go out with you!" I felt like I was getting a pep talk from a football coach or something. Whatever the reason, I felt a lot better after talking with him. My new motto was going to be "life, liberty, and the happiness of pursuit!" He told me to quit thinking of nothing but Stacy. I told him, "From now on, I'll be very broadminded. In fact, I'll think of nothing else!"

The very next day, a cute young girl named Amy stopped by my booth at the fair. Blond and in her early twenties. I was all over her like white on rice. I was determined to try out my new motto. "I am the King! What girl wouldn't want to go out with me?" We talked a bit and she and her friend hung around my booth for a while, then they left. Ah, but they came back! We talked some more, and found out we had quite a bit in common. In fact, a lot in common. She was just divorced at the same time Stacy had left me. She had gotten married on the same day Stacy and I had gotten married. We were both married less than a year. OK, so we didn't have a lot in common, but we were both on the rebound, and she was cute and I figured, "What the heck."

We exchanged phone numbers and then, lo and behold, she showed up back at the fair again the next day! We talked some more and then that evening I met her and some of her friends for dinner at a local Applebee's. Amy's friends seemed a little more thrilled to be around the King than she did, but that was okay. To me, this was like a date, so I thought I was really making progress.

Then, right there in front of everyone, I propositioned her! What I mean is, I told her I was looking for someone to go to Trinidad with me the next week and I thought she would be perfect. Her friends went crazy! "Oh my God, Amy! You've got to do it! What an opportunity! Think how much fun that would be!" They all chimed in and said she should go. And finally, she said she would!

The next day, I took Amy on a shopping spree to get some cool clothes for the trip. She was a bit apprehensive about going out to the ring with me, but I assured her she would be fine. All she had to do was walk out with me and look pretty, and for her, that should be no problem. I bought her about a thousand dollars' worth of clothes at the mall and then we went to have dinner at Kobe's Steak House. While we were eating and talking about the trip, we both suddenly realized something that would probably nix the whole deal. I had just taken it for granted that Amy had a passport. Of course, she didn't. The trip was doomed.

When you live in Memphis, Tennessee, trust me, it's impossible to get a passport in three days. That's what we needed. But sometimes, when you need to do the impossible, it's good to be the King. I called up my friend Congressman Harold Ford Jr. He was in Washington, but his office went right to work on it for me. Believe it or not, the next day, thanks to Congressman Ford and Federal Express, Amy had her passport! That night, to celebrate, we went out to dinner with her friends and at the end of the evening, someone suggested something really crazy. "Let's all go get a tattoo!"

It was a little after midnight, and I found myself in a car with Amy, her female roommate, and a young married couple who were friends with Amy, driving to downtown

Memphis to look for a tattoo parlor that was still open. As I said earlier, Amy was in her early twenties, as was her roommate. Her married friends looked to be around twenty-five. They all seemed gung ho about getting a tattoo, so I didn't want to seem like an old fuddy-duddy by objecting. But the truth is, I had always sworn I would never have a tattoo anywhere on my body. One, I always thought it was sorta low class or something, if you know what I mean. And, two, I have a low tolerance for pain outside the ring. I can't brush my teeth without crying. Sometimes I just use Whiteout. But I don't mean to offend anyone with tattoos. I realize they are all the rage right now and almost everyone has one. Plus, I was a new man now. Everything was different without Stacy, so why shouldn't I be different too? We found a tattoo parlor that was open late. Actually, I think all tattoo parlors are open late for people just such as us. People who, at the end of a fun night, decide to do something crazy.

We all started looking at the pictures on the wall and tried to pick out something appropriate. One of the coolest tattoos I'd ever seen, and one that I would have liked to have had, was the Superman logo. You know, the red "S" in the triangular shield. I've loved Superman since I was a child. But the guy Stacy ran off with has a Superman "S" tattooed on his arm, so that was definitely out.

Then it hit me. I reached into my wallet and pulled out one of my business cards. I asked the guy, "Can you put this on my wrist?" He said, "Sure." It was a crown—what else? It was perfect. Now I was excited. I sat down, and the artist went right to work on me. It hurt a little, but not too bad. The thing that made it bearable was the young lady right next to me with her blue jeans down to her knees. She was getting a dolphin tattooed right over her gimmick, and I got to watch! What a sight! She wasn't one of the girls in our party. Oh, did I mention that everyone else in our party chickened out, and I was the only one who went home with a tattoo? But I really like it. It's a cool tattoo. And the artist said he was so honored to do the King's first tattoo, he didn't even charge me!

Now it was the night before we were to leave for Trinidad. Amy was going to come to my house and spend the night because we had to leave at about six in the morning for the airport. I could tell she was a little nervous about spending the night. We had been out several times, and we had kissed a bit, but nothing more. She arrived at around nine o'clock with her roommate, who was going to share the guest bedroom with Amy and then drive us to the airport in the morning.

For some reason, Amy was acting really strange and I could tell she was having second thoughts about going. I think a lot of it had to do with the fact that all the times we had been out, it had been her, me, and her friends, but now it was going to be just her and me, and I think she was a little afraid.

Looking back on it, I can't say I blame her. We'd known each other for just a little over a week and here we were about to go out of the country together for a week. I knew I didn't want her to do anything she didn't feel one hundred percent comfortable with, so I told her I thought it would be best if she didn't go. Amy didn't get upset, but her roommate did. She started crying and apologizing to me for the way Amy was acting. I told her it was no big deal, even though I knew it was, and then Amy went out to her car and got all the clothes I had bought for her and brought them in for me to keep. At around ten, she and her roommate went home. Next morning, I went to Trinidad. Alone.

I was in a pretty lousy mood on that trip. The fact that I tore the rotator cuff in my right shoulder on the first move in my match with Buff Bagwell didn't help anything either. It wasn't Buff's fault, it was just one of those things. The bell rang to start the match. Buff posed a bit and showed off his big biceps, and then we locked up. I told Buff to shove me, and when he did I went backward and took a bump on my back. Except this time, for some reason, I landed on my elbow and I felt something pop in my shoulder. I finished the match but it hurt like crazy and it still bothers me, especially when I'm playing softball or football.

We only had to work the one show over there. The crowd was good and really into the matches, and the country was very pretty, but I couldn't wait to leave. When I got back home to Memphis from Trinidad, I had a whopping five days before I had to leave again for Australia.

My situation was looking pretty grim. There was no way on earth I was going to find a girl to take to Australia in less than a week. No ladies were being nice to me, especially not Lady Luck. During the five days, I had to do an autograph session with NASCAR drivers down on Beale Street for the Sam's Town 250 Race that was being held that weekend at Memphis Motorsports Speedway.

My car was running in that race. It got rained out.

I had to wrestle in Little Rock, Arkansas, the night before I flew out to Australia. On the way back from the show, I ran over something in the road, a tire, or wheel, or something, and tore the entire bottom out of my P.T. Cruiser. It had to be towed into Forrest City, Arkansas, and my son Brian had to drive seventy miles there to pick me up and bring me back to Memphis. And the capper of it all was, Stacy flew back to Memphis to see me for a day and try to settle our divorce with a one-on-one meeting. Three months earlier when she left me, she said she didn't want anything other than to live on her own. When she came back that day, she had some papers from her lawyer that said she wanted a quarter of a million dollars . . . in cash! It was not good to be the King that week.

I knew I was going to be miserable in Australia by myself so I made the only decision I felt I could live with. I wouldn't go. I had never canceled out of a wrestling booking in my life, but I just knew I couldn't go over there by myself. So I called the promoter, Andrew McManus, in Australia and told him of my decision. He panicked! He begged, he pleaded. He didn't want a no-show on his first event. He tried everything to persuade me to come, then he played his trump card. He said, "King, there are three girls to every man in Australia . . . and they're all beautiful! Wait till you see them. Plus, I just had Kiss over here last month and I still have all the numbers of the girls we had for Gene Simmons! I personally guarantee that if you come to Australia, you will not be lonely. I guarantee it!" Well, that was enough for me. Oh, not his personal guarantee, but the thought of having some of Gene Simmons's hot chicks! I told McManus I would be there. I was headed down under. Hopefully in more ways than one.

On Tuesday morning, October 16, 2001, I flew from Memphis to New York, a two-and-a-half-hour flight. I got off the plane, went into the city, and did a two-hour personal appearance at the Annual Toy Fair for Acclaim's Legends of Wrestling video. As soon as that was over, I rushed right back to the airport and flew from New York to Los Angeles, a six-hour flight. I got off one plane in L.A. and got right on another and flew from L.A. to Sydney, Australia, an eighteen-hour flight. When I landed in Sydney, I had to change planes and fly straight to Perth, Australia, where the first show was going to be—another four hours. A grand total of over thirty hours of flying to get there.

The first thing I realized was, Australian math is different from American math. Because if there are three girls to every one guy in Australia, I'll kiss Andrew McManus's butt in the middle of Sydney harbor, and give him an hour to draw a crowd!

I can't say I didn't have a good time in Australia. It is a really beautiful country, and the people there are wonderful. I said in an update on my web site that if I couldn't live in the United States, Australia is where I would want to live. But I didn't meet any girls there. I did finally see one very pretty girl at the matches on the last night I was there, but just got to say hello in passing. I found out later her name was Fiona. I hope I get back to Australia sometime in the future, because I have a feeling Fiona could make the long trip worthwhile.

On about the sixth day into the trip, I cornered Andrew and said, "Where are all those women you promised? Where are the Gene Simmons chicks?" He said, "Tonight, King, tonight!" Later that evening, I was in my hotel room—alone—when my phone rang. It was Andrew. He said, "King, come on down to the bar, I have a couple of girls who want to meet you."

I headed downstairs and went into the bar. I looked at the girls standing there with Andrew. I said, "Hello," then I grabbed Andrew by his elbow and pulled him aside. I said, "What should I do when I'm through with them . . .

kiss them good night, or just shake their paws?" I mean, these two girls had faces only a plastic surgeon could love. I'm not saying the one girl had a big snout, but compared to her, Pinocchio was snub-nosed. And I wanted to ask the other one, "Who did your makeup? Bozo?"

There were a lot of things I wanted to say, but what I really said was "I'd love to stay down here and talk to you all, but I'm expecting an important phone call from the States, so I must get on back up to my room." I got out of that bar, and a few days later, I got out of Australia, and the only girl I had talked to at length on the entire trip was . . . Stacy. Over a thousand dollars' worth of long-distance calls. I knew I shouldn't have gone on my own.

When I got back to Memphis, I was more lonely than ever. Then I finally caught a break. A beautiful young twenty-four-year-old girl named Briana called me up. I had actually known Briana since she was around thirteen. I was friends with her parents and I had watched her grow up. She and her dad had always liked wrestling and they had come to a lot of our matches over the years.

Briana

Well, Briana had grown up, and as a matter of fact, was just about two weeks away from getting married. She had already been given the bridal showers and she and her fiancé had picked out a house that they were going to move into. Then, something happened between them, and everything was off. No wedding, no house, no fiancé, nothing. She was calling to cry on my shoulder at the same time I needed a shoulder to cry on.

Briana and I hooked up and hung out together for a while. We went to movies, we went out to eat, we went shopping. She was really good for me and hopefully I helped her as well. We both did a lot of crying because we were both going through the same thing, but just having someone around so you wouldn't have to feel so alone was a tremendous help.

Another friend that I hung out with was a guy named Mark Amagliani. I'd known Mark since he went to school with Stacy to become a hair stylist. I guess it's true that misery loves company, because Mark and his woman had just split up too. He and I went out to a few clubs and looked for girls, but we got shot down so many times we needed parachutes. Now, believe it or not, my good friend Mark has hooked up with my good friend Briana and they have totally fallen in love. They are buying a house together and are the picture-perfect couple. I wish them all the luck in the world, they deserve it.

One night Briana and I were at a wrestling show we were doing every week at Harrah's Casino in Tunica, Mississippi. Briana was sitting out in the crowd with my mom and my brother and his wife, who had all ridden down to the show with us. I was backstage going over the matches with the wrestlers and getting ready to wrestle as well.

Someone told me there was someone who wanted to see me. I said, "Who is it?" and they said, "I don't know. It's a girl, though." I figured it was Briana com-

Joni, now those are some puppies.

ing backstage and wanting to talk to me about something, so I went out to see what she wanted. But it wasn't Briana. It was a gorgeous blonde who told me her name was Joni. Boy! Joni was a knockout! And get this, she was looking for a job . . . as a valet! For the past two months I had been searching frantically for a valet to work with me, and I had had no luck whatsoever. Now a raving beauty walks right in off the street.

I took Joni's phone number and called her a couple of days later and invited her up to my house to get better acquainted. She lives in Jackson, Mississippi, which is about two hundred miles from Memphis, and quite a drive. But she came up, along with a female friend of hers, and we sat in my den and watched *Shrek*. A couple of weeks later, Joni worked as my valet for the first time at a wrestling show in Lexington, Kentucky, and we have got together . . . working and playing.

And that brought me to mid-November, and the XWF. The XWF was a brand-new organization that I had gotten involved with. It had a pretty incredible talent list, names like Hulk Hogan, Roddy Piper, Curt Hennig, Jimmy Hart, Bobby Heenan, Gene Okerlund, the Nasty Boys, the Road Warriors, Rena and Marc Mero. I thought the XWF could be a serious contender in the world of wrestling. They looked like they had a good organization, good talent, and most importantly, enough money to compete with the WWE.

At the time, I said that everyone, including the WWE, wants another wrestling company in business. Competition is good for everyone. It's not good for the WWE to be the only wrestling company in existence. I've always said, "You can't be number one unless there is a number two."

The XWF was going to hold their initial TV tapings at Universal Studios in Orlando, Florida, on November, 13 and 14, 2001. Ironically, it was while I was in Florida at these tapings that the call came from the executive producer of WWE television, Kevin Dunn. He said they thought the timing was right for me to come back. It would fit perfectly in the story line for me to return to witness the end of the "Alliance." (According to the story line, the "Alliance," an outlaw organization of former WCW and ECW wrestlers, were out to destroy the WWE.) Not only did they want me to return to the WWE, but they wanted me there on the upcoming Monday's *Raw*!

My head was spinning. There was no way I could make it there on Monday, I was under contract to the

XWF. It would have been impossible for me to get out of my XWF contract unless they wanted to let me out. I was bound to them contractually for at least ninety days. I told Kevin Dunn I would talk to the XWF bosses and see what could be done. I met with Jimmy Hart and one of the XWF owners, and told them of my dilemma. I didn't want to put them in a bind, but everyone knew, especially Jimmy Hart, that the WWE is where I wanted to be.

It was decided that they didn't want to force anyone to be there if they would rather be somewhere else, and they let me out of the remaining forty-five days of my contract. I enjoyed my time with both the WWA and the XWF and I thought they were first-class organizations with a lot of really good people. But I felt I belonged back in the WWE. It was where I always wanted to be.

I called Kevin Dunn back and told him I could be there Monday. On that *Raw*, it was decided I would walk out and the "Alliance leader" Paul Heyman would be dragged off and "fired" by Vince. I knew it was going to be a classic!

I think a lot of people figured that because Paul was put into my spot after I left the WWE, there were hard feelings between Paul and myself. There was history between Paul and me, dating back to when he worked in the Tennessee territory for Jerry Jarrett and me that I've written about some. I had, when the ECW invaded the WWE a few years back, called ECW "extremely crappy wrestling." And people who heard or read some of the comments I made about Paul's color commentary work after taking my place thought there were hard feelings there.

The truth of the matter is I respect Paul's work, and I think he respects mine. That's part of what made my return to *Raw* so memorable. Paul's actions and expressions as he was being dragged past me couldn't have been better. They were only that good because he wanted them to be. He wanted my return to get over, to be well received by the fans as much as anyone did. And, thanks a great deal to Paul Heyman, my return got over big-time.

I don't want to speak out of school and I don't think I am but it was never a big secret as to what they wanted me to do. When I spoke to the WWE about coming back, they were intending to have me do just *Raw* and reunite J.R. and me. They would get that special chemistry going there and make *Raw* a special show and special combination. So the plan was for me to do just *Raw* and the PPVs.

But I guess that because *Raw* was so well received, Vince decided to have me go ahead and do *SmackDown!*, because he said my return felt like a breath of fresh air and he wanted to get that feeling going on all of the television programs, for a few weeks at least. That was before *Raw* and *SmackDown!* were split, of course, and J.R. and I went with *Raw*.

It had taken nine years for me to evolve into the more fun, entertaining type role. Jim Ross is the best at telling the story and selling the story to the audience, like telling all of the little details in the story, and he does it throughout the entire show. What happened with J.R. and Paul was, you had J.R. selling the product during the show and Paul doing the same thing but in a different way. When I go out there to do the show, I don't even know 90 percent of the time what the story line is and I don't have to know. J.R. can do all the selling that needs to be done because again he is the best at it. I'm just there to react to what I see and say what comes into my mind and have fun with it and try to be entertaining. J.R. is the information guy and I'm the entertainment guy.

I can't and don't want to take credit for the ratings going up after I came back. I would have felt horrible had they gone down. But that first show was great. I can't remember any show that was that much fun. It was a well-written show. Some people may not agree but the segment with Vince and William Regal, where Regal actually kissed Vince's bare ass on the air, may have been one of the funniest things I have ever seen on any *Raw* show. I personally enjoyed that and I thought it was great TV. It was a real edgy segment that could have come off as offensive but I think the way J.R. and I handled it made it fun. I thought the guys stepped it up a notch and it was just a great show.

So, in November 2001, I went right back to the demanding schedule for the WWE. Flying to Milwaukee to do *Raw* live on a Monday night. Driving across to Chicago for a *SmackDown!* taping the next night. Then flying on Wednesday to Stamford and the WWE Headquarters to do voice-over fixes for *SmackDown!* in the middle of the night and then make the forty-five miles down I-95 to La Guardia Airport in New York for a 6 A.M. flight home to Memphis. Ahhh.

But I was back.

Michael Cole on *SmackDown!*

WrestleMania is the WWE's SuperBowl. *WrestleMania X8*, in Toronto, was a huge success. The stadium sold out completely, meaning there were a record-breaking 68,237 fans in the SkyDome paying receipts of $3.9 million, or six billion Canadian. I mean million. There were 1.3–1.4 million Pay-Per-View buys. It's amazing for me to think I'm even a part of something as enormous and successful as that.

And my mother still always asks me, "When are you going to quit that mess?" But I tell her I feel like the luckiest person in the world. I've made a great living, had a great career doing something I would honestly have paid to do at one time. I don't feel like I've ever had a job in my life. Like professional athletes, I've been paid to play to make a living. You can't get much luckier than that.

There's always a certain amount of good fortune, or luck, involved in anybody's success. Plus a whole lot of blood, sweat, and tears, of course. As I said, a long series of events had to come together for me to get in the game. And a whole bunch of people had to help me out. They didn't have to put themselves out for me but what they did was put me in a position where I could take advantage of the opportunities that fell my way.

If you sit down and look at who helped me the most, number one was Lance Russell for showing those pictures of mine on TV. It was his decision to show them, it was his decision to call me up and have me come over and be on TV. Had he not done that, none of the other stuff would have taken place. I met Jackie Fargo at the TV station then. But Jackie, at that point, never even thought about my being in the wrestling business. Later, of course, when I was working for him at the sign company, he got me booked with Nick Gulas to get me away from the outlaw operation in Arkansas.

After Lance Russell, there was Jerry Vickers. He opened the next door, to the Avon Theatre in West Memphis, Arkansas, where I got my first match. And if Eddie Bond hadn't offered me the radio job, I wouldn't have got in with Jackie Fargo nor would I have been able to walk through the door Jerry Vickers opened. And if Scott Shannon hadn't been willing to help me, I would never have got the experience to get the radio job in the first place.

So I was in the right place at the right time with the right people. Had any one of these meetings not taken place, the whole thing could have been thrown out of sync or gone off in some other crazy direction, and instead of writing this book, I might have been drawing greeting cards for Hallmark. Even before Lance Russell, if my art teacher at Treadwell, Helen Stahl, hadn't saved my portfolio and pushed me and prodded me to get the art scholarship at Memphis State, I don't know what would have happened. My name may have been etched in the Vietnam Memorial Wall. . . . Who knows?

Jackie Fargo helped me most of anybody in my career. I was friends with Jackie but not really hanging-out friends. Very few people in the business are that. With Jackie it was really more of a father-son relationship. If I called him right now, I'd call him "Pop." He'd say, "Hi, son. What're you doing." Jackie provided the role model that I wanted to emulate and made sure I was set on a straight line when I got started.

Once I was wrestling for Nick Gulas, he helped me get ahead. By getting me sent down to Alabama, Jerry Jarrett helped me because I met Sam Bass when I was working for Bill Golden down there. And Jerry helped me again when I came back up and we went into business together. Later on, all the wrestlers I had matches with or booked or whose matches I called helped me with their professionalism and hard work. In that group, I include Andy Kaufman, with whom I had the best program of all and the most widely seen work I was ever involved with: the Letterman fight.

I have no idea what I would have ended up doing had these things not come to pass. I do know I wouldn't change any of the way it turned out.

The Natural is a movie about a person who was born to be a baseball player. As unlikely as I started, I sorta turned out to be a "natural" in the wrestling business. Almost everything about the wrestling business comes easy to me.

For the six months when I was switching off booking with Jerry Jarrett, I would write the hour-long TV show on my way back from wrestling in Blytheville, Arkansas, on a Friday night. I'd leave at eleven and get back at twelve-thirty, and in that time, I'd think of all the angles, think of everybody's interview. This kind of thing comes to me readily and it seems to work out pretty well. I know that Jerry, when he was doing it, would work all week long on the TV. Some writers sit and ponder and struggle. They'd get it done but it would take a long time. Others, the words just flow.

It's unusual because I didn't grow up in the business and my father wasn't in it or anything. It was like drawing. It's hard for me to comprehend that everybody can't

Mom

draw. I know people who say they can't even draw a stick person and that amazes me. I can sit down and draw your portrait, as easily as writing my name. Wrestling came naturally to me in the same way.

I always thought the point of the whole thing was entertainment, giving the fans what they want. That means you have to put everything you have into it. Make it the funniest or the most believable or even the grossest. Whatever it takes. My friend Kenny Bolin, who used to manage as "the King of Managers," said, "People believed what Lawler said in the ring. If the King said he was going to shove a stovepipe up Jackie Fargo's ass in an alley at five-thirty in the morning, you'd show up to see it happen." And my old friend and mentor Buddy Wayne said I could sell anything. He said I could take a broomstick into the ring and have a match with it.

While we're on the subject of me, Vince McMahon once said to somebody else in my presence, "King is the most talented person I have ever met in the wrestling business." That's a huge compliment. He later said to me, "There's not one aspect of this business that you can't do." I have done literally everything. From the wrestling, through the booking, the promoting, and the ownership, to the announcing, I've done it all and hopefully done it well.

But all that being said, I remember more than once being in a locker room with a veteran wrestler that we would call an "old timer." I was young and just getting started in the business and this guy would sit around and tell old war stories. Stories about matches or experiences he had had during his career. When he was through and had left the room for his match, I would roll my eyes and say, "If I ever get like that, where I just sit around telling those war stories . . . somebody please shoot me!" Somehow, right now, I have the feeling people are rolling their eyes and loading a gun.

The Mike Tyson–Lennox Lewis fight in Memphis in June 2002 was one of the biggest events in U.S. sports history, let alone the history of my hometown. The gate at the Pyramid alone was $23 million. The Pay-Per-View got 1.8 million buys, which, at $54.95 each, generated $103 million. The numbers are staggering.

As for myself, I didn't commit to whether I was going to go or not. A couple of people mentioned some things but I certainly wasn't going to pay $2,400, which was the price for one ringside seat. Somehow I figured someone would come up to me and say, "You're the King . . . you got to be at the fight! I'll get you in!"

As a matter of fact, a couple weeks before the fight, I did a press conference with Mayor Willie Herenton. We were talking about a "Tickets for Kids" program the mayor had started and the WWE was donating tickets to. After the press conference, the mayor asked if I were going to the fight. I told him I didn't have tickets. He said I needed to be there with him in his private luxury box. I thought to myself, "I'm in!" Unfortunately, the call to confirm never came from the mayor's office.

In the end, Joni and I got our names on the list to an HBO/Showtime prefight party at the Pyramid. My friend Lieutenant Ron Fittes of the Memphis Police Department set us up. The place was jammed with celebs. We stayed in the party right until the main event and went from there right down to the Pyramid floor. We were so close we could touch the ring. The $2,400 ringside seats were actually up off the floor on the first set of risers. Right on the floor were just certain VIP seats and the media. As we got ushered down there, Joni right behind me and right behind her was Magic Johnson. We're going along. "Hey, King. Hey, Magic," fans in the crowd were yelling.

We did a complete loop around the ring, as if we were in a parade. Samuel L. Jackson, Gregory Hines, Morgan Freeman, Emanuel Lewis, David Hasselhoff, Matt Dillon, Kevin Bacon, Val Kilmer, L.L. Cool J., Jerry West, Chris Webber, Tyra Banks, Chuck Zito, and The Rock. All of these big shots had been at the party with us and now we were all parading around the ring Tyson and Lewis were about to battle in.

I was looking up into the crowd at the fans, waving at no one in particular. I looked down and saw this guy standing by the ring and I said to Joni, "Hey, let me introduce you to Donald Trump." I walked up and tapped him on the shoulder. "Hey, Jerry, how're you doing," he said. I said I just wanted to welcome him to Memphis and introduce him to Joni. You'd have thought "the Donald" and "the King" were old buddies. I'd interviewed Donald Trump at Madison Square Garden for the WWE. Joni was like, "You know Donald Trump?"

As we walk away from Donald, I happen to glance up into the bleachers. I see some people I know. There, eight or ten rows up, all in a line, sit Vince McMahon; Linda McMahon; J.R.; Jan Ross; Shane McMahon; Stephanie McMahon; Triple H; Undertaker; and Sara, 'Taker's wife. I just wave up to them. In carny, the old roustabout's language, I shout up to Vince, "I'm just working the room." I wave again, and I turn and go on my way.

On that night, it was good to be the King.

acknowledgments

This is the part of the book where I get to say a special thanks to all the influential people in my life. People, who over the years lent me the encouragement and support needed to help me become someone even remotely worthy of having a book writen about their life. If I listed them all, this would be longer than the book itself, but I would feel guilty if I didn't give these people their due. Plus, I heard more people will buy a book if their name is in it somewhere! So here goes.

My love and special thanks to my Mom, my brother Larry, and my two sons, Brian and Kevin. Thanks to my three beautiful wives, Kay, Paula, and Stacy. Therese Branch, my wonderful housekeeper for over twenty-nine years, you know I'd be lost without you. Jackie Fargo, Lance Russell, Dave Brown, Buddy Wayne, and Guy Coffey, I could never find enough words to thank you all for helping to get me started on this crazy ride. Thanks to Bill Apter, you pushed me in the magazines and sent me Andy Kaufman.

Helen Stahl helped nurtured the creative spark inside me that helped make me an artist. Thanks to Jim Blake for being an art lover. Danny Dunn, your many years of friendship were always a great help. Thanks to Kevin Dunn and Sue Derosa at WWE for everything. To my own personal "dream team" of lawyers: Leonard Yelsky, Bill Massey, Joe Barton, Tim Dennison, Ralph

Holt, Russ Savory, and Wanda Shea, over the years you have kicked some serious butt for the King in the courtroom. Thanks to Frank Derry, my friend and Indians and Browns connection. Mick Foley, you gave me *Christmas Chaos,* many thanks. Ron Fittes, of the Memphis Police, not only have you been a friend, but you've proven everyday that you are Memphis's finest. Thanks to Ronnie Gossett who claims to be my only "real" friend. "Dangerous" Doug Hurt, thanks for countless adventures. Thanks to Randy Hales for years of hard work and dedication. Thanks to my friend and dentist, Ken Isaacman. My personal physician, Doc Sammons, has kept me in wrestling condition for all these many years.

Jerry Jarrett, for a twenty year partnership and friendship, thanking you just doesn't seem enough. "Downtown" Bruno Lauer, well . . . thanks for a whole bunch of stuff that's best left unsaid. Bobby Monica of the Browns, you're the best! Thanks to Corey Maclin for being my friend. Jimmy Hart you gave me the gift of one of the best wrestling feuds *ever.* Bob and Dot Caruth, in-law jokes aside, you are the best. Thanks to Michael O'Brien and Jonathan Gold for doing so much for me on the independent scene. Elliott Pollack thanks not just for friendship, but your advice, assistance and much more. Chip Pasley you keep me flying on Northwest. Thanks to Lori Stanley at Union Planters Bank. Big thanks to Alan Whitenton, my tireless webmaster for kinglawler.com.

Thanks to my friends and a wonderful family, the Gourgeot's. And a very heartfelt thanks to some wonderful, and beautiful girls who I have had the privilege of knowing over the years—some better than others, of course—April Butcher, Joni Horn, Briana Little, Beverly Hampton, Jenni Price, Terri Garcia, Chrissy Huebschman, Donna Celender, Pam Robbins, Amy Riley, Marian Huddleston, and Karen Underwood.

Thanks to the mighty men who came and went as members of my ball team, Lawler's Army: Robert Reed, Chris Elsworth, Mike Mashburn, Rudy Favati, Roy Henderson, Jerry Calhoun, Terry Pressgrove, Bobby Goss, Danny Stone, Jimmy Hampton, Dal Vowell, David Holcomb, Robert Burgess, Mike Gourgeot, Larry Sowell, Bip Cardosi, Wendel Ricard, Ricky Gresham, Dane Davidson, Paul Davidson, Dink Golding, Michael Deaton, Anthony Reasons, Mike Bryan, Lanny McBride, Brian Lawler, Danny Cloud, Larry Hale, Jason Stephens, Jimmy Guy, Stevie Wilson, Jerry Bryant, Mike Jewel, Calvin Burrows, Bailey Lowrey, Tommy Gann, Jimmy Harris, Jeff Mills, "Porky" Howard, and even Jimmy Hart.

And last, but certainly *not* least, a very special thanks to Vince McMahon and Jim Ross for believing in me. Thank you, thank you, thank you!

Doug Asheville would like to thank: Bill Apter, Jim Blake, Kenny Bolin, Brian Christopher, Jim Cornette, Jackie Fargo, Joni Horn, Hazel Lawler, Kevin Lawler, Larry Lawler, Sarah Lee, David Millican, Michael O'Brien, Bert Prentice, Lance Russell, Paula Caruth, and everyone concerned at Pocket Books and the WWE. And thanks to Jerry Lawler for his hospitality.